Navigating Semi-Colonialism

Harvard East Asian Monographs 410

Navigating Semi-Colonialism

Shipping, Sovereignty, and Nation-Building in China, 1860–1937

Anne Reinhardt

Published by the Harvard University Asia Center
Distributed by Harvard University Press
Cambridge (Massachusetts) and London 2018

Printed in the United States of America

The Harvard University Asia Center publishes a monograph series and, in coordination with the Fairbank Center for Chinese Studies, the Korea Institute, the Reischauer Institute of Japanese Studies, and other facilities and institutes, administers research projects designed to further scholarly understanding of China, Japan, Vietnam, Korea, and other Asian countries. The Center also sponsors projects addressing multidisciplinary and regional issues in Asia.

Studies of the Weatherhead East Asian Institute, Columbia University

The Studies of the Weatherhead East Asian Institute of Columbia University were inaugurated in 1962 to bring to a wider public the results of significant new research on modern and contemporary East Asia.

Library of Congress Cataloging-in-Publication Data

Names: Reinhardt, Anne, 1968– author.
Title: Navigating semi-colonialism : shipping, sovereignty, and nation-building in China, 1860–1937 / Anne Reinhardt.
Other titles: Harvard East Asian monographs ; 410.
Description: Cambridge, Massachusetts : Published by the Harvard University Asia Center, 2018. | Series: Harvard East Asian monographs ; 410 | Includes bibliographical references and index.
Identifiers: LCCN 2017029371 | ISBN 9780674983847 (hardcover : alk. paper)
Subjects: LCSH: Steamboat lines—China—Yangtze River—History. | Shipping—Government ownership—China—History—20th century. | China—Foreign relations. | Colonial companies—China—History—19th century. | Colonial companies—China—History—20th century. | China—History—1861–1912. | China—History—Republic, 1912–1949.
Classification: LCC HE894 .R45 2018 | DDC 386/.350951209034—dc23 LC record available at https://lccn.loc.gov/2017029371

Index by the author

♾ Printed on acid-free paper

Last figure below indicates year of this printing
27 26 25 24 23 22 21 20 19 18

To My Family

Contents

Maps, Tables, and Figures

Maps

Table

Figures

Acknowledgments

In the long years of working on this book, I have received much help and accrued many debts. It is my pleasure to finally acknowledge them here.

First, my graduate advisor, Susan Naquin, provided most generous guidance from the very beginnings of this project. I was also fortunate to work with Ruth Rogaski and Sheldon Garon, whose examples and mentorship have meant a great deal. Sherman Cochran, who served as an outside reader, introduced me to Lu Zuofu and offered several important research contacts in China. Moving further into the past, I am grateful for the opportunity to thank the many teachers who have helped me reach this point, particularly Alan Wachman, Peter Bol, Frederic Wakeman Jr., and Lydia H. Liu.

Research for this book has taken me to many different places in China, Taiwan, Japan, and the United Kingdom, and in each place I have received much help and advice. Zhu Yin'gui, currently of Fudan University, was a most patient advisor during my time at the Chinese Academy of Social Sciences in Beijing and beyond. Luo Zhitian, of Sichuan and Beijing Universities, did much to aid my dissertation research in Chengdu and continues to offer his help. Zhang Jin, of Chongqing University, has been a great friend and interlocutor, and her advice over many years has had an enormous impact on this project. I want to express my sincere appreciation to the Minsheng Shipping Company in Chongqing, its general manager, Mr. Lu Guoji, as well as Xiang Jingxi, Mu Li, and Cai Ailing of its Historical Research Division, who hosted me on numerous visits to Chongqing and kept me in contact with a community of historians interested in Lu Zuofu, particularly Zhao Xiaoling, Zhou Minmin, and Liu Chonglai. Thanks also to Huang Hanmin at the Shanghai Academy of Social Sciences and Fan Jinmin of Nanjing University and to the staffs of the Sichuan University Library and the Economics Library at the Chinese Academy of Social Sciences for their kind assistance.

In Taiwan, Ch'en Kuo-tung of Academia Sinica extended both help and hospitality on two separate trips, and Chuang Chi-fa of the Palace Museum offered expert guidance in navigating that collection. In Japan, I was fortunate to get advice from Hamashita Takeshi and access to the Tōa Bunka Kenkyujō collection at Tokyo University Library. Tatuski Mariko and Goto Mitsuya provided important introductions to Japanese shipping companies. I thank Matheson & Co., London, for permission to use the Jardine, Matheson & Company Archives at Cambridge University Library, and Julian Thorogood and Rob Jennings of John Swire & Sons, London, for allowing me to use materials from the collection at Swire House. The staffs at the Cambridge University Library and the Archival Collections Department of the School of Oriental and African Studies also provided much help and information.

Closer to home, Nancy Norton Tomasko was kind enough to allow me to use her private collection of Asian travel books and guidebooks. The staffs of Princeton University's Gest Library, the Harvard-Yenching Library, the University of Rochester Library, and the Williams College Library all offered useful assistance.

The research for this book has been supported by the following grant programs: Princeton University's James T. Liu Fellowship, the Chiang Ching-kuo Dissertation Fellowship, the Committee for Scholarly Communication with China dissertation grant, the An Wang Postdoctoral Fellowship at Harvard University's Fairbank Center, and the Hellman Fellows Program at Williams College. I also relied on research funds from the University of Rochester and Williams College.

I have learned much from those that have read sections of this work or commented on presentations of it: Paul Cohen, Henrietta Harrison, James Hevia, William Kirby, Philip Kuhn, Elizabeth Perry, Ezra Vogel, and Madeline Zelin. William D. Wray has been especially generous with advice, contacts, and sources. Thanks to Robert Bickers for including me in two projects that helped this book along, as well as for his generous advice and formidable command of sources. Karl Gerth, Eugenia Lean, and Elisabeth Köll all advocated for this project under a variety of circumstances, and I am grateful for their friendship and faith.

Friends have supplied all forms of support, including companionship abroad, translation help, steamship references, and countless conversations. Thanks to Dani Botsman, Dora C. Y. Ching, Nixi Cura, Charo D'Etcheverry, Crystal Feimster, Paize Keulemans, Hongming Liang, Yang Lu, Tom McGrath, Tracy Miller, Freda Murck, Allison Rottman, Ling Arey Shiao, Mark Swislocki, Arafaat Valiani, Di Wang, and Chuck Wooldridge. Special thanks to my cohort from the 2003–4 An Wang Fellowship year: Rob Culp, Dan Shao, Carlos Rojas, Eileen Otis, Shelley Drake Hawkes, Catherine Clayton, and Hsiu-hua Shen.

I have been fortunate to have academic appointments at the University of Rochester and Williams College. In both places, the history departments have offered much encouragement and support. Particular thanks to William B. Hauser, Mike Jarvis, Jean Pederson, and Joan Rubin at Rochester and Alexandra Garbarini, Kenda Mutongi, Christopher Nugent, Eiko Siniawer, and Anand Swamy at Williams. Sharron Macklin, formerly of Williams College Office of Information Technology, prepared the maps for this book. Student research assistants from both institutions helped complete particularly labor-intensive research tasks: Carl Filler, Elise Smith, Galen Jackson, and Daniel Kim.

Bob Graham of the Harvard University Asia Center has been truly patient as I have labored to conclude this project. Dan Rivero, of Columbia University's Weatherhead East Asian Institute, provided excellent publishing advice.

My parents, Paul and May C. Reinhardt, have always been a great source of support. In recent years, I have been thankful for my father and sisters' tolerance for brief and intermittent family events. My children, Bihu and Lalon, have provided much joy and pleasant distraction. I am grateful to their caregivers, particularly Karen McCarthy, for helping make it possible for me to commute, teach, and write during their early years. For my partner, Arindam Dutta, I reserve the final word. He has been with me almost as long as this project has, and for his contributions—intellectual, logistical, and personal—there is no sufficient thanks.

INTRODUCTION

> Building a new state is like building a new steamship. If we put in low-powered machinery, the speed of vessel will naturally be low, its freight capacity will be small, and profits from its running meager. But if we install high-powered machinery, the vessel will have a high rate of speed, will be able to carry heavy freight, and will bring in large profits. If we could build a steamship with a speed of 50 knots, then no other steamship could compete with it, and we would have the fastest and largest new steamship in the world.[1]
>
> —*Sun Yatsen,* Three Principles of the People, *1924*

Sun Yatsen's (1866–1925) famous speeches, *Three Principles of the People*, were written in the midst of the reorganization of the Guomindang in 1923–24, as China's continued subordination to foreign imperialism and the disintegration of the early Republican government demanded the reimagining of state and nation. The cutting-edge "ship of state" that Sun envisioned is readily recognizable as part of his enthusiasm for a China transformed by engineering and technology.[2] In this passage, however, Sun makes it clear that he was not seeking to achieve merely the modern or expertly engineered, but to transcend such benchmarks to create something unprecedented.

The ship of state is a well-used metaphor in twentieth-century China, from novelist Liu Tieyun's (1857–1909) depiction of the waning polity of the Qing dynasty (1644–1911) as a sinking ship in *The Travels of Lao Can* to Mao Zedong's sobriquet "the Great Helmsman."[3] As Michel Foucault has pointed out, the metaphor derives from an archaic image of government in which the object of governance is not merely territory but a "complex of men and things." Government thus resembles a ship's command in overseeing the vessel and the vessel's safe navigation as well as the people and relationships within it.[4] Sun's choice of a steamship to represent a future Chinese state invoked not only this metaphor but China's experience of imperialist penetration, in which the steamship was a mode of expansion into Chinese territory and a long-standing site of struggle between Chinese sovereignty and external domination. In envisioning the complete redesign of such a ship, Sun wrested it from this history, claiming the ultimate agency in determining the nation's future.

This book examines the steamship and steam navigation in Chinese waters in the nineteenth and twentieth centuries as a means of interrogating China's experience of Euro-American and Japanese imperialism. Brought to China by European navies and traders as early as the 1830s, steamships were instrumental in the British victory in the First Opium War (1839–42) and were subsequently used to transport opium and other goods along China's eastern coast. Within decades, they became an essential part of China's infrastructure, servicing the foreign trade that extended into the interior and transporting goods for domestic consumption and travelers bound for destinations within China. As an enduring mode of expansion and visible sign of foreign privilege in China, steamships were also objects of conflict and critique, becoming significant sites of nationalist mobilization in the twentieth century. By 1924, when Sun wrote the above passage, steamships were already ingrained within the physical and political landscapes of modern China.

The formal aspects of China's encounter with Western and Japanese imperialism before 1937 are well understood. Most of mainland China was not colonized by a single external power. Instead, a series of unequal treaties signed with several Western powers (and eventually Japan) secured a framework of economic and legal privileges for foreign nationals in China while leaving Chinese governments in place. Nearly every account of the period lists the treaty terms that infringed on Chinese sovereignty: the opening of treaty ports to foreign residence and trade, extraterritorial protection, fixed tariffs, and the most favored nation clause. Far less certain and more contentious is the question of how treaty provisions shaped the daily experience of most Chinese and the course of modern Chinese history. The "foreign presence" has been represented at times as a benign, modernizing influence and at other times as a mode of imperialist exploitation. It has been viewed as the central motor of change within modern Chinese history and a limited set of encounters confined to the peripheries of a vast empire.[5] Steam navigation was an element of the treaty system that bridged its abstractions and material realities, thus it can illuminate the conceptual and concrete aspects of this regime and its consequences.

To date, shipping has played a decidedly minor role in debates over imperialism in China. It is only occasionally included among the standard components of the treaty system. From 1860, however, foreign-flag shipping and soon thereafter steam shipping became constitutive elements of the treaty system with an incontrovertible significance for material life. Steam navigation linked the treaty ports together into a mechanized transport network that predated railway construction by several decades. It brought new possibilities for trade and travel, new opportunities and occupations, and new experiences of space and time. It formed a new sphere of enterprise characterized by intensive interaction between foreign shipping interests and Chinese clients, partners, and competitors. Steamships further furnished novel social spaces that placed disparate populations in close proximity and projected particular views of the social order. Although just one aspect of a multifaceted treaty system, the diverse dimensions of steam navigation can enliven our understanding of the dynamics of this system and the wider global processes of which it was part.

Semi-Colonialism and the Semi-Colonial Conundrum

This book uses the term "semi-colonialism" to refer to the relations of foreign and Chinese power in mainland China under the treaty system. It is not a new concept, having a long history and a variety of accrued meanings. Originating with early twentieth-century critics of imperialism such as J. A. Hobson (1858–1940) and Vladimir Lenin (1870–1924), the term was initially used to designate those areas of the world—including China, Persia, Siam, and the Ottoman empire—that were not formal colonies yet were clearly dominated by an external power or powers. In Lenin's formulation, such places occupied a "transitional stage" on the way to full colonial rule.[6] The same term was deployed within Chinese Marxist historiography, in which "semi-colonial" (*ban zhimindi*) is paired with "semi-feudal" (*ban fengjian*) to describe the socioeconomic formation that inhibited China's transition to full capitalism.[7] It currently remains a common way to refer to the particular formations of Western and Japanese imperialist power in China. The term has also had many detractors, from Sun Yatsen, who warned that Chinese people should not comfort themselves with the idea that China was "only" a semi-colony rather than a colony, to more recent scholarship questioning the term's capacity to capture the full range of phenomena resulting from China's encounter with imperialism.[8] Despite this range of interpretations, my choice to use the term is deliberate. I find it uniquely useful in that, keeping both sides of the hyphen under active consideration, it can encompass the particularity of China's experience, its comparability with colonial contexts, and its enmeshment within the process of the global ascent of European empires in the latter nineteenth century.[9]

My reading of the term is an effort to untangle the conundrum that prevails within contemporary scholarship on China's experience of imperialism: whether this experience can be understood through the same frameworks as colonialism or whether it was exceptional enough to require its own concepts and tools. This debate is particularly pronounced among China scholars engaged with the fields of colonial and postcolonial studies—the multidisciplinary efforts of the past forty years to explicate the complex relations between European expansion to other parts of the world and European notions of modernity. China scholars have been interested in the critical potential of these fields yet uncertain whether Chinese history can be accommodated within them.

Within this debate, the term "semi-colonialism" (often "semicolonialism") is usually used to demarcate difference between China's experience and that of the colonial world. Tani Barlow's essay "Colonialism's Career in Postwar China Studies," for example, even as it contends that scholarly practice has obscured the relevance of colonialism to Chinese history, distinguishes China from those places that were "outright European possessions" and calls instead for an "interrogation of the complexity of China's semicolonialism."[10] Barlow's analysis shows that the past categories and paradigms of academic China studies—such as a modernization approach that took indigenous "tradition" as its foil and a later emphasis on the economic impact of imperialism—were nearly identical to those used to study the colonial world, yet concludes that the "semi-" qualifier remains necessary to account for specific conditions in China.[11]

Other studies take this claim of difference further, emphasizing that the outcomes—most often the cultural effects—of semi-colonial rule in

China were distinct from those observed under colonial rule, most often using British India as a point of comparison. Shu-mei Shih's study of Republican-era literary modernism provides perhaps the most detailed account of the specific features of the semi-colonial order in China, emphasizing that multiple powers (rather than a single "colonizer") exercised control without the apparatus of a colonial state. This political fragmentation, she argues, produced a specific cultural result, allowing Chinese intellectuals to separate the "metropolitan West" (as worthy of emulation) from the "colonial West" (as deserving of critique). In Shih's argument, there is the subtle suggestion that this difference made Chinese intellectuals less effective critics of colonialism in that they did not produce an "authentic critique of post-Enlightenment rationality."[12] Bryna Goodman's article on the celebration of the 1893 Jubilee of Queen Victoria in Shanghai similarly links the form of external control in China to outcomes in the cultural sphere. Criticizing other scholars' failure to "substantively distinguish semicolonialism from colonialism," she argues that the presence of Chinese sovereignty and the limited exercise of foreign power in nineteenth-century China indeed made semi-colonialism qualitatively different from colonialism.[13] Her analysis concludes with the statement that in nineteenth-century Shanghai, Chinese did not view foreigners and their interactions with them "in terms of anything resembling colonized subjectivities."[14] In both of these studies, the specific mode of foreign political control is directly linked to cultural outcomes, therefore demanding an accounting of the specific nature of semi-colonialism.

In his book *English Lessons,* James Hevia provides the most explicit articulation of an opposing position, rejecting the need to calibrate the difference between colonialism and semi-colonialism. Hevia disaggregates what he calls colonialism's "hegemonic projects" from forms of colonial rule, pointing out that political control was only one aspect of European empire-building. His book details Britain's mid-nineteenth-century effort to instruct the Qing state and the Chinese people "how to function properly in a world dominated militarily and economically by European-based empires"—a process he describes as a form of colonization.[15] Hevia goes further, arguing that since no form of colonial domination was complete, we might consider "all the entities produced in the age of empire as forms of semicolonialism."[16] Other scholars have resisted making substantive distinctions between colonialism and semi-colonialism, but

Hevia is most unequivocal in interpreting Chinese history within this framework.[17]

Neither position in this debate is fully satisfying. The treaty system was a very specific political formation that left the Qing dynasty and later Chinese governments' sovereignty diminished but still intact. To gloss over this specificity sacrifices the variation and contingency that could permit deeper reflection on the global process of European expansion. Yet too great an insistence on the particularity or exceptionality of China's experience risks suggesting that China was separate or insulated from the broader processes identified with colonialism. A problem with the opposing positions is that they hinge on two different but overlapping conceptions of colonialism: first, colonialism as rule by a colonial state, and second, colonialism as the process of the imposition of European (or European-derived) forms of power/knowledge (the "hegemonic projects" of Hevia's argument). The scholarly practice of colonial studies over the preceding decades provides some explanation for the oscillation between these concepts. As Frederick Cooper has observed, one of the primary contributions of colonial studies was the "unbounding" of colonialism, the shift of the focus of inquiry away from the processes of acquiring and administering colonies to the dissemination of categories of Western power/knowledge, a shift that allowed colonial studies to offer critiques of the universalizing ideas of Western modernity and resist the idea that colonialism came to an end once former colonies achieved independence.[18] Yet as Cooper and others have noted, arguments for this unbounded colonialism have been overwhelmingly made through research into areas formally integrated into European empires, such as British India, French Africa, and Dutch Indonesia, making it difficult to disaggregate this more discursive definition of colonialism from rule by a colonial state.[19]

I use "semi-colonialism" in this book not to insist on difference but to make use of the term's particular and comparative attributes. In this investigation of the semi-colonial order in nineteenth- and twentieth-century China, the central questions extend in more than one direction. The book asks what was specific about semi-colonialism as a political formation as well as what was continuous with other contexts. It examines how semi-colonial China was imbricated in the broader processes of global European expansion throughout this period. Steam navigation is a specific yet empirically rich case that can elucidate many of semi-colonialism's central dynamics and its relationships to other places and contexts. Inevitably, such a choice of case privileges certain elements over others, but my intention is to offer a compelling fragment rather than an exhaustive model. A sharper historical portrait of semi-colonialism is important not only to advance the scholarly conversation but also because this period of Chinese history continues to invite strongly opposed uses and interpretations in the present: its struggles may be all too easily dismissed as irrelevant in this moment of assertive Chinese power and prosperity, or conversely marshaled to create a useful past, such as the fostering of contemporary patriotic sensibilities in the People's Republic of China through state narratives of "One Hundred Years of National Humiliation."[20]

The Steamship and Semi-Colonialism

In taking up steam navigation as a case through which to understand semi-colonial China, this book departs from previous English-language studies of modern shipping that primarily focus on steamship companies—either their individual entrepreneurial achievements or the relations between Chinese shipping companies and the state.[21] It views steam navigation as a wider arena comprising intertwined political, economic, social, and cultural elements. The book examines the expansion of steam navigation in the Qing empire, the shifting organization of the steam shipping business and identities of its participants, and the steamship as a social space. It extends the investigation of these aspects into the twentieth century through the nationalist responses to and critiques of them. Finally, the book sustains a comparison of different facets of steam shipping in China and India, not only to ponder the particularities and continuities between semi-colonial and colonial formations but to consider the ways both places participated in processes of global expansion that extended beyond each specific context.

The view into the semi-colonial order that steam navigation provides is not comprehensive, but it is strikingly rich and varied. In the political and commercial realms, it reveals the workings of an impaired yet active Chinese sovereignty and the concrete ways the asymmetrical relationships between Chinese governments and the treaty powers constrained this sovereignty. In the social and cultural arenas, the social space of the steamship highlights the construction and reinforcement of racial hierarchies and exclusions. In furnishing a focal point through which to investigate Republican-era nationalism, contests over steam navigation demonstrate the robustness of Chinese critiques of the semi-colonial order.

Rather than attempt an exhaustive history of steam navigation in Chinese waters, this study focuses on China's primary nineteenth- and twentieth-century domestic shipping network, linking its eastern coast with the Yangzi River (*Changjiang*). Numerous overseas and regional shipping networks also included Chinese ports, but the Yangzi River and coastal network was an artifact of the evolving treaty system, particularly the treaty regime that followed the 1860 Treaty of Tianjin, and best exemplifies the semi-colonial formation that is the subject of this book.

SOVEREIGNTY AND COLLABORATION

The expansion of steam navigation into Chinese waters was both a political and a commercial process. The carriage of Chinese-owned goods in foreign-flag sailing ships began as an informal means of extending Western commercial activity along China's coast in the 1840s and 1850s, but following the Second Opium War (1856–60), the right of foreign ships to navigate China's inland and coastal waters was enshrined in the unequal treaties. Subsequently, as steam navigation began to replace sail along these routes, all questions of foreign steamships' access to different parts of the Qing empire were adjudicated through the treaty system. The treaty powers—particularly Great Britain—consistently pressed the dynasty to extend the reach of steam navigation and the scope of steam transport networks. By the dynasty's end in 1911, the steam network and the shipping privileges granted to treaty powers had grown substantially. Occurring simultaneously to these negotiations of treaty terms was the extension of foreign steamship enterprises throughout the shipping network. Initially, these enterprises were located and financed in the treaty ports, but by the late 1870s, they were replaced by powerful companies backed by British capital. After 1895, government-subsidized Japanese firms also became important contenders in Chinese waters.

These political and commercial expansions, however, were not simply enacted on a passive or unaware China. The Qing state was a particularly important participant and interpellator in these processes. Qing officials were deeply concerned with the expansion of foreign shipping privilege and worked to limit it to preserve areas of dynastic autonomy and control, efforts that affected the shape and scope of the steam network. As the power of foreign shipping companies grew, the Qing state intervened in the commercial sphere as well, supporting a merchant shipping firm under the Qing flag to check the rapid development of foreign enterprise. This company—the China Merchants Steam Navigation Company—became an enduring competitor in the shipping business.

The margin of sovereignty and agency left to an indigenous government is one of the clearest distinctions between a semi-colonial formation and a formal colony, but the significance of this margin is not always clear. It could be dismissed as merely symbolic, a convenient cover under which the treaty powers could exploit China, or it could be interpreted as a capacity for resistance, which immediately leads to the question of why Chinese governments were not more effective resistors. This study analyzes Chinese sovereignty under semi-colonialism within the framework of collaboration. "Collaboration" is a controversial term, but it permits the examination of the significant porosity and contingency in the relations between Chinese governments and the treaty powers, to better understand the benefits and vantages each sought to gain, and to witness the assertions and limitations of Chinese sovereignty within semi-colonialism.

Collaboration is a familiar but problematic concept for historians of imperialism: its moral inflection can easily overwhelm the interactions it seeks to describe. It immediately calls to mind collaborators who assisted Japanese or German military regimes during World War II; within the historiography of imperialism, it often serves as an accusatory label affixed to individuals or groups who abetted the rise of colonial regimes.[22] In these contexts, the collaborator is charged with betraying his or her country or people for narrow or self-serving gains. Historians of China often identify compradors—the Chinese merchants who mediated between foreign businesses and local markets—as collaborators.[23] In the Marxist historiography of modern China, collaboration is at the heart of the "semi-feudal, semi-colonial" economic base, attributed to alliances between foreign imperialists, compradors, officials, warlords, and large landlords—all considered "enemies of the people."[24]

A rigorous account of semi-colonialism, however, cannot avoid discussion of the negotiation of external and local power. Despite the term's strong moral overtones, collaboration focuses our attention on these relations of power. In his 1972 essay "Non-European Foundations of European Imperialism: Sketch for a Theory of Collaboration," Ronald Robinson presented a view of collaboration that emphasized its functions over its moral implications. He identified collaborators as the mediators between imperialist powers and a local political situation, allowing that such a position could be unwelcome or involuntary.[25] He stressed the interdependence of indigenous collaborators and imperialist regimes, arguing that the extent of foreign authority depended on collaborators' ability to intercede with local society. If external powers made too-extreme demands, they might discredit their collaborators and unravel the system altogether.[26] His essay identified an enormous range of relationships under multiple forms of imperial control as befitting the term, but in discussing nineteenth-century China, he attributed this mediating role to "Chinese mandarins" (Qing officials).[27]

Drawing on Robinson's view of collaboration, this book details several collaborative mechanisms in both the politics and the business of steam navigation in semi-colonial China. I emphasize these mechanisms over the identification of particular persons or groups as collaborators so as to explicate the terms and dynamics of collaboration. Although collaboration was always based on some measure of shared interest, it also embodied profoundly unequal power relations, which shaped the actions and choices of the participants. The collaborative mechanisms significant to steam navigation share several characteristics. First, the external participants (the treaty powers) determined the terms of collaboration. Second and consequently, the external participants often had greater experience in the context of the collaboration and better access to information and resources related to it than did indigenous participants. Because of this imbalance, over time, collaborations reinforced the inequities between the external and indigenous participants and forwarded the imperialist/expansionist project. Third, indigenous participation in collaboration was often the result of a choice to preserve or defend existing structures or institutions rather than simple opportunism. Finally, despite the evident inequities, the outcomes of indigenous participation were not unequivocally negative: collaborative mechanisms could support the exercise of indigenous sovereignty and agency, but always within the unequal framework of the mechanism. Understanding the constraints of the collaborative mechanism is thus critical to understanding the motives and choices of indigenous participants, who are too often anachronistically vilified for their failure to forward modern-day goals such as national autonomy, modernization, or development.

Between 1860 and 1911, the treaty system itself was a collaborative mechanism. Following the Qing's defeat in the Second Opium War, the conduct of the treaty system was imposed from without, via the Treaty of Tianjin (1858–60), which dictated almost the entire system of diplomatic relations.[28] Nevertheless, the Western signatories and Qing officials were both invested in supporting Qing sovereignty—the treaty powers to avoid the costs of conquest and rule, the Qing to ensure its own survival.[29] The powers depended on the still-sovereign dynasty to uphold and enforce the terms of the treaties. Therefore, at the same time the treaty system diminished Qing sovereignty, its remaining margin was indispensable to the functioning of the system. The process of extending foreign shipping privileges into Chinese waters allows us to view this margin of sovereignty in action over the remainder of the dynasty. At times, Qing officials succeeded in curbing foreign demands, limiting and defining the transport networks produced through this process. At other times, however, they were unable to halt or reverse the momentum of expansion and had to accept conditions that further eroded their authority. Examining the collaborative mechanism within the treaty system thus permits a mapping of the imbalances of power that both enabled and constrained Qing sovereign action between 1860 and 1911.

Attention to collaboration within the treaty system reveals change within the semi-colonial order. The treaty system remained in place well after the Qing dynasty's fall in 1911, but its central collaborative mechanism collapsed just a few years after the dynasty's end. During the Warlord Era (1916–27), when China split into competing militarist regimes, there was no central government on which the treaty powers could rely to enforce treaty terms and privileges across the country.[30] Rather than intervene with greater force to secure a new collaborator, the treaty powers suspended the continuous pressure for expansion that had characterized their relationship to the Qing dynasty. After securing the revenue of the Maritime Customs and Salt Administrations, they ceased to make new demands for shipping privileges. Whereas individual instances of collaboration—such as agreements between individual militarists and foreign powers—can be identified in the early Republican period (1911–27), there was no longer a comprehensive political collaborative mechanism. Accompanying this change was a new climate of far more open conflict between foreign and Chinese interests. Foreign powers resorted to shows of military force to defend treaty privileges; Chinese citizens staged demonstrations and boycotts to protest their presence. In the past, the Qing government had acted as the primary locus of resistance to foreign expansion, but in the Republican period this role was more widely shared throughout Chinese society, with workers, intellectuals, professional organizations, entrepreneurs, and even militarist regimes participating in nationalist activity. Absent a central collaborator, this resistance was far less constrained than it had been under the Qing. This shift in the terms of collaboration between the Qing and Republican periods provides the chronological framing of this book.

The diplomatic processes of the treaty system set the parameters of the steam transport network in Chinese waters, but the steamship enterprises that worked within it set the pace of trade and travel. The growth of steamship enterprise in Chinese waters yields several different types of collaboration between Chinese and foreign interests. In the shipping business of the 1860s and 1870s, there was a classic instance in which Chinese merchants invested in foreign steamship companies as a means of shielding their wealth from the Qing state. As the shipping business changed, this form was soon displaced by a more enduring collaborative mechanism that, like the treaty system, provides a view into the complex relations between foreign expansionism and Qing agency. This mechanism was a shipping conference initiated in 1877 between the three most powerful steamship companies on the Yangzi River and coast: the Qing-sponsored China Merchants Steam Navigation Company and the British China Navigation and Indo-China Steam Navigation Companies. Through the 1870s, all three firms competed fiercely, fueled by state support in the case of the China Merchants Company and the worldwide expansion of British shipping in the case of the others. By the end of the decade, these firms chose to resolve their struggle through a shipping conference: an oligopolistic cartel that set freight rates and divided the trade and profits among them. Within the shipping conference, the companies worked together to ensure their mutual survival and prosperity. It was an institution that persisted, with varying levels of strength and influence, until the Second Sino-Japanese War (1937–45).

Like the treaty system, the shipping conference deepened the asymmetries between its participants over time. The British firms were its most obvious beneficiaries. The conference was modeled on similar agreements made among British overseas steamship lines and was promoted in China by the head of the British merchant firm that ran the China Navigation Company. Initially, the conference kept the three steamship companies on relatively equal terms, but over time the British firms were able to take advantage of superior access to capital and connections to resources that allowed them to diversify and develop new trades that the China Merchants Company could not match. Within Chinese waters, the British firms' share of the conference steadily grew while the China Merchants Company's declined.

In 1877, the China Merchants Company was by far the largest steamship company in Chinese waters, but by 1911 it was clearly subordinate to British rivals. Historians have often criticized the company's leaders' decision to join the shipping conference, as it meant abandoning the company's early "proto-nationalist" goal to take back merchant shipping in Chinese waters from foreign firms.[31] As a collaborative mechanism, however, the conference was not entirely inimical to Qing (and later Chinese) sovereign interests. Whereas by the turn of the twentieth century the company had fallen behind its British counterparts in the size of its fleet, market share on key routes, and scope of operations, the secure business and profit that the conference guaranteed helped the company survive a rocky history that included management problems, accusations of corruption from the bureaucracy, declining state support, and an onslaught of new competition on major routes from German, Japanese, and French shipping firms after 1895. In other words, even as the conference reinforced the inequities between the British firms and the China Merchants Company, it also provided the Chinese company some much-needed protection. Subsequently, the China Merchants Company endured several transformations—it was privatized in 1911 and nationalized in 1933—but it remained a viable and significant merchant steamship company under the Chinese flag (both Qing and Republican) through 1937.

SOCIAL SPACE

Circulating among the ports of the network, steamships were novel physical and social spaces, distinguished by greater numbers of people working and traveling in close proximity. The confines of their interiors demanded an explicit organization of the space that facilitated command and control, molding many of the actions and interactions that could take place within them. With its deliberately constructed features, the steamship provides a context in which foreign and Chinese employees and passengers shared its sometimes impersonal and sometimes peculiarly intimate spaces. Whereas the questions of sovereignty and collaboration highlight some of the particularities of the semi-colonial formation, an investigation of steamships as social spaces reveals an arena easily recognizable within a colonial studies paradigm of confrontation with Western power /knowledge: the production and reinforcement of racial categories and hierarchies.

The space of the steamship was marked by hierarchies of racial privilege in the arenas of work and travel. In steamship crews, Europeans (or Japanese in Japanese companies) held the positions of highest authority and those requiring technical knowledge, while Chinese workers invariably held the less skilled positions. Steamship passenger accommodations distinguished between "foreign" and "Chinese" classes of travel, with the most expensive and luxurious class designated "foreign," and three or four cheaper classes with fewer amenities marked for "Chinese." The existence of such hierarchies is not in itself particularly revealing; the more significant question is how they were understood and maintained over time in a shipping field composed of British, Japanese, and Chinese companies. Steamship companies did not have explicit policies barring Chinese seamen from technical positions or Chinese passengers from the foreign first class. Management practices offer a partial explanation for the perpetuation of hierarchies and exclusions, but the conceptions and constructs of race and competence that underlay them are most often revealed outside the company archive, culled from the writings of outside observers, travel writers, and journalists who attested to and interpreted their personal experiences of the space.

The consistency of these practices across the shipping field provides yet another perspective from which to view collaboration in semi-colonial China. The spaces were structured in very similar ways on the China Merchants Company's ships as they were on Japanese and British companies', with only slight variations in management practices. This uniformity was in part a product of the shipping conference, and in part the result of the primacy of foreign companies in this business shaping the standards and expectations to which the later-arriving Chinese and Japanese firms adhered. Both the mechanism of the shipping conference and the perception of some of these practices as the standards in the field made sharp departures from them difficult, and hence they were perpetuated to some degree by all of the steamship companies in Chinese waters.

Racial exclusion in semi-colonial China can appear unreal in that there were few tangible traces of it. There is no colonial state archive whose laws or policies make distinctions between metropolitan citizen and colonial subject.[32] It is more evident within the institutions of the variety of foreign communities of the treaty ports—clubs, schools, or centers of worship—and the varying approaches of these communities to interactions with the Chinese. In such cases, exclusion is often articulated in terms of the preferences of a specific community, and therefore within a very particular and personalized sphere.[33] Familiar cases remind us that exclusions could become contentious if the social spaces in which they occurred blurred the line between communal and public. The infamous "No Dogs and Chinese Allowed" sign at the Shanghai Public Garden may have been apocryphal, but the principle that the Public Garden (in spite of its name) should be maintained for the exclusive use of the foreign community was in place for much of the park's history.[34]

Steamships were another space that blurred this line: was the "foreign" first class reserved for the foreign community, or was the entire ship open to anyone able to purchase a ticket? Significantly, it was not just the possibility of exclusion from this most elite class of travel that Chinese passengers protested, but also the ways companies managed the spaces designated "Chinese." They objected to the practice of contracting out the management of the Chinese passenger classes to a comprador, as it absolved the companies of any responsibility for conditions within these classes. Since the comprador was a fellow Chinese, this practice reinforced the idea that the dirt, disorder, and overcrowding in these accommodations represented the actual preferences of Chinese travelers. As steamships circulated among the ports, they rendered such racial constructions and hierarchies inescapably concrete. In the 1920s and 1930s, the social spaces of steamships became targets of nationalist criticism and reform, with advocates looking to reformulate the space to convey their own visions of the Chinese nation.

SHIPPING NATIONALISM: REPUBLICAN-ERA CRITIQUES OF SEMI-COLONIALISM

Nationalist discourse and protest so saturate the sources of Republican Chinese history that they have engendered a certain skepticism about the harms that they tried to redress. In its most extreme form, this skepticism has been expressed through arguments that minimize the historical significance of semi-colonial domination, casting it as an invention of Chinese nationalists. Rhoads Murphey, for instance, argued that Chinese nationalists overstated the economic efficacy of foreign domination to blame it for China's unsatisfactory economic and political progress.[35] Even scholars deeply engaged with Republican-era nationalism have struggled to reconcile the intensity of nationalist discourse and the limited extent of the foreign presence. In his rigorous study of the Nationalist Revolution, John Fitzgerald referenced this apparent disjuncture, although he also cautioned that "any attempt to devise an accurate measure of foreign economic or political influence in China in an attempt to explain or justify the strength of anti-imperialist sentiment is likely to be misplaced."[36]

It is likely the juxtaposition of a totalized "foreign presence" against a similarly totalized Chinese nationalism that has produced these doubts about the proportions of impact and response. Steam shipping, again as one element of the semi-colonial order, provides a specific context in which to investigate how the concrete effects of semi-colonialism provided crucial building blocks for the nationalist imaginary to follow. During the Republic, the field of steam navigation was a site of concentrated nationalist activity. Although the Chinese nationalists involved in it undeniably indulged in polemics, their arguments and proposals addressed specific conditions within the field. Any involvement in Republican-era shipping made it impossible to ignore the dominance of foreign-flag ships on major routes and the treaty privileges that underwrote their presence.

Mainstream nationalist arguments coalesced around the related ideas of shipping rights recovery and shipping autonomy. Emerging from the late Qing, the discourse of shipping rights recovery shifted the discussion of Chinese sovereignty from the Qing-era problematic of protecting existing systems of governance to one where China sought to claim its sovereign rights as a nation-state and participate in regimes of international law. Arguments for shipping autonomy focused on eradicating foreign shipping power in Chinese waters and replacing it with self-sufficient Chinese shipping enterprises. These concepts were at the heart of Republican-era shipping nationalism, although the courses of action proposed from different locales and institutions were varied and sometimes contradictory.

Commitment to shipping nationalism was particularly strong among a new generation of private Chinese shipping companies that emerged in the late Qing and early Republic. Even as foreign shipping enterprise continued to grow in Chinese waters during these years, new Chinese companies began to challenge it in major trades. In their struggle to gain entry to these trades, Chinese companies readily deployed the language and tactics of the nationalist movement to their advantage. The founders of several of these new companies also consciously cultivated images of themselves and their companies as nationalist, adhering to a common praxis in the development of their companies and their public personas. Although these firms did not displace the dominant companies and the shipping conference system, they did become a significant presence on the Yangzi River and coastal routes.

The shipping nationalism of the Republican period was not well coordinated with the state-building efforts of the Nationalist government. Shipping nationalism emerged among steamship companies and activists during the early Republic without much state involvement or support. The establishment of the Nationalist government in Nanjing in 1927, with its claim to represent the central government of China, made shipping once again an arena of state intervention. Nanjing exerted its authority over shipping regulation and administration in addition to pursuing treaty revision. The Nanjing regime's questionable control over the country, however, made it just one among many entities pursuing the goals of shipping nationalism. Between 1929 and 1938, the semi-independent militarist Liu Xiang (1888–1938) implemented his own program for shipping autonomy on the Upper Yangzi River in Sichuan Province. Liu was surprisingly effective at diminishing the power of foreign shipping and increasing the presence of Chinese companies on the Upper Yangzi, but his actions clashed with—and likely helped undermine—the Nationalist government's plans for treaty revision. Despite the Nationalist government's uncertain control, however, advocates of shipping nationalism continued to hope that the state would play a central role in pursuing its goals. Ship owners' associations lobbied the government to adopt the shipping rights recovery agenda that challenged foreign navigation rights in Chinese waters. Private shipping firms anticipated state aid that would sustain them in their fight against foreign companies. Eventually, both were disappointed by what they perceived as Nanjing's limited outlook in these areas.

The social space of the steamship within the context of shipping nationalism became both a new object of scrutiny and a target of urgent reform. All steamship companies, Chinese and foreign, responded in some way to the nationalist politics of the Republican period. Considerations of cost, improvements in the technical training and licensing of Chinese seamen, and increased labor activism provided incentives for steamship companies to dissolve the formerly rigid division between foreign skilled personnel and Chinese workers. Some companies—both Chinese and non-Chinese alike—sought to downplay the distinctions between foreign and Chinese classes of travel, providing a new range of options to an increasingly demanding Chinese clientele. Yet for some nationalist reformers of this period, the need to transform steamship space was far more pressing than small adjustments and gradual improvements would satisfy: for them the space was a site in which to project new visions of the Chinese nation and its citizens. The most dramatic instance of the transformation of steamship space was carried out by the Chongqing-based Minsheng Industrial Company under its founder, Lu Zuofu (1893–1952). Minsheng rejected the prevailing practices of the shipping business and replaced them with new management techniques that reconstructed the relationships between employees and the company and those between the company and the traveling public. In his particular revision of steamship space, Lu attacked not just the inefficiencies of the older organization but also their representations of race and Chineseness. The later adoption of Lu's methods by Jiang Jieshi's (1887–1975) New Life Movement (initiated in 1934) and their transmission to other Chinese shipping companies underscored the efficacy of Lu's riposte to the social spaces created by semi-colonialism.

The multiple strands of shipping nationalism in the Republican period were cut short by the outbreak of the Second Sino-Japanese War and the radical reorganization of shipping made necessary by wartime conditions. The shipping nationalism of the Republic thus did not advance a linear process of national emancipation, although many of its principles were revived after the war, particularly in the first years of the People's Republic. The importance of Republican shipping nationalism was its ability to organize productive efforts against and generate precise critiques of semi-colonialism.

CHINA AND INDIA

The development of steam transport networks, growth of steamship enterprise, social spaces of steamships, and nationalist responses to a foreign-dominated shipping sector provide discrete points of comparison between China and British India over the 1860–1937 period. These comparisons help sharpen the book's arguments for the particularity and comparability of semi-colonialism by furnishing continuities and distinctions between these two contexts.[37] More significantly, the comparisons also render visible how China's and India's histories were intertwined in this period. Several of the comparisons herein make evident Robert Bickers's and James Hevia's observations that British India played a profound role in shaping the British presence in China, supplying personnel, practices, anxieties, and expectations that affected British decisions and behavior in China.[38] Furthermore, they show China and India to have been both subject to and participant in the global rise of British shipping power in the mid-nineteenth century, a process facilitated by the colonization of India and one that far transcended the bounds of any one colony or other imperial formation. The intention of these comparisons, therefore, is to articulate the specificities of semi-colonial China and simultaneously situate it within the broader history of the global intensification of Western expansionism in the nineteenth and twentieth centuries.

The book is organized into two major sections that correspond to the two distinct periods of semi-colonialism in China between 1860 and 1937. Within each section, chapters address the major themes of politics of shipping, the organization of the shipping business, and the social space of the steamship. The first section examines the period from the implementation of the Treaty of Tianjin (1860) to the fall of the Qing dynasty (1911). In this period, the central dynamic of semi-colonialism is the close interaction between the Qing state and the treaty system. The second period, from founding of the Republic of China (1912) to the beginning of the Second Sino-Japanese War (1937), is characterized by the disintegration of China into competing warlord regimes, the prolonged difficulty in restoring a central government, and the rise of a widespread nationalist movement. The book concludes with the outbreak of the Second Sino-Japanese War in 1937. Wartime conditions presented a sharp break with and a considerable disruption of the processes examined here. The question of shipping autonomy in China, however, would not be fully resolved until the early years of the People's Republic, a process detailed in the conclusion.

CHAPTER 1

Sovereign Concerns

The Formation of a Semi-Colonial Steam Transport Network, 1860–1911

Rutherford Alcock (1809–97), the British consul at Shanghai in 1848, commented on the increasing traffic in foreign-flag ships along China's coast: "In a political point of view the transfer of the more valuable portion of their junk trade to foreign bottoms is highly desirable, as tending more than any measures of Government to improve our position by impressing the Chinese people and rulers with a sense of dependence on the nations of the West for great and material advantages, and thus rebuking effectually the pride and arrogance which lie at the root of all their hostility to foreigners."[1] For Alcock, the Chinese demand for these foreign shipping services provided the proof of a particular relationship he envisioned between Britain and the Qing dynasty, one wherein the Chinese acknowledged the superiority of and depended on the West. Shipping Chinese goods in foreign vessels was a means of persuasion, a wedge that would crack the Qing dynasty's reluctance and doubt about such a relationship. Foreign shipping may never have fulfilled the political mission Alcock assigned to it, but his account of the demand for it was not mistaken: in the years following the First Opium War, the carriage of Chinese cargoes in foreign vessels along the coast became a profitable trade, and Western ship owners brought vessels to China specifically to engage in it. After the Second Opium War, the activity of foreign-flag shipping in Qing waters was formalized and extended by the unequal treaties. Shipping remained a mode of foreign expansion into the Qing dynasty through its fall in 1911.

As the once informal and unsanctioned "coasting trade" in foreign ships became a part of the treaty system, Qing officials acted to restrict these ships to open ports alone, a decision that defined a shipping network along the eastern coast of China and into the Yangzi River Valley. Within this treaty-port network, steamships overtook sailing vessels within a short time, and the network became as important to trade and travel within the empire as it was for overseas trade.[2] The network continued to grow over the latter nineteenth century, becoming denser along existing routes and incorporating new areas into it. It was the only modern transport network in Qing China before the initiation of railway construction in the 1890s.

As the expansion of this shipping network was adjudicated through the treaty system, the process illuminates key interactions between the Qing state and the interested treaty powers. Between 1860 and 1895, the steam shipping network was primarily the product of Qing relations with a single power—Great Britain. Britain consistently initiated negotiations or demanded the concessions that expanded the scope of foreign shipping in China. British predominance in this arena was both the outcome of the leadership role the country had assumed among the treaty powers and a sign of its growing power and interest in shipping worldwide. After 1895, as Japan asserted itself as a shipping power in Qing waters and on overseas routes, it joined Britain in pursuing shipping concessions from the dynasty.

These interactions reveal the operations of Qing sovereignty within the semi-colonial formation. This sovereignty had been damaged by the Opium Wars and the treaty settlements, but by 1860 the powers had rejected conquest and colonization in favor of the treaty system, and supported continued Qing rule to limit their commitments in China. Fundamental to this system was the principle that a viable central government would ensure the enforcement of treaty terms.[3] Qing officials worked within the treaty system to limit more extreme demands for and curb the undesirable effects of the expansion of foreign-flag shipping. The policy of the newly established Qing Office for Managing Affairs with Various Countries (Zongli geguo shiwu *yamen*, or Zongli *yamen*) remained consistent for several decades: the protection of those areas in which Qing governance remained in place, unaffected by the potentially destabilizing consequences of foreign shipping and trade. Foreign observers often interpreted Qing officials' defense of these sovereign concerns as a failure to appreciate the benefits of technology and progress, yet in the process, Qing agency significantly shaped the emerging shipping network.

From 1860 to 1911, the treaty powers pressed the dynasty for greater and greater shipping privileges within the empire as Qing officials sought to contain the growth of foreign shipping. This dynamic underscores that the treaty system was a collaborative mechanism but a particularly tense and conflicted one. Both sides were invested in the preservation of Qing sovereignty but clashed over the expansion or containment of foreign shipping privileges. The asymmetrical power relations were evident from the collaboration's earliest days and can help explain the limitations of Qing resistance: at the same time that Qing decisions shaped the network, the dynasty was compelled to legitimize informal extensions of foreign privilege when it could not reverse or eradicate them. Furthermore, disagreements among British interests over the limitations of Britain's role in China subjected the Qing to constant pressure to expand the steam network between 1860 and 1911. Qing officials' argument for containing foreign shipping remained consistent, although Britain and later Japan succeeded in steadily expanding the scope of their privileges throughout this period.

Origins: The Coasting Trade as Informal Expansion, 1842–60

The steamship did not become a significant presence in China's coastal and river shipping until the early 1860s, but the shipping network that it eventually dominated originated from the activities of foreign-flag sailing ships on the coast between the Opium Wars. During this interval, European and U.S. sailing ships took advantage of the new conditions established by the Treaty of Nanjing (1842) to become carriers in China's coastal trade. Ships under foreign flags were no longer merely conveyances for the import and export trade between the Qing dynasty and places abroad: foreign-flag shipping had become a service sold to Chinese merchants and traders operating domestically. This new shipping trade had not been anticipated by the European or Chinese formulators of the Treaty of Nanjing, but it grew exponentially through informal channels during the interwar years.

The Treaty of Nanjing's six open ports and decentralized administration provided scope for this new trade. The Canton system (1757–1842) had confined European traders to the port of Canton so that their ships only entered and cleared this single port. The additional five open ports of the new treaty regime made it possible for foreign ships to circulate among them. The ships, often in search of the best markets for their cargoes, began to do so almost immediately. A further significant feature of this treaty regime was that conflicts, disputes, and problems within the trading system were addressed to Qing imperial commissioners who resided in the open ports, which meant there was often considerable variation in the administration of treaty terms among the different ports. Because there were no treaty provisions governing the movement of foreign ships among the open ports, the details were decided in practice.

Since at first most of these ships carried import and export cargoes, their movements along the coast raised the question of whether they had to pay import/export duty at all ports at which they stopped or only at their port of entry. After some confusion, imperial commissioners began to issue "exemption certificates" attesting that ships had paid full duty at one port and excusing them from paying at others. Subsequent treaties between the Qing and foreign powers, such as the Sino-American Treaty of Wangxia and the Sino-French Treaty of Whampoa (both signed in 1844) included provisions that explicitly sanctioned the movement of foreign ships among the open ports.[4]

As this framework developed, foreign-flag ships immediately began to exceed it by providing shipping services to Chinese merchants. In addition to their own trading activities, ships could earn freight by carrying Chinese-owned cargoes among the open ports. To Chinese merchants, foreign-flag ships offered the advantages of greater speed and armed protection in coastal areas disturbed by piracy and the outbreak of the Taiping Rebellion (1850–64). They also offered marine insurance, an amenity not available in junk shipping. This trade became profitable enough that it was soon more than a supplement to other trading activities: Europeans began bringing ships to the China coast specifically to engage in the shipping trade. Some Chinese merchants chartered whole foreign vessels and sublet the cargo space to other merchants.[5] English-language sources refer to providing shipping services to Chinese merchants among the ports as the "coasting trade."[6] In the 1840s, foreign-flag ships also engaged in a convoy trade, in which heavily armed schooners and lorchas (European-style hulls with Chinese-style rigs) protected fleets of Chinese fishing and cargo junks from pirates for substantial—some said extortionate—fees.[7]

The coasting trade engendered some outright violations of the treaty, the most prominent of which was foreign-flag ships transporting goods to places outside of the treaty ports. Captains justified this practice by arguing that their ships were under charter to Chinese merchants and were needed for carrying goods to places where junk shipping was unsafe. They interpreted local Qing authorities' silence on the matter as permission to continue.[8]

Even when ships stuck to the open ports, the carriage of Chinese merchant cargoes in foreign-flag ships muddied the distinction between the systems for administering foreign and domestic trade. The Qing dynasty collected duties on foreign trade through the Maritime Customs (*haiguan*) system and on domestic trade through the Domestic Customs (*changguan*) system. Under the Maritime Customs system, foreign-owned cargoes paid import or export duty only once, since they were presumably entering from or clearing for places abroad. Under the Domestic Customs system, Chinese-owned cargoes paid duties at multiple barriers along trade routes, albeit at rates far lower than those of the Maritime Customs. It was not clear which system applied to Chinese merchant cargoes transported in foreign-flag ships, and the question was settled differently by individual imperial commissioners in the ports. Commissioners complained that the participants in this trade tried to manipulate the distinction between the two systems for their own benefit.[9] In 1847, an exchange of notes between the British governor of Hong Kong and the imperial commissioner Qiying (1787–1858) tacitly recognized the coasting trade, both sides agreeing that Chinese merchants could ship their goods in foreign-flag ships as long as they paid the correct duties, although they did not specify how to determine these duties.[10] By the late 1850s, a consensus emerged among treaty-port commissioners in which foreign-flag vessels paid Maritime Customs duties regardless of the ownership of the cargo. This method was probably the simplest way to avoid verifying ownership of multiple cargoes aboard a single ship.[11]

The coasting trade furnished a reliable source of profit to European merchants under otherwise disappointing trade conditions. By many European accounts, the concessions obtained under the Treaty of Nanjing had not improved the trade as hoped. Of the treaty ports, only Shanghai and Canton sustained a substantial direct trade abroad. Others, such as Xiamen, Fuzhou, and Ningbo, had almost none. The strong demand for coasting trade services, however, had "proved [these ports'] salvation" as sources of profit.[12] Upon the Qing's defeat in the Second Opium War, British merchant groups lobbied to make their participation in the coasting trade a new treaty right.

Lord Elgin (James Bruce, 1811–63) was the British official charged with negotiating the terms of the new treaty settlement. He refused the merchants' request to raise the topic of the coasting trade in treaty negotiations, citing the principle of international law under which the carriage of domestic produce from port to port within a nation (cabotage) was generally reserved for the ships of that nation. Foreign participation in the cabotage of another nation "was not a right so recognized by international practice in Europe as to justify imposing it by force."[13] Neither the 1858 Treaty of Tianjin nor the 1860 Peking Convention contained any mention of the coasting trade.[14] Elgin's acknowledgment that this trade infringed on Qing sovereignty signified only his unwillingness to discuss it in formal negotiations. Neither he nor any other European diplomatic official made any effort to stop the coasting trade, and it continued apace through the Second Opium War and into the 1860s.

Formalization: The Shipping Network under the Treaty of Tianjin, 1860–70

The Treaty of Tianjin, the settlement that concluded the Second Opium War, brought significant change to many aspects of the relations between the Qing and the treaty powers and the administration of foreign trade and shipping in China.[15] Under the new treaty regime, the shipping networks of the coasting trade—the unanticipated consequence of the previous regime—were recognized, formalized, and subsumed into the treaty system. The formalization of this network happened not during the treaty negotiations but just afterward, as Qing and British officials worked through the problems and inconsistencies they encountered in implementing the treaty regime. Three key decisions in this process established the parameters of the shipping network: the recognition of the coasting trade, the limitation of foreign-flag shipping to the treaty ports, and the decision to subject Chinese-owned ships of Western design (steamships or clippers) to the same restrictions as foreign-owned ships. The first two decisions were made in 1861, immediately after the treaty went into effect. The Zongli *yamen* announced the third in 1867, when Chinese participation in steamship ventures had become impossible to ignore.

The negotiated solutions to the problems of implementing the treaty were themselves a product of the new regime. The Treaty of Tianjin permitted European powers to post diplomatic legations with resident ministers in Beijing and required the Qing dynasty to abandon its earlier protocols of foreign relations and adopt European notions of interstate diplomacy.[16] Whereas under the Treaty of Nanjing foreign consuls addressed complaints and concerns to imperial commissioners in the treaty ports, such issues were now adjudicated in the capital between the diplomatic representatives of the powers and the dynasty. The British formulators of the treaty believed that bringing the "central government of China" into the process would minimize the arbitrariness and inconsistencies of the previous system and ensure greater compliance with treaty terms.[17]

Although the Qing dynasty famously resisted posting diplomatic legations in the capital until the bitter end of the Second Opium War, soon thereafter it made the institutional adaptations necessary to participate in this new system of relations. It established the Zongli *yamen* in January 1861 to manage affairs with the treaty powers, led by the emperor's brother Prince Gong (Yixin, 1833–98).[18] In significant policy matters, the Zongli *yamen* sought the counsel of a group of Qing officials with experience in "Western Affairs" (*yangwu*). This group included the famous leaders of the Taiping suppression (and military modernizers) Zeng Guofan (1811–72), Li Hongzhang (1823–1901), and Zuo Zongtang (1812–85), as well as provincial governors and governors-general in maritime provinces and trade commissioners and customs officials in the treaty ports.[19]

The treaty extended the Foreign Inspectorate of the Chinese Imperial Maritime Customs to all of the open ports and established an inspector-general in Beijing. The Foreign Inspectorate had begun as an ad hoc arrangement under which foreign consuls collected duties on behalf of Qing officials during a period of unrest in Shanghai in 1854, but because it offered better returns to the dynasty and greater consistency in the collection of duties to foreign traders, the new treaty replaced the earlier system of collecting Maritime Customs duties with this newly centralized bureaucracy.[20] Although its inspectors-general were British and much of its staff European, it was an agency of the Qing state, collecting revenue on its behalf. Like the officials of the Zongli *yamen*, Robert Hart (1835–1911), who became officiating inspector-general in 1859 and inspector-general in 1863, was closely engaged with the administration of the new treaty regime.[21]

One of the first issues the new Qing agencies negotiated with British diplomats in summer and fall 1861 was the opening of the Yangzi River. Within this discussion, they reached resolutions to several questions related to the status of the coasting trade. These negotiations resulted in a set of rules—the Yangzi Regulations—announced in October 1861. These regulations established important parameters for foreign-flag navigation, which within the decade became the parameters for all steam navigation in Qing waters.

The coasting trade was not the central concern of the negotiators, but it presented enough obstacles to implementing the new treaty regime that they addressed it in these talks. The impetus came from the new Maritime Customs administration, which now confronted the problem of how to collect duties on Chinese-owned cargoes transported in foreign-flag ships. Hart brought the question to the Zongli *yamen*, and after much deliberation, he and *yamen* officials devised a system for collecting duties on the coasting trade, which they then proposed to the British and French ministers. Similar to interwar practice, coasting trade cargoes in this system were classified by the nationality of the ship rather than the owner of the goods, so foreign-flag ships always paid Maritime Customs rather than Domestic Customs duties or other local taxes. The Maritime Customs further assessed an additional half-duty on ships that had paid import/export duty at one treaty port and moved on to a second (called a coast-trade duty). After this was paid, the cargo was exempt from further taxation if it went on to other ports. Once approved by the British and French, the new system was included in the 1861 Yangzi Regulations.[22]

This system for collecting duties on the coasting trade amounted to an official recognition of a trade that had developed through extra-treaty channels, and brought it into the formal treaty regime. In the aftermath of the Second Opium War, Qing officials believed it would be both politically and logistically impossible to eradicate this trade. Recognizing and bringing it into the treaty system allowed the dynasty to both supervise it and collect and distribute its revenue. The decision was a considerable blow to Qing sovereignty nevertheless. The recognition of the coasting trade signified the dynasty's renunciation of its claim to the empire's cabotage. Subsequently, nations seeking commercial treaties with the Qing claimed participation in the coasting trade as a treaty right: treaties with Denmark (1863), Spain (1864), and Belgium (1865) all included such provisions.[23]

The negotiations over the Yangzi Regulations, however, were not a complete loss for the Qing. Related to the central issue of the Yangzi River, the Zongli *yamen* was able to use the process to shut down further avenues of informal expansion within the system of foreign navigation and trade. The regulations definitively limited foreign navigation to the open treaty ports: foreign-flag ships could not anchor or trade anywhere other than those ports named in the treaties. This decision was most immediately a response to the opening of the Yangzi River when many parts of the surrounding area were under Taiping control, but it also halted what had been an illegal but largely tolerated practice in the interwar coasting trade—for foreign-flag ships to transport cargo to places not opened by treaty.

The Treaty of Tianjin's Article X declared the Yangzi River open to foreign navigation and trade, but stipulated that the river would remain closed until the Taiping Rebellion had been suppressed completely. In November 1860, Lord Elgin, then in Beijing as commander of the British military forces, and his brother Frederick Bruce (1814–67), the newly appointed British minister to China, proposed to open the river early, making the argument to Prince Gong that foreign trade would help revive commerce in war-stricken areas and aid the suppression effort by increasing the dynasty's revenues. The prince agreed to their proposal.[24]

The intense anticipation of European merchants may have prompted the brothers' request. The prospect of access to this central river had raised enormous expectations for the prospects of steam navigation in Chinese waters. The interwar coasting trade had been carried on predominantly in sailing ships; only a few large trading houses used steamships to transport valuable cargoes like opium rapidly along the coast.[25] River navigation would justify the considerable expense of building and fueling steamships because it would make use of their capacity to travel quickly against a current. New sources of coal discovered in Japan and Australia, and rumors of coalfields along the Yangzi itself, also promised to lower the cost of steam navigation.[26] Well before the official opening of the river, large firms and individual traders began to bring steamships to China from other parts of the world.

With permission obtained from the dynasty, Elgin and Bruce took steps to open the Yangzi River, although each proceeded in a different manner. The Treaty of Tianjin had named the three river ports of Zhenjiang, Jiujiang, and Hankou as treaty ports. In Beijing, Bruce drafted a set of provisional rules specifying that trade was allowed at these ports and strictly prohibiting any trade in arms or ammunition with the Taipings.[27] Elgin and his forces stopped in Shanghai as they withdrew from China early in 1861, and from Shanghai he moved to open the river on somewhat different terms. Elgin sent Admiral James Hope (1808–81) and Consul Harry Parkes (1828–85) on a mission upriver from Shanghai to secure agreements from Taiping leaders not to attack foreign ships or interfere with foreign trade.[28] In his instructions to Parkes, Elgin specified that he did not want British vessels to be limited to specific ports but intended instead to "throw open to them the general coasting trade of the river."[29] When Parkes declared the Yangzi open to foreign trade by consular notification on March 18, 1861, his notification stated that the river was closed between Shanghai and Zhenjiang because of the heavy Taiping presence, but that ships were permitted to "discharge or load legal merchandise at ports or places on the river above [Zhenjiang]," a phrase understood to mean that trade was allowed at all points on the river between Zhenjiang and Hankou. For the months in which these regulations remained in effect, foreign merchants and ship owners enjoyed what they called "free trade" along the Yangzi above Zhenjiang.[30]

The interval of several months of free trade on the Yangzi more than fulfilled the high expectations of European traders for shipping profits, particularly from steamships. Because steamships could traverse Taiping-occupied territories rapidly, they could charge steep rates to carry cargo and passengers and tow sailing ships upriver. Alexander Michie (1833–1902), a British merchant resident in Shanghai at the time, described the rush of activity: "The interior of China had for years been dammed up like a reservoir by the Taipings, so that when once tapped, the stream of commerce gushed out, much beyond the capacity of any existing transport. The demand for steamers was therefore sudden, and everything that was able to burn coal was enlisted in the service."[31] Others noted that steamships were paying for themselves because of the enormous demand for their services.[32]

The opening of the Yangzi under Elgin's orders, however, drew immediate protests from Qing officials. Although trade with the Taipings was expressly forbidden, Qing officials reported foreign-flag ships carrying on a flagrant trade in food and arms to rebel areas.[33] They complained of Chinese merchants using foreign-flag ships to smuggle salt and evade tax barriers.[34] Since the *lijin* tax, a transit tax levied on Chinese trade, was a major source of funds for the Taiping suppression campaigns, compromising this revenue could have dire consequences for the Qing.[35] When Frederick Bruce and the Zongli *yamen* began negotiations over the implementation of the treaty in the summer of 1861, their first action was to rescind the provision of the Hope-Parkes regulations that allowed foreign-flag ships to land anywhere above Zhenjiang. New rules announced that foreign trade on the Yangzi would henceforth be confined to the three treaty ports of Zhenjiang, Jiujiang, and Hankou. A later set of revised regulations announced that "shipment or discharge of cargo at any other point on the river is prohibited and violation of the prohibition renders ship and cargo liable to confiscation."[36]

The decision drew loud protests from the European merchant community. British chambers of commerce in the treaty ports argued that the new regulations had rescinded a "right" that had already been obtained from the Qing.[37] An editorial in the *North China Herald* claimed that the restriction of trade to the treaty ports was contrary to the "spirit" of the Treaty of Tianjin.[38] Another complained that Qing officials had destroyed a flourishing trade by enforcing the rule against ships landing cargo at nontreaty ports "too vigorously."[39] Minister Bruce responded that

Elgin, Hope, and Parkes had been too hasty in opening the river and insufficiently aware of the Qing's concerns.[40] He emphasized his own approval of the regulations' ability to limit British involvement in illegal trading activities, to which he referred as "a formidable bar to pacific progress."[41] Despite vocal merchant opposition to the regulations, the British Foreign Office backed Bruce's decision.[42]

The 1861 Yangzi Regulations formalized the foreign-flag shipping network in Chinese waters and made it part of the treaty system. The coasting trade, initially an extra-treaty development, was officially acknowledged and its revenue collection systematized. The limitation of foreign navigation to the treaty ports foreclosed the possibilities of expansion through the regime of free trade along the Yangzi and clearly outlawed the earlier practice of foreign ships landing at nontreaty places. These decisions brought foreign-flag shipping in Qing waters from an amorphous set of practices into a sharply defined network: foreign ships could circulate among the treaty ports, paying duty at Maritime Customs stations and carrying cargoes for both foreign and domestic trade, but they could not extend beyond the treaty ports. Any expansion of this network would require opening a new treaty port and would thus have to proceed through formal negotiations in the Qing capital. The significance of these decisions would become even clearer as steamships became more prevalent within the network.

The negotiations for the Yangzi Regulations exemplify the dynamics of collaboration under the treaty system. In this process, the exercise of Qing sovereignty and the limitations it encountered are apparent. As the limitation of foreign navigation to the treaty ports shows, Qing officials could reverse foreign policies that threatened dynastic control; such actions in turn had a profound effect on the constitution of the shipping network. But this sovereignty could only be exercised within certain constraints. Qing officials acknowledged that they lacked the power to eradicate the coasting trade and thus chose to recognize and regulate it. In doing so, they relinquished any potential to use international law to claim the Qing empire's cabotage for indigenous ships.

After 1861, the circulation of ships within the network of treaty ports became progressively more significant. In important ports like Shanghai and Canton, although some of the cargoes entering and clearing these ports were coming from or going to places abroad, a growing number were coming from or going to another treaty port. An 1861 report estimated that 50 percent of the steam traffic coming through Shanghai was destined for other treaty ports rather than for places abroad, and by 1863 that figure had reached 70 percent.[43] Many of the open ports carried on very little foreign trade but derived their significance from shipping. The British consul at Zhenjiang, for example, complained that its commerce was "fortuitous and accidental," and that it served as a calling station for Yangzi steamers.[44] Over the course of the 1860s, steamships had taken over much of the traffic among the treaty ports from foreign-flag sailing vessels.[45]

The decision that transformed the treaty-port network from one defined by foreign navigation to one defined by steam navigation was made by the Zongli *yamen* in 1867. It was a resolution to subject steamships (and other ships of Western design, such as clippers) owned by Chinese merchants to the same conditions as those owned by foreigners: limiting them to the treaty ports and having them pay duty at the Maritime Customs. With this decision, all steamships in Qing waters were tied to the same network of open ports.

The Zongli *yamen* reached this conclusion in the process of addressing the somewhat different problem of bringing Chinese ownership of Western-style ships under government control. Legally, Qing subjects were prohibited from purchasing or owning steamships (or other ships of Western design), but many merchants in the treaty ports owned such ships, often operating them under a purchased foreign registration and flag.[46] Chinese merchants were also often owners, part-owners, or shareholders in the steamships (and later steamship companies) that Western trading firms operated in the treaty ports.[47] Qing officials saw the purchase of foreign registrations as a means to shield criminal behavior and evade taxation, while the purchase of shares in foreign steamships allowed merchants to conceal their wealth from official view and protect it from exactions.[48] Officials expressed concern that Chinese merchants would be cheated or foreign governments might make claims on Chinese businesses.[49]

By formulating regulations for Chinese owners of Western-style ships, the Zongli *yamen* hoped to bring these activities under government supervision.

The Zongli *yamen* polled officials in Shanghai, Fujian, and Guangdong for their opinions on the regulations, and in the course of that discussion, a further question arose of how Qing authorities should treat steamships owned by Qing subjects: should they be treated like foreign-flag ships or like Chinese junks and other indigenous craft? If considered closer to foreign-owned ships, they would be confined to the treaty ports and pay duty at the Maritime Customs; if classified as Chinese craft, they could move freely through the empire's waterways and pay duty at Domestic Customs and *lijin* barriers. Although a number of the officials polled argued that treating Chinese-owned steamships like other Chinese craft would give them an advantage over foreign steamships, the final regulations published in 1867 subjected all Chinese-owned ships of Western design to the same rules that governed foreign-flag ships.[50] The rationale for this decision came from Li Hongzhang, who argued that offering Chinese-owned steamships any privileges beyond those given to foreign ships would only make foreigners demand the same privileges.[51] Therefore, the 1867 "Regulations for Chinese Purchasers and Charterers of Steamships, Clippers, etc." (*Huashang maiyong yangshang huolun xiaban deng chuan xiang zhangcheng*) stipulated that these ships were also confined to the treaty ports and paid duty at the Maritime Customs.

The Zongli *yamen*'s regulations did not have much of an immediate impact: no merchant ever registered a steamship with the Qing authorities under these rules, and they did not end the purchases of foreign registrations or shares in foreign steamships.[52] In 1872, however, when the dynasty approved the establishment of a government-sponsored commercial steamship company, the China Merchants Steam Navigation Company (Lunchuan zhaoshang ju), its ships were subject to the same restrictions. Although one of the goals of this company was to compete with foreign steamship firms, China Merchants ships were not allowed to travel beyond the treaty ports and paid duty at the Maritime Customs. The text of the new company's rules echoed Li Hongzhang's concern: China Merchants ships were subject to these restrictions "to avoid Western merchants making a pretext of it" to gain greater access to Qing waterways.[53]

The Zongli *yamen*'s decision to limit Chinese-owned steamships to the treaty ports appears to deny Chinese ship owners advantages that indigenous shipping might have enjoyed, and several contemporary studies interpret the 1867 regulations as evidence of the repression of commercial activity under Qing rule.[54] Yet such an interpretation is insufficiently attentive to the position of the dynasty within the collaborative mechanism. The decision was based on the conviction that foreign demands for shipping privileges would continue and intensify—a concern that far outweighed any thought to improve conditions for indigenous merchants. By denying Chinese-owned ships an advantage, the Qing officials' intent was to foreclose further demands that might be pursued through the treaty system. In this instance, Qing officials may have been acting against the interests of Chinese merchants, but their priority was to check foreign expansion.

The result of these regulations was that as steam navigation was growing on the Yangzi River and coast, all steamships—not just those under a foreign flag—were restricted to the treaty ports. The treaty port thus became a vital part of shipping infrastructure—the node where steamships could anchor, load and unload, and pay duty. This full identification of steam navigation with the treaty ports meant that the future development of the steam transport network had to take place through the diplomatic channels of the treaty system, since it would require opening a new treaty port or extending formal treaty privileges. This characteristic imposed certain limitations on steam navigation in China. After 1860 there were thirteen treaty ports connected to one another and to ports abroad by the speed, power, and reliability of steam navigation, whereas intermediate points were not accessible by steam (see map 1.1). This relatively sparse network displaced some preexisting long-distance transport trades—most dramatically the sand boats (*shachuan*) that carried tribute grain from the Yangzi provinces to Tianjin—but increased levels of junk transport between treaty ports and intermediate places.[55] The restriction of steam navigation to the open ports made casual steam tramp trades unprofitable, and instead favored the development of liner companies in which coordinated fleets carried high-value goods at regular intervals among the ports.[56]

The network covered great distances, linking ports on the northern coast to those in the south, and linking these coastal places to the central heartland of the Yangzi River Valley. Because Shanghai was situated at the confluence of these river, coastal, and international shipping routes, it quickly became the linchpin of the network and the central market for the import-export trade. The Yangzi ports of Hankou and Jiujiang had been chosen as treaty ports because of their proximity to black and green tea–producing districts, yet in the 1860s most of the trade in teas from these districts took place in Shanghai, since steamships could transport

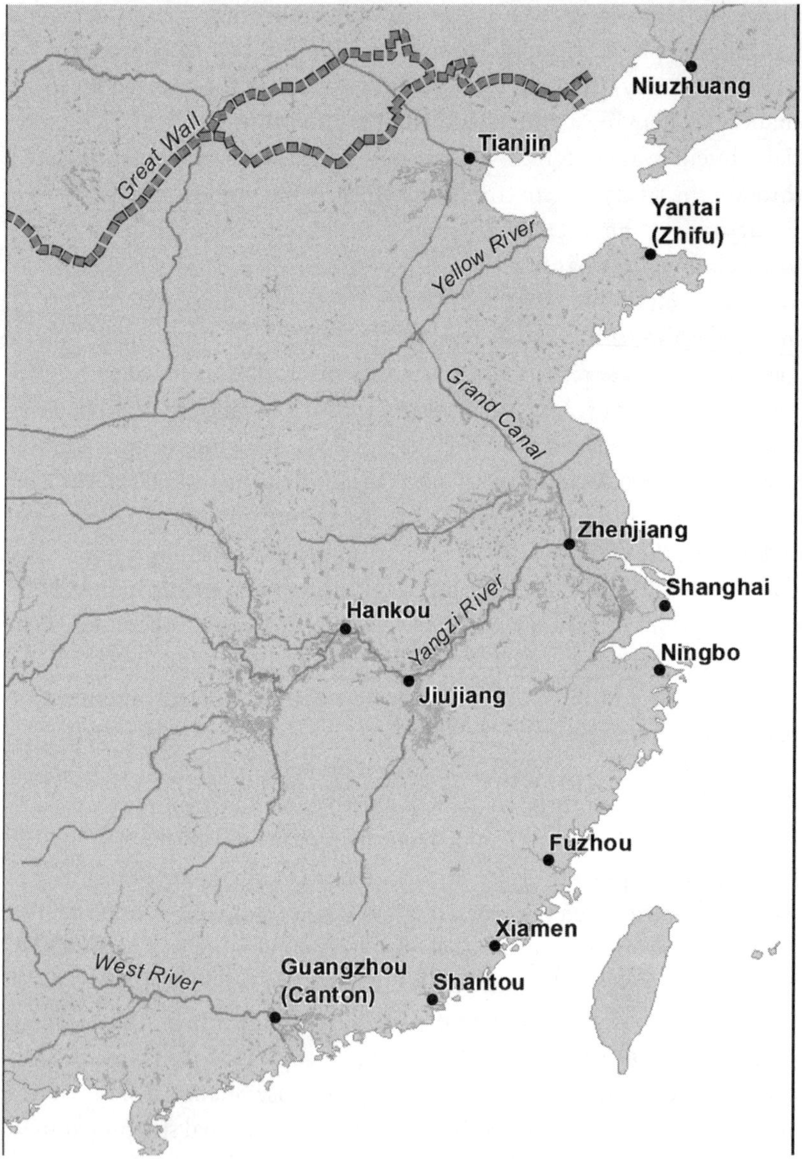

MAP 1.1 Open Treaty Ports, 1860–77. Adapted from K.C. Liu, *Anglo-American Steamship Rivalry*, 5.

crops to Shanghai rapidly.[57] Consuls at coastal ports such as Tianjin and Canton reported that the majority of ships entering and clearing these ports were coming from or heading to Shanghai.[58]

The solidification of the steam network in the 1860s also transformed the import-export trade. Foreign traders complained that the availability of steam transport had allowed Chinese merchants to take over the distribution of the key commodities of the import-export trade—opium, tea, and textiles—from European trading houses. Although many trading firms had set up branch offices or agencies in the newly opened treaty ports after 1860, they found that Chinese merchants, who had lower overhead costs and better market information, made use of steam transport to distribute and sell these goods at a lower cost than they could.[59] The *North China Herald* reported that since Chinese merchants had begun to use steamships, any advantages in the "rapidity of transit and returns" once enjoyed by foreign merchants now belonged to the Chinese.[60]

By the end of the decade, steam navigation and the steam transport network were becoming significant components of the Qing dynasty's domestic commerce. Steamships were initially concentrated in the import-export trade, carrying goods of high value and low volume like opium, silk, and cotton cloth, but by the late 1860s they were increasingly participating in China's interregional trades. Chinese passengers—such as merchants accompanying cargoes to market or examination candidates traveling to the capital—became a source of profit for steamship companies in addition to the transport of domestic staple goods, such as raw cotton and rice.[61] Within the decade, the steam network had become a central transport infrastructure in the Qing empire, one whose significance continued to grow through the early twentieth century.

Sovereignty, Technology, and Expansion, 1864–70

The Yangzi Regulations of 1861 and the Zongli *yamen*'s decision to subject Chinese-owned steamships to the same limitations as foreign steamships identified steam navigation with the treaty ports. Although this principle endured through the mid-twentieth century, it was constantly challenged, particularly through the Qing dynasty's remaining years. Steam navigation remained a critical mode of foreign expansion in China, and Qing officials were under constant pressure to extend the existing network and free foreign-flag ships from its constraints. Before the Sino-Japanese War (1894–95), nearly all such demands came from Great Britain. Through a variety of opportunities to revise treaties and make new demands, Britain enlarged this network well beyond its initial bounds.

The contours of the conflict between Britain and the Qing dynasty over the expansion of steam navigation in Chinese waters were apparent during the 1861 negotiation and persisted through the end of the dynasty. The Zongli *yamen* and Qing official position remained consistent: it sought to contain foreign navigation to the greatest extent possible, closing down potential avenues of informal expansion and keeping foreign-flag shipping from extending to new regions of the empire. In so doing, the Zongli *yamen* and Western Affairs officials' foremost concern was Qing sovereignty, defined in very concrete terms. They focused on ensuring that dynastic authority, systems of governance, and systems of revenue collection remained as undisturbed as possible in areas that had not already been integrated into the treaty system. The introduction of foreign shipping under extraterritorial protection to new areas could change the balance between central and provincial government finance: Beijing received a portion of Maritime Customs revenue and provincial governments retained greater control of Domestic Customs, *lijin*, and other trade taxes. When foreign navigation extended to a new place, not only did foreign-flag ships pay Maritime Customs duties but if they were to put local shipping trades out of business, they could disturb a province's revenue streams.[62] For Qing officials, foreign trade and navigation also raised the incidence of tax evasion, threatened existing shipping systems vital to Qing interests, and increased the possibility of conflict between Qing subjects and foreigners. Qing officials repeatedly articulated these sovereign concerns in response to expansionist demands.

The British pressure to extend foreign shipping privileges in China did not originate with a specific policy but was the product of inveterate tensions between British commercial interests and diplomatic representatives over Britain's role in China. There was a conviction among merchant groups that restrictions imposed by the Qing undermined their trade and greater access to China would redeem it. At the same time, the

British Foreign Office and diplomatic establishment in China did not see the potential of the China trade as significant enough to warrant the cost of deeper imperial commitments.[63] Nathan Pelcovits named these merchant groups—which included members of trading firms such as Jardine, Matheson & Company; British chambers of commerce in Shanghai, Hong Kong, and the treaty ports; as well as commercial organizations in London and Manchester—the "old China Hands." Treaty-port publications such as the *North China Herald* provided platforms for their views.[64] Confronting official skepticism about the potential of their trade, the China Hands consistently lobbied the British government to secure greater privileges for them.[65] The China Hands' agenda was unapologetically expansionist and at times verged on calls for the colonization of China.

British diplomats never explicitly endorsed the China Hands' proposals, but they also did not ignore them. The Foreign Office and British diplomats in China consistently consulted these merchant groups when they had opportunities to engage the Qing diplomatically or press for further concessions, adapting elements of the agenda to fit each circumstance. The expansion of steam navigation in the Qing empire through the turn of the twentieth century was propelled by this intermittent diplomatic attention to the China Hands' views. In the 1860s, British diplomats were committed to the Cooperative policy in China, under which they undertook to settle disputes through negotiation and support the Qing dynasty's "legitimate interests" in return for the dynasty's enforcement of the treaties. At this time in particular, the diplomats tended to support the Qing's sovereign concerns over the more extreme of the China Hands' claims.[66]

In conflicts over steam navigation and shipping privilege in the 1860s, the China Hands' arguments represented their desire for expansion as inevitable and beneficial technological progress and Qing objections to expansion as a fear or misapprehension of technology. In the wider history of colonial discourse, deploying technology in an expansionist argument is not unusual: the "civilizing" power of technologies like steamships and railways was often used as justification for European colonial projects.[67] Yet given how insistently past historiography has presented Qing officials in precisely this mode—as conservatives whose commitment to tradition precluded their appreciation of Western modernity—it is striking that any discussion or debate on technology in these cases was confined entirely to the China Hands' own writings. The Qing sources on these incidents never engage with questions of technology and its power or potential. For them, steamship technology was apparently not a significant problem: they were far more preoccupied with immediate challenges to dynastic order and control that the expansion of steam navigation—and thus extension of the foreign trade system—entailed.

Characteristic patterns of interaction between Qing officials, British diplomats, and the China Hands were visible in the negotiations for the 1861 Yangzi Regulations: Qing officials insisted on the limitation of foreign navigation to the treaty ports, British merchants protested that the Qing were rescinding a "right" (to free trade on the Yangzi) it had already conceded, and British diplomats backed the dynasty. The pattern was repeated several years later when the Qing attempted to enforce the principle of restricting foreign-flag ships to the open ports. In 1864–65, Li Hongzhang, as acting Liangjiang governor-general, shut down a foreign steam launch trade on the rivers and creeks between Hangzhou, Suzhou, and Shanghai.

This trade had started during the Taiping occupation of the Jiangnan area, when steam launches under foreign flags could carry goods such as silk and cash between the Jiangnan cities and Shanghai with relative safety. Once the Taiping Rebellion was suppressed, Li Hongzhang stopped the trade because the launches were landing at places outside of the treaty ports.[68] The British, French, and U.S. merchants involved in this trade argued that since Qing officials had failed to stop the trade earlier, it was a right they had obtained in practice. Some launch owners tried to argue that the Treaty of Tianjin's consular passport system sanctioned their trade, since it permitted foreigners to travel throughout the Qing empire.[69] The new British minister in Beijing, Rutherford Alcock, dismissed this as an excessively liberal interpretation of the treaty clause and upheld Li's ban.[70]

A *North China Herald* editorial on this incident represented the cancellation of the launch trade as Qing officials' inability to appreciate the benefits of the steamship and other transport technologies:

> Beyond the same instinctive desire to oppose foreign intercourse which first suggested the endeavour to oust us altogether, and now impels them to restrict as much as possible our movements, the real reason why the officials

> oppose the introduction of either steamers or railways is the dread lest the boating class be deprived of their occupation. And when we consider how recently the operatives of our large manufacturing towns in England destroyed the machine which they feared was destined to supersede handicraft, it is not surprising that they should entertain this apprehension. Experience can only teach them, as it has taught us, that improvement in mechanical appliances does actually rather increase rather than diminish the demand for labour.[71]

This account shifts the conflict from one over the limitation of foreign-flag ships to the treaty ports to one over steamship technology. Not only is Qing opposition presented as instinctive rather than reasoned, the passage implies that it derives from inexperience with, and therefore fear of, new technology, comparable to the Luddite opposition to textile mechanization in England.

In Li Hongzhang's correspondence with the Zongli *yamen* about this ban, steamships were not the central focus. He discussed instead the anticipated complications of the extension of the foreign trade system into an area recovering from the Taiping occupation. Additional traffic on the Jiangnan waterways would impede the restoration of the salt monopoly and grain tribute systems in this wealthy area. Foreign-flag navigation would increase the likelihood that Chinese merchants would use such ships to avoid *lijin* barriers, threatening the revenue source for reconstruction efforts.[72] Li voiced some concern that the steam launches would threaten the junk trade on these waterways, but his interest was not for the livelihood of the "boating class" but to secure a reliable fleet to resume the grain tribute and salt monopoly. Beyond his anxieties about reconstruction, Li emphasized the importance of reinforcing the principle of restricting foreign-flag navigation to the treaty ports: unruly foreigners could use the opportunity to go outside of the ports to escape the jurisdiction of their consuls, and if any exception were made for this particular trade, other foreigners would soon demand this privilege for themselves.[73]

In shutting down the steam launch trade, Li Hongzhang exercised the margin of sovereignty afforded to Qing officials under the treaty system, the defense of the dynasty's "legitimate interests," and the use of the terms of the treaties to check foreign expansion. This precise action was interpreted by the *North China Herald* as a moral position on the steamship itself: the dread of the consequences for "time-honored" traditions with the introduction of a new technology. In Li's discussion of the ban, however, there is no trace of such philosophical consideration of the demands or consequences of tradition and progress; his is a pragmatic argument for the containment of the foreign presence, both to ensure the progress of post-Taiping reconstruction and to reduce the likelihood of future demands.

British Minister Rutherford Alcock backed Qing sovereign interests over the objections of the China Hands in the case of the steam launch ban, but he subsequently sought the advice of these British merchant groups in formulating new demands to bring to the dynasty. The Treaty of Tianjin was scheduled for revision in 1869, and as early as 1867 Alcock began touring the treaty ports, soliciting suggestions for the new treaty. British merchant groups submitted petitions to the Foreign Office and published articles in the *North China Herald* that detailed their dissatisfaction with the existing treaty regime and proposed changes to it.[74] This interval gave the China Hands an opportunity to formulate an agenda for change to the treaty system, and theirs was an unabashedly expansionist one, the central principle of which was the removal of nearly all restrictions on foreign trade.

The consensus among the various organizations of China Hands was that the Treaty of Tianjin had failed to benefit British business and trade in China. Advocates pointed to the expanding role of Chinese merchants in the distribution and sale of import and export products and expressed frustration with the inefficiency and expense of distributing their goods beyond the treaty ports, problems they attributed to insufficient transport and "irregular and excessive" Qing taxation.[75] The key remedy proposed by numerous petitions and articles was removing the barrier of the treaty ports, providing full access to all parts of the Qing empire. As one editorial put it, "free access, as *settlers*, to all parts of China—leaving the ports to buy directly from producers and sell directly to consumers."[76] Along with this privilege, the China Hands also demanded the right of "inland navigation" by which they meant "free and full permission to any foreign vessel to enter any Chinese port."[77] The China Hands petitions contended that such an expansion of their presence in the Qing empire would ultimately benefit both foreign and Chinese trade, as it would permit them to develop the empire through technologies such as steamships, railways, mines, and telegraphs.[78]

As these arguments emerged in the treaty-port press, the Zongli *yamen* made its own preparations for treaty revision. It sent a secret letter to officials who held the rank of governor or higher and had experience with the treaty system, requesting their responses to the key points of the China Hands agenda. The original letter indicated that the Zongli *yamen* had no plans to entertain these proposals, stating that the only way foreigners would be allowed beyond the treaty ports would be if they were to give up extraterritoriality and were treated as Chinese traders.[79] The respondents to the letter echoed this stance. Most of the respondents also dismissed inland navigation as posing too great a threat to Qing sovereignty and territorial control: compromising the empire's military integrity and inviting disorder, whether through Chinese merchants using the foreign trade system to evade tax barriers or the complications of supervising foreign traders beyond the treaty ports.[80]

The officials' responses to the China Hands' proposal to develop the Qing empire through Western technologies again reveal the absence of any connection between the technological justification for expansion and Qing officials' concrete concerns. Most respondents dismissed the idea that the large-scale introduction of Western technologies would ultimately benefit Qing subjects, but not because they objected to technological change itself. They argued instead that the intended changes did not support the Qing state's priorities. In arguing for extending steam navigation, for example, the China Hands repeatedly contended that Qing officials need not fear the demise of the junk trade because steamships would provide employment for even larger numbers of Chinese workers.[81] Several respondents to the secret letter scoffed at this argument, declaring that the fate of the common worker was not their concern. In objecting to the proposal for inland navigation, they cited instead the large-scale junk shipping trades that had serviced the tribute grain system and the salt monopoly and had declined in competition with steam navigation on the coast. These trades were crucial to state interests and entitled to state protection, as well as being trades in which many Qing officials had financial interests.[82] Qing resistance to this proposed "technological development" was neither moralistic nor sentimental: officials objected to the ways the foreign trade system had already disrupted or undermined the dynasty's sovereignty.

Conscious of the extent of Qing opposition, Alcock did not press the China Hands' agenda in the 1869 treaty revision. Rather than raising demands such as inland navigation or the right to build railways, telegraphs, and mines throughout the country, the Foreign Office and British minister opted for a gradual approach to addressing trade grievances. The revision agreement, known as the Alcock Convention, consisted of mostly adjustments to the existing system, and included no provisions for extending steam navigation other than the opening of two new treaty ports.[83] The diplomats' disregard of the China Hands' agenda, however, proved costly. The Alcock Convention caused an uproar, particularly in London, for its failure to extract greater concessions from the Qing, and merchant organizations blocked its ratification by the British government. Debates between Alcock, the Foreign Office, and chambers of commerce in London continued for over a year, but ultimately the Alcock Convention was never ratified or implemented in China.[84]

The events of the 1860s such as the ban on steam launches and the 1869 treaty revision set up many of the dynamics of expansion of the steam network in subsequent decades: the extreme expansionism of the China Hands, the struggle of Qing officials to anticipate and contain this expansion, and diplomatic attempts to mediate. In the 1860s, the diplomats were attentive to Qing objections, but after the 1870 Tianjin Massacre and their subsequent abandonment of the Cooperative policy, the dynasty could no longer count on such support. The China Hands' agenda continued to be a source for new proposals to extend steam navigation and the foreign trade system.

The representation of Qing officials within the expansionist discourse of the 1860s as naively fearful of technology unquestionably elided any acknowledgment or consideration of Qing sovereignty. Lydia H. Liu has argued that the historiographical position that tradition-bound Qing officials were unable to meet the challenges posed by the modern West trivializes Qing resistance to European expansion by representing it not as a reasoned response to an unprecedented political situation but as a traditionalist's opposition to social change.[85] The expansionist discourse of the China Hands anticipated this position precisely. Not only was Qing opposition to the extension of steam navigation a concrete and pragmatic defense of the dynasty's sovereign concerns with its own control, order, and revenue streams at stake, but the very Zongli *yamen* and Western

Affairs officials who argued against extension of foreign navigation were instrumental in the actual deployment of steamship technology in Qing China.[86] They used steamships to transport soldiers and tribute grain during the Taiping suppression and to patrol for smugglers and pirates in the Canton delta. They initiated the military self-strengthening programs at the Fuzhou Shipyard and the Jiangnan Arsenal, where the first steamships were built in China. Many were involved in the establishment of the Qing-sponsored China Merchants Steam Navigation Company.[87] The view that Qing officials' commitments to "tradition" prevented an adequate response to the modern West has long been subject to critique, but its origins in the expansionist discourse of the 1860s are worth acknowledging.[88]

Struggle over the Interior, 1870–95

The failure to ratify the 1869 revision of the Treaty of Tianjin meant that many of the questions raised in the process—particularly that of greater British access to the Qing empire—were not resolved conclusively. Over the subsequent two and a half decades, the pressure on the Qing to expand the foreign trade system and steam network persisted. Distinguishing this period from the 1860s was the new position of British diplomats. The China Hands remained consistent in their advocacy of expansion, but the diplomats were no longer as supportive of the Qing dynasty's interests. After the Tianjin Massacre, Britain and other treaty powers withdrew the Cooperative policy, and were more likely to demand punitive concessions or attempt to hold the Qing accountable for evading treaty obligations.[89] This shift in the diplomats' position gave the China Hands a greater voice than they had in the previous decade: as the diplomats found new opportunities to press the Qing for concessions, they returned again and again to the China Hands' agenda to formulate them.

Debates over expansion centered on access to the "interior" of the Qing empire. This term had two slightly different but equally significant meanings at the time. One referred to areas located far inland in China that had become known to Europeans through expeditions undertaken in the 1860s under the Treaty of Tianjin's consular passport system. New knowledge of this interior raised the seductive possibility that the true commercial potential of China lay beyond the areas open to European traders. The second meaning was part of the idiosyncratic lexicon of the treaties, in which "interior" (*neidi*) referred to any place within the empire that had not been opened as a treaty port. The China Hands pressed for access to this interior as well, hoping for the removal of the barrier of the treaty ports. Qing officials also used the word *neidi* in arguments for maintaining its integrity under the continual push for expansion: for them, it meant the places where the treaty system did not reach and in which Qing systems of governance and revenue collection were not complicated by foreign trade, even if these places were situated along a coast or river. Between 1870 and 1895, the British made demands for access to new areas and continued to challenge the boundary of the treaty ports.

From the late 1860s, the publication of geographical and economic intelligence gathered by numerous expeditions to remote areas of the Qing empire added color and urgency to arguments for expanded access. The Treaty of Tianjin had made it possible for Europeans to travel throughout the empire under consular passports, and many had taken the opportunity to go to new places. Some of these expeditions were undertaken with grand imperial ambitions, such as finding routes that could link China with British possessions in India or besting Russia and France in the race for power and territory worldwide. Transport technologies played an important role as explorers tried to identify routes suitable for steam navigation or railroads that would facilitate these connections. Several expeditions—such as one headed by British Navy Captain Thomas Blakiston (1832–91) in 1861 and another led by Calcutta Chamber of Commerce member Thomas T. Cooper (1839–78) in 1868—focused on the Yangzi River, intending to trace the river to its source in the Himalayas and locate efficient transport routes linking China, Burma, and India.

One of the concrete demands that emerged from this wave of exploration was the idea of extending foreign trade to Sichuan Province, particularly to the port of Chongqing on the upper reaches of the Yangzi River. Blakiston, Cooper, and others reported on the rich commercial possibilities at Chongqing, noting the convergence in the port of traders from Sichuan, Yunnan, and Guizhou Provinces and comparing its trade to that of important treaty ports like Shanghai, Hankou, and Canton.

Detracting only slightly from the exciting possibility of an undiscovered trade entrepôt so deep in the interior of China was the problem that Chongqing could not be reached by steamship. It was separated from the navigable lower portions of the river by the scenic Three Gorges area, which also hosted dangerous rapids, whirlpools, and shoals that made steam navigation treacherous.[90] The explorers concurred that although current steamship technology was not adequate to navigate this area safely, if the problem could be solved, the extension of steam navigation would allow Europeans to tap the rich commerce of Chongqing.[91]

British Minister Alcock commissioned a navigational and commercial survey of the Yangzi River in 1868, which concluded that the best means of accessing the promising trade of Chongqing would be to open the Hubei port of Yichang, the highest point on the river that could be easily reached by steamship. At Yichang, goods could be trans-shipped from steamers to junks and sent on to Chongqing, until a steamship could be devised that could navigate the Upper Yangzi rapids.[92]

The idea that access to Chongqing would provide the much-needed boost to the Europe–China trade became so popular that in January 1872 the Associated Chambers of Commerce in Britain petitioned the Foreign Office to procure the right to navigate the Upper Yangzi, arguing that "the richest and most industrious province of China [would be] brought into almost direct communication with Europe."[93] Later that year, newly appointed British Minister Thomas Wade (1818–95) proposed this to the Zongli *yamen* as part of a short-lived attempt to negotiate commercial concessions outside of the treaty revision process. The Zongli *yamen* refused Wade's request on the grounds of protecting provincial finance: Sichuan's provincial officials did not want foreign trade and ships to compromise their collection of *lijin* and Domestic Customs revenues.[94]

Both Blakiston's and Cooper's expeditions were halted by unrest or local opposition on the Qing empire's western borders. This tendency for explorations under consular passport to run into trouble in the far reaches of the empire was what provided British officials with a fresh opportunity to pursue diplomatic and commercial concessions. In 1875, A. R. Margary (1846–75), a junior member of the British consular service, was killed by Shan tribesmen in a remote area of Yunnan Province while on an expedition searching for railway routes connecting Yunnan to British possessions in Burma.[95] Minister Thomas Wade sought redress from the Qing on the grounds that the government had failed to ensure Margary's safety while under consular passport. For this failure, Wade said, he intended to "extract privilege as a penalty."[96] The Chefoo (Zhifou) Convention, negotiated in 1876, settled the Margary affair.

Overall, the penalties imposed by the Chefoo Convention were not significant departures from the trade system of the 1860s, but they extended the steam network and made it denser along existing routes. Although the China Hands had rejected the idea that trade could be improved by gradually opening more treaty ports, the Chefoo Convention did just that, establishing five new treaty ports—Wenzhou and Beihai on the coast and Wuhu, Yichang, and Chongqing on the Yangzi River—in addition to recognizing six ports of call along the Yangzi River. The opening of Wuhu in Anhui Province had the benefit of situating a Maritime Customs house in a new province, which helped regularize the collection of duties on the import-export trade as it passed through Anhui.[97] The Yangzi River ports of call—Shashi, Luxikou, Wuxue, Hukou, Anqing, and Datong—were large towns situated at points between Yangzi treaty ports where steamships had been observed landing passengers for several years.[98] Their recognition as ports of call allowed the Zongli *yamen* to oversee and limit foreign activity in them. To prevent foreigners from building warehouses or settling in these ports, the convention ruled that steamships could only load or unload passengers—but not cargo—at ports of call. Steamships were not permitted to anchor in port but had to transfer passengers onto registered junks in the middle of the river.[99]

The Chefoo Convention also attempted to fix the idiosyncratic use of the term "interior"/*neidi* in the context of the treaty system. The convention stipulated that the word applied to places on the coast or rivers as well as actual inland places, signifying all places beyond the treaty ports that were not (as yet) opened to foreign trade.[100]

With the opening of Yichang and Chongqing, the Chefoo Convention answered the desire for the extension of foreign trade into the deep interior, but only provisionally. Because steamships could easily reach Yichang, it became the western terminus of the Yangzi steam network. The convention stationed a British consul in Chongqing but stipulated that the port would not be fully open to foreign trade until it could be reached by steamship.[101] This provisional opening thus challenged all those eager to reach Chongqing to devise a steamship that could traverse the Upper Yangzi.

Qing officials may have agreed to the provisional opening of the port in hopes of delaying the extension of the steam network and trade system to Sichuan. After the Chefoo Convention was signed, the Zongli *yamen* refused requests from established steamship companies, including Jardine, Matheson's Indo-China Steam Navigation Company and the Qing-sponsored China Merchants Steam Navigation Company to survey the Upper Yangzi and assess its navigability. It considered Sichuan too unstable for foreign trade, as banditry, secret society activity, and violence against missionaries and Chinese Christians had increased in the province.[102] Following a series of attacks on missionaries in the Chongqing area, the Zongli *yamen* argued that the appearance or even rumors of a steamship's arrival might cause further antiforeign agitation and violence, the types of incidents for which Qing officials now knew they could be forced to account.[103]

But such measures did not deter those convinced of the benefits of opening Western China to foreign trade. Archibald Little (1838–1908), a British tea taster and trader, wrote a popular book promoting this cause that argued extending steam navigation to Chongqing would "create another Shanghai in Western China."[104] Little raised funds in England to build a steamship designed for the Upper Yangzi: a ship of light enough draft to pass over its rocks and shoals but with sufficient power to steam upriver through the rapids. In 1887, he brought this ship to China, intending to use it to secure the full opening of Chongqing.[105] The Zongli *yamen* requested that British Minister John Walsham (1830–1905) prevent Little from taking his ship upriver, but Walsham suspected the Zongli *yamen* was using the reports of unrest in Sichuan to avoid fulfilling the provisions of the Chefoo Convention. Walsham refused to stop Little, insisting that the convention sanctioned his effort.[106]

Unable to stop the venture, the Zongli *yamen* ordered local officials in Hubei and Sichuan provinces to take measures to prevent their riverine populations from interfering with Little's ship.[107] It also insisted that the British consul at Yichang and deputies of the Huguang and Sichuan governors-general draw up rules for preventing collisions between steamships and junks on the Upper Yangzi before Little's ship could proceed. Negotiations over these rules, however, took so long that Little accepted a substantial payment from Qing officials for his ship in exchange for a promise not to make another attempt at Upper Yangzi navigation for ten years.[108] Little claimed that he had run out of funds, but some speculated that the ship had not proven suitable for Upper Yangzi conditions. The British Foreign Office objected to this settlement as a Qing attempt to evade a treaty obligation and instructed Walsham to make a formal demand to open Chongqing. The demand resulted in the signing of an additional article to the Chefoo Convention on March 31, 1890.

The additional article officially opened Chongqing without the condition of steam navigation. As a concession to Qing concerns, it stated that foreign steamships could only navigate the Upper Yangzi after Qing-flag steamers established a presence there. Since there was no immediate prospect of steam communication, the additional article established a system of "chartered junks" to carry goods between Yichang and Chongqing. These were specially designated Chinese craft that flew the flags of their charterers and paid duty at the Maritime Customs.[109] Predictably, the chartered junk system raised the concerns of provincial officials: Huguang Governor-General Zhang Zhidong (1837–1909) argued that it provided yet another opportunity for Chinese merchants to use foreign flags to evade tax barriers.[110] To protect provincial revenue, Sichuan Governor Liu Bingzhang (1826–1905) demanded that provincial governments be allowed to increase duties on opium carried in foreign-flag ships and decrease *lijin* rates paid by Chinese merchants, a suggestion that was incorporated into the final version of the additional article.[111]

The extension of steam navigation through the Yangzi gorges to Chongqing was perhaps the only point in the steam network's development at which technical obstacles were more significant than political obstacles. It was nearly twenty years before regular commercial steam navigation was established on this route. In 1898 and 1899, Archibald Little made two successful steam voyages through the gorges, but his ships were too small to be commercially viable. In 1900, the spectacular wreck of a German steamer in the rapids and plans for a railway in Sichuan discouraged further attempts, and Upper Yangzi steam navigation was limited to British and French gunboats of extremely light draft. In

1909, however, a company started by Sichuanese provincial officials established regular steam communication between Yichang and Chongqing, using ships designed by the Maritime Customs' Upper Yangzi River Inspector Cornell Plant (d. 1921).

The general desire of the China Hands to transcend the limitations the treaty system placed on their trade was condensed into the project of extending foreign trade and steam navigation deep into the interior, to the port of Chongqing. Qing officials remained consistent in their aim of containing the destabilizing effects of foreign trade and navigation, in this case particularly to places where it was completely unfamiliar. Although these positions were quite similar to what had come before, the shift in the stance of the Foreign Office from supporting Qing sovereign concerns to suspicion of Qing motives meant that collaboration under the treaty system had become increasingly tense. The Zongli *yamen* and other Qing officials were under nearly constant pressure to expand the network. Although they retained some power to regulate, deflect, or slow down the expansion process, the steam network increased in size and density over this period.

Eclipse of the Interior: The Steam Network in the "Scramble for Concessions," 1895–1911

Following the Sino-Japanese War of 1894–95, other powers challenged Britain's position as the principal author of the steam network and predominant foreign power in China. Within a climate of interpower rivalry and demands for exclusive concessions from the Qing, in 1898 Britain pressed for the right of inland navigation, defined in the same way as the China Hands had articulated it in the late 1860s: "free and full permission to any foreign vessel to enter any Chinese port."[112] In theory, inland navigation would eradicate the treaty ports and eclipse any distinction between the treaty ports and the interior. Yet as dramatic as the consequences of such a concession might have been, once Britain obtained it, the Maritime Customs, Zongli *yamen*, and the Qing government succeeded in taking countermeasures that curbed its repercussions. After 1898, treaty ports were no longer the absolute limit of the steam network, but they remained central to the treaty system and the trade of the Qing empire.

The context for Britain's demand was the "scramble for concessions" that followed the conclusion of the Sino-Japanese War. Prompted by the Treaty of Shimonoseki's granting of exclusive territorial concessions to Japan, powers such as Germany, Russia, and France began to demand exclusive concessions from the Qing, including demands for leased territories and "spheres of influence" in which a power enjoyed exclusive rights to build railways, mines, and industries. This atmosphere of competition among the powers, combined with the Qing dynasty's weakening diplomatic leverage following the war and the Boxer Rebellion (1899–1901), gave the powers new incentives and opportunities to secure greater commercial concessions as well.

Britain had reigned as a "first among equals" among the treaty powers for decades, as shown by the leading position it had taken in negotiating and expanding the steam network. The new territorial concessions other powers obtained raised the possibility of Britain losing its dominant position in central China. The China Association, a merchant organization based in London, advocated for Britain to answer this threat by claiming the entire Yangzi Valley as its own sphere of influence and, several years later, proposed that Britain establish a protectorate in the Yangzi Valley. The Foreign Office chose instead to sign a nonalienation agreement, in which the Qing agreed not to cede the territory to a competing power.[113] In addition, the Treaty of Shimonoseki clearly communicated Japan's plans to contest Britain's shipping power in China. Through the treaty, Japan secured shipping rights in two places over which the British and Qing had struggled: the Upper Yangzi (without waiting for Chinese steamships to reach the area first) and the inland waterways between Shanghai, Suzhou, and Hangzhou.

It was probably the pressure from these new rival powers that prompted Britain to press the Qing for the right to inland navigation, a concession that went well beyond the earlier framework for foreign trade and navigation under the treaties. Britain obtained the right to navigate all of China's inland waters when it demanded compensation for the dynasty's refusal to accept a guaranteed loan in 1898. Subsequent commercial treaties between the Qing and Britain (1902) and Japan (1903) lifted additional restrictions on inland navigation and granted foreigners the right to rent docks and warehouses in places formerly designated the "interior" of the Qing empire.[114]

Inland navigation should have rendered the steam network obsolete, because ships had obtained the right to anchor and trade anywhere in China. In reality, the effects were much narrower in scope. The provision did extend the range of places to which foreign ships could go, but in a way that strengthened the treaty-port network rather than destroying it. Qing officials managed to curb the effects of the inland navigation provision. Immediately after the signing of the 1898 treaty, the Zongli *yamen* issued regulations that limited inland navigation and made it a system separate from navigation between the treaty ports. The regulations restricted inland navigation to only those provinces with open ports and controlled the size of ships that could be taken inland. More significant, the regulations stated that steamships working in the interior had to trade on the same basis as Chinese craft: they would be required to pay duties at all Domestic Customs and *lijin* stations en route. The inspector-general of the Maritime Customs, Robert Hart, helped draft these regulations. He saw it as his responsibility to prevent inland navigation from becoming "an orgy of unlicensed carriage of goods into the interior in defiance of [Qing] national and provincial interests."[115]

British Minister Claude MacDonald (1852–1915) protested the regulations, insisting that there should be no difference between inland navigation and navigation between the treaty ports. He further asserted that in conceding the right to inland navigation, the Qing had also extended foreign extraterritorial privilege into the interior, an idea that Qing officials strenuously opposed.[116] MacDonald and the Zongli *yamen* were unable to resolve this conflict before the questions were raised afresh during the negotiations for a Sino-British commercial treaty following the Boxer Rebellion. The 1902 Mackay Treaty contained language that eclipsed the distinction between "inland waters" and "coast and river" navigation, but the central question of the extension of extraterritorial privilege outside of the treaty ports remained unresolved.[117]

Although MacDonald was able to impose his definition of inland navigation in the 1902 treaty, once again the procedures devised for inland navigation by the Maritime Customs and the New Policies–era

(1901–11) Qing ministries tempered its effects. The Qing Foreign Ministry (Waiwu bu) stipulated that those who wanted to extend steam navigation to new routes had to apply to the nearest Maritime Customs commissioner, who then awaited approval and instructions from the Ministry of Commerce (Shangwu chu).[118] These procedures allowed the ministries to veto any proposed route. As such, the reality of inland navigation never approached the China Hands ideal of a Qing empire completely open to their ships. As before, any expansion of foreign navigation had to be negotiated.[119]

Applications from shipping firms for inland waters certificates in 1904–5 show that obtaining the necessary approval for an inland waters route was difficult. Provincial and Maritime Customs officials refused requests on the basis of familiar criteria: disturbed conditions in certain provinces, prior participation of steamers in smuggling operations, or simply because steam navigation had not previously extended to a particular area.[120] The last years of the Qing saw only a gradual development of inland waters navigation on specific routes, usually in the hinterlands of treaty ports.[121] There were clusters of inland waters companies in the Canton area, on the newly opened West River, at Shanghai (serving the Hangzhou-Suzhou-Shanghai triangle) and at Hankou (connecting cities along the Xiang River in Hunan to the treaty port), on the Grand Canal between Zhenjiang and Yangzhou, the Han River, and the Poyang Lake between Jiujiang and Nanchang.[122] Inland waters navigation had thus become a discrete channel through which steam navigation occasionally extended rather than the complete opening of the interior of China.[123]

A further step the dynasty took to contain the impact of inland waters navigation was to encourage the formation of Qing-flag shipping companies on inland waters routes. After establishing the China Merchants Steam Navigation Company in 1872, the government helped it maintain a de facto monopoly on Qing-flag steam carriage within the treaty-port network by routinely refusing permission to other Qing subjects wanting to form other companies.[124] In 1896, the government began to encourage Chinese merchants to establish steamship companies on the Shanghai-Hangzhou-Suzhou route to prevent foreign shipping firms from "seizing the advantage." In 1898, it further relaxed restrictions on private shipping companies.[125] The Qing state did not support these companies to the extent that it had the China Merchants Company, but it fostered their growth to keep the inland waters routes from being overrun with foreign concerns. Between 1895 and 1911, the China Merchants Company remained the sole Qing-flag company working among the treaty ports, but a new generation of small-scale Chinese-owned shipping firms emerged on inland waters routes and made up 90 percent of inland traffic by one estimate.[126]

Although the intention behind inland navigation had been to remove the "obstacles" of the treaty ports to trade, once in place it appeared to only confirm the significance of the treaty-port and steam network. Treaty ports remained the most important junctures of the network, even as it occasionally extended onto inland waters routes. The British and Japanese demanded the formal opening of new ports such as Wanxian (1902) on the Upper Yangzi and Changsha (1904) in Hunan Province, even though access to such places might have been pursued under inland waters provisions. Treaty-port facilities, particularly Maritime Customs houses, could stabilize shipping and trade operations in new areas and improved the chance that Qing authorities would approve inland navigation routes in the area.[127] In 1898, the Qing dynasty began to open some ports voluntarily as a means of increasing trade and Maritime Customs revenues. In some cases, it is not entirely clear how voluntary the decision was: the Qing classified the ports of Yuezhou, Changsha, and Changde (all in Hunan Province) as "voluntarily opened ports," yet Japanese or British pressure played some role in the choice of all three.[128] The ability of a Maritime Customs house in a treaty port to bring new revenue to the center, however, was likely an important motivation for the voluntarily opened ports, both to fund the state-building efforts of the New Policies period and to make payments on the Qing's war indemnities.[129] By the fall of the dynasty, the steam network was considerably larger, denser, and more complex than it had been before 1895, but it continued to operate on almost the same terms as it had before.

The case of inland waters navigation at the turn of the twentieth century underscores the consistency of the dynamics of collaboration under the treaty system. As in the past, Qing agency remained significant: British and Japanese demands for inland navigation rights were imposed on the Qing, but in the process of implementing this provision, Qing officials dramatically tempered its possible consequences. Tensions between British and Qing officials over the adherence to and implementation of treaty terms had increased since 1870, but the British remained committed enough to Qing sovereignty to countenance—perhaps grudgingly—Qing efforts to parry their expansionist demands. The British and Japanese did not obtain the full extension of navigation rights or extraterritorial protection in the interior, but it would be a mistake to argue that Qing officials could effectively check foreign expansion. Fueled by the scramble for concessions, the entire foreign presence grew exponentially between 1895 and 1911. Apart from the new territorial bases and "spheres of influence," the treaty-port network itself grew, incorporating no fewer than twenty-one new ports and extending onto the West River in Guangdong and Guangxi and north into Manchuria (map 1.2).

From the inauguration of the Treaty of Tianjin's new regime to nearly the end of the dynasty, the pressure on the Qing to expand the steam network had been constant and the demands increased. Even as diplomatic relations between the Qing and the British grew frostier after the 1860s, Qing officials remained reliable collaborators, engaging with British demands and trying to adhere to the treaties while protecting their own interests. These relations continued through the end of the dynasty and a short time beyond. After 1911, the treaty system remained firmly in place, but what disappeared—particularly after 1916—was a central Chinese government that could enforce treaty terms across the country. The political fragmentation of China among competing militarists after 1916 rendered the earlier mode of collaboration impossible because the powers lacked a viable collaborator. The most palpable consequence in the shipping field was a halt of the forward momentum of the expansion so evident in the final decades of the Qing dynasty. After 1911, the powers demanded no further extensions or modifications of the steam network other than the occasional pursuit of a new inland waters route.[130] Other possible explanations for this stoppage might include that the network had reached its maximum potential or that the powers were distracted by war in Europe, but without a central collaborator, concessions could not necessarily be enforced. Collaboration did not simply abet expansion under semi-colonialism, it enabled it.

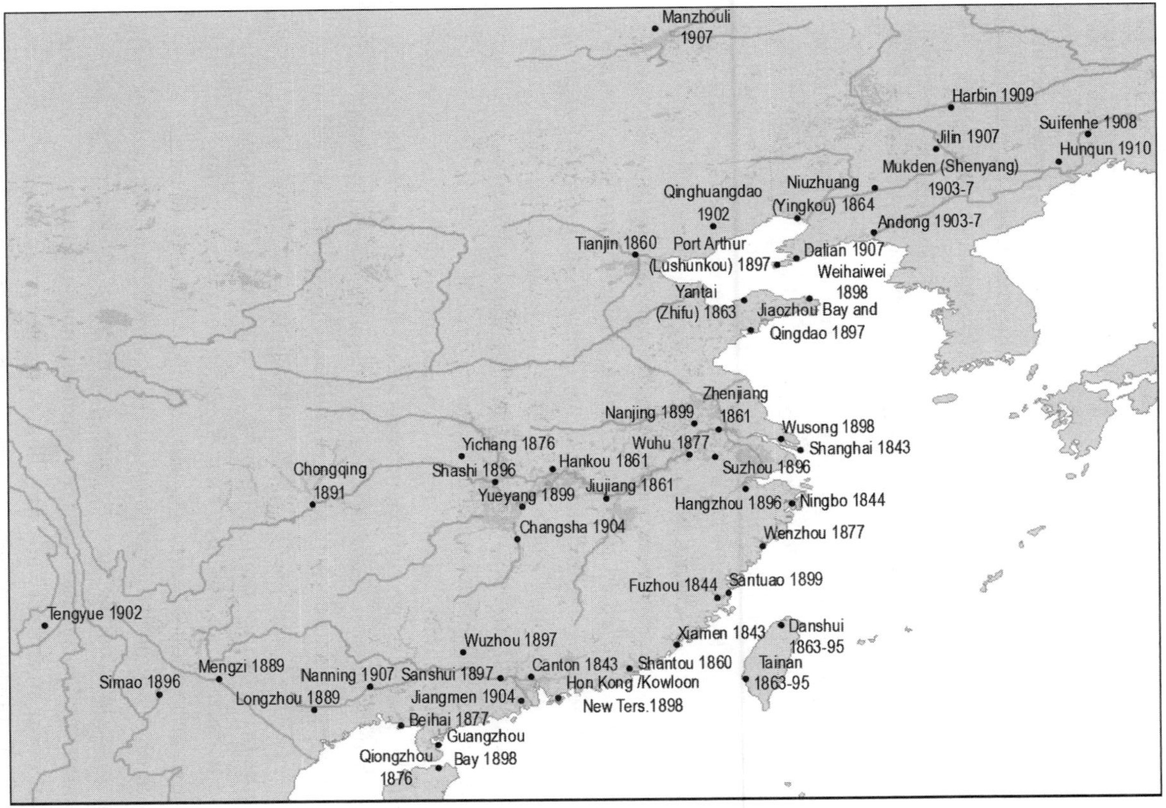

MAP 1.2 Open Treaty Ports, 1911. Adapted from Albert Feuerwerker, "The Foreign Presence in China," 130.

Conclusion

The development of this steam transport network between 1860 and 1911 reveals the operations of and the constraints on Qing sovereignty under semi-colonialism. Whereas the dynasty lacked the power to expel foreign-flag ships from its waters, its officials could limit ships' mobility and reach within the empire, shaping the effects of the steam network within that space. Under continuous pressure to expand the shipping network and foreign shipping privilege, Qing officials worked to defend the dynasty's sovereign concerns. Under the treaty system, the Qing and the treaty powers were invested in preserving the remnants of Qing sovereignty, yet the collaboration was conflicted and inequitable. Qing officials made several decisions that could be interpreted as compromising the dynasty's autonomy, such as recognizing the coasting trade and subjecting Chinese-owned ships to the same restrictions as foreign ones. These moves, however, were not made in ignorance or to placate the powers but were calculated to preserve dynastic authority under the certain pressure the powers would make further demands and in anticipation of potential future foreign violence. To judge such decisions as deficient by anachronistically nationalist or modernizing standards is to overlook the centrality of collaboration under the treaty system.

The development of the steam transport network between 1860 and 1911 also suggests a new spatial perspective on the treaty ports by presenting them as nodes in a dynamic transport system rather than individual urban centers. Although treaty ports were at the cutting edge of modern developments in nineteenth- and twentieth-century China and have been the primary loci for examining the social and cultural history of semi-colonialism, the charge that they are exceptional spaces that offer little insight into conditions across China remains difficult to counter.[131] A network of treaty ports linked by steam navigation, however, underscores the roles these ports and the treaty system more broadly played in the fundamental social and material transformations of modern China. The treaty-port steam network was the first modern mechanized transport network, predating railway construction by several decades. Even after railway construction began in earnest in the 1890s, the network remained a crucial component of China's developing transport infrastructure, with almost all major rail lines built before the 1930s intersecting with rather than running parallel to the Yangzi River shipping route.[132]

Although a complete mapping of the complex social, economic, spatial, and temporal effects of the incorporation of treaty ports into the steam network is beyond the scope of this book, changes that affected not only individual ports but their relationships to one another and to their hinterlands are readily visible. These changes were the results of the development of steam transport rather than that of a foreign presence or foreign trade.[133] Zhenjiang, from which consuls and customs commissioners long bemoaned a meager foreign trade, became the point from which Yangzi Valley rice was shipped to the southern ports of Fuzhou and Canton. Following the Chefoo Convention, Zhenjiang lost this status to newly opened Wuhu, which was closer to the producing districts.[134] Migrants also responded to shifts within the network: sojourning populations sought seasonal labor not only on the docks in the great port of Shanghai but in the smaller "outports" as well: the Maritime Customs commissioner in Wuhu described the seasonal influx of temporary workers from other places.[135] Such examples suggest that treaty ports were much more than foreign enclaves, they were the nodes of an expanding transport network, experiencing the full range of social and economic changes resulting from its development.[136]

A comparison between the steam network developed in Qing China and the one emerging in British India around the same time shows the distinct and concrete outcomes of the imperial formations of each context for the transport networks. In some important respects, the Chinese and Indian steam networks were similar. In both places, steamships were introduced into large economies that were highly commercialized and regionally integrated.[137] This introduction was overwhelmingly a British project. Steam transport was rapidly adopted in both places and quickly became as significant to domestic trade and transport as to overseas communication.[138] Yet the reach of these networks and the processes through which they were developed were quite different.

In contrast to the Chinese network, in which steam communication was restricted to ports formally opened by treaty and modifications had to be negotiated through the treaty system, the Indian network was malleable. Without restrictions on the movement of ships within the subcontinent, ports could be incorporated or avoided to suit either profit or convenience.[139] The Indian steam network developed alongside the formidable Indian Railway, both aiding in its construction and offering complementary transport services. As both transport networks grew, the major nodes of the steam network were increasingly coastal ports, to which the railway connected inland places.[140] The Indian steam network could support both liner and tramp trades: maintaining scheduled services among important coastal ports, while allowing casual tramp steamers to collect freight among smaller ports and river systems.[141] Because of the restriction of steam navigation to open ports, steam shipping within the Chinese network was predominantly in liner trades.

These distinctions between the networks appear to be based on access to territory, and it is thus tempting to attribute the major differences between them to differing degrees of territorial control in colonial India and semi-colonial China. But this factor is only a minor part of the story: the far more significant difference between these networks was the speed and urgency with which they were built and correspondingly the different degrees of official investment in each.

In India, the formation of the network was rapid and immediate, proceeding from an intimate alliance between the government of India and British enterprise. It was the product of the government's needs for communications, security, and revenue collection. Following the 1857 Mutiny, the newly installed government decided to eliminate the East India Company's Indian navy as a cost-saving measure, turning the task of maritime defense over to the Royal Navy and contracting with private shipping companies to meet its own transport needs.[142] Beginning in 1862, it offered a series of mail contracts to a British-owned, sterling-backed firm called the British India Steam Navigation Company.[143] The company was charged with delivering the mail on schedule, maintaining certain speeds on mail routes, and making its ships available to the government in emergencies. In exchange, the British India Company received a subsidy for its operating costs and exclusive rights to transport government passengers, arms, cash, and other goods at set rates.[144] The government's communication needs thus determined the basic structure of the coastal steam network, but the financial security of the contract allowed the British India Company to develop commercial steam navigation within and around it, identifying the best ports or most lucrative trades and opening or closing routes depending on their profitability.[145] The British India

Company was not the only steamship company in Indian coastal waters in the 1860s, but it quickly defeated most of its competitors. In 1873, the company was able to amalgamate its various government contracts into a single ten-year contract, which gave it an almost complete monopoly on transport work for the Indian authorities and further eliminated competitors. From this alliance, the government of India got a transport system that reliably met its requirements, and the British India Company received support that allowed it to dominate steam transport on the Indian coast, and later extend beyond it to short-distance routes within Asia and overseas shipping.[146]

In China, British officials also played a central role in expanding and developing the steam network. Despite the forward momentum of this expansion through the turn of the twentieth century, compared with the Indian network it was a gradual process conducted through piecemeal demands and diplomatic deliberations. In their choices of new treaty ports, British officials in China almost certainly had strategic and trade considerations in mind, yet none of these considerations appeared as urgent as the demands of colonial transport infrastructure in India. As chapter 2 will show, British steamship companies became a powerful presence in the treaty-port network, but there is no evidence of the sort of close cooperation between British officials and British business in China that the growth of the British India Company exemplifies. From the 1840s, the British government supplied the Peninsular & Oriental Company, an overseas steamship line, with contracts to transport mail between Britain and China, but no contracts were ever extended to the companies working within the treaty-port network.[147] Powerful as they were, British steamship companies in China never dominated the network as completely as the British India Company on the Indian coast; they constantly faced competition from others, including the Qing-sponsored China Merchants Steam Navigation Company. Arguably, the entire treaty system provided a means for British officials to support British businesses in China, but as the case of the steam network demonstrates, these officials entertained British traders' requests only occasionally and selectively. The differences between the Chinese and Indian steam networks were thus much more than the products of differing degrees of territorial control and access: strategically, institutionally, and ideologically, Britain's imperial investments were very different in each place.

Given the importance of Qing sovereignty and agency in its formation, the dynamics of collaboration within the treaty system, and the particular configuration of British power and investment that it evinces, the history of the steam network in Chinese waters makes a case for investigating semi-colonialism as a distinct imperial formation, one that is not easily encompassed within broad definitions of colonialism. In the steam network, it is possible to see the concrete and palpable effects of this formation on the emerging transport system in China. The comparison with the Indian coastal network highlights the two distinct historical contexts more than it provides any comprehensive account of the differences between colonial and semi-colonial rule, but it underscores how different the outcomes from these formations could be.

At the same time, it is important to acknowledge that semi-colonial and colonial rule were not unrelated or mutually exclusive models of exogenous control. They existed together in space and time and informed one another. As is evident in the process of expanding the Chinese network, the possibility of full colonial control consistently informed the China Hands agenda for expansion, and British India was the example to which they constantly referred. In India, their visions of technological and commercial expansion would not be impeded by an inconvenient local sovereignty. An 1866 *North China Herald* article complained: "But whatever our success in India, it has been attained because our position has enabled us to introduce the appliances of modern science, despite the apathy or opposition of the people; and the latter learn from practical demonstration. In China, where the case is reversed, where we have to convince the native mind of the values of these appliances as preliminary to their introduction, it is different."[148] As the China Hands bridled against both the restrictions imposed by the still-sovereign Qing dynasty and the limitations of Britain's commitment in China, they propelled the expansion of the steam network forward through the turn of the twentieth century.

CHAPTER 2

Aligning Capital and Flag

The Steam Shipping Business, 1860–82

The demands, negotiations, and concessions of the treaty system laid out the parameters of the steam network, setting possibilities for and limitations on the places to which steamships could travel in the Qing empire. The network's overall shape, however, was just one of its dimensions: the speed of circulation, the relative importance of the ports it encompassed, and the types of trades carried on within it were determined by the steamship enterprises established in China between the 1860s and 1880s.

During the first decade after 1860, the political arena of the treaty system and the commercial arena of the steamship business bore slight resemblance to one another. In the 1860s, when British diplomats and Zongli *yamen* officials were engaged in formal negotiations over the administrative problems posed by the coasting trade and shipping in the interior of China, the shipping business was fluid and centered in treaty-port business communities. Steamships of many nations came to Shanghai to take advantage of the newly opened Yangzi River. Chinese merchants and a variety of foreign investors in the treaty ports supported the new steamship ventures of trading firms. By the 1870s, however, the shipping business had taken on the polarities of the treaty system: British- and Qing-flag steamship companies had become the most powerful within the network and competed with each other for larger shares of its trade. An 1877 *North China Herald* article reflected on this transformation of the shipping business by mourning the disappearance of what it called the "cosmopolitan" steamship companies in Chinese waters: those backed by treaty-port capital of such diverse national origins that the ships' flags were, "an accident rather than an essential."[1]

By the 1870s, an alignment of capital and flag in the shipping business made the flags that steamships flew undeniably essential. This transformation was the result of two interrelated processes: the dramatic growth of British shipping worldwide and the intervention of the Qing state into the shipping business in Chinese waters. British shipping power grew within the "communications revolution" of the early 1870s. The opening of the Suez Canal (1869) increased the use of steamships in overseas trade, and the establishment of direct telegraphic communication between Europe and Asia brought Europe into much closer and faster communication with China. Britain's technological and financial power put it in a position to benefit from these changes: British ships dominated overseas lines, and Britain itself became the world center of finance, shipping, and insurance. Although there had been an important British presence in the coastal and river shipping of the 1860s, Britain's growing global shipping and financial power provided plenty of capital, enthusiasm, and expertise for entirely British-backed firms to establish strong positions within the steam network. The China Navigation Company (est. 1873) was a new arrival that enjoyed close connections to powerful British shipping and shipbuilding interests. The Indo-China Steam Navigation Company (est. 1882) was a reorganization and consolidation of Jardine, Matheson & Company's previous shipping businesses, supported by capital from Britain.

The Qing intervention into the shipping business proceeded from the growing conviction of Western Affairs officials of the strategic, political, and economic significance of commercial shipping in Chinese waters. They established the China Merchants Steam Navigation Company, a commercial shipping firm overseen by officials, with the primary aim of taking back the profits accumulating to foreign shipping companies on the river and coast. A secondary goal was to disrupt a prevalent form of collaboration in which Chinese merchants invested in foreign shipping firms as a way to hide their wealth from the Qing state. The *North China Herald*'s complaint about the disappearance of "cosmopolitan" steamship companies was a response to the purchase of the largest of those companies by the China Merchants Company, an event that made the Qing-flag firm the largest steamship concern in Chinese waters.

Through the 1870s, these companies competed fiercely, yet in another way the shipping business came to resemble the politics of the treaty system, by the end of the decade; the companies opted for collaboration over prolonged conflict. Between 1877 and 1882, the two British firms and the China Merchants Company made a series of agreements to divide the trade in a way that allowed all three to survive and eventually prosper in the steam network. These agreements formed the basis of a shipping conference that, along with these "Three Companies," became a central, defining feature of the shipping business in China up until the start of World War II.

"Cosmopolitan" Capital in the Shipping Field, 1860–72

After the opening of the Yangzi River in 1861, British and U.S. trading firms took the primary initiative in establishing steamship companies for the treaty-port network. These were firms that sold Indian opium, European textiles, and other imported goods in China and exported teas, silks, and other wares to Europe and the United States, originating with the private traders under the East India Company's monopoly and the agency houses of the Canton system and extending into the open ports following the First Opium War.[2] Some of the larger firms, such as the British Jardine, Matheson & Company and the U.S. Russell & Company, had used steamships on occasion in the 1850s for the rapid transport of opium and correspondence between the coastal ports or on the river route between Hong Kong and Canton, but the anticipated shipping boom following the Yangzi River's opening brought all kinds of ships in great numbers to Shanghai, particularly steamships.[3] In January 1862, after the river had been open for six months, there were seventeen steamers running between Shanghai and Hankou. By September 1862, there were fifty-eight, with an estimated twenty trading firms involved in steamship operations.[4]

These trading firms managed the ships but often were not the sole owners of any particular steamship. Significant capital was needed to purchase and operate steamships, and firms were usually unwilling to commit their trading funds to shipping ventures. In the early 1860s, therefore, most steamships were owned in shares: a firm held a portion of the shares and sold the remainder to foreign and Chinese merchants in the treaty ports. Chinese investors were most often compradors, export merchants, or others with close business connections to foreign trading firms. The involvement of these investors might range from owning just a few shares in a ship to owning the majority stake. For example, Augustine Heard & Company's ship *Fire Dart* was owned in twenty shares, of which the firm held thirteen, the ship's captain two, and individual investors (including several Chinese merchants) the remaining five.[5] The comprador Chen Yüchang had put up 85 percent of the purchase price of the same firm's steamship *Shantung*.[6] Other trading firms, such as Jardine, Matheson & Company, Glover & Company, and Morris, Lewis & Company, ran steamships that were owned in part by other foreign and Chinese treaty-port investors.[7] These steamships flew the national flag of the trading firm that managed them, but a significant portion of the capital behind these early shipping ventures was recruited in the treaty ports from investors of various national origins.

One such early venture by the U.S. trading firm of Russell & Company extended this form of ownership of individual ships into a larger-scale joint-stock steamship company. One of the firm's partners, Edward Cunningham, was concerned with the decline in Russell's commission business in the early 1860s and wanted to diversify into shipping. Finding the firm unwilling to commit its capital, Cunningham sought investors in Shanghai, Hong Kong, and from among Russell's partners outside of China to underwrite the purchase of three steamers. Many of the Shanghai investors were the firm's "old Chinese friends."[8] With these ships, he formed the Shanghai Steam Navigation Company in 1862.

Cunningham was not satisfied with the capital he had managed to recruit initially. Most firms at the time ran two or three steamers at irregular intervals on the Yangzi and coast, but he envisioned a company of five river and five coastal steamers that could maintain a regular schedule of departures from the open ports. To realize this expansion, he sought out more investors, turning particularly to Chinese merchants in

Shanghai, many of whom he knew personally from his tenure as Russell's representative there. He appealed to investors from small British trading firms by arguing that the new company would free them from dependence on larger British firms for shipping services. Later that year, Cunningham had collected capital of one million *taels* for the Shanghai Steam Navigation Company, including investments from at least nine Chinese merchants, eight British merchants connected with small firms, various other European and U.S. treaty-port merchants, and several members of Russell & Company who invested as individuals. Cunningham had delved so deeply into the available treaty-port capital that some rivals complained there was little left for competing ventures. The Shanghai Steam Navigation Company became a joint-stock company and an ownership organization for which Russell & Company acted as managing agent.[9]

By the mid-1860s, the Shanghai Steam Navigation Company dominated the steam shipping business, nearly monopolizing steam carriage on the Yangzi River and coast. Cunningham's insistence on a regular liner service helped the company survive a contraction in the shipping market in 1864 that destroyed many competing steamship ventures. Freight rates on the Yangzi and some coastal routes fell sharply after the suppression of the Taiping Rebellion, when peacetime levels of junk transport returned to these routes. In 1864 alone, the number of steamship enterprises on the Yangzi River dropped from twenty to ten. By this time, the Shanghai Steam Navigation Company was maintaining a schedule of regular twice-weekly departures from Shanghai at one end of the Yangzi route and Hankou at the other. It maintained one steamer in port at either end, which allowed shippers to load cargo any day of the week. As competition intensified, the regularity and efficiency of the Shanghai Steam Navigation Company's liner service became a great advantage.[10]

Furthermore, the company's careful cultivation of a clientele of Chinese shippers allowed it to benefit from changes in the interport trade. After 1860, Chinese merchants increasingly took over the distribution of import-export items such as teas, cotton textiles, and opium from foreign firms, and began using steamships to transport domestic commodities such as sugar, silk piece goods, copper cash, raw cotton, wood oil, and tobacco. In 1863, the Shanghai Steam Navigation Company began offering Chinese merchants free storage and docking service for cargoes and a 1 percent return on freights paid. Two years later, Russell & Company hired Chen Yüchang as the firm's comprador, using Chen's connections to expand the company's Chinese business even more. By appealing so directly to Chinese shippers, the Shanghai Steam Navigation Company benefited from what was otherwise a decline in the trading business of Russell & Company and other foreign firms. The Russell partner F. B. Forbes (1839–1908) boasted that the business from the shipping company's Chinese clients alone more than covered its expenses.[11]

By 1867, the Shanghai Steam Navigation Company was the largest competitor on the Yangzi River and Shanghai–Tianjin and Shanghai–Ningbo coastal routes. On the Yangzi, its rivals had contracted from twenty firms in 1862 to four in 1865, and it further grew by buying up the fleets of failed competitors. At this time, it was in a strong enough position to make an agreement with Jardine, Matheson & Company to divide the steamship trades: it promised to stay off the Shanghai–Fuzhou route in exchange for Jardine's promise to stay off the Yangzi River. Between 1867 and 1872, the Shanghai Steam Navigation Company could set monopoly rates of freight on its three major coastal and river routes. Its only rivals were smaller companies, to which it could dictate terms.[12]

After 1867, the Shanghai Steam Navigation Company was the model for new steamship ventures. New companies imitated its organization, establishing joint-stock shipping firms backed by the combined investments of trading firms and treaty-port merchants. The British firm Glover & Company started the Union Steam Navigation Company in 1867 for the Yangzi River trade. Its largest shareholders were Chinese merchants.[13] In the North China Steamer Company, established in 1868 for the Shanghai–Tianjin route, one-third of the capital was subscribed by Chinese merchants involved in trade with the northern coastal ports, one-third by a trading firm, and the last third by European residents of Tianjin and Shanghai.[14] In 1872, Jardine, Matheson & Company organized the China Coast Steam Navigation Company for the Shanghai–Tianjin route. Jardine owned a 64.2 percent majority stake, Chinese investors 20.3 percent, and other foreign investors 15.5 percent. The company's fleet included ships formerly owned by Jardine's chief Shanghai comprador Tang Tingshu (Tong Kingsing, 1832–92), and its investors included Chinese merchants recruited by Tang and the firm's Fuzhou comprador.[15]

Together, this generation of steamship companies made up the "cosmopolitan" firms that would disappear within the decade.

Characterizing these shipping companies as cosmopolitan neatly captures some of their distinctive aspects but glosses over the more complex power relations within them. Because their capital derived from the treaty ports and their investors were of multiple national origins, the steamships' flags appeared "accidental" or arbitrary. Yet this term does not do justice to the relations between Chinese investors and the foreign firms. Although this generation of companies shows that the steamship business in Chinese waters depended heavily on the investment and continued support of Chinese merchants of substantial capital, Chinese investors did not necessarily share with their European and U.S. counterparts the ability to direct and administer the companies.

Scholarship on Chinese investment in the treaty ports echoes this cosmopolitan characterization. Chinese investments in the steamship business have been included as part of a broader trend of share affiliation (*fugu*) in the treaty ports of the late nineteenth century. Detailing how treaty-port Chinese purchased shares in a wide range of Western enterprises, including banking, insurance, and industry as well as shipping, the scholarship on share affiliation interprets these investments as evidence of the availability of capital in the treaty ports and the entrepreneurial acumen of Chinese investors.[16] Scholars acknowledge that these investments provided a means for merchants to shield their wealth from Qing official exactions or interference, yet they do not dwell on the political significance of share affiliation.[17]

To Qing officials, however, share affiliation in the steam shipping business represented a deeply objectionable form of collaboration with foreign merchants. Before 1867, when the Qing promulgated its Regulations for Chinese Owners and Charterers of Steamships, Qing subjects were prohibited from purchasing or operating steamships. Shareholding in individual ships or shipping firms was a means by which Chinese merchants could sidestep these restrictions to participate in this new, lucrative business. Yet even after the dynasty reversed this policy, Chinese investments in foreign-flag shipping firms continued to grow, and no ships were ever registered under Qing regulations.[18] Qing officials wanted to stop the practice. In 1872, one of the arguments that Li Hongzhang made in favor of establishing a government-sponsored commercial shipping firm was that it could attract the Chinese merchant capital invested in foreign firms back into the service of the Qing state.[19]

Li's criticism of share affiliation, however, went well beyond the idea that the Qing state had a claim to merchants' capital. He also emphasized the vulnerability of Chinese investors, noting that the profits from the shipping business were enormous, but because the investments were not officially sanctioned, Chinese investors would have no legal recourse if they were cheated by foreign firms.[20] As he articulated it, share affiliation had the potential to disadvantage its Chinese participants vis-à-vis their foreign partners.

A closer examination of the organization of companies like the Shanghai Steam Navigation Company shows that Li's concern was not misplaced. It also indicates that this form of collaboration, although seemingly based on the shared interests of Chinese and foreign merchants, had the potential to privilege the foreign interests at the Chinese merchants' expense. Although there are no accounts of Chinese shareholders deprived of their dividends, they did not always enjoy the same rights as foreign investors in the governance of steamship companies. In the Shanghai Steam Navigation Company, the partners of Russell & Company owned less than one-third of the steamship company's stock but exercised considerable control over its board of directors.[21] The board was composed of the managing partner of Russell & Company, one other member of the firm, and two directors elected from among the European or U.S. shareholders who were not firm members. Not only did Chinese shareholders have no direct representation on the board, they were presumed loyal to the firm's interests. It was taken for granted that the Chinese shareholders backed the firm partners' decisions. Since the Russell partners—along with the Chinese shareholders—owned 60–70 percent of the company, the partners enjoyed a majority on the board that allowed them to resist occasional opposition from outside directors and shareholders and control the company's governance.[22]

The Russell partners may have presumed that the Chinese shareholders would back them because many shareholders probably had close personal ties with the partners. Share affiliation was relatively new in the 1860s, and Chinese investors tended to rely on regional, family, or friendship networks to choose the businesses they backed.[23] Nevertheless, the company's structure did not treat the Chinese shareholders in the same way as even the "outside" European/U.S. shareholders: they had no voice independent of the Russell partners to decide company policies and rates of freight. This may not have been true of all of the cosmopolitan steamship companies: Jardine's comprador Tang Tingshu was elected to the China Coast Company's board of directors in 1867.[24] Yet the Shanghai Steam Navigation Company's organization indicates how even within a form of collaboration in which the interests of foreign businesses and Chinese investors appeared to be equivalent, Chinese investors could still be marginalized. Thus, to describe such a company as "cosmopolitan" elides these power imbalances and the Russell partners' determination to retain control of the company. The U.S. flag on the Shanghai Steam Navigation Company's ships was perhaps not accidental at all.

Share affiliation in other businesses continued and grew over the remainder of the nineteenth century, but this form of collaboration within the steam shipping business contracted sharply by the 1880s. The cosmopolitan shipping companies modeled on the Shanghai Steam Navigation Company were gradually defeated by firms in which flag and capital were very obviously aligned. First, the Qing carried out its plan of establishing a government-sponsored commercial shipping firm in which shareholding was restricted to Qing subjects. Li Hongzhang's hope of rallying Chinese capital behind such a company was only partially realized, but the rapid expansion of this company in the 1870s was sufficient to drive many smaller firms out of the field. Equally significant was the arrival of one new and one substantially reorganized British steamship company financed almost exclusively by British capital. By the early 1880s, there were very few prospects for share affiliation within the steam shipping business.

Aligning Capital and Flag: British and Chinese Shipping Companies, 1872–82

The global communications revolution of the late 1860s and early 1870s and the increasing interest and concern of the Qing government in the arena of merchant steam shipping brought the three new steamship companies to Chinese waters that defeated the generation of cosmopolitan firms. Their arrival ushered in a period of particularly fierce competition and growth. By 1882, these three companies dominated the major coastal and Yangzi River routes.

The communications revolution followed the mid-century expansion of the British empire and made Britain the preeminent world shipping power. British innovations in steamship construction, such as Alfred Holt's (1829–1911) 1865 demonstration that steamships could compete effectively with sail in long-distance cargo trades, coupled with the conditions in the Suez Canal that favored steam over sail, increased the use of steamships in international trade and prompted a wave of steamship construction worldwide. Britain was at the forefront of this wave, enjoying the wealthiest money market in the world, well-developed iron and mechanical industries, and supplies of excellent, inexpensive steamer coal. By the 1880s, four-fifths of the tonnage passing through the Suez Canal was British. Coupled with the establishment of direct telegraph communication between Europe and Asia in 1870, in which Britain controlled most of the new submarine telegraph cable, the communications revolution extended British shipping power across the world.[25]

In China, the communications revolution was initially experienced as a decrease in the amount of time necessary for goods, people, and information to travel between Europe and China. The opening of the Suez Canal had reduced travel times between London and Shanghai from four months to two, and in the 1870s, the time was further reduced to twenty-nine days.[26] By the mid-1870s, five new overseas steamship lines (four of them private British firms) had joined the older, subsidized mail lines of the British Peninsular & Oriental Company and the French Messageries Imperiales in running regularly between Europe and China.[27] The new prominence of British shipbuilding was also evident in Chinese waters: the U.S.-flag Shanghai Steam Navigation Company, which still dominated the interport trade in the early 1870s, replaced its U.S.-built wooden-hulled steamships with British-built iron-hulled ships.[28] Telegraphic communication made it possible to transmit news and market information within days, a development that transformed the business of trading firms, as they no longer needed to maintain large capital reserves for purchases in China or large stocks of tea, silks, and other goods in Western markets.[29] Newcomers without the capital of the older firms could make use of shipping, telegraph, and banking facilities to carry out business with lower overhead costs. Increased competition precipitated the failure of many established trading houses, whereas others survived by diversifying into services like shipping, insurance, banking, and utilities.[30]

As these changes transformed external trade and communications, the market for steam shipping services within China boomed. In the 1860s, steamships primarily serviced the import-export trade, carrying goods of high value and low volume, such as opium, silk, and cotton textiles. By the end of the decade, steamships were becoming integrated into interregional trades. Chinese passengers—such as merchants accompanying cargoes to market or examination candidates traveling to the capital—had become a significant source of profit for steamship companies.[31] Even more promising were several instances in which steamship companies realized huge profits from the interregional transport of staple goods. Between 1867 and 1871, floods on the Upper Yangzi River destroyed cotton crops in Sichuan, Hunan, and Hubei Provinces, and steamships transported the surplus of Jiangsu's cotton crop from Shanghai to Hankou to supply the handicraft industries of the flooded provinces on the upper river. The cotton shipments in turn stimulated the downriver shipment of Sichuan produce, such as wood oil, vegetable tallow, white wax, and silk, from Hankou to Shanghai.[32] These flood years were a windfall for the Shanghai Steam Navigation Company, whose ships left each year "piled as full as the use of every available space could make them" with raw cotton.[33] Again in 1871–72, bad weather damaged rice crops in the north and south while the Yangzi Valley enjoyed an abundant harvest, and steamships transported rice from the Lower Yangzi Valley north to Tianjin and south to Canton and Shantou. The scale of this rice trade was so vast that steamship companies had to charter ocean steamers to supplement their fleets.[34] Such incidents demonstrated the potential for expanding steam transport on the Yangzi and coast and brought new companies into the shipping field.

During these years, Qing officials had become keenly aware of the economic and strategic significance of commercial steam shipping. They were facing a crisis in the transportation of the tribute grain from the Lower Yangzi provinces to Beijing. After damage to the ancient Grand Canal in the 1840s, the government had contracted with oceangoing merchant junks to carry the grain, but in the 1860s many of the junk operators had abandoned their trade because of competition with steamships, and the government struggled to find a way to transport this crucial revenue. In 1872, Western Affairs officials resurrected a much-contested proposal from 1865 to use steamships to deliver the tribute grain. The proposal was reworked to support two Western Affairs projects that were under attack from Grand Secretary Song Jin: the Jiangnan Arsenal and Fuzhou Shipyard, both of which built modern weapons for China's defense. In response to Song's challenge that these endeavors were costly and corrupt, the arsenal's founder Zeng Guofan drew up a plan in which the arsenal and shipyard would build a fleet of steamships that could carry the tribute grain in season, transport troops and supplies in wartime, and be rented to merchants in peacetime. When Zeng died later that year, Li Hongzhang, then superintendent of the northern ports and governor-general of Zhili, took over this project. Li transformed it into a primarily commercial venture intended to compete with foreign shipping companies. He envisioned a state-supported steamship company managed by merchants that would carry tribute grain and troops for the government, but whose principal task was to "take back" the Yangzi and coast from foreign companies.[35]

Three new shipping companies entered the Yangzi and coast trades as a result of these developments. The China Navigation Company was a British shipping company started by the newly established trading firm of Butterfield & Swire. Shipping company and trading firm were closely connected to the British shipping interests central to the communications revolution, and China Navigation was founded specifically to take advantage of the expanding market for domestic steam shipping in China. The China Merchants Steam Navigation Company was the product of Zeng Guofan's and Li Hongzhang's arguments to the throne; an officially supervised, merchant-managed shipping company that performed transport services for the state at favorable rates and competed with foreign shipping companies on major routes. The Indo-China Steam Navigation Company was established somewhat later (1882). It was the reorganization and consolidation of the various shipping interests of the venerable trading firm of Jardine, Matheson & Company. The Indo-China Company brought Jardine's various fleets under the management of a single organization and expanded them, a process funded primarily by British capital. The entrance of these new companies into the steamship trade in

Chinese waters resulted in periods of intense competition, in which the newcomers displaced or absorbed the preexisting companies. When the three new firms began to compete with each other, they expanded the scope of the steam shipping business on the Yangzi and coast by working to match one another's services.

BUTTERFIELD & SWIRE: THE CHINA NAVIGATION COMPANY

Butterfield & Swire's organization of the China Navigation Company illustrates how British trading firms could take advantage of the new British preeminence in worldwide shipping to extend their activities in China. The trading firm was formed only in 1866, and was a relative newcomer to the China trade. Based in the cotton and shipping center of Liverpool, it was initially a partnership formed between John Samuel Swire (1825–98), head of the firm of John Swire & Sons, and British wool merchant Richard Butterfield (1806–69), to sell British textiles in China.[36] When it opened its Shanghai office in 1867, Butterfield & Swire sold cotton textiles and acted as agent for Alfred Holt's Ocean Steamship Company. A significant part of the firm's business became the development of the Ocean Steamship Company's business in China and Japan. After a visit to China in 1867, Swire tried to persuade the Holt family to establish a steamship company on the Yangzi River to act as a feeder for its overseas line. Finding the Holts unwilling, Swire organized the company himself by purchasing the two ships and the shore properties of the Union Steam Navigation Company (previously the Shanghai Steam Navigation Company's sole competitor on the Yangzi). Three new ships ordered from Britain rounded out the fleet of the new China Navigation Company as it entered the Yangzi trade in 1872.[37]

The China Navigation Company resembled firms like the Shanghai Steam Navigation Company in that it was a free-standing ownership organization for which Butterfield & Swire held the management contract, yet the crucial difference was that all of China Navigation's shares were bought and sold in Britain without the involvement of Chinese or foreign treaty-port investors. Swire was aware of treaty-port communities as potential sources of capital, but he never tried to tap them. Instead, China Navigation's capital was drawn from a close-knit Liverpool-based group of family and business associates. Swire, his brother William Hudson Swire (1830–84), and William Lang (the Butterfield & Swire partner in Shanghai) owned a block of shares, as did Alfred Holt and other members of the Holt family. Shipbuilder John Scott (1830–1903) and Liverpool ship owners such as the Rathbone family and Ismay, Imrie & Company and other merchants interested in textiles and insurance invested in the China Navigation Company. Within this group, the Swire, Holt, and Scott families worked particularly closely to promote one another's business interests. Scott's shipyard built ships for both the Holt companies and China Navigation, Butterfield & Swire acted as the Holts' agent in China and Japan, and members of the Scott family became partners in Butterfield & Swire.[38] The China Navigation Company exemplified the trend for British trading firms to float new ventures on British capital markets, but it was more than just evidence for the general availability of capital in Britain; it was a project launched by tightly connected British shipping and trade interests. As these interests became more prominent, the parent firm of John Swire & Sons moved from Liverpool to London for better access to the city's financial services and information.[39]

The China Navigation Company's capital strength was the key to its competitive power in China. The year 1872, when it entered the Yangzi shipping trade, had been one of peak performance for the Shanghai Steam Navigation Company. Operating a fleet of seventeen ships on the Yangzi River and coast, the U.S. company could dictate rates of freight and terms to its small-scale opponents and enjoyed record profits from the interregional staple trades in cotton and rice. To break this monopoly, Swire put five China Navigation steamships on the Yangzi. The following year, despite sustaining losses, China Navigation's managers rejected an agreement with the other firm that would have limited the size of China Navigation's fleet as well as an offer to purchase it outright. By 1874, the Shanghai Steam Navigation Company was forced to concede to a more equitable arrangement in which both firms agreed on rates, maintained fleets of equal size, and scheduled equal numbers of departures from Shanghai and Hankou (three times a week per company).[40] The U.S. firm's retreat from its previous, aggressive stance was the result of its recognition of the wealth behind China Navigation. The Russell & Company partner Paul Siemen Forbes had been impressed by the availability of capital in London on a recent visit there and saw behind China Navigation "[a] practically unlimited supply of British pride and capital."[41]

As it established its place in the Yangzi trade, the China Navigation Company introduced new business practices that quickly became standard in the shipping field. First, it determinedly cultivated Chinese shippers to a degree that unnerved its competitors. The company recruited freight brokers by offering well-known Chinese traders commissions and other incentives to solicit freight for its ships. China Navigation paid its brokers a 5 percent commission on cargoes obtained and returned another 5 percent to loyal shippers through these brokers after a six-month period. In the past, Shanghai Steam Navigation had offered a 10 percent return on shipments only to their Chinese shareholders, but it soon adopted China Navigation's more generous system of commissions and returns.[42] When China Navigation offered direct booking of cargoes from China Navigation ships onto the Ocean Steamship Company's overseas lines, it likewise prompted Shanghai Steam Navigation to make an agreement with the Peninsular & Oriental line providing through shipments between the treaty ports and London.[43]

Within two years, the China Navigation Company had made sufficient inroads into the Yangzi trade to deal with the Shanghai Steam Navigation Company on nearly equal terms. This tentative equilibrium was extremely short-lived, however, as the Qing-sponsored China Merchants Steam Navigation Company entered the coastal and river trades in 1873–74 and open competition once again returned to the field.

THE QING STATE AND THE CHINA MERCHANTS STEAM NAVIGATION COMPANY

The China Merchants Steam Navigation Company was the English name of the steamship company set up under Qing official auspices in 1873. It had originated in proposals to use steamships to carry the grain tribute and save the embattled Jiangnan Arsenal and Fuzhou Shipyard, but the proposal the emperor approved in 1872 was a more explicit expression of Qing power and sovereignty. Organized by Qing officials and developed and managed by prominent merchants, China Merchants was a Qing-flag merchant steamship company intended to challenge the dominance of foreign companies in coastal and river shipping. Between 1873 and 1882, it did not achieve all the goals its founders had envisioned, but it made the Qing flag a significant presence in the steam network.

In early 1872, Li Hongzhang submitted a memorial that gained approval from the throne. In it, he detailed a steamship company financed and managed by merchants and supervised by Qing officials.[44] The company would have exclusive rights to carry a portion of the tribute grain at a special rate, providing the state with an essential service while ensuring a level of profit Li hoped would make the company competitive and attract investors. In his justifications for such a company, Li drew on the idea of "commercial warfare" (*shangzhan*), first articulated by Western Affairs officials like Zeng Guofan in the 1860s, who argued that the best way to resist foreign expansion into China was to allow Chinese merchants to outcompete foreign ones through a combination of the merchants' superior knowledge of local conditions and the adoption of certain Western practices and technologies, thus depriving Western businesses of the source of their interest in China.[45] Li observed that "the profits of our rivers and coasts have been completely usurped by Westerners," and he stated that the goal of this steamship company would be the "gradual recovery of profits" (*jian shou liquan*).[46] The term "profits" or "material prerogatives" (*liquan*) originally referred to the state's ability to derive revenue from systems such as the salt monopoly or grain tribute. By the dynasty's last years, it would take on the expanded meaning of "economic rights" as foreigners and Chinese struggled over control of telegraph lines, mines, and the Maritime Customs revenue.[47] In the 1870s, however, it signified the state's claim to the economic benefits of the burgeoning shipping business in Chinese waters. It implied that the company, if successful, would eventually drive foreign steamship companies out of Chinese waters.

Integral to Li's proposal was the idea that the company would be financed and run by merchants. He wanted to recruit the Chinese merchants who owned shares in foreign shipping companies to the new firm, and he proposed an organization he hoped would appeal to them. Shareholding would be restricted to Qing subjects; no foreign investors would be allowed.[48] Qing officials would exercise some supervision over the company, but it would be run by merchant managers who would determine its regulations and daily operations.[49] To make it clear the company would be competitive with foreign-owned companies, Li decided that its ships would be subject to taxation by the Maritime Customs on the same terms as foreign-flag ships.[50] The significance of the intended role for these merchants is evident from the Chinese name for the enterprise—Lunchuan zhaoshang ju—which translates as the "Steamship Bureau for Recruiting Merchants."

The China Merchants Company's organization, known as "official supervision and merchant management" (*guandu shangban*), was an attempt to reconcile the political and strategic importance of shipping with the need for a commercially viable enterprise. The official supervision of the China Merchants Company was carried out by Li Hongzhang himself, from his concurrent positions as superintendent of the northern ports and governor-general of Zhili. Li championed the autonomy of the merchant managers, but he retained the right to appoint and dismiss them. He appointed Sheng Xuanhuai (1844–1916), an official from his own entourage, to the company to assist it in its relations with the government. The model of official oversight over a merchant-funded enterprise became the template for a number of modern enterprises Li Hongzhang established in the 1870s, including the Hubei Coal Mining Company (1875), the Kaiping Mines (1877), and the Shanghai Cotton Cloth Mill (1878).[51]

Once Li's plan was approved, the process of recruiting merchants to the company proved complicated. After an initial attempt to enlist prominent Zhejiang merchants through tribute grain commissioner Zhu Qi'ang (d. 1877) failed, Li appointed the compradors Tang Tingshu and Xu Run (1838–1911) merchant managers, charging them with collecting an investment capital of one million *taels*.[52] Tang and Xu had extensive experience in foreign steamship ventures. Tang had been Jardine, Matheson & Company's Shanghai comprador since 1861, responsible for soliciting freight for the company's shipping ventures. He also held a direct or joint interest in five or six steamships operated by foreign companies and was on the board of directors for the Union and North China Steamer Companies. Xu served as comprador for Dent & Company, owned shares in the Union and Shanghai Steam Navigation Companies, and had interests in Shanghai real estate, native banks, and the tea, silk, opium, and cotton trades.[53]

Both men invested their own capital in the nascent China Merchants Company and recruited more investors through their business and native-place networks. Tang and Xu were from Xiangshan County in

Guangdong Province and had close ties to other Cantonese merchants in the treaty ports. Tang was a leader of the Cantonese native-place association in Shanghai, the Guangzhao huiguan. Many Cantonese merchants were involved in interport shipping, particularly moving goods between Shanghai and the northern ports opened by the Treaty of Tianjin, and many owned shares in foreign shipping firms. Drawing on their connections with these merchants, Tang and Xu increased the company's paid-up share capital from 180,000 to 476,000 *taels*.[54] At this time, 20–30 percent of China Merchants shares were held by Li Hongzhang; his deputy, Sheng Xuanhuai; and families of junk owners interested in the carriage of the tribute grain; 60–70 percent of the stock was held by Tang and Xu, members of their families, and their associates in the treaty ports.[55]

After 1873, Tang and Xu struggled to find more investors for the China Merchants Company. Between 1873 and 1876, they collected only 209,000 *taels* in new merchant shares, leaving the total paid-up capital well short of the million *taels* goal.[56] In particular, the Chinese investors in foreign shipping firms outside of Tang and Xu's personal and native-place networks remained unenthusiastic about the China Merchants Company, and Chinese shareholding in the Shanghai Steam Navigation Company peaked at precisely this time.[57] Many potential investors were wary of the official presence in the China Merchants Company, as shareholding in this company would not shield capital from official view. Long-standing conflicts between Cantonese compradors and those from Jiangsu and Zhejiang Provinces may have made other investors hostile to the dominance of Cantonese at all levels of the company, from managers Tang and Xu to the shareholders who served as branch managers and the native-place association members acting as freight brokers.[58] Merchants with close ties to foreign firms may have been reluctant to damage these relationships by investing in a company the *North China Herald* called "a thoroughly anti-foreign affair."[59] Whatever the exact reason for their reticence, actual investment in the China Merchants Company had fallen well short of Li Hongzhang's hope of uniting all Chinese capital invested in foreign shipping companies behind the state-sponsored firm. The company relied on government loans to make up the shortfall in its capital through the end of the decade.[60]

Tang and Xu's company prospectus and reports to shareholders continued to represent the company as one whose Chinese identity provided an advantage in competition and was capable of "taking back" the river and coast from foreign shipping. They argued that China Merchants Company had the special advantage of being able to negotiate with fellow countrymen to provide lower-cost warehousing and labor than foreign companies could arrange.[61] They contended that its services would be more attractive to Chinese shippers, because unlike foreign firms, the China Merchants Company would provide fair compensation in cases of loss of cargo or collision and a more sensitive response to local conditions (like drought or famine) in setting freight rates. Competition from the China Merchants Company would prevent foreign companies from setting unfairly high rates of freight in the short term, and over the long run the company would completely regain control of the carrying trade from foreign companies.[62]

In its first years of operation, the China Merchants Company competed aggressively. In 1873–74, its ships entered three major routes—the Yangzi River, Shanghai–Tianjin, and Shanghai–Ningbo—offering rates 30 percent below others' as well as large rebates to shippers. It actively expanded its fleet, adding eight new steamers to its original fleet of six and operating three more on consignment from Chinese ship owners. These actions destroyed the careful agreements struck between the Shanghai Steam Navigation and China Navigation Companies on the Yangzi, as well as others made between the U.S. firm and Jardine's China Coast Company on coastal routes, precipitating a new round of open competition during which all suffered losses. Several firms contemplated selling out to the China Merchants Company, but it was the former hegemon of the steam network, the Shanghai Steam Navigation Company, that proposed such a sale in fall 1876. In January 1877, Tang Tingshu signed an agreement to buy the ships and shore properties of the Shanghai Steam Navigation Company for 2,220,000 *taels*.[63]

This purchase made the China Merchants Company the largest steamship company in China. It owned a total of thirty-three ships, a fleet that dwarfed those of its competitors. It ran ten steamers on the Yangzi River compared with China Navigation's three, and eleven on the Shanghai–Tianjin route compared with the China Coast Company's four. With newly acquired ships, it invaded routes that had been previously considered the preserves of particular companies, such as Jardine's Shanghai–Fuzhou route and a route Butterfield & Swire had initiated between the Manchurian port of Niuzhuang and Shantou on the southeast coast. China Merchants ships also made trips between Shanghai and Hong Kong and made forays into the emigrant trade between South China ports and Singapore.[64]

Viewing the formidable size and aggressive tactics of the China Merchants Company, the treaty-port press raised the alarm that it would soon succeed in driving foreign-flag shipping companies from coastal and river routes.[65] One *North China Herald* article called on British ship owners to defend their treaty right to participate in this trade.[66] Such arguments, however, were usually based on the assumption that the China Merchants Company enjoyed unassailable support from the Qing government, when in fact the company's relationship to the government was complex and tenuous. For all of its belligerence, the company was in a delicate position politically and financially after its 1877 purchase of the Shanghai Steam Navigation Company.

The Qing government never invested directly in the China Merchants Company. The company received support from the Qing dynasty in the forms of contracts at remunerative rates of freight, in addition to various tax concessions and other privileges—a relationship similar to that between the British India Steam Navigation Company and the government of India. The most important government contract was the transportation of the tribute grain from Shanghai to Tianjin at double the prevailing freight rate on this route. China Merchants carried increasing amounts of the tribute grain over its initial years of operation.[67] Between 1877 and 1899, the state granted the company a number of further concessions that similarly acted as operating subsidies, including exemptions from customs duty and *lijin* in the copper and tea trades for the Mongolian and Russian markets and a monopoly on official freight sent from the provinces to Tianjin. The government used China Merchants ships to carry military supplies and troops.[68] Although the China Merchants Company's rules did not mention formal monopoly rights, it enjoyed a de facto monopoly on steam carriage under the Qing flag through the end of the nineteenth century. Qing officials repeatedly refused requests from other subjects to register new shipping companies. Li Hongzhang defeated Shanghai merchants' attempts to establish private steamship companies in 1877 and 1882, and the ships of a steamship enterprise started by Taiwan Governor Liu Mingchuan (1836–96) in 1888 were barred from routes worked by the China Merchants Company.[69] The monopoly helped ensure the company's viability and allowed it to remain competitive with foreign companies.[70] Although all of these measures supported the company and helped subsidize its operating costs, the Qing government never funded it directly.

Furthermore, the China Merchants Company was not integrated into the Qing bureaucracy, nor did it come under the authority of any of the Qing boards. The company had been initiated by Qing officials, and officials exercised some oversight over its operations, but it was not part of the government's formal structure. In its first several decades of operation, Li Hongzhang himself supervised it from his concurrent positions as superintendent of the northern ports and governor-general of Zhili. Li's role was primarily that of patron or protector. His patronage proved vital to the company's development because he was able to secure loans and special concessions from the government at crucial junctures, but his support was contingent on his political standing and was not institutionalized over the long run. In later years, as Li's political fortunes declined, he was unable to advocate for and protect the company in the same way.[71]

The rapid expansion of the China Merchants Company between 1873 and 1877 shows both the significance and the limitations of Li Hongzhang's patronage and the company's official connections. This expansion was mostly enabled by Li's ability to secure loans from government treasuries at low interest. Part of the company's authorized capital remained unsubscribed as it was engaged in intense competition with foreign-flag firms, and neither the China Merchants' capital nor its earnings could cover the cost of new ships. Its considerable earnings from the grain tribute were offset by its losses in competition and its policy of paying a guaranteed dividend of 10 percent to shareholders (intended to attract more merchant investors). The purchases of new steamers in these years were financed in part by loans from native banks arranged by Tang and Xu and in part by loans from the provincial treasuries of Jiangsu, Zhejiang, Zhili, and Shandong, negotiated by Li. In 1877, when the China Merchants Company wanted to purchase the Shanghai Steam Navigation Company, Li and Sheng Xuanhuai secured further loans from provincial treasuries. These loans were a limited form of assistance, as the company had to pay them back within a short period at 8–10 percent interest. The China Merchants Company had to pay Russell & Company the balance of the purchase price at the same time as the interest on its government loans came due, putting it in precarious financial straits at the moment that it appeared to be at the height of its power.[72]

Tang Tingshu begged Li Hongzhang to arrange to defer repayment of the government loans, but Li was unable to secure such terms from provincial treasuries. As the China Merchants Company was engaged in rate wars with China Navigation and Jardine's companies on several routes, its financial position was very insecure. Under these conditions, the China Merchants Company retreated from its formerly aggressive and competitive stance to ensure its own survival. Tang Tingshu worked with China Navigation and Jardine's to negotiate rate agreements and divisions of trades, ending open competition among these companies and ensuring a stable level of earnings for all participants.[73] This agreement signified the China Merchants' retreat from its goal of taking back the river and coast from foreign shipping firms: it had to postpone the pursuit of this aim to remain in business.

The China Merchants agreement with the British firms helped stabilize its earnings, which in turn helped it expand its investment capital. The new shareholders did not come from the expected sources: after its purchase of the Shanghai Steam Navigation Company, Tang and Xu had anticipated that the U.S. firm's Chinese shareholders would transfer their shares to the China Merchants Company, but these shareholders continued to resist. Many simply declined to buy shares, and some deflected official "invitations" to do so by substituting large contributions to famine relief in Shandong.[74] A group of Zhejiangese merchants led an effort by former Shanghai Steam Navigation shareholders to establish a new steamship company under the U.S. flag, suggesting continued misgivings about the China Merchants' official connections, suspicion of its Cantonese leadership, or both.[75] Despite the disinterest of this particular population, however, the demand for China Merchants shares among other Chinese investors exploded. By 1880, the China Merchants Company had sold enough shares to achieve its planned capitalization of one million *taels*. Within three years, it was able to double that amount and even had to turn away some prospective investors.[76] This increased interest may have been the effect of the stabilization of the company's earnings or the growing familiarity with shareholding among Chinese with capital.[77]

The China Merchants Steam Navigation Company's entrance to the steam shipping business in 1873 brought even greater change than China Navigation's the year earlier. China Merchants enjoyed enough support from official sources to make an aggressive entrance and immediately secure a significant position in a field dominated by foreign-flag firms. Within a few years, it purchased its most powerful rival, the Shanghai Steam Navigation Company, making it the largest company on the Yangzi and coast. Although the company's relationship to the government was not as close as foreign observers imagined it to be, securing a substantial presence within the steam network was both a commercial achievement and a sovereign action on the part of Qing officials. In this period, the company fulfilled neither of its initial aspirations to take back shipping profits from foreign companies nor mobilize Chinese capital invested in foreign firms, but it had become a powerful and established enterprise and remained so through 1937.

JARDINE, MATHESON & COMPANY: THE INDO-CHINA STEAM NAVIGATION COMPANY

Another effect on the steam shipping business of the 1877 sale of the Shanghai Steam Navigation Company to the China Merchants Company was that the steamship companies run by the British trading firm of Jardine, Matheson & Company became the only major companies remaining that were financed by treaty-port capital in the cosmopolitan mode. Chinese and foreign treaty-port investors held a 38.5 percent share in the firm's China Coast Steam Navigation Company (est. 1872). Earning record profits between 1877 and 1880, Jardine's established a new Yangtze Steam Navigation Company (1879) and built new ships for the Niuzhuang–Shantou trade, recruiting treaty-port investors for both ventures.[78] In 1881, however, the firm consolidated its various shipping interests into the Indo-China Steam Navigation Company, a merger that shifted the bulk of investment in Jardine's shipping interests from China to Britain.

The Indo-China Steam Navigation Company was Jardine, Matheson & Company's response to the greater availability of capital in Britain.

The new company's fleet of thirteen ships amalgamated the ships of the China Coast Steam Navigation Company, Yangtze Steam Navigation Company, the ships built for the Niuzhuang–Shantou trade, and three ships the firm ran between Hong Kong and Calcutta.[79] To finance the merger, Jardine's William Keswick (1834–1912) turned to his hometown of Glasgow, selling shares to associates there with interests in British shipping and shipbuilding. James MacGregor of the London and Glasgow Shipping and Engineering Company, a shipyard that had built some of the firm's new ships, along with Thomas Reid, head of another prominent Glasgow firm, became the Indo-China Company's largest shareholders.[80] One of the company's first directors was the senior partner of MacGregor Gow & Holland, founders of the Glen Line of steamers.[81] Shares in denominations of £10 were held by an unspecified "British investing public."[82] The network of shipping and shipbuilding interests that backed the Indo-China Steam Navigation Company was perhaps less tightly integrated than that behind the China Navigation Company, but both companies enjoyed the support of British shipbuilders and overseas steamship lines.

In making this change, Jardine's did not completely abandon its treaty-port shareholders. Of the company's initial capital of £449,800, £210,000 in shares was held by British investors. Approximately £200,000 in Indo-China shares—almost half the initial capital—was reserved for investors in Hong Kong and China. Half of these reserved shares, however, were held by Jardine, Matheson & Company itself, with only the remaining £100,000 going to the treaty-port investors in the China Coast and Yangtze Steam Navigation Companies.[83] Despite its recognition of its treaty-port shareholders in the new structure, there is no evidence the company continued to seek investors in China. Indo-China's new British identity was unmistakable: the combination of the firm's shares and British shares accounted for nearly three-quarters of its capital, and the company's offices and directors were located in London.

Jardine's merger was the final step in the transformation of the steam shipping business in Chinese waters. Not only were capital and flag consistent in the China Navigation, China Merchants, and Indo-China companies but they operated on a much larger scale than steamship companies had in the past. They maintained larger fleets, and by the early 1880s, all three offered roughly parallel services on the major coastal and river routes. In the past, it had been common for a single company to dominate or monopolize a route or set of routes, but as China Navigation, China Merchants, and the Jardine's shipping companies competed with one another between 1877 and 1882, each began to invade routes that had formerly belonged to other firms. After its purchase of the Shanghai Steam Navigation Company, the China Merchants Company used its enlarged fleet to enter routes that had been recognized as preserves of China Navigation or Jardine's companies. The British companies did the same: when Jardine's entered the Yangzi trade in 1879, China Navigation put ships on Jardine's Shanghai–Tianjin route. Jardine's began to build ships for the Niuzhuang–Shantou route, on which China Navigation competed with the China Merchants Company.[84] By 1882, all three companies maintained services on the Yangzi River, Shanghai–Tianjin, and Niuzhuang–Shantou routes, while Indo-China and the China Merchants competed on the Shanghai–Fuzhou route and China Navigation and the China Merchants competed on the Shanghai–Ningbo route (map 2.1). Although the services each company offered were slightly different, there was no major shipping route that remained the exclusive preserve of a single company.

Once the companies had reached a comparable size and scope, they stepped away from open competition, choosing instead to control it through agreements on routes and rates of freight. This kind of controlled competition was not unprecedented in the shipping network: agreements on rates, divisions of the trade, and claims to particular routes had been common since the late 1860s. What was new was the comprehensiveness of the agreements, which now pooled profits and divided sailings according to specific proportions on shared routes. A set of such agreements made in 1877 earned the China Merchants, China Navigation, and soon-to-be Indo-China Companies the moniker "the Three Companies" (*san gongsi*). A subsequent agreement in 1882 made adjustments for the Three Companies' expansions and consolidations, dividing the trade carefully among them on the most significant Yangzi and Shanghai–Tianjin routes. With these agreements, the Three Companies formed a shipping conference, an organization that helped maintain their status as the most powerful companies over the next six decades and definitively shaped the steam shipping business in Chinese waters.

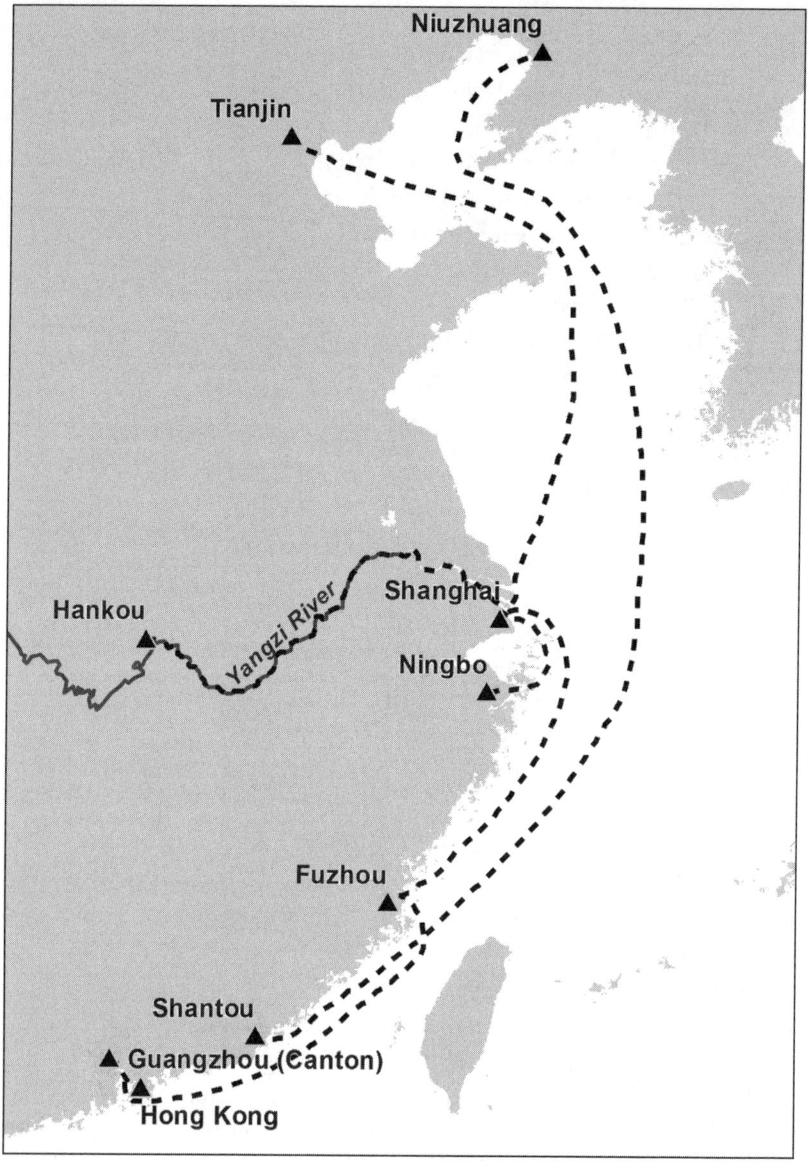

MAP 2.1 Major Steamship Routes of the Yangzi and Coast, 1870s. Map adapted from K.-C. Liu, *Anglo-American Steamship Rivalry*, 5.

Jardine's reorganization of its shipping interests into the Indo-China Steam Navigation Company struck a final blow to the erstwhile cosmopolitanism of the steamship business in Chinese waters. Neither of the two British firms actively sought treaty-port shareholders, and the China Merchants Company prohibited foreign investors from buying its shares. As these three expanding companies came to dominate the steam network, the flags their ships flew had become reliable indicators of the interests behind them. The practice of share affiliation did not completely disappear from the steamship business, as witnessed by the minority of shares reserved for treaty-port investors in the Indo-China Company and a few, occasional new steamship ventures floated in the treaty ports in the 1880s and 1890s. These new ventures were minor and often short-lived, however, as the Three Companies drew on much deeper reserves of capital and power.[85] The steam shipping business is therefore an exception to the argument that share affiliation increased over the 1880s and 1890s. Although share affiliation grew in fields such as banking, insurance, textiles, export processing, and light industry, merchant steam shipping within the treaty-port network never again became an important arena for this type of investment.[86] The alignment of capital and flag that took place between 1872 and 1882 resulted from new political and economic conditions affecting the steam network: the worldwide expansion of British shipping and British companies' turn to Britain as a source of capital, and the Qing dynasty's interest in reclaiming coastal and river shipping through the China Merchants Company.

Conclusion

The transformation of the steam shipping business in the 1870s and 1880s brought the realm of business more closely into line with the politics of the treaty system. Replacing a treaty port–based, multinational realm of investment and interest in steam shipping was a conflict between British and Qing interests. In business and in politics, the impending terminal conflict resolved into a new form of collaboration: the Three Companies' shipping conference.

Chapter 3 provides an analysis of the shipping conference as a form of collaboration in the 1880s and beyond. In the 1860s and 1870s, the significant instance of collaboration was the more stereotypical case: the investments of treaty-port Chinese merchants in foreign shipping firms. This form of collaboration was based on a shared economic interest taken by Chinese merchants without regard to—or in defiance of—indigenous authority and sovereignty. Although Li Hongzhang and the other founders of the China Merchants Company never entirely succeeded in recruiting these particular merchants to the China Merchants Company's cause, their attempt to intervene in this collaboration hastened the sharp contraction of the practice of share affiliation in merchant steam shipping. The China Merchants Company eventually joined the shipping conference, but even then Chinese interests were concentrated in this state-sanctioned company, and the company maintained the presence of the Qing flag in Chinese waters, on a considerable scale, for the duration of the dynasty.

A comparison of the development of the steam shipping businesses in Indian and Chinese waters between 1860 and 1882 illuminates the historical relationship between the two businesses, indicating that colonial state-building in India in the 1860s facilitated the extension of British shipping power to China in subsequent decades. More generally, the colonization of India gave British shipping there the power to surpass the boundaries of the colony and become a global force. Daniel Headrick has argued that the colonization of India was essential to Britain's rise as the dominant world shipping power in the second half of the nineteenth century: India balanced Britain's worldwide trade and provided a nearly captive market for British shipping services and commodities, making Britain the center of world finance, shipping, and insurance.[87] This new role had a profound impact on China and many other parts of the world.

The steamship business on the Indian coast in the 1850s and early 1860s closely resembled that of China's cosmopolitan companies of the 1860s. Most of the capital for steamship enterprises was raised in India itself from both Indian and European merchants, often in partnership with each other. Indian merchants who made fortunes during the boom in the Bombay and Ahmedabad textile industries during the U.S. Civil War or Parsi merchants involved in the China trade invested in steamship lines.[88] By the end of the decade, however, nearly all of the locally financed ventures failed in competition with the British India Steam Navigation Company, which was supported by government mail contracts, British capital, and British-built ships.[89]

The British India Company's mail contract with the government of India was central to achieving this dominant position and extending well beyond it. After 1862, the mail contract helped the firm raise capital in Britain, fueling its expansion. The firm's access to capital allowed it to maintain large reserves and continuously update its fleet, which further strengthened its competitive position in India.[90] Furthermore, the company's rapid development through the 1860s put the British India Company in a position to anticipate and profit from the changes in world shipping resulting from the communications revolution. Predicting that the Suez Canal would bring both more advanced steamship technology and more efficiently managed companies to India, the British India Company prepared carefully, stocking its coal supplies, refitting many of its ships, and paring down its crews.[91] Following the opening of the canal, it made through-traffic agreements with new overseas steamship lines that allowed it to retain control over its Indian coastal routes, further discouraging the entrance of new companies.[92] Subsequently, the company extended its contracts and connections with the government of India.[93] The British India Company thus became the primary beneficiary of the growth in India's maritime foreign and country trades that resulted from the communications revolution. Its prosperity allowed it to extend services to the Indonesian archipelago (1866) and the East African coast (1872) and establish an overseas line to Europe (1874, 1876) and a service between India and Australia (1881). By 1882, the British India Company possessed the largest fleet owned by a single company in the world.[94] By contracting with the colonial government to provide mail services and secure the colonial communications network, it extended beyond the Indian coast to become a world shipping power.

The growth and expansion of the British India Company predated the arrival of the new British companies in China by a full decade, but in many other respects, these companies were quite similar. The Scottish merchant trading house that started the British India Company—Mackinnon, Mackenzie & Company—had a similar history to those of Butterfield & Swire and Jardine, Matheson & Company in China. It transformed from a trade intermediary in Asia to a more diversified firm whose connections to the British home economy gave it a competitive advantage abroad. The founding partners of Mackinnon, Mackenzie & Company were from the same town in Scotland and set up the firm in

Calcutta in 1847. In the 1850s and 1860s, it began to move from trade into shipping, eventually consolidating its different shipping ventures into the British India Company. As shipping played a larger and larger role in its business, Mackinnon, Mackenzie & Company's strength derived less from its location in (and hence access to information in) India and increasingly on its access to capital and support in Britain for new ventures in India. The firm relied on a close network of family and business associates in Glasgow as shareholders and staff and purchased its ships from Clyde River shipbuilders in Scotland.[95] It is not difficult to see how the meteoric rise of the British India Company helped establish the conditions through which the trading firms of Butterfield & Swire and Jardine, Matheson & Company might find ample funds at home for their ventures in Chinese waters.

The steam shipping fields in China and India emerged on either end of the nineteenth-century communications revolution, and both contributed to the expansion of British shipping power across the globe in the nineteenth century. The time relationship between the two contexts suggests that colonial state-building was an important impetus for this process. The colonial state provided the British India Company a context in which it could expand rapidly and profit maximally, making investment in other overseas shipping ventures an attractive prospect in Britain and thus expanding British shipping beyond the borders of its formal empire.

The outstanding difference between the Indian and Chinese shipping businesses in the 1870s, however, was that the British India Company faced almost no opposition on Indian coastal routes, whereas the British companies in China contended with fierce competition from the China Merchants Company. By the end of the decade, it was clear that individually or together, the China Navigation Company and Jardine's shipping companies could not oust the China Merchants Company, nor could it defeat them. The situation was eventually resolved with the establishment of a shipping conference. In both places, the shape the business assumed in this decade remained in place for a long time, with the British India Company all but unopposed through World War I and the Three Companies of the shipping conference assuming a constant presence on the Yangzi and coast through World War II. As Baldev Raj Nayar has shown, there was little scope for indigenous shipping in colonial India because the colonial government and British shipping interests were so closely entwined. Nayar argues that "the sovereignty of the state, more importantly the exercise of that sovereignty, is thus fundamental to the survival of a national merchant fleet."[96] China was hardly exempt from the rise in British shipping power, but the intervention of the Qing state, in the form of the China Merchants Steam Navigation Company, ensured the existence of a merchant fleet under the Qing flag.

CHAPTER 3

The Shipping Conference as Collaboration, 1882–1913

In March 1883, John Samuel Swire of the China Navigation Company described the transformation of the relationship among the "Three Companies" under their new agreement: "We are now developing the various trades in unison, and to our mutual advantage. We may have had family quarrels, incompatibility or temper may cause temporary separations but there will not be a divorce. In future, we must share the same bed. Celestials and terrestrials."[1] Swire was correct that the shipping conference would become a permanent fixture of the shipping business in China from the 1880s through 1937. This alliance of "celestials and terrestrials" at times dominated the business completely and at other times struggled against challenges from newcomers, but it remained a central institution of the treaty-port network. The conference shaped the shipping business and the pace and rhythms of steam transport in Chinese waters. As a significant collaborative mechanism, the conference also highlights the paradoxical qualities of collaboration in semi-colonial China.

The important role this shipping conference played on China's Yangzi River and coast is quite unique, because such conferences are overwhelmingly associated with international shipping lines of the late nineteenth century. Conferences are cartels that at a minimum fix freight rates to protect members' market shares from outside competition. They were seen as necessary to protect the business of liner companies—that had made huge investments in ships and in establishing regular services—from irregular carriers who might take profitable cargoes without providing regular services. Conferences became widespread on international routes in the 1880s, most often introduced by British ship owners, and by the turn of the twentieth century, they controlled most international trade routes.[2] John Samuel Swire had negotiated a number of conference agreements on international lines for Holt's Ocean Steamship Company, and he actively promoted the conference agreement in Chinese waters. The adoption of the conference system in China proceeded from the increasing British presence in the steamship business and the companies' liner organization, which was similar to those of overseas companies.

The shipping conference among the Three Companies—China Merchants, China Navigation, and Indo-China—was at the height of its power in the years between 1882 and 1895, and it definitively structured the shipping field at that time. It stabilized and increased all three companies' earnings after many years of competition, and it regularized the pace of the steam traffic, established a schedule, and set uniform rates. During these years, the institution of the conference could readily accommodate occasional competitors and competition among its members. The Three Companies conference had advocates who appreciated the stability it brought to the business and critics who believed it curtailed the extension of steam navigation within the Qing empire.

The shipping conference also presents a particularly trenchant instance of semi-colonial collaboration. Critics of the China Merchants Company see its decision to enter into agreements with the British companies as a betrayal of its original mission to "take back" the rivers and coast from foreign companies, yet the actual impact of the conference on the Qing-flag company was far more complex. Like other forms of collaboration, its effects were paradoxical: over the 1882–95 period, as a result of conference involvement, asymmetries emerged between the China Merchants Company and the British companies that indisputably favored the latter. At the same time, the stability of trade and earnings resulting from the conference agreements had a protective effect on the China Merchants Company, allowing it to weather political vulnerabilities and managerial upheaval to remain a viable shipping venture. It continued to contribute to the cause of Qing sovereignty even if it never managed to expel foreign shipping companies from Chinese waters.

After the Sino-Japanese War of 1895, a new group of steamship companies contested the conference's control of the treaty-port network. These new companies came from Japan, Germany, and France and were subsidized by their home governments to establish national presences in Chinese waters. Between 1895 and 1911, the scope and pace of the steamship network increased as the result of new competition and new concessions treaty powers obtained from the Qing. The conditions of this period challenged the conference organization, but it survived, retaining most of its earlier power. By 1911, the only new competitor to the Three Companies able to secure a comparable place in Chinese waters was the Japanese Nisshin Kisen Kaisha, which joined the conference in 1913.

During these years of intense competition and instability in the shipping field, the effects of collaboration within the conference became even more pronounced for the China Merchants Company. By the time of the 1913 agreement, China Merchants' market share had dropped below those of the British and Japanese companies, and it was unable to participate in significant new trades these companies had developed. At the same time, the conference organization continued to buoy the China Merchants Company as its relationship with the Qing state dissipated over these years. The Qing not only ceased providing the profitable concessions that it had in the past, but also began demanding payments or using company funds for other purposes. In 1911, the China Merchants Company severed its relationship with the government completely, registering as a private firm. By the last years of the dynasty, it was clear that shipping was no longer the same arena of sovereign concern for the Qing that it had been in years past. Nevertheless, it was likely the functionality and viability of the China Merchants Company as a conference participant that allowed the government to turn to other priorities in these years of dynastic crisis. In the end, the China Merchants Company and the conference system outlived the dynasty, and the China Merchants Company continued to fly the Chinese flag within the steam network through the start of the Second Sino-Japanese War.

The Shipping Conference in China, 1882–95

The shipping conference was most powerful in Chinese waters between 1882 and 1895. The conference practices on which the Three Companies relied defined the shipping business and shaped the experience of steam transport in general. Not only did the conference diminish competition and bring stability to trade and traffic within the network, but the conference companies' agreements to reciprocally accept passenger tickets, forward cargo, and resist the intrusions of outsiders provided a relatively uniform shipping service. Although there were agreements among competing steamship companies in the 1860s and 1870s, the 1882 conference stands out for its comprehensiveness in regulating the trade and its parallels with rising shipping conferences on overseas lines throughout the world.

The emergence of a conference organization among shipping companies on China's coast and river was linked to the development of conferences on international shipping lines in the 1870s. These conferences, also called cartels or rings, were formed among overseas liner companies in the newly competitive conditions in steam navigation following the opening of the Suez Canal. Conferences were designed to limit competition among participants and deter newcomers from entering the trade. British shipping firms dominated the conference system that emerged in the late 1870s, beginning with the Calcutta Conference of 1875. The participants in the Far East Conference (1879) provided liner services from Europe to China and Japan. Apart from the French Messageries Maritimes, they were all British shipping firms.[3] By the turn of the twentieth century, British-led conferences dominated most international trade routes. These included routes to Australia (1884), South Africa (1886), West Africa (1895), Brazil (1895–96), and the west coast of South America (1904).[4] These conferences defined the international shipping regime of the late nineteenth and early twentieth centuries.

The rationale behind conferences was that they ensured the profitability of liner trades. Technological improvements in ocean-going steamships in the 1860s and 1870s had made regularly scheduled overseas shipping services possible. Liner companies specialized in scheduled transport on specific routes, carrying high-value goods like manufactures or time-sensitive goods like fruits. Because their ships required heavy capital outlays and their fixed costs were high (up to 75 percent of the total cost of the voyage), these companies relied on speed and efficient organization to make profits. Liner companies were particularly vulnerable to shifts in supply and demand, seasonal fluctuations in trade, and competition. As a result of the boom in steamship construction in the 1870s, they endured stiff competition from newcomers and tramp steamers or "casuals"—individual ships that could invade liner routes at peak season and undercut the freight rates of the regulars. Conferences among the liner companies sharing a particular route were a means of limiting both types of competition and increasing the earnings of participants.

Because steam shipping in China was restricted to the open ports, the steamship companies active in the network after the mid-1860s most often operated as liner companies and were thus similarly vulnerable to competition and seasonal changes. As the U.S.-flag Shanghai Steam Navigation Company grew in size and influence from the mid-1860s, its managers initiated agreements with rival companies to maintain uniform rates of freight or to divide shipping routes on many occasions.[5] Following the entrance of the China Navigation Company to the Yangzi in 1872, John Samuel Swire took the lead in introducing even stronger accords to limit competition on key routes. He arranged to divide the Yangzi trade with the Shanghai Steam Navigation Company in 1874 and the China Merchants Company in 1877 through "rate pools" in which the companies charged uniform rates, maintained a strict schedule of departures, pooled their profits, and divided the receipts among the participants at the end of a specified period.[6] His biographers contend that his experience of the stabilizing effects of such arrangements in river and coastal shipping in China convinced him of their utility for overseas lines. Since John Swire & Sons acted as agent for Holt's Ocean Steamship Company, Swire helped establish the Far East Conference and organized other conferences on routes between Europe and Asia.[7] Although agreements that limited competition were not new to the steam network, by the late 1870s Swire's experience in China fueled the launch of British-led conferences worldwide, and the Three Companies followed suit with a conference-style agreement in 1877 and a more comprehensive agreement in 1882.

Conferences reduced competition among participants by maintaining internal controls to which all participants were subject. They determined freight rates, but they might also implement pooling arrangements: predetermining the division of trade on a specific route among the participating companies, with each company entitled to a share of the total profits based on the size, tonnage, or efficiency of its fleet. At the end of a season, the conference companies would redistribute the total profits based on these proportions. A comprehensive set of pooling agreements was at the heart of the Three Companies conference. By 1882, the China Navigation, China Merchants, and Indo-China companies had expanded to the point that the size of their fleets and scope of their routes were comparable. The conference set the numbers of sailings and pooled earnings on the major Yangzi River and Shanghai–Tianjin routes. On the Yangzi, the China Merchants Company was entitled to 42 percent of the profits, China Navigation 38 percent, and Indo-China 20 percent. On the Shanghai–Tianjin route China Merchants received 44 percent, and China Navigation and Indo-China 28 percent each. The companies consented to stay off certain routes that others had developed: thus the Shanghai–Wenzhou route was recognized as the China Merchants' and the Hong Kong–Calcutta route as Indo-China's. China Navigation agreed not to enter the Shanghai–Fuzhou route, and Indo-China agreed to stay away from the Shanghai–Ningbo and Hong Kong–Canton routes on which the other two companies competed.[8]

In addition to internal controls, conferences also employed exclusionary measures to deter new competitors. The most common device was the deferred rebate, which provided shippers an incentive to remain loyal to conference ships. Companies would refund shippers 5–10 percent of the freight they had paid after a certain period of time (usually six months to a year), on condition that they shipped exclusively by conference ships within that period. The practice of "fighting ships" was directed against new companies attempting to enter conference routes. The conference would dispatch a member's ship offering low freights to match every departure of new competitors' ships, thus using participants' financial resources to run newer arrivals off thc route. The Three Companies offered a 5 percent rebate at the end of a set period to shippers for remaining faithful to conference ships, and they responded with simultaneous sailings or sudden dropping of freight rates when new ships came on the line. They also refused the services they provided to one another, such as accepting other companies' passenger tickets or towing ships in trouble, to newcomers.

The 1882 conference stabilized and eventually increased the Three Companies' earnings.[9] It also ensured that steam transport among the treaty ports was carried out on a regular schedule at uniform rates. Yangzi ports, for example, enjoyed the regularity of the daily steamer—one ship departing from each of the termini of Shanghai and Hankou per day between Monday and Saturday. Each company made two scheduled departures per week from either end of the route: China Merchants Company ships left Shanghai on Mondays and Thursdays, China Navigation's on Wednesdays and Saturdays, and Indo-China's on Tuesdays and Fridays.[10] The Three Companies also cooperated to keep services running smoothly, allowing first-class passengers to make return trips on any conference ship, forwarding goods on another company's ship in case of a problem or delay, and assisting one another in towing ships run aground.[11] As British overseas shipping lines became known as the "Ocean Railway" in this period, so did the daily steamer on China's river and coast maintain a regular pace of communication among the treaty ports.

Shipping conferences could diminish competition, but they could not eradicate it completely. Over the 1882–95 period, the Three Companies sometimes incorporated newcomers as affiliate conference members. Affiliates were required to abide by conference schedules and freight rates, but they lacked voting rights in the organization. Although affiliation with the conference allowed new companies to participate in the trade without being attacked, the conference set limits on affiliates' growth, restricting the number and tonnage of their ships as well as the routes on which they were allowed to work.[12] In the 1880s and 1890s, there were two small British-flag firms on the Yangzi that accepted this affiliate status: McBain & Company and the Hong'an Company. Both companies' fleets and operations were much smaller than those of the Three Companies.[13] Their ships were permitted two departures a week from Shanghai and Hankou but were required to overlap with departures of the Three Companies' ships.[14] As the *North China Herald* described, "they are carefully regulated so as to provide only a semblance of opposition to the main lines."[15]

The history of the Hong'an Company shows how even an opponent intent on competing against the conference might eventually succumb to its power. This company was organized in the late 1880s to challenge conference hegemony. It was financed by local Chinese and British capital, including investments from compradors and brokers once associated with the Three Companies. Initially the company had eleven ships and provided services on the Yangzi River, Shanghai–Tianjin, and Shantou–Taiwan routes. After several years of competition, its operations had contracted to four small ships running on the Yangzi River, and it joined the conference as an affiliate in 1897.[16]

The conference organization provided some scope for competition among members. The Three Companies competed with one another to maximize profits by running the most efficient ships, which in turn allowed a company to invest in newer, better-equipped ships. Over time, changes in the size and capacity of one company's fleet might prompt it to demand the renegotiation of conference terms. China Navigation expanded its fleet over the course of the 1880s. When the original conference agreement lapsed in 1889, John Samuel Swire demanded that the new agreement recognize China Navigation's strengthened position. The other companies disagreed and temporarily dissolved the conference agreement, which resulted in open competition among the Three Companies between 1890 and 1892. They referred to the period of open competition as a "rate war," in which each company tried to undercut its opponents, and rates of freight on shared lines dropped so low that the companies could not cover costs. At this time each of the Three Companies invaded routes they had previously agreed to cede: Indo-China put a ship to the Shanghai–Ningbo line, China Merchants added one to the Canton River, and China Navigation added to the Shanghai–Fuzhou line.[17] Not until 1893 did the companies settle on a new conference agreement that recognized the expansion of China Navigation's fleet and by this time the growth of Indo-China's as well. This translated into adjustments of each company's share of important trades: China Navigation gained a 4 percent greater share on the Yangzi and northern coast routes, and Indo-China 1 percent, while the China Merchants lost 5 percent. This agreement was renewed in 1896 and lasted until 1901.[18]

On international lines and in China, the conference system was controversial. In Britain, many criticized it as anticompetitive, monopolistic, and a departure from the idea of freedom of the seas that free trade advocates had used to overturn the British Navigation Acts in 1847.[19] Defenders of the conference system claimed that it was necessary to provide regular and efficient services on routes vulnerable to different types of fluctuation in availability of cargoes.[20] They contended that conferences benefited shippers and consumers because they provided greater stability in freight rates, and thus allowed for greater predictability in markets.[21]

Supporters emphasized the checks and balances within the system: conferences could not raise rates too high or "casuals" might invade the routes, and they could not fix membership, so successful new competitors could eventually gain admission.[22] Because of their anticompetitive qualities, the legality of conferences was challenged several times in British courts between 1885 and 1890, but the courts and major government studies, such as the British Royal Commission and Shipping Rings Report (1909) and the U.S. Alexander Report (1914), found them to be legally acceptable means of organizing ocean shipping.[23]

In China, some complained that the absence of open competition—the steadiness of the daily steamer—inhibited the development of steam navigation. A British consul's report on the trade of Hankou from 1888 noted that the pace of steam traffic in and out of the port was steady, but the large volumes of junk and lorcha traffic suggested greater potential for steam transport in the area.[24] Advocates of extending steam shipping to Sichuan Province saw the conference as impeding the development of that route. The Three Companies conference agreement had made the Upper Yangzi route the exclusive provenance of the China Merchants Company, and that company only ran an occasional steamer above Hankou.[25] For those eager to extend steam navigation to new areas of the Qing empire, conference agreements that preserved the status quo for several years at a time slowed this process even further.

Despite the frustration of some with the sleepy pace of the daily steamer, many extolled the benefits of the predictable and efficient services under the conference system. The value of this system in maintaining order in trade and transport was made obvious when the conference agreement dissolved suddenly during 1890–92. The volatility of freight rates caused shippers to delay their shipments, thus slowing down the trade.[26] The very low passenger fares available during the rate war resulted in a sudden increase in the volume of travelers, on which many observers blamed outbreaks of crime and disturbances. The customs commissioner at Wuhu commented that "the almost nominal steamer fares enabled bands of thieves and other bad characters to move from place to place and concentrate on any port they liked."[27] These disturbances took on a clearer shape in a series of anti-Christian riots that took place in Yangzi treaty ports and calling stations in May 1891. The riots moved progressively upriver from Yangzhou to Wuhu, Nanjing, Anqing, Danyang,

Wuxue, Jiujiang, and Yichang. The instigators were said to be members of the Brothers and Elders Society (*Gelaohui*) and disbanded soldiers. Low fares allowed them to travel upriver to escape capture and instigate further riots and demonstrations.[28] When the rate war was over and a conference agreement restored, many were relieved to see these volatile conditions end.

Shippers, both internationally and in China, opposed the power conferences had to determine rates and procedures. The organization of Chinese commodity traders into guilds based on specific trades and/or native places provided a platform from which shippers could protest and negotiate with the Three Companies. Even prior to the development of the full-fledged conference system, Chinese guilds had organized "taboos" (boycotts) of particular shipping firms to protest policies they found unfair. Such actions were organized quietly among guild members, who simply ceased to send goods via the errant company's ships.[29] Because most of these guilds had branches throughout the network of open ports, a taboo could be active in many places at once. The Shandong guild, for example, organized a taboo of the Shanghai Steam Navigation Company's steamers in the summer of 1873 in response to the company's refusal to compensate a guild member for goods lost in a shipping accident. The company had to settle with guild branches in both Shanghai and Tianjin to end it.[30] With the advent of the conference system, the guilds tended to single out one of the Three Companies in protests against conference policies, putting the burden on that company to negotiate a compromise between the guild and the other two firms. Although the conference mechanism ensured that even a boycotted company could collect its share of profits, a taboo was a blow to the company's business and reputation and might provide an opportunity for an outsider to challenge conference power by meeting the guild's demands.[31] The Three Companies took taboos very seriously and worked to reach agreements with guilds: they only rarely used their collective power to break a taboo for fear of completely alienating the guild behind it.[32] The conference was unquestionably powerful, but guild taboos provided a check on the demands it could make of shippers.

Between 1882 and 1895, the Three Companies' conference defined the steam shipping business on the Yangzi River and coast. Beyond maintaining the powerful position of the Three Companies, it also set the pace of trade and travel within the steam network. Some contemporaries appreciated its stabilizing effects and others criticized its lack of dynamism, but it remained the central institution of the business.

The Conference as Collaboration

The China Merchants Company's history of aggressive expansion in the 1870s and its founding intention to take back the rivers and coasts from foreign shipping firms suggest that the company's decision to participate in shipping conferences in 1877 and 1882 was a dramatic reversal of its original aims. Many historians have criticized the company's apparent abandonment of its proto-nationalist stance in favor of compromise with foreign shipping interests. Fan Baichuan, for example, author of a wide-ranging history of modern Chinese shipping, attributed the reversal to China Merchants leaders such as Tang Tingshu, Xu Run, and Li Hongzhang, who he characterized as insufficiently tolerant of business competition and ready to join the conference to forestall personal financial losses.[33] In a more recent study of conference agreements, Chen Chao argues that the China Merchants Company's decision to join the conference also inhibited the potential development of other Chinese shipping enterprises, as it cooperated with foreign firms to monopolize the shipping business.[34] In both accounts, the China Merchants' decision is represented as favoring its own narrow interests at the expense of a larger task of national development—either maintaining its own independence or allowing the modern Chinese shipping sector to expand.

To judge the China Merchants Company's role in the shipping conference in these terms, however, overlooks the conference's complex, almost paradoxical impact on the Qing-flag company and the nuances of semi-colonial collaboration. China Merchants did reverse its initial position, joining the conference to survive a financial crisis, but the impact of conference participation on the company was not entirely negative from the perspective of its own development or its role in fostering Qing sovereignty. Like the treaty system and other forms of collaboration, the shipping conference produced inequalities among its participants. Between 1882 and 1895, the British companies' shares of various trades grew steadily as the China Merchants' shares contracted. Nevertheless, conference participation also protected and sustained the China Merchants Company through a particularly turbulent period in its internal affairs and in its relations with the government.

The China Merchants Company's rapid expansion in the 1870s and its purchase of the Shanghai Steam Navigation Company left it deeply in debt to Qing government sources, Russell & Company, native banks, and other private creditors. By the early 1880s, the company could no longer delay the repayment of its government loans or its debts to Russell & Company. The conference's guarantee of stable conditions and steady profits allowed China Merchants to resolve this crisis. Between 1882 and 1895, it repaid its sizable debts and had enough surplus to update its fleet, if not at the same rate as the other conference companies in the same period.[35]

The China Merchants Company's position within the conference changed between 1882 and 1895. In 1882, China Merchants enjoyed the largest fleet and the greatest share of profits on most routes. By the time the Three Companies renegotiated the conference agreement in 1893–94, its fleet was the smallest, and it lost 5 percent of its pooled profits to the other companies. In 1882, the China Merchants operated thirty-three ships to China Navigation's twenty and Indo-China's thirteen. By 1894 its fleet had shrunk to twenty-six ships, and its total tonnage contracted slightly (23,697 to 23,284 tons). Over the same interval, the British companies had consistently expanded and updated their fleets. China Navigation's fleet increased from twenty to twenty-nine ships (22,151 tons to 34,543 tons), and Indo-China's fleet grew from thirteen to twenty-two ships (12,571 tons to 23,953 tons).[36] Although the new agreement evinced more of a reshuffling of positions than a sharp decline for the China Merchants Company, it had lost some ground to its rivals.

Scholarly explanations for this change tend to attribute it to the China Merchants' business decisions or management style without taking into account the effects of conference participation. K.-C. Liu blamed the diminishment of the China Merchants position on its policy of guaranteeing a 10 percent dividend to shareholders each year between 1873 and 1893, a dividend paid regardless of the company's performance. Liu viewed this policy as evidence of the managers privileging short-term gains over the long-term health of the company and failing to reinvest profits in capital equipment, contrasting it with the practices of the British companies, which allocated earnings to cover depreciation and built reserves before paying dividends to shareholders.[37] Another argument, that the company's fortunes declined when the official Sheng Xuanhuai replaced merchant managers Tang Tingshu and Xu Run in 1883–84, contrasts the relative autonomy with which Tang and Xu ran the enterprise with Sheng's more bureaucratic leadership, under which its business is said to have stagnated.[38] Although specific business practices and management style probably influenced the company's performance in this period, its participation in the conference also affected its prospects.

Within Chinese waters, the Three Companies conference agreements held each company to a specific number of sailings, share of profits, and division of routes. Once beyond Chinese waters, however, the apparent equivalence of the conference arrangement disappeared. All three companies operated in a global context in which Britain dominated shipping, trade, and finance, and many of the inequalities that developed between the British firms and the China Merchants Company between 1882 and 1895 resulted from the British firms' greater access to the resources of Britain's shipping power. In this context, the China Merchants Company experienced a double impediment: not only was it impossible for it to replicate the relationships through which the British companies gained this access, it was also dependent, even in Chinese waters, on a British-dominated shipping infrastructure that included shipbuilding, insurance, repairs, and fuel supply. The wider field in which the Three Companies operated was far from level, and thus the China Merchants Company's internal policies and management are at best only partial explanations for the shift in its competitive position in these years.

An examination of the development of the China Navigation and Indo-China Companies between 1882 and 1895 reveals key aspects of their privileged position. The trading firms that oversaw these companies expanded into diversified businesses that benefited the shipping ventures and extended their services from the China coast to overseas lines. In both areas, the firms' close relationships with other British business and shipping interests were essential to their expansion. In 1882, Butterfield & Swire established Taikoo Sugar, an affiliated sugar refinery in Hong Kong. China Navigation ships brought raw sugar from Java and the Philippines to Hong Kong, and dispatched cargoes of refined sugar for sale in China,

Japan, and Australia, making the carriage of sugar an important source of revenue for the shipping company.[39] Through the 1880s, China Navigation further extended its overseas services on lines to Manila, Saigon, Bangkok, Java, Japan, Australia, and the eastern coast of Russia.[40] Jardine, Matheson & Company established a sugar refinery and an ice factory in Hong Kong and extended its business interests into insurance and wharf companies in Hong Kong and Shanghai.[41] The Indo-China Steam Navigation Company provided shipping services to the Straits Settlements and Calcutta.[42] By the 1890s, both of the British shipping firms had exceeded the bounds of the treaty-port steam network to develop new business concerns and overseas services connecting China to Southeast Asia and beyond. Although the bulk of this expansion took place beyond Chinese waters, these new transport connections and lines of business enhanced the companies' carriage on the Yangzi River and coast.

During the 1880s, the British-dominated conference system began to monopolize international shipping routes, and central to China Navigation and Indo-China's expansions were their close relationships to British overseas shipping interests. China Navigation and Indo-China held agencies for major British overseas lines, and the owners of these lines held shares in these firms. Butterfield & Swire had long acted as agent for Holt's Ocean Steamship Company in Asia, and the Holt family owned shares in China Navigation and Taikoo Sugar. Jardine, Matheson & Company maintained close ties, including shareholding, with the Peninsular & Oriental Company.[43] The trading firms held agencies for other international shipping lines, insurance companies, and banks.[44] When these China-based shipping companies extended onto overseas lines, they were not outsiders fighting for a foothold in conference-dominated trades but had the information and connections to negotiate and secure places in the trades that would benefit them. Furthermore, their relationships with overseas shipping lines allowed them to offer convenient connections between their services in China and major overseas routes.

It was no coincidence that the 1880s was also the decade in which the China Merchants Company abandoned its efforts to establish overseas lines. Whereas the British companies were able to leverage their connections to extend beyond the Yangzi River and coast, similar initiatives by the China Merchants Company crumbled under opposition from shipping conferences and other protectionist measures abroad. Developing overseas lines had been a goal of the China Merchants Company since its founding: as early as 1873, it sent ships to Kobe and Nagasaki to carry passengers and obtain inexpensive coal.[45] In the early 1880s, it began a service between China and Southeast Asian ports such as Manila, Singapore, Haiphong, and Saigon. China Merchants even attempted to enter the routes connecting China, Europe, and North America, sending a ship to Honolulu in 1879 and ships to San Francisco and London in 1880. The company issued new stock worth 200,000 *taels* to overseas Chinese in Hawaii and the United States to support the proposed overseas lines.[46] On the Southeast Asian and European routes, China Merchants capitulated to the opposition of organized shipping conferences. In U.S. and Japanese ports, its ships were excluded by government measures designed to protect national shipping.[47] By 1882, the only overseas route on which the China Merchants Company remained active connected China to Haiphong and Saigon, but this service ended with the start of the Sino-French War in 1883.[48] To break into conference-dominated routes, the China Merchants Company needed either a large reserve of capital or significant government subsidies to weather the opposition, and it had neither. Li Hongzhang refused a request by China Merchants managers to resume overseas operations in 1890 because, as he explained, the aid they would need to enter competitive overseas routes was not forthcoming from the government.[49] In contrast to the British firms, by the mid-1880s the China Merchants Company had no overseas services or connections to overseas lines, an inequality that was compounded in subsequent decades.

The China Merchants Company also tried to create a network of affiliated businesses in the 1870s that would support its shipping business and free it from dependence on foreign-owned (often British-owned) services such as repairs, insurance, and fuel supply. These businesses, however, either failed or did not maintain close enough ties to the company to provide much assistance. In 1874, Tang Tingshu and Xu Run established two concerns: the Tongmao Ironworks, to allow the company to repair its own ships rather than sending them to foreign-owned shipyards in Shanghai, and the Renhe Insurance Company, to save on high rates charged by foreign insurance firms. Neither business was able to fulfill its mission: the Tongmao Ironworks was dismantled in a managerial reorganization of the China Merchants Company in 1879, and although the insurance company did insure the company's fleet briefly, the greater coverage needed after the Shanghai Steam Navigation Company purchase necessitated a return to foreign insurers.[50] In 1877, Tang Tingshu was involved in establishing the Kaiping Mines under Li Hongzhang's patronage. The mine was an officially sponsored, merchant-managed enterprise intended to provide a domestic substitute for the imported coal used in steamships and provide return cargoes for China Merchants ships carrying tribute grain to Tianjin. By the time the mines began operations in the mid-1880s, Tang had been dismissed from the position of China Merchants manager and the two companies did not maintain close relations.[51] Another enterprise set up under Li's patronage, the Shanghai Cotton Cloth Mill (est. 1878, later the Huasheng Mill) might have provided cargoes for the China Merchants Company, but it encountered stiff competition from foreign textile mills following the Sino-Japanese War and never became a source of profit.[52] By the 1890s, not only did China Merchants lack affiliated ventures that could enhance its business, it remained dependent on many foreign services.

The clearest example of the China Merchants Company's dependence in this period was its reliance on British-built ships. The company's founders had hoped it would support the shipbuilding programs of the Jiangnan and Fuzhou Arsenals, but they soon discovered that the ships built at these facilities were inadequate for commercial competition. Apart from the ships acquired from the Shanghai Steam Navigation Company, all new ships for the China Merchants Company's Yangzi River and coastal fleets before 1912 were purchased—at high prices—from British shipyards on the Clyde River.[53] This dependence on British-built ships has been interpreted as a case of mismanagement within the company since the majority of these purchases were made by a single British marine superintendent said to have amassed a personal fortune by overcharging the company for ships built at his brother's shipyard.[54] This superintendent may have lined his own pockets, but the China Merchants Company had little choice but to buy ships that could keep pace with its British competitors. In contrast, the China Navigation and Indo-China Companies needed no such intermediaries because Clyde River shipbuilders owned shares in both firms.[55] It was not until 1912 that the China Merchants Company was able to purchase a ship from a Chinese-owned facility, the Jiangnan Dock and Engineering Works in Shanghai.[56] Before this point, the considerable expansion of steam shipping on China's river and coastal routes after 1870 benefited British shipbuilders almost exclusively and presents another parallel between the Chinese and Indian steam networks as Indian routes were supplied by the same shipbuilders.[57]

The asymmetries that emerged among the Three Companies between 1882 and 1895 were stark. The British firm extended onto overseas lines where the China Merchants Company was mostly confined to the Yangzi and coast. China Merchants also encountered greater difficulties building auxiliary business and remained dependent on British services and shipbuilding. Although the contraction in the China Merchants Company's business over this period was slight, in subsequent years these inequalities became more pronounced and had greater consequences for the Qing-flag company. The shipping conference nominally placed the Three Companies "in the same bed," but their very different access to worldwide shipping resources had marked effects on their future prospects.

As significant as the asymmetries resulting from conference participation were, the conference's protective effect on the China Merchants Company was also undeniable. The conference helped the company weather a number of crises in the short term and maintain the presence of Qing-flag shipping in Chinese waters over the long run.[58] The stable business and earnings the conference guaranteed kept the China Merchants Company a viable enterprise even as it endured investigations of corruption initiated by the Qing bureaucracy and upheavals in its management and leadership.

The China Merchants Company's particular relationship to the Qing government made it vulnerable to bureaucratic interference, usually in the form of accusations of and investigations into financial malfeasance originating with officials outside of the company. The company's indebtedness to provincial treasuries and other official sources opened it to this type of scrutiny, and in 1877 and 1880, imperial censors initiated reviews of corrupt practices in the China Merchants Company. In his study of the company within Qing bureaucratic culture, Yi Li describes these investigations as stemming from a "tacit code of bureaucratic functioning" around enterprises connected to the bureaucracy, such as the salt monopoly or grain tribute transport. Li argues that the officials and merchants involved in these enterprises were expected to derive some personal profit from them, but if these profits accrued too much to one person or one particular group, competing factions within the bureaucracy would bring charges of corruption against the enterprise to redistribute profits to a broader group.[59] The investigations into the China Merchants Company in 1877 and 1880 were challenges to Li Hongzhang's control of the company's profits, and both demanded greater bureaucratic supervision of the company.[60] At the time, Li was powerful enough to maintain his position, but the China Merchants Company had to accept changes to its management and organization as a result.

In the mid-1880s, the impending Sino-French War caused a more thorough restructuring of the China Merchants Company's leadership and personnel. In 1883, growing Sino-French tensions over Indochina caused a financial panic in Shanghai, during which the personal finances of managers Tang Tingshu and Xu Run collapsed. The panic exposed these men as having borrowed considerable sums from the China Merchants Company to invest in other ventures. After a decade of leading the company, Tang and Xu were dismissed from their positions and their personal stock confiscated. This upheaval was followed by a temporary sale of the entire China Merchants' fleet to Russell & Company in advance of the war with France. In 1885, when the fleet returned and business resumed, Sheng Xuanhuai took charge of the China Merchants Company in place of Tang and Xu. The company came under much closer bureaucratic supervision than in the past and had to submit information on its business to the Board of Revenue. The intense criticism directed at Li Hongzhang during the Sino-French War and subsequent peace negotiations diminished his political standing, and he could not be as effective a patron as before. Li was no longer able to obtain favors for the company, such as the official loans that had helped China Merchants expand in the 1870s.[61]

The chaotic internal history of the company in these years suggests that conference participation was important to maintaining the China Merchants Company's profitability through the 1882–95 period. Although it never replicated the rapid expansion of the 1870s, the firm's performance remained steady through the 1880s and 1890s despite upheaval and restructuring. It did not match the British companies' rates of growth, but the China Merchants Company's business between 1882 and 1895 was good: it carried more than its allotted share of the trade each year between 1883 and 1889 and enjoyed substantial earnings. It added sixteen new ships to its fleet before 1893, even if these additions did not fully compensate for losses and depreciation or match its competitors' rates of expansion.[62] It continued to operate on the broadest range of coastal routes, commanding the largest percentages of the major Yangzi River and northern coast trades in the 1893 conference agreement. Sheng Xuanhuai was able to reduce the company's indebtedness, which offered it some protection from further bureaucratic attacks.[63] The China Merchants Company's competitive position had declined by 1893, but the change was modest, and despite the company's internal turmoil, it remained one of the three most powerful shipping companies in China.

In maintaining the viability of the China Merchants Company, the conference also helped support the objectives of the Qing state. Throughout the 1882–95 period, China Merchants continued to service the grain tribute, carry special government commodities, and transport troops for the state, for which the state continued to compensate it well. Although it cooperated closely with the British firms, the China Merchants Company could still forward state objectives like containing foreign-flag shipping within the constraints of the conference. For example, as part of the 1882 conference agreement, the company secured exclusive rights to work the route between Hankou and Yichang on the Yangzi River. Yichang, opened by the 1877 Chefoo Convention, was at the entrance to the Three Gorges and the gateway to the Sichuan trade. The Zongli *yamen* considered this area sensitive and was wary of allowing foreign ships to travel that far upriver. For nearly a decade after 1882, the only commercial steamships that reached Yichang were China Merchants ships. The desultory pace of China Merchants service frustrated foreign merchants eager to enter the Sichuan trade, but it helped the Zongli *yamen* keep foreign ships out. It wasn't until 1891, when Chongqing was formally opened as a treaty port, that the British companies put ships on this route.[64] Even then, the Qing government provided the China Merchants Company special concessions to help it maintain its powerful position. The eastern Sichuan circuit intendant (*Chuandong daotai*) exempted goods sent by China Merchants ships from certain types of taxation. Shippers preferred to send heavily taxed goods like opium via China Merchants ships, and the company continued to enjoy the largest share of the Upper Yangzi trade in subsequent years.[65] In 1895, Zongli *yamen* officials defended the China Merchants Company from yet another censorial indictment on charges of corruption, citing the "conspicuous role it had played in recovering economic rights."[66]

As a collaborative mechanism, the conference had more in common with the treaty system than with the collaboration between Chinese treaty-port merchants and foreign trading firms in the 1860s. Promoted by British ship owners, the conference ultimately forwarded the goal of foreign expansion into China by facilitating the rapid expansion of British shipping firms in the 1880s. Yet in its protective effects, the conference resembled the treaty system in that it provided a degree of support to Qing sovereign interests. Although the relationship between the Qing state and the China Merchants Company could be tenuous and fraught, the company was an artifact of Qing agency and power. In joining the conference, the China Merchants Company had to give up its aspiration to recover coastal and river shipping from foreign companies, but the conference also helped the company survive as a merchant steam fleet under the Qing flag. Even within the constraints of the conference, the company could also further Qing agendas, such as forestalling the extension of foreign shipping to the Upper Yangzi. Although the China Merchants Company never enjoyed the same prospects for development as its British rivals, the continuous presence of a significant indigenous merchant steamship company was a feature that set the steam network in semi-colonial China apart from its counterpart in colonial India.

The Conference Challenged, 1895–1913

New shipping interests challenged the Three Companies' secure hold on China's coastal and river routes in the years between the First Sino-Japanese War (1894–95) and the fall of the Qing dynasty (1911). The Three Companies continued to work together but now had to resist the attempts of well-financed newcomers to gain shares of their trades. The new conditions in the shipping field were a direct result of the interpower competition of the "scramble for concessions" following the Sino-Japanese War. The Japanese, German, and French governments subsidized shipping companies to support them against the exclusionary tactics of the Three Companies conference and establish national presences in the steamship networks of the Yangzi River and coast.

Although closely tied to political and economic developments within China, these new conditions also reflected growing competition in shipping worldwide. Not long after major overseas routes came under the control of British-dominated liner conferences, new government-subsidized merchant steamship companies contested their position.[67] As early as the 1880s, the United States, France, Italy, Japan, and Germany formed new overseas lines to promote national-flag shipping and counter British hegemony, subsidizing the new lines so they could weather conference opposition. Not all of these companies were successful, but some of them were strong enough to force the existing conferences to admit them as members. By 1900, the Far East Conference, originally entirely British except for the French Messageries Maritimes, had admitted German, Austrian, Italian, and Japanese lines.[68]

In Chinese waters, the arrival of these new shipping companies brought an influx of tonnage to the Yangzi and coast. There were more ships working within the steam network than in the preceding decade, and the new competition meant far less stability and predictability. These new conditions, along with new shipping concessions these powers obtained from the Qing, rapidly developed many shipping routes well beyond the previous routine of the daily steamer, and prompted new areas of competition among the shipping firms.

The Yangzi River route provides a particularly useful context within which to examine the new conditions and competition in the steam shipping field. This route traversed many rapidly developing areas in the interior of China, particularly the Middle (Hankou–Yichang) and Upper Yangzi (Yichang–Chongqing) regions. After 1895, the Qing had initiated north–south railway lines that would intersect with the Yangzi River at Hankou, making it even more promising for transport. For new and veteran steamship companies, a strong Yangzi River trade promised cargoes sufficient to feed coastal and overseas shipping lines. Moreover, at the time when new treaty powers were demanding exclusive concessions from the Qing dynasty, the Yangzi was seen as the stronghold of British power in China. Although the Foreign Office had refused merchant demands to have the region recognized as a British sphere of influence, it was an ideal site for newcomers to contest the dominance of British shipping.[69]

The interpower rivalry and new subsidized steamship lines of the 1895–1913 period ultimately did not destroy or even displace the Three Companies shipping conference. Throughout this period, the Three Companies maintained agreements among themselves, although occasionally these were modified or suspended when competition grew too fierce. After this interval, the Three Companies never regained the level of dominance within the steam network that they had between 1882 and 1895: in 1913 they admitted the Japanese Nisshin Kisen Kaisha as a full conference member, sharing routes, trades, and profits among four companies rather than three. Although the Three Companies had prevailed under the new conditions in the shipping field, before and after 1913 they faced a far more dynamic opposition than they had in the past.

Japanese steamship companies were the first "outsiders" to enter the steam network after 1895, and they did so on a considerable scale. The Treaty of Shimonoseki (1895) had extended to Japan the shipping rights enjoyed by other treaty powers and new shipping privileges in China's interior. The new treaty terms included formal navigation rights to the Upper Yangzi River, a new treaty port at Shashi (on the Yangzi in Hubei Province), and navigation rights to inland river routes between Shanghai, Hangzhou, and Suzhou. Soon after the treaty was signed, several Japanese shipping companies began operations in China.

These companies took advantage of increased support from the Japanese government to shipping enterprises after the Sino-Japanese War. As early as the 1870s, the Meiji government was uncomfortable with the prominence of European and U.S. steamship companies in Japan's coastal and overseas trades and began to support the development of a Japanese merchant steam fleet that could also aid the military. The government offered subsidies to shipping firms like Mitsubishi, and in 1885 backed a merger between Mitsubishi and some of its competitors to form the Nippon Yūsen Kaisha (Japan Mail Steamship Company), which received regular government subsidies. Nippon Yūsen operated on Japanese coastal routes and routes within East Asia and initiated a line from Japanese ports that called at Shanghai and Tianjin. During the Sino-Japanese War, the government discovered that this merchant fleet still fell short of the state's military transport needs. The large indemnity that Japan obtained from China in the settlement of the war supplied further financial resources for developing Japanese shipping. In 1896, the government established an expanded program that made subsidies available to any Japanese shipping company calling at overseas ports whose fleet met government standards for size and speed.[70] These subsidies helped several Japanese shipping firms begin operations in Chinese waters.

Large Japanese companies like the Osaka Shōsen Kaisha (Osaka Commercial Steamship Company, est. 1885) and the Nippon Yūsen Kaisha used government subsidies to link services within the steam network to their regional and overseas lines. In 1897, the Osaka Shōsen Kaisha obtained a subsidy for the Yangzi River and in 1899 one for the Shanghai–Tianjin route that allowed it to establish a direct service between China's northern ports and Japan.[71] In 1900, the company raised capital and expanded its Yangzi fleet, replacing its original ships (of about 600 tons each) with three newly built ships of over 2,000 tons for the Shanghai–Hankou and Hankou–Yichang lines. These new ships gave Osaka Shōsen the largest tonnage of any company on the river and increased the frequency of its services to twice-weekly trips between Shanghai and Hankou and six monthly trips to Yichang.[72] Nippon Yūsen initially used the new subsidy program to develop overseas lines to India and Europe. The company found it could easily fill ships returning to Japan from Europe, but there was not enough Japanese cargo to fill ships traveling in the other direction. Nippon Yūsen found plenty of Europe-bound cargoes in Shanghai, however, and began to use Shanghai (rather than Yokohama or Kobe) as a hub for its lines to Europe, North America, and Australia after 1899. In 1900, it joined Osaka Shōsen on the Yangzi and on the Shanghai–Tianjin routes to speed the movement of Chinese cargoes to this hub.[73] In 1903, it purchased the property of McBain & Company (a small British firm that had been an affiliate conference member) and began building new ships for the Yangzi line.[74]

Smaller Japanese firms took advantage of the new opportunities for transport in China's interior. In 1904, after the city of Changsha on the Xiang River in Hunan Province had been opened as a treaty port, the Kōnan Kisen Kaisha (Hunan Steamship Company) initiated a new route connecting the main Yangzi line with the Xiang River through Dongting Lake. There had been no foreign navigation in Hunan Province before this point, and the company's investors believed the area was ripe for development. The Daito Kisen Kaisha was formed to provide services in the newly opened inland river routes connecting Shanghai, Suzhou, and Hangzhou.[75]

German shipping companies also initiated shipping services in Chinese waters at the same time. A German government policy in place since the 1880s offered subsidies to shipping companies to compete against British shipping power. In China, Germany matched its demands for the permanent occupation of Jiaozhou Bay and sphere of influence in Shandong Province (1898) with subsidized shipping services on major routes. In 1898, the Rickmers, Hamburg-Amerika, and North German Lloyd lines established a joint freight and mail service from Hamburg to Chinese coastal ports.[76] The Hamburg-Amerika and North German Lloyd lines initiated a joint service on the Yangzi River in 1900 that competed on the Shanghai–Hankou and Hankou–Yichang routes.[77] The German government paid a subsidy equivalent to £18,750 a year to these companies between 1900 and 1904 for their Yangzi lines.[78]

On those routes where they faced Japanese and German opposition, the Three Companies deployed the full range of conference tactics against their new rivals: dropping freight rates, raising the deferred rebate from 5 to 10 percent, and denying reciprocal services to new opponents.[79] These attempts were not immediately effective, as Japanese and German subsidies were intended to counter them. Competition further intensified as the new companies lowered rates and offered special terms to attract shippers, the Osaka Shōsen Kaisha advertising a 15 percent rebate.[80] As the battles wore on, Japanese and German firms nearly doubled the Yangzi River tonnage. Several observers commented that this increase was driven not by demand but by these companies' need to maintain a position in the trade.[81] In the process, the pace of the Yangzi River traffic increased. Previously, each of the Three Companies made two departures a week from either end of the route, but now the daily steamer faced a competing German or Japanese ship on most days of the week.

The German companies made a formal request for admission to the shipping conference when the Three Companies Yangzi River agreement came up for renewal in 1902. Since both German and Japanese firms had begun to connect their Yangzi and coastal services, approaching the scale of the conference companies, the Three Companies were interested in coming to terms with them. Yet the German companies found the conference's offer of admission too restrictive as it limited their routes and tonnage, granting them a share of the Yangzi trade smaller than they believed they deserved. The Three Companies renewed their agreement in August 1902, but the German and Japanese firms remained "outsiders."[82]

Subsequently, Yangzi River competition further escalated with the arrival of subsidized tonnage from France. In 1906, the Compagnie Asiatique de Navigation added two steamers to the Shanghai–Hankou route and one to the Shanghai–Ningbo line.[83] This company received a yearly subsidy from the French government as part of a program to increase the nation's economic presence in China.[84] The company intended to build high-speed ships that would make connections with the Beijing–Hankou Railway, and use the Yangzi line to extend French influence into the Upper Yangzi and western China.[85] The addition of the French ships and an expanded Nippon Yūsen fleet in 1906 brought the total number of steamers working the Shanghai–Hankou route to thirty-three. Passenger fares and freight rates declined by more than 40 percent.[86] An editorial in the *North China Herald* warned against unchecked competition, sounding nostalgic for the days of conference hegemony:

> A wholesale reduction of rates of passage money and freights, to Japan, up and down the Yangtze, and along the coast, is the immediate prospect on this declaration of hostilities and the shipper and holiday-makers will lightheartedly avail themselves of those benefits, careless who bears the immediate loss. Yet in the long run the unhealthy abnormal conditions produced by an industrial conflict must react more or less on the community at large. Cut-throat competition is eventually as demoralizing to trade generally as the operations of monopolies and trusts.[87]

Despite this dour assessment, one of the effects of the prolonged competition on the Yangzi River was that the active shipping network extended well beyond its pre-1895 limits. All companies were eager to develop services in the Middle Yangzi region of Hankou, as the construction of the Beijing–Hankou and Hankou–Canton railway lines promised enormous opportunities for trans-shipment.[88] Conference companies tried to match the initiatives of their rivals: China Navigation and Indo-China started "Hunan Rivers" services between Hankou and

Xiangtan in 1903 to compete with that of the Kōnan Kisen Kaisha.[89] The Hankou–Yichang route also developed rapidly under these competitive conditions, becoming a regular feature of all companies' Yangzi services. Under the 1882 conference agreement, the route belonged to the China Merchants Company, which ran only one steamer on it at irregular intervals. The British companies had begun to make occasional trips to Yichang by 1897, but it was not until the Osaka Shōsen Kaisha and North German Lloyd built new ships specifically for this route in 1900 that all companies began providing matching services to Yichang (map 3.1).[90]

In this period, the British companies went outside of the conference to enlist the aid of British diplomatic officials to check the expansion of subsidized rivals—probably a sign of how embattled they felt under these competitive conditions. China Navigation and Indo-China appealed to British consuls in the Yangzi ports and officials in Beijing and London to maintain control of key waterfront properties in Yangzi ports. When the Nippon Yūsen Kaisha purchased the McBain properties in 1903, the British companies tried to keep the Japanese firm from taking possession of McBain's berthing facilities in Hankou's British concession by applying for the leases themselves. Although there had been no restriction on the nationality of leaseholders in this British concession in the past, the companies now argued that frontage in a British concession should not be ceded to foreign interests. They succeeded in convincing the British Foreign Office to support their bid for the leases, which prevented the Nippon Yūsen from making use of these convenient wharf facilities for its Yangzi line. It took Nippon Yūsen several years to find comparable facilities in Hankou's French concession.[91] The British companies adopted a similar strategy in the Yangzi ports of Zhenjiang and Jiujiang in 1907, protesting the lease of wharves that had formerly belonged to McBain & Company to the French Compagnie Asiatique de Navigation, once again obtaining these properties for themselves.[92] The Jiujiang customs commissioner observed that this action had an immediate negative impact on Compagnie Asiatique's business, as shippers were unwilling to pay additional charges to tow cargo out to the French ships.[93] Although they had done nothing like this in the past, the British firms used their nationality to monopolize the best facilities and constrain the business of new rivals.[94]

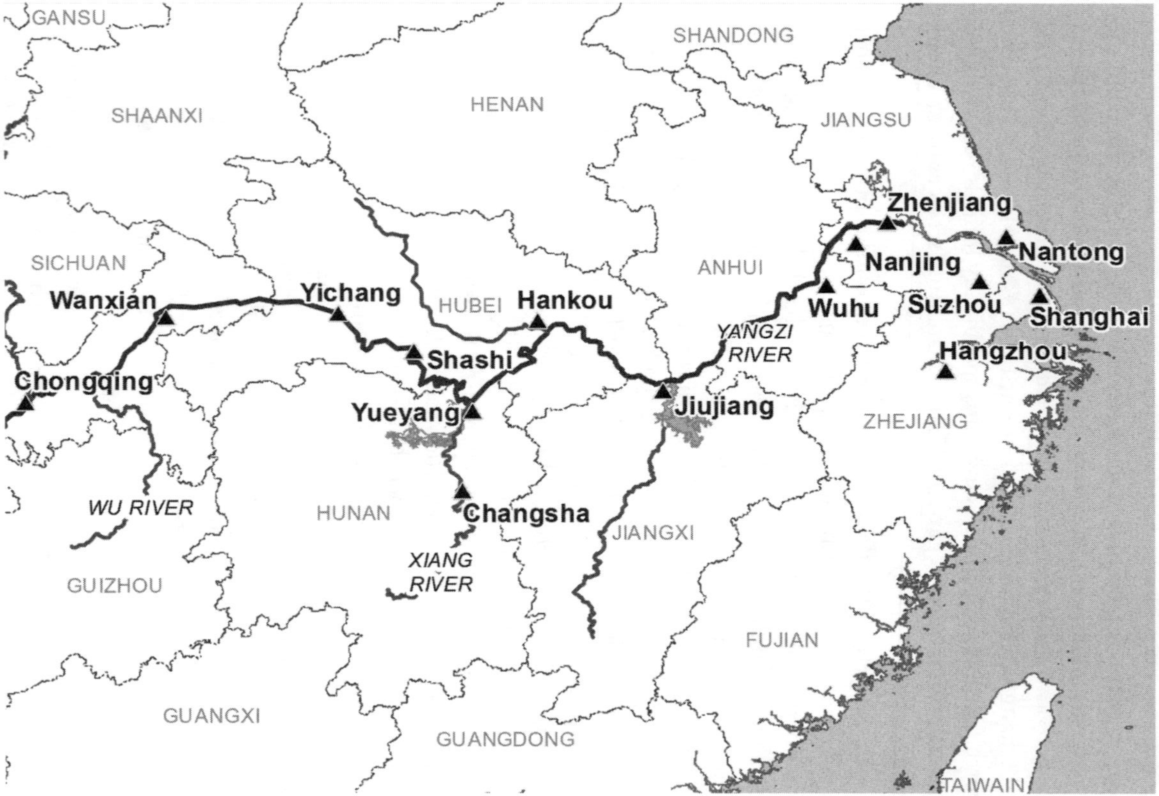

MAP 3.1 Treaty Ports on the Yangzi River, ca. 1911. Map adapted from David H. Grover, *American Merchant Ships*, xiv.

The extreme competition on the Yangzi River was eventually diminished first by the intensification of Japanese government investment in Yangzi shipping and later by the withdrawal of the German and French companies. In 1907, Japan's Ministry of Communications proposed to merge the Yangzi services of all Japanese companies into a single new firm, the Nisshin Kisen Kaisha (Japan-China Steamship Company). The government wanted to strengthen the Japanese presence in the interior of China and prevent competition among the four active Japanese firms.[95] The Nisshin Kisen Kaisha became the fourth largest Japanese shipping company, with a capital stock of ¥8.1 million. The Japanese government was more closely involved in the Nisshin Kisen Kaisha than it had been in earlier subsidized companies. Nisshin received a yearly subsidy of ¥800,000, in exchange for which it followed government stipulations for its organization, the number of monthly voyages its ships made, and the ships' tonnage and speeds. The government could requisition its ships and seamen at any time. Its president was a member of the Ministry of Communications' Shipping Division, and officials from the ministry, along with the executives of the original four companies, oversaw its operations. The ministry had to approve any modifications of the company's rules and could audit Nisshin's branch offices in China. These branch offices also reported to the ministry on commercial conditions in China.[96]

The Nisshin Kisen Kaisha has been described as a "national policy company" (*kokusaku kaisha*), a partnership between the Japanese government and large firms that served the government's strategic needs and commercial purposes.[97] It is often compared with the South Manchurian Railway Company, also established just after the Russo-Japanese War. Just as the railway company intensified economic links between South Manchuria and Japan, the Nisshin Kisen Kaisha was intended to expand the trade between central China and Japan and maintain a significant Japanese presence in the competitive Yangzi traffic.[98]

Well subsidized and with the resources of four shipping companies under its control, the Nisshin Kisen Kaisha became a formidable force on the Yangzi. After the merger, it had the largest fleet on the river (the 28,000 tons stipulated by the Japanese government) and the most advanced ships.[99] Initially, this fleet was larger than the company could use profitably, but it used its excess tonnage to provide services that would attract shippers. For example, Nisshin guaranteed the delivery of upriver export cargoes to Shanghai in the low-water season when the other companies could not and covered the cost of towing cargo from the British, French, and German concessions in Hankou to its own docks in the Russian concession. Nisshin also offered an expedited trans-shipment of cargoes from its Yangzi lines to the Osaka Shōsen and Nippon Yūsen Kaisha's overseas lines, which allowed the company to profit from the growth in Chinese exports, an area that was expanding more rapidly than domestic trade at the time. Most cargoes that Nisshin carried—90 percent in 1910—were bound for overseas rather than Chinese ports. The British steamship companies scrambled to provide comparable connections to overseas services. Nisshin depended on subsidies to get it through its first few years, but by 1910 its profits were greater than the subsidy. In 1903, Japanese ships had accounted for 23.7 percent of Yangzi River tonnage; by 1911, the Nisshin Kisen Kaisha's fleet made up 46.6 percent.[100]

Whether intimidated by the prospect of a huge Japanese company or simply weary of the prolonged competition on the Yangzi, the German and French companies began to withdraw from the river around the time Nisshin Kisen Kaisha was formed. In 1906, Hamburg-Amerika sold two of its Yangzi steamships to the Hong Kong, Canton, and Macao Steamboat Company, and in 1907 withdrew from the river entirely to concentrate on coastal shipping. By 1911, there were only three remaining German ships on the river. In the same year, the Compagnie Asiatique sold its three river ships to China Navigation and Indo-China.[101] The Hong'an Steamship Company, a small conference affiliate, ceased operations for several years.[102] By the last years of the Qing dynasty, competition on the Yangzi River centered on the Three Companies and the Nisshin Kisen Kaisha.

The Three Companies had survived the trial of the earlier generation of subsidized companies, but the Nisshin Kisen Kaisha presented a threat not only to their businesses but to the conference organization itself. Nisshin refused invitations to join the conference in 1908 and 1910, which in the Three Companies' view prolonged open competition and resulted in losses to all.[103] But the conditions stipulated by the Japanese government made it impossible for the company to accept the limits on routes and tonnage imposed by conference agreements. In competition with the Nisshin Kisen Kaisha, these agreements proved constraining even for the

British firms, which wanted to expand their fleets quickly enough to challenge Nisshin in the overseas trans-shipment trade. China Navigation and Indo-China had to ask for the China Merchants Company's permission to violate the conference agreement to add ships to the Yangzi River line.[104]

In 1913, after nearly two decades of continuous competition, the Three Companies and the Nisshin Kisen Kaisha finally reached an agreement that brought all of them into the conference organization. The agreement secured only a brief peace: three years later, new requirements from the Japanese government prompted Nisshin Kisen to leave the organization.[105] For this short span, the Three had become Four Companies. Despite the stability that the new agreement brought to the trade, many Chinese shippers objected to it, threatening a taboo against the Nisshin Kisen Kaisha. Since it had not been a conference member in the past, the company had always tried to offer shippers favorable rates. The new conference agreement raised Nisshin's freight rates and storage fees by 50 percent. The issue was eventually resolved through a compromise made by all four companies and the Shanghai General Chamber of Commerce.[106]

The 1895–1913 period began as a confrontation between the established Three Companies and subsidized newcomers and ended in a somewhat uneasy truce between the Three Companies and their conference organization and the Japanese "national policy company," the Nisshin Kisen Kaisha. Despite the volatility and intensive competition in the shipping business, the period was one of rapid development of Yangzi River and coastal shipping. On the Yangzi, the "daily steamer" that had stopped at ports and calling stations between Shanghai and Hankou gave way to a greater concentration of ships and an expanded network. By 1913, there were regular steamship services in the inland rivers around Shanghai, on the Hunan Rivers, and on the Middle Yangzi between Hankou and Yichang. Even after German and French steamships abandoned the river trade, Yangzi tonnage was at least twice what it had been before 1895. The Four Companies also made twice as many departures from key ports as the Three Companies had before 1895, with improved connections to coastal and overseas lines.[107]

In the battle between the Three Companies conference and the new, subsidized shipping lines, neither side could claim an absolute victory. Even the outsized, government-backed Nisshin Kisen Kaisha could not destroy the conference: the Three Companies maintained agreements with one another through this period and retained their commanding positions in the trade despite the inclusion of a new and powerful company. But the conference never regained the power it had enjoyed in the past. Over the next three decades a variety of agreements structured the trade, but the Nisshin Kisen Kaisha never became a permanent conference member. Instead it continued to join and leave the conference in response to government mandates and commercial opportunities.

Collaboration Revisited: The China Merchants Company, 1895–1913

The Three Companies conference, as an institution, remained relatively healthy throughout the 1895–1913 period, but the relations among the companies within it changed. The British companies continued to grow and after 1907 were particularly focused on competing with the Nisshin Kisen Kaisha. The China Merchants Company did not fare as well: by 1913 it was by far the weakest conference participant and no longer operated on a scale comparable to that of the other members. The China Merchants Company's experience in this period highlights the effects of collaboration in the conference over time. The asymmetries that had emerged among the Three Companies between 1882 and 1895 became even more pronounced, making it impossible for the China Merchants Company to keep pace with the other companies. Simultaneously, the Qing government withdrew most of the aid it had extended to the company since the 1870s, in some cases actually extracting funds from the company for other purposes. Under these conditions, the conference became even more important to the company's viability and survival. The China Merchants Company endured a difficult interval but outlasted the Qing dynasty and remained an important presence within the steam network until 1937 and after. It never fully regained the status of equal competitor with its British and Japanese counterparts, but it continued to participate in conference agreements as one of the four largest steamship companies in China.

The competitive conditions of the 1895–1913 period compounded the inequalities between the China Merchants Company and the British companies that had emerged before 1895. The China Merchants Company's share of major trades shrunk. By one calculation, the company's tonnage on the Yangzi River dropped from 27.1 percent of the total in 1903 to 16.1 percent in 1911.[108] The influx of new tonnage, particularly the Nisshin Kisen Kaisha's, was an immediate cause, but perhaps more significant was that the primary arena of growth and competition between the British and Japanese companies had become the direct overseas trade. Without overseas lines and connections, the China Merchants Company was cut out of this trade completely.

Although its position was declining, the China Merchants Company did not fade into insignificance. It could no longer match its rivals' growth and did not attempt to match the other companies' new services on the Hunan Rivers routes or in the direct overseas trade from the Yangzi region.[109] Far from remaining static, the China Merchants Company consolidated its position in these years, expanding selectively into new areas and making investments in its strongest trades. In 1902, the company launched a new subsidiary, the Inland Rivers China Merchants Company (Neihe lunchuan zhaoshang ju) on the Shanghai–Suzhou–Hangzhou triangle. Run from the Shanghai China Merchants office, this company acquired a fleet of thirty steamships by 1911 and extended its services north of the Yangzi to the Huai River, taking advantage of the new inland waters regulations to become one of the largest inland shipping enterprises in China.[110] On the Shanghai–Hankou route that had always been central to China Merchants business, the company kept up with the intensified pace of trade. In 1903, three steamship companies made two departures a week from either end of this route, and by 1914 four steamship companies made four departures a week.[111] China Merchants invested in new, larger ships for this route, matching the other companies' additions of at least two ships of over 3,000 tons after 1904.[112] On the Hankou–Yichang line, the China Merchants Company's two ships were smaller and older than those of the British and Japanese firms, but it matched the other companies in making four monthly departures on this route.[113] A proposal for the 1913 Yangzi conference agreement confirms the viability of the China Merchants Company: it was awarded the largest share of the Shanghai–Hankou traffic: 28.8 percent against 24 percent to the Nisshin Kisen Kaisha and 23.5 percent to each of the British companies.[114]

While the asymmetries between the China Merchants Company and the British and Japanese companies intensified in these years, so did the protection the conference provided the Qing-flag company. After 1895, its guarantee of stable earnings allowed the company to survive a dramatic withdrawal of Qing government support. Since the company's founding, the Qing had provided a variety of special concessions: either paying the company high rates to carry government goods and personnel or granting it tax exemptions. After 1895, however, many of these concessions had become burdensome obligations. The China Merchants Company continued to carry the tribute grain, for example, but in 1898 the court cut freight rates while demanding the company carry more grain. By 1911, the company was providing this service at a loss. Similarly, the compensation for transporting troops, supplies, and official materials was reduced to the point that these services drained company resources.[115] At the same time that the China Merchants Company was confronting subsidized foreign companies in Chinese waters, it had lost the government's financial support while retaining the obligation to perform services for it.

Furthermore, the Qing dynasty began to demand "surplus" funds from the China Merchants Company to support other projects. These payments were called "efforts to return the imperial grace" (*baoxiao*) and were understood as obligations incurred by the aid the government had already granted the company. The Qing began to require this type of payment early in the 1890s, in 1891 appropriating the interest on a government loan in the China Merchants Company's reserve fund for famine relief, and in 1894 extracting "contributions" totaling 100,000 *taels* for the birthday celebrations of the empress dowager.[116] Following the Sino-Japanese War, the Qing's deteriorating finances made the company even more of a target for such demands. In 1899, Sheng Xuanhuai received an imperial edict dictating that the "surplus profits" of the China Merchants Company and other officially supervised–merchant managed enterprises he oversaw be paid regularly into the government treasury. Sheng was able to negotiate a reduction of the payment to an annual 60,000 *taels*, but the demands continued. In 1904, China Merchants had to make regular payments in support of the newly established Ministry of Commerce.[117] In years the company earned no surplus, payments were made from its depreciation fund, limiting its ability to replace outdated ships and facilities.[118]

In the wake of the Sino-Japanese War and the Boxer Rebellion, the Qing's weakened finances might offer a simple explanation for its withdrawal of support from the shipping company. The continuous, extractive demands on the company, however, suggest that it was perceived to be a reliable source of funds. Sheng Xuanhuai also made use of China Merchants Company funds to support other enterprises he oversaw. After 1896, China Merchants funds helped underwrite the Imperial Bank of China, the Pingxiang Coal Mines, the Hanyang Ironworks (later merged as the Hanyeping Coal and Iron Corporation), and the Jiangsu, Zhejiang, and Hankou–Canton Railways. This particular use of China Merchants funds is sometimes interpreted as Sheng's attempt to enrich himself, but it also suggests sufficient confidence in the China Merchants Company earnings that its resources could be used elsewhere without destroying the company.[119]

Qing shipping policies also indicate that the government no longer subscribed to the idea of channeling support to a single company to compete with foreign firms. After 1895, the dynasty began to encourage the formation of Qing-flag inland waters shipping companies to counter the push by Japan and Britain into inland waters navigation.[120] This decision dissolved the China Merchants Company's de facto monopoly on steam navigation in Chinese waters, although the new companies were overwhelmingly small concerns and did not compete on major routes.[121] Furthermore, the government did not offer these new companies the support and protection that it had once furnished the China Merchants Company. Qing officials had ensured that the China Merchants Company was subjected to the same conditions as foreign firms—traveling only between open ports and paying duty at the Maritime Customs—but the inland waters companies had to pay *lijin*, from which foreign-flag ships were exempt. This disparity, combined with the tendency for provincial officials to extract payments from new steamship companies, revived the practice of Chinese-owned steamship companies operating under purchased foreign registrations and flags.[122] The Qing dynasty had sought to expand the modern shipping sector with these new companies, but it no longer provided much support or protection to them or the China Merchants Company.

Political struggles at the end of the Qing dynasty so adversely affected the China Merchants Company leadership that its shareholders finally cut all government ties, registering it as a private commercial firm in 1911. Patron Li Hongzhang's reputation suffered further after the Sino-Japanese

War, and he could no longer help the company. After Li was removed from the post of commissioner of the northern ports at this time, none of his immediate successors—Wang Wenshao (1830–1908), Ronglu (1836–1903), or Yülu (d. 1900)—took an active interest in the company's affairs. After Li's death in November 1901, Yuan Shikai (1859–1916) became commissioner of the northern ports and intervened in company affairs, immediately clashing with Sheng Xuanhuai. In 1903, Yuan took advantage of the mourning period for Sheng's father to replace the China Merchants managers with his own protégés—most notably Xu Run, who had been dismissed in 1884. In 1907, Sheng used his influence as the company's largest shareholder to lead a movement to register the company as a private commercial firm under the Qing's Company Law.[123] Sheng did not succeed, but he regained control of the company later that year when Yuan Shikai was removed from his post. In 1909, an imperial edict ordered the China Merchants Company removed from the jurisdiction of the commissioner of the northern ports and placed under the new Ministry of Posts and Communications (Youchuan bu). Although Sheng held a position in that ministry, he backed an effort by China Merchants shareholders to elect a board of directors and secure a greater role for them in company governance. Between 1909 and 1911, the shareholders struggled with ministry officials over control of the company, a situation that did not end until the dynasty fell. In 1911, the board of directors assumed full control of the company, and after decades of official supervision, the China Merchants Company became a private commercial firm. It remained a private concern until 1927.[124]

Between 1895 and 1913, the steady business and profits guaranteed by conference agreements protected the China Merchants Company as the Qing withdrew its support of the company and deployed company resources for other purposes. Despite this significant change in its relationship to the Qing state, the China Merchants Company remained a viable enterprise through this time and a major force within the steamship business. Examining the company's changing relationship to the government together with its involvement in the conference reveals some of the ironies of its position. First, it was likely the very functionality of the company as a conference participant that allowed the state to see it as a source of funds. Second, despite the deterioration of the company's relationship with the government, the conference's protection also enabled the company to prevail as an expression of Qing sovereignty. The China Merchants Company maintained the Qing flag as an important presence on the Yangzi River and coast through the end of the dynasty and beyond.

Conclusion

Describing the conference in 1883, John Samuel Swire was correct to declare that there would be no "divorce" among the Three Companies that formed it. From the heights of the conference's power in 1882–95 to the intense competition it faced from new companies in 1895–1913, it remained the central structure of the steam shipping business in Chinese waters. At the time, Swire may not have been able to predict the expansion of Japanese shipping companies in China and their eventual place alongside the Three Companies. He also might not have anticipated the change in the fortunes of the China Merchants Company: the largest company in 1882 was in a subordinate position in 1913.

The conference's history encapsulates the paradoxes of semi-colonial collaboration. The main function of the conference was to control competition and stabilize the shipping business in Chinese waters. This forwarded British expansionism by giving the British companies the opportunity to connect and leverage other resources of the British empire to their shipping concerns and extend from there, magnifying the differences in access to these worldwide resources between themselves and the China Merchants Company. At the same time, the conference's stability was also a lifeline for an increasingly beleaguered China Merchants Company facing internal turmoil and a loss of support from the Qing state. Therefore, it is possible to say that the conference aided the expansionist project and that it helped maintain the China Merchants fleet as an expression of indigenous sovereignty. These two aspects may appear incompatible, but under this collaborative mechanism, they occurred simultaneously.

The China Merchants Company's performance in the late nineteenth and early twentieth centuries might be found wanting in entrepreneurial or nationalist terms, yet the significance of its long-term and central presence in coastal and river shipping should not be underestimated. The sharpest contrast between the steam shipping businesses in semi-colonial China and colonial India was that British domination of the Indian coast was nearly complete. As it grew with the support of its government mail contracts, the British India Company was able to almost completely eradicate Indian capital from coastal shipping. There was no presence of Indian-backed shipping companies comparable to the China Merchants Company. This absence set an extremely high bar for Indian shipping enterprises as they tried to break into coastal and overseas lines dominated by the British India Company or British-led conferences. At times, the colonial government intervened to support British shipping interests against Indian ones. Indian entrepreneurs faced both commercial and political barriers when they tried to enter the shipping field in the late nineteenth and early twentieth centuries.

As the British India Company's power grew, it tolerated a small opposition, forging agreements and dividing routes with a few companies. These "opponents," however, were most often British firms, including the Glasgow-based Todd, Findlay & Co. in Burma and the Liverpool-based Turner, Morrison & Co. in the Bay of Bengal.[125] The one exception to this rule was the Bombay Steam Navigation Company, with whom the British India Company shared the Bombay–Karachi route. Originally founded by Indian merchants in the 1840s, this company was taken over by British owners in the 1860s and reorganized once again under both British and Indian partners in 1869. The company's Indian ownership proved a liability when it bid against the British India Company for the Bombay–Karachi mail contract in 1884. The Bombay Steam Navigation Company submitted a lower bid, but the post office official who made the decision deemed the company "unreliable" precisely because it had Indian partners. He granted the contract to the British India Company, which had already held it for many years.[126]

The overseas lines that connected Indian ports to others in Asia were controlled by British-led conferences that could set unfavorable terms for the Indian businesses that relied on them for transport. In the mid-1890s, Indian industrialist J. N. Tata (1839–1904) objected to the high freight rates the Peninsular & Oriental Company charged him to ship cotton and cotton yarn to Japan and China, particularly after he discovered that the company offered rebates to his rivals.[127] Finding the P & O unresponsive to his protests, Tata tried to enlist the help of newly arrived "outsiders"—such as the Italian Rubbatino (Navigazione Generale Italiana) and Austrian Lloyd companies—to oppose it, but was disappointed when they joined the conference and charged even higher rates. In 1894, Tata tried to evade the conference by forming an alliance with Japanese shipping companies and cotton goods exporters. He went to Japan and met with the Nippon Yūsen Kaisha and the Japanese Spinners Association, proposing a competing shipping line run jointly by Tata and Nippon Yūsen. Tata secured promises from Indian shippers to provide guaranteed cargo for the new firm, and Nippon Yūsen secured similar promises from Japanese thread exporters. This new collaborative line was met with a rate war by the conference companies—which offered to carry cotton yarn to Japan free of charge—and attempts to discredit its ships on the insurance market. Tata had to withdraw the following year.[128] The venture had a different outcome for the Nippon Yūsen Kaisha, however: coming at the conclusion of the 1894–95 Sino-Japanese War, the company could now take advantage of increased Japanese government subsidies that allowed it to establish a place on the route between Japan and India. In 1896, it joined the conference on the Bombay–Kobe Line.[129]

On the coast, Indian ventures such as the Bombay-based Shah Line and the Burmese Bengal Steamship Company were destroyed by rate wars with the British India Company.[130] During the Swadeshi Movement (1905–8), an Indian shipping enterprise with an overt nationalist agenda was met with the combined opposition of the company and the government. The Swadeshi Steam Navigation Company was started in 1906 by the Tamil leader V. O. Chidambaram Pillai (1872–1936) to work the routes between Tuticorin, Colombo, Bombay, and Calcutta. Its shares were held exclusively by Indians. Not only did the British India Company greet this initiative with a fierce rate war in which it carried passengers for free, but government officials were ordered to boycott the line, and its ships were held up in port until after the departures of British India ships. In 1908, Pillai was arrested for attending a political meeting, after which the company failed.[131]

It was not until after World War I that Indian-backed shipping companies were able to establish themselves as competitors to the British India Company on major routes or challenge conference control of overseas lines. This exclusion was not limited to shipping, but was a part of what Rajat K. Ray has called the "division of economic space" on the subcontinent in which British businesses headquartered in Britain dominated trade, finance, and shipping, making it difficult for Indians to enter into these fields.[132] In China, the division was not absolute, as the China Merchants Company remained one of the leading carriers on the Yangzi and coast. The company's lack of overseas connections may have confined it to Chinese waters, but within them it maintained this position until 1937. Like in India, the indigenous shipping sector in China grew after World War I, with once small inland waters companies extending onto major routes and new Chinese firms challenging the conference companies in many places. Throughout, the China Merchants Company remained the largest Chinese concern and provided the basis for a national merchant marine.

CHAPTER 4

The Steamship as Social Space, 1860–1925

Beyond being instruments of foreign economic expansion and new foci of enterprise in semi-colonial China, steamships were novel social spaces circulating within the treaty-port network. They were larger and more technologically complex conveyances than sailing ships, transporting larger numbers of passengers and carrying more specialized crews. Although capacious, steamships were highly delimited spaces in which a spectrum of persons, processes, and interactions had to be provisioned, coordinated, and controlled. The space was both segmented and hierarchized, regulating and orchestrating the movements and relationships of both workers and passengers. Steamship travel was not a universal experience in nineteenth- and twentieth-century China, but it was common enough that many people experienced and engaged with this space.

One of the most unmistakable features of the steamship space was its obvious hierarchies of racial and class privilege in work and travel. On steamship crews, the positions of highest authority, requiring technical knowledge, were held almost exclusively by Europeans. Chinese workers invariably held unskilled positions. When Japanese companies arrived in the 1890s, this hierarchy was modified only to place Japanese nationals in the skilled positions on Japanese ships. Travel accommodations distinguished between "foreign" and "Chinese" classes, with the most expensive and luxurious class designated "foreign," and three or four classes offering passage at lower rates and with fewer amenities designated "Chinese." Despite the multinational origins of the four major steamship companies, each followed this general pattern in the organization of their work and passenger space with only minor variations, rendering these hierarchies palpable and concrete.

The articulations of racial hierarchy and the practices of exclusion within the steamship space were not specific to semi-colonial China. In this space, race was expressed as competence, both technical and cultural. Boundaries were enforced out of anxieties over proximity and intimacy between races. Not only were similar organizations of social space present in colonial contexts, it was also consonant with racial discourses and ideologies that exceeded the boundaries of formal colonies. The case of the steamship space indicates that in spite of the particular dynamics and characteristics of semi-colonialism, China could not be insulated or distanced from the hegemonic projects of colonial power/knowledge.

This investigation of steamship space is more specific to China in its excavation of how these particular hierarchies were constructed and perpetuated on steamships in Chinese waters. Steamship companies did not articulate rules or principles that justified the organization of the space; explanations must instead be sought through the structures and practices that undergirded it, and these were often particular to the steam shipping field in China. The parallel management structures of the major steamship companies, particularly in their relations with Chinese markets for labor, cargo, and passengers, provide one type of explanation. Another significant factor was the precedence of foreign (British or U.S.) models of company organization and their entrenchment as standards through the conference system. The conference's demand for commensurability among participating companies discouraged challenges to such standards. Apart from these structures were the daily practices—formal and informal, consistent and inconsistent—of overseeing disparate spaces aboard the steamship.

The perceptions and interpretations of the steamship space by those who encountered it are an additional means of assessing its meaning and impact. A common interpretation of the steamship's social space in many contexts emphasized its replication or reflection of the outside world within the ship's hold: transatlantic steamships were known as "floating cities," for example, and Louis Hunter called the U.S. river steamboat a "world in miniature," where "the essential processes of living went on, keyed to a higher pitch than the ordinary course of landbound existence."[1]

In contrast, Michel Foucault saw ships—among other social spaces—as "heterotopias": real spaces can challenge or disrupt the social relations of the culture that produces them. Although he identified gardens, prisons, brothels, and boarding schools as examples of heterotopia, Foucault called the ship the "heterotopia par excellence."[2] In late nineteenth- and early twentieth-century China, journalists and travelers echoed this range of interpretation in their writings. Many foreign travelers wrote about steamships as "worlds in miniature" that confirmed their expectations of the social order and their place within it. Nineteenth-century Chinese journalists furnished a very different view as they worked to fathom the steamship space—particularly the accommodation provided to Chinese passengers—as it completely confounded their expectations of social relations. By the late 1920s, journalists' prior confusion with the treatment of Chinese passengers aboard steamships had given way to a more politicized interpretation in which the steamship space had become emblematic of China's geopolitical condition, and encounters with it opened paths to nationalist awakening.

Shared Practices: The Organization and Management of Steamship Companies

This chapter's identification of a single, characteristic social space of the steamship in Chinese waters may appear to be an oversimplification given the multinational origins of the four major steamship companies. Although national origins do account for some variation, the more striking result of an investigation of steamships' social space is the overwhelming parallels between the ships of the Four Companies. Despite the various flags they flew, the major companies were organized and managed in similar ways, and these practices structured the social spaces of their ships. This consistent organization derived from several factors, most prominently the demands of the shipping business in China but also the historical development of the business and the disciplinary institution of the shipping conference.

Sherman Cochran's study of British, Japanese, and Chinese businesses in Republican China criticizes the notion that different national cultures produce characteristic business organizations, specifically taking on the argument that Western and Japanese businesses tended to be organized along hierarchical, corporate lines, while Chinese businesses tended to be organized through lateral social networks. Cochran's research shows that Western, Japanese, and Chinese businesses active in Republican China made use of both forms of organization for different purposes at different times.[3] That British, Chinese, and Japanese steamship companies in late Qing and Republican China were predominantly structured along network lines further underscores Cochran's point about the contingency of national culture in business organization. These firms relied on social networks to recruit their core managers and to establish presences in Chinese markets. This was a low-cost, minimalist management strategy that allowed the companies to extend their operations over as broad a geographical area as possible. Albert Feuerwerker's argument that the failure of enterprises like the China Merchants Company to industrialize China can be attributed to the "deficien[cy] in the rationalized organization, functional specialization, and impersonal discipline associated with the development of modern industry in the West," would therefore apply equally to the British steamship companies.[4] The latest arrival, the Nisshin Kisen Kaisha, adopted some corporate hierarchies in its upper management, but like the other companies relied heavily on networks to make inroads into Chinese markets.

China Navigation, Indo-China, the China Merchants Company, and the Nisshin Kisen Kaisha employed a few core managers who oversaw the company's operations from select locations, generally a main office in Shanghai and branch offices in other treaty ports. In the British and Japanese firms, these core managers were expatriates who maintained close contact with the companies' home offices in London or Tokyo.[5] Locally recruited, mostly Chinese clerical staffs and other workers assisted these managers, but there were few opportunities for these employees to advance into management positions.[6] In addition, the shipping companies maintained salaried technical staffs, usually headed by a marine superintendent who hired captains and engineers and oversaw the fleet. The remainder of the day-to-day operations of their shipping business was contracted out to local compradors (*maiban*).

In the British and China Merchants companies, personal ties were crucial to recruiting core managers. As chapter 2 described, Indo-China's and China Navigation's capital was raised primarily from business networks of shipping and shipbuilding enterprises centered in Glasgow (for Indo-China) and Liverpool (for China Navigation). The trading firms of Butterfield & Swire and Jardine, Matheson & Company furnished their expatriate managerial personnel.[7] In these firms, expatriate managers were recruited in Britain, usually through personal recommendation or acquaintance with the firm's directors, and staff members often shared native-place or family ties with their superiors and colleagues. Jardine's described its supply of expatriate managers as "friends and relations," hailing almost exclusively from Scotland. Similarly, many Butterfield & Swire employees were relations of one of its shareholding families, the Swires, Holts, and Scotts.[8] These employees were not professional managers; they were trained on the job first in the company's home offices and later in China.[9] The close personal ties among these managers helped maintain trust over the distance between Britain and China.

In the China Merchants Company, there were two levels of managers recruited from overlapping networks. The general manager of the company's main Shanghai office and his assistants were official appointees charged with mediating between the shareholders and the bureaucracy. Below this level were the "business managers" who ran specific departments, such as shipping, finance, and administration or branch offices in the treaty ports. Business managers were recruited from among the company's shareholders.[10] The distinction between official and shareholding networks was imprecise, as many of the company's shareholders, particularly in its early years, were the friends and relations of its official patron, Li Hongzhang, and its merchant managers, Tang Tingshu and Xu Run. The government-mandated reorganization of the China Merchants Company in 1885 demanded turnover among the general managers, but the business and branch office managers retained their positions through these transitions. The close networks of the China Merchants Company helped bridge the bureaucratic and commercial spheres and in the company's early years helped raise the necessary share capital to begin operations.

Like the China Merchants Company, there was a significant official presence among the managers of the Nisshin Kisen Kaisha. The substantial government subsidies the company received were contingent on the appointment of an official of the Japanese Ministry of Communications

Shipping Division as its president. Other core managers came from the four original Japanese firms that merged to form Nisshin. Its methods of recruiting its expatriate staff were more open than those of the other companies. It employed two different types of Japanese staff: some who were elite recruits from Japanese universities, and others recruited from Japanese settler communities in China. Although paid less initially than the university graduates, local hires had some opportunity to rise through the company's ranks.[11]

These companies could conduct business across China with only these small and tightly knit staffs of core managers because they made extensive use of Chinese compradors to oversee all aspects of the steamship company's daily business. Compradors recruited cargo and passengers, managed warehouses and docks in port, and supervised the business of each steamship. Compradors were not company employees; they were contractors who undertook an aspect of the shipping business on the company's behalf and assumed some of the risk of it themselves. They were businessmen in their own right: the companies selected men in each locality who they believed possessed market knowledge and connections robust enough to generate maximum business for the firm. The exigencies of the shipping business can explain why compradors were so important to these companies: capital equipment was expensive and costs per voyage were high, and the shipping companies needed to generate business across the entire treaty-port network, accounting for local variations of dialect, trade practice, and currency. Rather than hiring and training a large staff to do this work, the companies contracted with compradors to make use of their existing knowledge and business networks. Compradors thus provided a low-cost means for the companies to extend their operations across China.

In shipping companies, company or "land" compradors worked in the companies' offices in the treaty ports, canvassing for Chinese cargo and passengers. These compradors cultivated relationships with transshipping companies and freight brokerages (*baoguan hang*) to obtain cargoes from Chinese merchants. They arranged delivery of cargoes to the ships and collected freights from shippers. Company compradors could earn informal income by collecting interest on freight and passage money advanced to them (before they paid it to the company) or by underreporting freight and passenger earnings. Warehouse compradors collected and guaranteed the payment of storage fees for the warehouses, and in some companies they made arrangements with dock laborers or boats to load and unload cargo. Ship compradors attended to the cargo and passenger businesses of each ship. They recruited passengers and cargo in port, supervised the cargo from the time it came onto the ship until it was unloaded, sold passenger tickets, and managed the passenger accommodation, including providing meals.[12] Although different types of compradors fulfilled similar functions in locating cargo and cultivating clients, they did so in different contexts and at different levels of the market, such that each comprador's particular web of clients and contacts helped the companies cover as much ground as possible.

The general terms of comprador contracts were consistent across these occupations. Contracts usually specified a certain amount or percentage of the earnings of the business the comprador undertook to be remitted regularly to the company. The comprador was responsible for any irregularities or shortfalls in these remittances. Compradors often deposited a substantial sum or real estate deed with the company as a security. They earned commissions on the transactions they undertook on the company's behalf and received a small salary. Compradors hired, guaranteed, and paid their own assistants, saving the companies the effort of recruiting, paying, and managing large numbers of Chinese employees. To offset the risk the comprador undertook, most positions provided a means for the comprador to generate informal income outside of the terms of his contract. The low cost of using compradors was balanced against substantial problems of control for the companies, the most common of which was the concern that compradors cut into profits by habitually underreporting earnings.

The extensive—and routine—use of compradors in steamship companies suggests an alternative interpretation to that of a "bridge between East and West" in Yen-p'ing Hao's classic study. Hao's research focused on compradors who provided foreign businesses in the treaty ports a necessary entrée into the Chinese commercial world and in turn channeled the wealth and knowledge of Western business practices they accumulated into the modernization of China's economy and society.[13] This characterization is appropriate to describe the careers of very prominent compradors like Tang Tingshu, Yu Xiaqing (1861–1945), or Robert Ho Tung (1862–1956, of Jardine, Matheson & Company, Hong Kong), but it does not capture the routine use of compradors at many different levels of shipping, banking, insurance, or trading companies in semi-colonial China.[14] In these contexts, compradors were contractors who assumed responsibility for a specific aspect of the business, allowing the companies to extend their activities over a broad area and minimizing expenses and risk or liability in transactions with clients. Compradors helped foreign and Chinese businesses negotiate local markets. The China Merchants Company employed compradors in the same ways as did the British or Japanese firms. Although this company's managers were Chinese, they were not necessarily well versed in the variations of dialect, business practice, market conditions, and currency systems in ports across China.[15]

The very similar organizations of the Four Companies make it possible to examine a characteristic social space of the steamship in China. Their minimalist management strategy of a small core staff supported by the extensive use of compradors in all aspects of the business played a particularly important role in shaping that space, as subsequent sections of this chapter will show. The demands of the shipping business provide some explanation for the utility of this structure to all companies, but other factors also influenced its widespread adoption. The first steamship companies in Chinese waters were those organized by British and U.S. trading firms in the 1860s, and these served as models for new arrivals. In the 1870s, as companies like the China Navigation Company and the China Merchants Company entered the trade, they based their organization on the Shanghai Steam Navigation Company or Jardine, Matheson & Company's early shipping ventures. In some cases, there was a direct transfer of personnel and knowledge from one company to another: the first merchant managers of the China Merchants Company, Tang Tingshu and Xu Run, previously worked as compradors for Jardine's and Dent & Company.[16] Japanese steamship companies looking to enter the shipping business in China at the turn of the twentieth century actively researched the practices of the existing firms and implemented many aspects of their organization.[17] In addition to the primacy of these models, the conference organization reinforced uniformity within the field. Conference agreements presumed that the Four Companies' services and facilities were comparable and interchangeable. In such a context, too extreme a departure from standard practices could be a risk to an individual company's business and a risk to the conference agreement if the change were either too great a failure or success. These features of the steam shipping field in China can help account for the relatively uniform practices evident among shipping companies of different national origins in organizing work and travel aboard their ships.

Steamship Crews: Hierarchies of Race and Skill

The steamship was a place of work for the crews that kept the ships in motion. In all four companies, steamship crews were very clearly stratified along lines of race and training/education. Before the 1920s, Europeans and Japanese invariably held positions such as captains, officers, and engineers—positions that required technical knowledge and training as well as the ability to command. The rest of the crew, performing the less skilled tasks related to navigation or the running of the ship's engine, were Chinese. There was very little possibility for mobility between these levels of ship's crews. This characteristic hierarchy derived from the conditions of steam navigation in general and from the shared practices of the Four Companies in Chinese waters. Throughout the nineteenth and early twentieth centuries, steamship crews evinced a hierarchy that conflated technical competence with race.

One of the key questions about this aspect of social space is why the China Merchants Company perpetuated this hierarchy on its steamships from the 1870s through the 1920s. It employed nearly exclusively European captains, officers, and engineers and Europeans in other supervisory positions requiring technical knowledge, such as company marine superintendent and chief engineer.[18] In the company's early days, there were few Chinese with the appropriate skills to serve as captain or engineer; in later years, a combination of the power of British shipping and insurance and the Qing and early Republican governments' lack of initiative in this area kept even those Chinese who had acquired the necessary skills out of these positions.

The requirements of steam navigation made steamship crews far more stratified than the crews of sailing ships had been. With the necessity of navigating the ship and running its engine as well as coordinating these processes, steamship crews were larger and performed more specialized but also more routinized tasks than the crews of sailing vessels. A steamship had a deck crew for navigation and an engine room crew. The deck crew included the captain, officers, and pilots, assisted by the boatswain, quartermaster, carpenter, and sailors. The engine room crew consisted of a chief engineer and two to four assistant engineers, supported by fitters, water-tenders, oilers, and stokers. In both crews, the racial line was drawn between those who were technically skilled and trained and those who assisted them. Historians of shipping have pointed out that the lower ranks of ships' crews became "proletarianized" with the advent of steam: the tasks they performed were more routinized and required less skill, closer to industrial labor than the work of crews on sailing vessels had been, and they accordingly commanded lower wages than those crews.[19]

Crew members lived and worked closely together within the confines of the ship, and although living space was carefully apportioned according to one's status in the hierarchy, it seems plausible that these less skilled workers might acquire the technical skills and knowledge necessary to serve as a captain or engineer. On steamships in China, however, the divide between the European/Japanese and Chinese crew was firm: although a Chinese sailor or fireman might advance through the ranks to lead the unskilled segment of the crew, it was nearly impossible for him to break into the ranks of captains, officers, or engineers.

The lack of mobility within the crew was the result of the different employment conditions for European/Japanese skilled personnel and Chinese crew members. Each steamship company had a marine department that oversaw the technical aspects of its business, such as the construction and repair of ships. This department hired and supervised ship captains and engineers. In all four companies, marine department staff members were European or Japanese expatriates, even in the China Merchants Company. Coming under the authority of this department, captains, officers, and engineers were salaried employees of the steamship companies. Knowledgeable and competent captains and engineers were in very high demand among the steamship companies, and the companies invested heavily in them. Most were compensated as expatriate staff and thus paid higher salaries to work in China than they would have been paid for the same work in their home countries. They were often granted additional allowances and home leaves with free passage at regular intervals.[20]

In contrast, members of the Chinese crew were not formal employees of the steamship companies. The companies relied on brokers to recruit them, and crews were hired on a seasonal rather than a permanent basis. Sometimes the broker was a crew member who negotiated the whole crew's employment, and sometimes the broker was a middleman who specialized in furnishing crews to steamship companies. The broker, rather than the company, was the worker's primary employer. Companies paid wages to the broker rather than to the individual crew members. Workers paid the broker a fee—sometimes the equivalent of several months' wages—for a place on a crew, and the broker could deduct payments from their monthly earnings toward that amount. Some brokers deepened this debt relationship by charging crews for housing and entertainment onshore and advancing more loans.[21] Chinese crews were paid much less than comparable crews composed of Europeans; they were understood to require less space on board the ship and less expense to feed. The broker, rather than the company, took responsibility if crews were unemployed due to seasonal fluctuations in shipping and saved the company the cost and trouble of recruiting, training, and maintaining discipline within crews by tapping into the existing structures of China's labor market.[22]

These structures discouraged mobility between Chinese crews and the technically skilled positions usually held by foreigners. As in other sectors of treaty-port labor markets, steamship crews tended to hail from a single native place and share that tie with the broker. Yangzi River crews, for example, were usually signed in Shanghai and composed of natives of the Ningbo area of coastal Zhejiang Province.[23] Such ties allowed for ready communication of the skills and protocol necessary for the work and helped maintain discipline and control within the crew, as each worker was involved in kinship or other obligational relationships that might extend back to his home area. Like the use of compradors in other aspects of the shipping business, hiring crews through brokers allowed the steamship companies to access Chinese labor at low cost. Despite the physical proximity of crew members at all levels, there were few opportunities for Chinese crew members to acquire the skills necessary to advance to technically skilled positions. The seasonal hiring of crews made long-term relationships in which specialized skills might be transferred unlikely. Even daily interactions between these strata of the crew were mediated by the broker relationship: usually only the boatswain or head fireman spoke enough pidgin English to communicate with the ship's officers, who relied on these intermediaries to translate orders to the Chinese-speaking crew.[24]

Conditions of employment thus worked against Chinese crew members acquiring the skills to become captains or engineers, but this explanation cannot fully account for the persistence of the racial line in steamship crews. Although there may have been few qualified Chinese navigators in the 1860s and 1870s, after that time, merchant shipping companies, particularly the China Merchants Company, could have hired former Qing naval officers in such positions. A 1908 Ministry of Posts and Communications survey shows that such a circumstance was very rare. At that time all thirty-one China Merchants Company ships had European captains, and the vast majority of officers and engineers were also European. Of 179 technical personnel, there were only 4 Chinese that held the position of third or fourth engineer.[25] One S. C. Zhang (d. 1887), commander of the *Jiangfu*, was the company's only Chinese captain before 1913.[26]

The maritime laws of some nations, such as the United States and Japan, stipulated that captains and officers of ships flying the national flag be citizens or hold some form of national certification. The prevalence of foreign-flag companies in Chinese waters thus meant that those in command were often foreign nationals, but shipping firms did not always follow these laws in China. The steamship companies valued familiarity with navigational conditions over nationality in their choices of captains and engineers, thus foreign-flag shipping companies often employed personnel of nationalities other than their own. When the China Navigation Company sent its first steamships to China in 1872, it replaced the British captains that commanded the ships on their outward voyage with captains that had been hired away from existing Yangzi River steamship companies, several of whom were Americans.[27] This practice was so prevalent that in 1877, the U.S. consul-general in Shanghai apologized to U.S. ship owners for enforcing the law requiring captains and officers to be citizens, acknowledging that it "interfered with American trade interests in China."[28] In China, it was common for U.S. companies to employ British captains or British companies to employ Norwegian captains, but such reciprocity was not extended to Chinese mariners.

Insurance standards were another factor that excluded Chinese from these positions. The extended employment of European technical personnel in the China Merchants Company is often cited as an example of the mismanagement of the company, as the salaries of foreign employees were one of the company's largest expenses.[29] Yet over the China Merchants history, there was no shortage of proposals for replacing European captains and engineers with Chinese. The earliest was a plan composed by Tang Tingshu and Xu Run in 1873, to train "capable Chinese" to take over these positions from Europeans, but the managers acknowledged that such a program was contingent on the company becoming self-insuring because the foreign insurance firms on which the company relied would not insure ships commanded by Chinese.[30] The failure of the short-lived Renhe Insurance Company (see chapter 3), and the company's return to foreign insurers likely halted this plan.[31] In the 1890s, the China Merchants manager Zheng Guanying (1842–1921) proposed a similar plan to recruit and train former naval officers and Chinese with experience on ships for these posts, since he found that the company's foreign employees were paid at least eight times what a Chinese would be paid under these circumstances.[32] After the company became a private concern in 1912, its shareholders voted to replace European captains with Chinese, but this decision was blocked by the company's board of directors, who argued that it would be too difficult for the company to insure its ships.[33] Similar resolutions passed in 1919 and 1924 resulted in the hiring of only four Chinese captains for the company's Yangzi River fleet.[34] Throughout this period, it was clear that company leaders were well aware of the desirability of replacing their European staff with Chinese, but insurance difficulties were the obstacle cited most often.

The rationale behind the foreign insurance companies' refusal to insure ships commanded by Chinese is not entirely clear, but a significant difference between European/Japanese and Chinese mariners during this period was that Europeans and Japanese could obtain formal certifications from their home governments, whereas neither the Qing nor the early Republican governments had made legal provisions for certifying Chinese as merchant steamship captains and engineers. The few Chinese who served in such positions before the 1920s were graduates of naval academies or navy veterans.[35] It was not until 1929 that the Nationalist government set up certification procedures for merchant seamen.[36] If there was a stereotype that Chinese were less able commanders than were Europeans, the long absence of a certification process almost certainly reinforced it. Many of the small Chinese shipping companies started around the turn of the twentieth century hired Chinese of uncertain qualifications to command their ships, and the number of accidents that resulted from inexperienced captains and engineers deepened the association between a foreign captain and a "safe" ship.[37] As late as 1931, some insurance companies still refused to insure Upper Yangzi ships unless they were commanded by Europeans.[38]

The China Merchants Company remained dependent on foreign insurance and foreign technical personnel throughout this period, despite its leaders' awareness of the problems these caused for the company. A comparison with the Japanese state's effort to promote shipping independence from European personnel in the nineteenth century underscores the difficulty of reversing such dependence in a world dominated by British shipping and insurance. In the 1870s, Japanese steamship companies employed mostly European captains and engineers. In 1875, the Meiji government initiated a program to train Japanese for these positions, providing Mitsubishi with a subsidy to start a school for merchant mariners (later the National Tokyo Commercial Shipping Academy). The government established legal procedures to certify Japanese captains and engineers and stipulated that both European and Japanese personnel on steamships had to obtain Japanese government certifications. The government offered one type of certification for graduates of the training school and another for those who could pass a competency exam based on experience.[39]

These measures alone were not enough to replace Europeans with Japanese on Japanese-flag ships. British insurers refused to recognize Japanese certificates, so the government established its own marine insurance companies. Most difficult was challenging the widespread association of European commanders with "safe" ships in the market. Some Japanese companies resisted hiring Japanese captains because they feared losing the faith of their shippers. After the Sino-Japanese War, when the government expanded its shipping subsidies, it offered additional funds to companies who employed Japanese captains exclusively. It also mandated that all steamship companies had to equalize the salaries paid to European and Japanese employees. Most Japanese shipping firms employed only Japanese personnel by 1914, yet even at this late date, a few continued to use European captains on highly competitive overseas routes.[40] The reversal of Japanese dependence on European technical personnel was thus a long-term process that required not only an infrastructure for educating and certifying mariners but also an independent insurance business and strong incentives for companies to bear the risk that their ships would not be considered as safe as those commanded by Europeans.

The China Merchants Company had little of the sustained state support that eventually reversed Japanese companies' dependence on foreign personnel. Under conditions in which there was little hope of challenging the wider foreign dominance in shipping, there was a distinct rationality to the company's employment of Europeans that belies the charge of poor management. Both inside and outside of the conference, the China Merchants Company's competitors were all foreign-flag companies. The employment of Europeans allowed the company to redress some of the asymmetries it faced in the foreign-dominated context. Although the China Merchants spent heavily on European salaries, its employment of European captains allowed it to insure its ships at rates comparable to those paid by its competitors.[41] European captains allowed the company to avoid the additional burden of convincing customers that ships commanded by Chinese were as safe as its British or Japanese competitors'. Furthermore, since European employees (even on Qing-flag ships) enjoyed extraterritorial protection, any legal actions taken against China Merchants captains would be prosecuted in the consular courts rather than in Qing or Republican courts. These actions were most often disputes with Chinese plaintiffs over loss of property, and consular courts had a reputation for resolving them in the captain's or steamship company's favor.[42] Whether or not this reputation was justified, the employment of European captains ensured that legal cases against China Merchants captains were prosecuted under conditions comparable to captains in the other companies.

For the China Merchants Company, participation in the collaborative mechanism of the conference could be both a constraint and a support. The presumed equivalence or comparability of the conference companies overlay an actual situation in which the Chinese company did not have the same access to the resources of the shipping world, in this case insurance and trained technical personnel, as did its British or Japanese counterparts. Without significant support outside the conference structure—such as from the government—it was very difficult for the China Merchants Company to challenge the prevailing practices in the shipping field without appearing deficient in comparison to the other companies. The China Merchants Company's ships therefore replicated the same hierarchy of race and skill so evident on British and Japanese ships and indirectly contributed to the conflation of race and skill in the steam-shipping business.

The hierarchy of race and skill on steamships was not unique to China: it could be seen on steamship lines throughout the world. On numerous British, U.S., and German overseas lines, steamship captains, engineers, and officers were overwhelmingly educated, middle-class graduates of European training programs, while "native" crews of Asians, Arabs, or Africans were paid lower wages and accommodated under more meager conditions than European crews could command.[43] The same hierarchy was visible in shipping companies in India, where captains and engineers were unfailingly British, overseeing Indian crews hired through middlemen known as *serangs* or *ghat serangs*. The relationship of the *serang* to the workers was nearly identical to that between the Chinese brokers and steamship crews.[44] Steamships across the world thus reproduced a social space of work that conflated race and skill, particularly technical competence. The assumed connection between race and technical competence was replicated in departments of the colonial Indian government, including the Railways, Telegraph, Public Works, the Geological Survey, and the Forest Service, in which managerial and technical posts were given to recruits from Britain, mid-level skilled and supervisory jobs to Anglo-Indians, and unskilled jobs to Indians.[45] The organization of work on steamships in China thus departed little from hierarchies of race and skill visible elsewhere in the world.

Race and the Passenger Space

The passenger trade was central to the steamship business in China. Following its introduction, steamship travel became a common convenience for Chinese passengers: Qing officials traveled to new posts, examination candidates traveled to provincial capitals and Beijing, merchants accompanied goods to market, and Yangzi junk crews caught quick passages upriver on the steamship. By the 1870s, the passenger trade had become so profitable that steamship companies began to set their schedules according to Chinese travel patterns, adding extra ships at the time of Chinese New Year, metropolitan and provincial examinations, and during the first, fifth, and eighth lunar months when merchants traditionally traveled to settle debts.[46] Chinese travelers made up the majority of steamship passengers, but foreign merchants, missionaries, consuls, Maritime Customs officials, and tourists also traveled by steamship among the treaty ports. The passenger trade expanded steadily over time: on the Yangzi River, it grew from tens of thousands of passengers each year in the 1860s to several million on the Lower Yangzi alone in the 1930s.[47]

Like the composition of steamship crews, the organization of passengers on steamships in Chinese waters reflected colonial racial categories and hierarchies, but the lineaments of the passenger space were more ambiguous than the clear chains of command within the crew. The design and management of the passenger accommodation made overt distinctions between the accommodations designated for foreign and Chinese passengers. The privileging of foreign passengers was evident in the allotment of space on the ships, ticket pricing, and in the separate management of the foreign and Chinese classes. This organization was evident on the ships of all four major steamship companies. Nevertheless, the existence of such structures is only part of the story: looking beyond them to the daily supervision and management of these spaces, it is possible to see variation among the companies and identify particular constructions of race and concerns over proximity and exclusion. This examination of passenger space thus delves into the presumptive passenger space of steamships and into the question of how boundaries between "foreign" and "Chinese" classes of travel were maintained in practice.

THE PRESUMPTIVE PASSENGER SPACE: DESIGN, PRICING, AND MANAGEMENT

The physical space of ships is so finite that the distribution of space among different groups on board—in amount and quality—speaks to the presumed relations among these groups. The obvious difference between the quarters provided to the captain and those provided to an ordinary sailor reflected their different statuses in the chain of command. In the same way, the design of passenger accommodation on China's river and coast steamships distinguished foreign and Chinese passengers. In steamships built in the 1860s and 1870s, the "foreign" accommodation consisted of cabins arranged around a saloon, whereas the "Chinese" accommodation was like steerage in other contexts: a single large cabin supplied with berths. Steamships of this vintage accommodated up to 50 foreign passengers and 200 or more Chinese passengers. As the companies updated their fleets over time, the Chinese accommodation became more elaborate, first with the addition of enclosed cabins for female passengers and later with the development of three Chinese passenger classes. Chinese first class offered shared cabins for two to four, second class had cabins with six berths, while steerage remained a large open cabin. These later ships often furnished a "Chinese saloon," a dining room where Chinese passengers in all classes could eat.[48] Even as the configuration of the Chinese accommodation became more complex, the categories of foreign and Chinese passengers remained separate, with almost no spaces on board shared between them. For example, the specifications for a ship of the late 1920s with a 1,000-passenger capacity stipulated separate ladies' saloons and smoking rooms for the foreign and Chinese first classes.[49] The foreign accommodation consistently occupied the most advantageous position on the ship—on the uppermost deck at the bow—the area that was best ventilated and least affected by the heat and vibration of the ship's engine. In some ships, all three Chinese classes were arranged on the second deck, with first class at the bow, second class in the middle, and third class at the back. In other ships, the steerage accommodation might be placed on an even lower deck, or sometimes below deck altogether (see figures 4.1, 4.2, and 4.3).[50]

Ticket prices not only underscored the distance between the foreign and Chinese accommodation but also presumed a significant difference in economic power between these groups. Tickets for the foreign accommodation cost from three to four times the Chinese first-class fare, and this proportional difference was maintained over time and through the different currencies in use in China. In 1900, a traveler reported the cost of a foreign first-class ticket between Shanghai and Hankou as $40 Mexican, whereas a Chinese first-class ticket cost $10.40 Mexican.[51] By 1924, this gap had narrowed only slightly: a foreign first-class ticket from

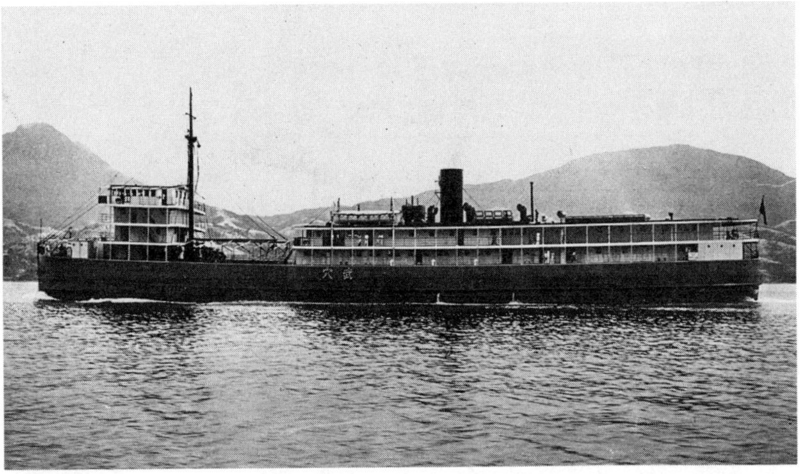

FIGURE 4.1 The China Navigation Company ship, *Wusueh* (1931–52). Courtesy of John Swire & Sons, London.

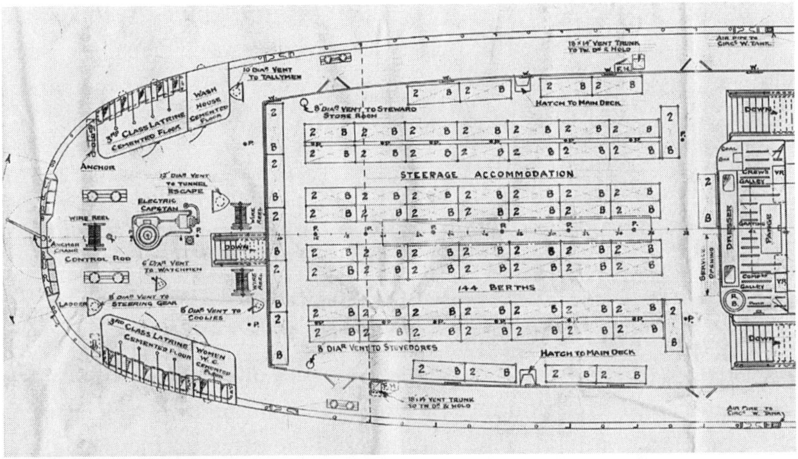

FIGURE 4.2 Steerage Accommodation. Detail of Plan of China Navigation Company's *Wusueh* (I) Ships 244. Courtesy of John Swire & Sons, London. The *Wusueh* was a later ship than most of those discussed in this chapter and had some differences in design. These images show the use of space in different classes.

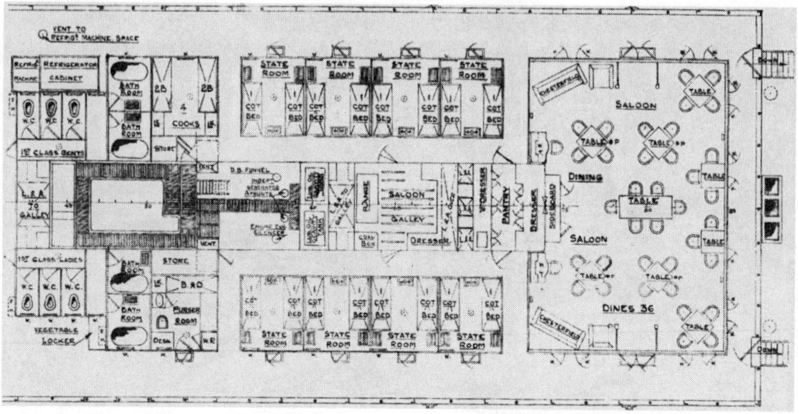

FIGURE 4.3 Saloon Accommodation. Detail of Plan of China Navigation Company's *Wusueh* (II), Ships 244. Courtesy of John Swire & Sons, London.

Shanghai to Hankou cost 50 *yuan*, and a Chinese first-class ticket 17.6 *yuan*. The price differences between fares within the Chinese accommodation were smaller—the same 1924 report lists the Chinese second-class ticket as 12 *yuan* and the third-class ticket as 5.4 *yuan*.[52] Thus, the three Chinese classes were relatively close in price while the foreign accommodation was significantly more expensive than even the first-class Chinese fare.

The foreign and Chinese passenger classes were also managed separately and differently. Each ship's captain took charge of the foreign accommodation. Passengers bought tickets at company offices in treaty ports or directly from the captain. The captain hired a staff of cooks and stewards, who were paid members of the crew, furnishing European-style food and service to the ship's foreign passengers, officers, and engineers.[53] The ship comprador's contract included oversight of all three classes of the Chinese accommodation in addition to the cargo business. Like the captain, the comprador was responsible for recruiting passengers, selling tickets, and providing food for passengers, but the terms of the contract required him to bear greater risk. The captain was a salaried employee of the company who collected an additional allowance to purchase food and secure services for the foreign staff and passengers. Although he might earn a little profit from selling tickets, it was not his primary livelihood. In contrast, the nominal salaries and commissions that compradors received were rarely enough to meet their expenses and make remittances to the company. Compradors depended on profits they earned from the spaces of the ship under their control to meet the terms of their contracts. Among these, the Chinese passenger business was often the most important source of income. Often compradors were expected to cover costs from the cargo business—such as compensation to shippers for loss or damage to cargo—out of their earnings from the passenger business.[54]

The differences in management between these types of accommodation were reflected in the very disparate experiences that travelers recorded in each. Because Chinese passenger fares were the mainstay of ship compradors' incomes, compradors competed fiercely to attract passengers and had the authority to lower fares if necessary. They commonly overloaded the Chinese passenger accommodation, packing as many people onto the ship as possible, allowing them to settle on deck or in the crew's cabins. Passengers constantly complained of overcrowding, with so many packed into the accommodation that there was barely room for them to sit, sleep, or move about comfortably. The crowding led to other annoyances: the steerage cabin, often located close to the ship's engine, could be unbearably hot in warm weather and reeked of perspiration. Even after the development of Chinese first and second classes, passengers complained that the cabins booked so quickly that they were difficult to obtain and that the common space of the Chinese saloon was noisy with constant gambling, filled with the smoke of passengers' tobacco and opium pipes, and often crowded with people unable to find a berth in steerage.[55] Compradors almost always sold more tickets than there were berths on board and did not keep detailed records of passengers in the Chinese accommodation, which allowed them to underreport their earnings to the company.[56]

The comprador's incentive to maximize earnings also led him to other economies that directly affected passenger experience. Food was an expense on which he could skimp: a writer for the Shanghai newspaper *Shen bao* complained, "Why serve prison fare to paying customers?"[57] Rather than paying a staff of stewards, compradors hired "teaboys" (*chafang*) to serve passengers. Teaboys did not receive regular wages; they were expected to earn a living from tips. Furthermore, compradors profited from their employment by charging each teaboy a down payment for a position on the ship and collecting a regular cut from his tips thereafter.[58] Chinese passengers suffered the consequences of the teaboys' terms of employment, as the teaboys were famously aggressive in demanding tips and payment for every service rendered.[59]

Compradors also sought an increase in earnings by selling concessions to vendors of snacks, books, opium, and organizers of gambling operations as well as to hotel touts and others who added to the crowding and annoyances on board. The result was a hectic and freewheeling space, but one that could also be full of threats. Travelers recalled having to remain vigilant against a full spectrum of dangers or swindles: gangs of ruffians who kicked passengers out of their cabins or berths, thieves posing as passengers who robbed travelers' luggage, and hotel touts and porters who badgered passengers into accepting their services and later cheated them.[60] As the steamship company had contracted the Chinese passenger business out to the comprador, it rarely intervened in the management of the Chinese accommodation beyond occasional measures to control underreporting or falsifying passenger returns.

In sharp contrast, passengers in the foreign accommodation inevitably praised its opulence. One claimed that Yangzi River steamers were "perhaps the most luxurious steamers in the world."[61] Others remarked on the excellent cuisine, scrupulous cleanliness, and impressive furnishings, which included white enamel, mirrors, gilding, electric light, and fine carpets.[62] Travelers in the 1920s and 1930s compared the amenities and food on these ships favorably with those on a first-class ocean steamer.[63] Passengers in this class reported very few fellow passengers on their steamship journeys: the foreign accommodation in many steamships was designed for as many as fifty passengers, but passenger lists consistently reported very small numbers—rarely more than five or six—of passengers in the foreign accommodation of any one ship at a time.[64] The captains and officers took a leading role in the social life of the foreign passengers on board and saw to their comfort and convenience, sharing regular meals and cocktail hours. The foreign personnel of the ship ensured an intimate and convivial atmosphere among the passengers. For example, on the China Navigation steamer *Ngankin*, the captain and engineer played the piano and flute to entertain passengers.[65] The famous Victorian traveler Isabella Bird (1831–1904) recalled that a ship's chief engineer helped her tone photographs in the saloon.[66]

The separate management of the foreign and Chinese passenger classes underlay the very different experiences passengers had in each. The captain's low-risk oversight of the foreign accommodation allowed him to maintain high levels of luxury and service, run it nearly empty, and cultivate an atmosphere of exclusivity and intimate sociability among the passengers and high-ranking crew. In contrast, the higher risk borne by the comprador gave him a strong incentive to maximize earnings at any cost, crowding the accommodation, skimping on food and other services, and exposing the passengers to various dangers and annoyances. In general, the hierarchical distinction between foreign and Chinese accommodation suggested by the differences in their placement on the ships and ticket prices were borne out by the experiences of travelers within them.

The four major steamship companies shared these elements of ship design, pricing, and separate management of the foreign and Chinese accommodation. These elements formed the presumptive organization of the social space that constructed foreign passengers as invariably well off and demanding luxury and service, and Chinese passengers as economically diverse but requiring less space and fewer comforts overall. This presumptive organization reveals very little about the actual social spaces on board ships. It cannot impart what the categories of "foreign" and "Chinese" meant in practice or whether the boundary between the two types of accommodation was rigidly enforced or permeable. This organization of passenger classes could indicate a commitment to racial separation or reflect market conditions in which foreign travelers were willing to pay for space and luxury while Chinese travelers preferred more austere conditions at lower rates. The daily management of the passenger accommodation—the policies of shipping companies, the practices of their employees, the experiences of travelers and observers of the industry—provides greater access to the texture of relations within this social space. At the level of daily management, variations among the steamship companies emerge, revealing a range of approaches to the social space of the passenger accommodation.

THE AMBIGUITIES OF EXCLUSION: RACE AND THE FOREIGN FIRST CLASS

Compared with the overall numbers of steamship passengers, the foreign first class served only a small minority. However, this class is central to understanding the significance of race within the social space of the passenger accommodation. Practices of admitting passengers to and excluding them from this class can flesh out the implications and meaning of the presumptive organization of the steamship space. Were those willing to pay the fare admitted regardless of race, or were Chinese passengers uniformly excluded? Travelers' experiences and reports on the practices of different shipping companies show that there was no single or standard policy: Chinese passengers traveled in the foreign first class, but they also encountered exclusion from it. The presumptive structure of the passenger classes was consistent among the steamship companies, but practices of admission and exclusion varied among the companies and even within the same company. The omnipresent and often unspoken question informing these practices was one of tolerance for the social intimacy across races that the accommodation demanded, and the question was most often addressed on an informal or individual basis rather than enshrined in policy.

The nomenclature of steamship passenger classes reveals the ambiguity of the boundaries between them. The English-language correspondence of the China Navigation Company, for example, makes an explicit distinction between the foreign first class and the remaining Chinese classes. This distinction is reflected by Japanese observers in the late nineteenth century, who clearly identified a "foreign first class" (*gaikokujin shōtō*) or "Western first class" (*yōjin shōtō*).[67] The Chinese terms for passenger classes in all companies made no distinction between foreign and Chinese. The Chinese equivalent of what appears in English-language sources as "foreign first class" was *da canjian cang* (lit. "large dining room" or saloon class) and "Chinese first class" was *guan cang* ("official" class, often translated as "mandarin class"). The terms for the Chinese second and third classes were similarly descriptive: *fang cang* ("cabin class") and *tong cang* ("joint" class, usually translated as steerage). The steamship companies thus did not communicate a foreign/Chinese distinction through the Chinese terms. Moreover, it was a relatively common occurrence for

Chinese passengers to travel in the foreign first class. Passenger lists published in the *North China Daily News* recorded the names of passengers in this class only, and these often included Chinese names: "Mrs. Ah-yan and infant," "H.E. Governor Pan & suite," "one mandarin," "Three Chinese Gentlemen."[68]

Despite the apparent neutrality of the Chinese terms, many anecdotes describe Chinese passengers as routinely excluded from the foreign first class. An 1896 survey of the shipping field conducted by a commercial association from Nagoya, Japan, reported that such exclusions were a matter of course, "those wearing Chinese dress, even if they are gentlemen (*shinshi*) are refused passage in the foreign first class."[69] A twentieth-century memoir stated, "the first class was for Europeans only."[70] One explanation for this contrast was the different ways the steamship companies managed the boundaries between passenger classes. Incidents of exclusion from the foreign first class were most often associated with the British China Navigation and Indo-China companies and very rarely with the Nisshin Kisen Kaisha or the China Merchants Company. Yet a company's provenance cannot fully explain the different ways of conceiving and managing this space. Exclusionary practices are particularly difficult to parse in this context because they almost always occurred in informal or individualized settings rather than at the level of company policy. None of the companies ever admitted to a policy or rule that explicitly barred Chinese passengers from the foreign accommodation, yet anecdotal evidence shows that in its daily supervision by captains or pursers, this class was often treated as the space of a foreign community that excluded Chinese.

The British companies had the clearest reputation for excluding Chinese passengers from the foreign first class. The evidence that underlay this reputation reveals a powerful discomfort with proximity—physical and social—between European and Chinese passengers in this class of travel, likely stemming from the British perception of themselves as colonial elites in China. In his study of the British settler community in Shanghai, Robert Bickers describes the commonly held belief that physical and social distance from the Chinese was necessary to maintain British racial superiority and "position" in China, while overfamiliarity with the Chinese was a threat to British dignity.[71] In the management of the foreign first class on British ships, this preoccupation was often in tension with the companies' official policies that this class of travel was open to all.

The official passenger policies of both China Navigation and Indo-China permitted Chinese passengers to choose any class of travel but limited European passengers to the foreign first class alone.[72] This policy appears solicitous of the preferences of Chinese travelers, yet it also communicates anxiety about proximity between Europeans and Chinese. Regardless of which group was restricted, the policy's effect was to limit the possibilities for close contact between European and Chinese travelers to the most expensive class of travel. China Navigation explained its policy as an attempt to prevent missionaries from annoying Chinese passengers by preaching during the journey, yet the missionaries' eagerness to interact with Chinese passengers may have been more disturbing to the European passengers and crew than to Chinese travelers.[73] The policy ensured that European passengers traveled together in the best-appointed class, apart from the vast majority of Chinese passengers.

Despite the circumspection of the policy, the Nagoya survey reports that the British companies excluded Chinese passengers from the foreign first class as a matter of course. Significantly, it identifies exclusion occurring at the moment Chinese passengers attempted to purchase tickets. Foreign first-class tickets could be obtained only by personal application at the steamship company's office or to the ship's captain. Therefore, although the official policy did not bar Chinese from the accommodation, the company's agent or the captain might do so on an individual basis. The requirement that a passenger apply in person for a ticket indicated that some examination of his or her body—rather than name, status, or credentials—was considered necessary for admission. The Nagoya survey is even more specific, citing dress as the essential criterion, "those wearing Chinese dress, even if they are gentlemen, are refused passage in the foreign first class."[74] In such a case, exclusions were made not in principle (i.e., "no Chinese allowed") but in person as a European employee of the steamship company scrutinized and judged the Chinese applicant.

Steamship company employees such as captains or pursers appeared to take on the unofficial role of policing contact between European and Chinese passengers on British ships. In cases where Chinese passengers succeeded in purchasing foreign first-class tickets, captains or pursers might deny them access to certain spaces within the accommodation, such as the dining table or ladies' saloon.[75] Such incidents suggest that the employees who oversaw the accommodation were willing to furnish Chinese passengers with cabins but were not willing to admit them to the common spaces in which the intimate socializing described by so many European travelers took place.

Further evidence from the day-to-day supervision of the space communicates fears that Chinese passengers would threaten an atmosphere of European-style civility expected there. A set of rules posted in Chinese in the foreign first class of a British ship stipulated that passengers must dress appropriately at dinner and forbade spitting, bringing one's own food or utensils to the dining table, or smoking opium except in designated areas.[76] These rules had no English-language counterpart and reflected the stereotypical observations that European travelers made of Chinese steamship passengers in other classes: beyond the ubiquitous disgust with spitting were the common reports of Chinese passengers wearing pajamas during the day and consuming opium openly on board.[77] Not only did the rules target presumed "Chinese" habits, they made passengers aware that their behavior would be monitored according to European standards. Li Boyuan's (1867–1906) 1905 novel *Modern Times* contains a scene in which a steamship captain recites a similar list of prohibitions to a Chinese government official traveling to the United States. When the official boards the ship, the captain informs him that he is forbidden to smoke opium and that any visible smoking equipment will be tossed overboard. When eating in the dining saloon, he "must on no account scratch his head, clean his fingernails, or do anything that might be regarded as repugnant by the other passengers." Although the official takes careful note of these rules, he is still ridiculed by the other passengers at dinner for his unfamiliarity with Western food and table manners.[78] Li Boyuan may have intended to mock the pretensions of the official as much as criticize the assumptions of the captain or other passengers, but this incident renders concrete what the list of rules only implies: those who supervised the space on a daily basis intended to enforce European standards of deportment and civility. Not only were the habits of Chinese passengers presumed to threaten these norms, but once they entered this space, their behavior would also be closely scrutinized to ensure that it did not.

The anecdotal evidence of exclusion on British ships reveals a disjuncture between the official policy that the foreign first class was open to Chinese passengers and the informal practices of the employees who oversaw this space. Although not officially acknowledged, these workers made daily decisions about which passengers could purchase foreign first-class tickets or enjoy the common areas of the accommodation. They might also make a passenger conscious of his or her behavior in the space. Although such decisions were informal and variable, common among them was the privileging of the sensibilities of European passengers, particularly the concern for maintaining a social distance from the Chinese. Although the companies were unwilling to state it as a matter of principle or policy, captains, pursers, and ticket sellers often took on the role of enforcing the European quality of the space by excluding Chinese passengers in some way. As many passengers noted, these practices might vary among ships of the same company and even on different voyages of the same ship.

The references to deportment and dress that surround the issue of proximity between foreign and Chinese passengers were articulations of racial difference that drew on wider racial discourses in semi-colonial China. John Fitzgerald has excavated the "colonial critique of John Chinaman," which linked the European distaste for Chinese habits of body and hygiene, such as spitting and nose blowing in public, to doubts about Chinese competencies, most significantly, their ability to govern themselves.[79] John Chinaman's inability to meet European standards of deportment or civility was evidence of Chinese subordination and inferiority. Social intimacy in the foreign first class between Europeans and Chinese passengers who evoked the John Chinaman stereotype was thus an intolerable transgression of the racial order. The alleged reliance on dress as the criterion for exclusion was also a means of articulating racial distinction. In other instances in nineteenth-century China, dress was a way to distinguish Qing subjects from other East Asians—such as Japanese or ethnic Chinese from the Straits Settlements—who were under British protection.[80] The fact that "those wearing Chinese dress" could be excluded suggests that anxieties about proximity were focused on Qing subjects in particular and that "Chinese dress" was a metonym for the deficiencies of John Chinaman.[81] To a steamship captain or company agent, dress indicated whether a passenger was capable of meeting the standards of civility in the foreign accommodation. The focus on behavior and dress demanded scrutiny of Chinese bodies, yet neither of these articulations made explicit reference to skin color or facial features usually associated with racial identity. This type of oblique racial discourse was not unique to China: Ann Laura Stoler has observed that colonial laws tended to distinguish European citizens from colonial subjects not through their physiological characteristics but through perceived cultural competencies.[82]

Underscoring the point that deportment and dress were means of representing race rather than specific criteria for inclusion in the space are instances in which even the most "Westernized" Chinese were barely tolerated in the foreign first class. A request from one of Butterfield & Swire's Chinese compradors for steamship tickets for his children illustrates the contradictions of this articulation of race. The comprador asked for foreign first-class accommodation for his children's return from missionary schools in Shanghai, since "they have to a great extent been brought up to foreign ways." He also suggested that they be assigned to cabins in the hall near the ship comprador's room rather than in the main saloon because there "they would not be in the way of foreign passengers or feel any restraint."[83] The comprador makes an argument for his children's qualifications for admission to the space—their familiarity with "foreign ways"—yet acknowledges the probability that their presence would be unwelcome and they would be made aware of it.

The possibility of social contact between Europeans and Chinese was a vexed enough problem on British steamships, but evidence of sexual intimacy between races was even more intolerable. Bickers identifies a sexual taboo in British settler culture—the condemnation of those who married or had sexual relationships with Chinese and others outside of the European community.[84] Such mores were reflected in cases in which captains or pursers insisted that interracial couples travel separately in different classes, the European partner invariably placed in the foreign first class. Han Suyin's (1916–2012) memoir *The Crippled Tree* describes an incident in which her Chinese father and Belgian mother were made to travel apart on a trip from Shanghai to Chongqing. As her father put it, "the first class was for Europeans only, there was no other steamer."[85] A Chinese traveler in the 1920s reported sharing the Chinese first-class accommodation on a British ship with a Japanese woman whose European husband had been moved to the foreign first class.[86] Despite the policy that Chinese passengers were free to choose their class of travel, in neither case was the non-European partner given the option of joining their spouse in the foreign first class. That the ship's staff took the initiative to separate these couples suggests that they wished to render the evidence of interracial intimacy invisible to foreign first-class passengers in particular.

On British ships in China, there were two views of the social space of the foreign accommodation that existed uneasily alongside one another. The companies articulated a policy in which Chinese passengers had unrestricted choice in their accommodations, yet in their daily management of the space, employees such as captains and pursers might implement a view of this space as one of the European community, catering exclusively to its modes of civility or tolerance for proximity. As neither view of the space was enforced consistently, passengers' experience of exclusion varied widely.

A case brought before the Hong Kong Supreme Court in 1879 attempted to penetrate the ambiguities experienced by Chinese travelers with regard to access to the foreign first class. In June 1879, Hong Kong resident Cheong Wan sued the captain of the *Ichang* (a China Navigation ship plying between Hong Kong and Canton) for refusing to seat him at the "cabin table" (the dining table in the foreign first class) when he had purchased a foreign first-class ticket and ordered a meal. According to Cheong's lawyer, the point of the case was not to claim monetary damages but to "test the right" that the purchase of a foreign first-class ticket entitled the bearer to a meal at the cabin table—in other words, the same privileges that other foreign first-class ticket holders enjoyed. The lawyer contended that since Cheong was a paying passenger the captain had infringed upon his rights by refusing to seat him there.[87]

Although Cheong was permitted to buy a foreign first-class ticket, testimony in the case revealed the captain of the *Ichang* granting or denying Cheong and his wife access to the spaces of the accommodation in a manner that suggests he was concerned with preventing them from coming into direct contact with foreign passengers. For example, the captain testified that he had allowed Cheong's wife to sit in the ladies' cabin, "as there were no foreign ladies on board." Had there been foreign women on board who might have used the space, she presumably would not have been allowed to sit there. When Cheong ordered his meal from the purser, the purser told him, "You had better ask the captain." The captain claimed he had not denied Cheong a meal but had directed him to eat his meal in the "Parsee cabin." Cheong denied he was offered this option. That this ship had a separate cabin for (Indian) Parsis may reflect the prevalence and importance of Parsi merchants in this part of China and the strict dietary rules this community followed in addition to the need to separate them from European passengers.[88] For this captain, the cabin provided an alternate location for a passenger unwelcome at the main table to eat a meal.

Cheong and his lawyers focused on the point that the segregation of spaces he experienced was not uniformly enforced on ships on the route. Cheong testified that he had taken meals at the cabin table on other ships on the same route. Other Hong Kong Chinese witnesses—including barrister Wu Tingfang (1842–1922)—testified that they had eaten at the *Ichang*'s cabin table in the past, and thus the lawyers argued that Cheong had every reason to expect that he would be served there. When asked to explain the inconsistency, the *Ichang*'s captain replied that he had only ever allowed three Chinese passengers to eat at the cabin table: one had been accompanied by a European and the other two had been "known to him." His lawyer elaborated on this point, explaining that "the Captain had a perfect right to refuse any one a seat at the cabin table," and "the question of admitting Chinese to the cabin indiscriminately was a very serious one," citing a case in which Chinese pirates had boarded a ship dressed as well-to-do passengers. The captain and his lawyer's response to this line of questioning reveals that the captain regarded excluding Chinese passengers from his table as normal, unless he or another European knew them personally, and that this practice could be justified by the potential danger to the safety of the ship or other passengers that an unknown Chinese passenger posed.

The judge ruled in favor of the captain, with costs. His decision focused on whether Cheong Wan could claim the meal as a "right" attendant on the purchase of a foreign first-class ticket. Concluding that it was the captain himself, rather than the steamship company, who provided and profited from the meals, the judge ruled that there was no connection between the ticket and the meal. The captain "kept a *private* table" (emphasis added) and thus not all were entitled to a meal there. Referring to the inconsistencies of admission to this table, the judge argued that the fact that some Chinese passengers had eaten there in the past did not entitle all to do so, as "a custom is not a right." In articulating this principle, the judge reinforced the idea Cheong Wan and other Chinese passengers in this position were not simply "paying customers," and that access to the different spaces of the foreign accommodation depended on the captain's discretion. The judge's decision was nearly identical to the steamship company's response to Cheong Wan's complaint. Butterfield & Swire, China Navigation's managing agency, told Cheong that "they had nothing to do with the matter as the Captain had full power to deal with the situation as he saw fit."

Particularly striking in this case is the relegation of a question of racial exclusion to an informal sphere of personal prerogative and discrimination. The captain's, the judge's, and the steamship company's positions aligned closely to deny the obvious logic of Cheong's argument that a foreign first-class ticket entitled him to a meal at the cabin table. The captain's testimony acknowledged that the Cheongs' proximity to other passengers was a problem he managed actively during the voyage, yet neither the captain nor those who took his part attempted to explain or defend any principles behind these exclusionary practices (save the lawyer's intimation that unknown Chinese passengers could be dangerous). Instead, the captain, the judge, and the company uniformly defended the captain's personal authority to manage the space as he wished. In contrast to a public space in which principles of exclusion might need to be articulated and justified, the captain's table was deemed private, and thus his criteria for exclusion remained so as well. By making access to the space a captain's personal decision, the company could retain its inclusive policy while captains or other employees could maintain it as an exclusively European space.

The experience of African American abolitionist Frederick Douglass (1818–95) on transatlantic steamships in the 1840s evinces a nearly identical tension between certain accommodations as open to paying customers and as social spaces restricted to particular communities. Douglass, by that time a prominent writer and speaker, was barred from purchasing a first-class passage on a Cunard Line steamer to Britain. The company's agent offered him a second-class ticket instead, as "American passengers would object to such social intimacy across races." Returning to the

United States two years later, Cunard's Liverpool agent allowed him to purchase a first-class ticket on condition that he take a cabin by himself, eat his meals alone, and refrain from mingling with the other passengers. Despite their somewhat different solutions to the problem, the Cunard agents were consistent in their efforts to prevent racial mixing in the first class. After Douglass's treatment was detailed in the press, however, Samuel Cunard himself apologized and promised that it would never happen again on his ships.[89] The inconsistency between Cunard's apology and the uniform practices of the company's agents evinces an unwillingness to acknowledge racial exclusion at the level of the company and a conception of this space as one that necessitated it.

A China Navigation captain active in the 1920s and 1930s observed that "Chinese could travel 'foreign' if they wished, but rarely did so."[90] Chinese passengers entering the foreign first class of the British companies' ships risked encountering the racial anxieties of those who oversaw the accommodation, whether expressed through outright exclusion, intensive scrutiny, or restriction from certain areas of the accommodation. It was perhaps even more confounding that these exclusions were unspoken and inconsistent, as they were recognized only as the result of an individual's personal judgment. The foreign first class of the British companies' ships demonstrates not only the significance of colonial racial ideology in this social space but the deep ambivalence about its articulation there: it was both inescapable and unacknowledged.

The Nisshin Kisen Kaisha's and China Merchants Company's ships evince no parallel practices of exclusion from the foreign first class, yet these social spaces were clearly affected by a similar racial ideology. British precedence and preeminence in the shipping field ensured that although the other companies might not replicate these practices, they were influenced by them. There is no evidence of exclusion of Chinese passengers by the Nisshin Kisen Kaisha, but its management of the passenger accommodation was based on British practices. Nisshin's foreign first class was designed to appeal to Japanese passengers as a space of their expatriate community. It provided Japanese-style meals and baths. Travel accounts by Tōa Dōbun Shoin students further suggest that Nisshin captains cultivated an intimate atmosphere: the students describe being welcomed and offered discounted fares by captains who were fellow graduates of the school.[91]

Nisshin's passenger policy was similar to that of the British companies in that it also allowed Chinese passengers to choose any class of accommodation but did not allow European and Japanese passengers to travel in steerage.[92] Like the British policy, the restriction was placed on foreign rather than Chinese passengers, but it permitted a broader margin of interaction between passengers than the British policy did. Foreign passengers could travel in the Chinese first and second classes on Nisshin's ships. Graduating students from the Tōa Dōbun Shoin, for example, almost always traveled in Nisshin's Chinese first class on their trips to survey economic conditions across China. Student travelogues suggest that they saw these steamship journeys as important opportunities to interact with Chinese passengers and experience Chinese culture and cuisine.[93] The greater range of ticket options available to foreign passengers on Nisshin ships may reflect what Mark Peattie has described as the generally more modest lifestyle of Japanese settlers in China compared with their European counterparts, since the company did not require all foreign passengers to pay the most expensive fare.[94] Although the policy allowed for both some economic diversity among foreign passengers and some social interaction between foreign and Chinese passengers, neither extended to the level of the steerage accommodation. Japanese travel accounts often repeat the point implicit in the policy that the conditions in the steerage accommodation were unacceptable for Japanese. One commentator wrote in the 1890s that steerage conditions "would be difficult for our countrymen to tolerate," and even the budding "China hands" of the Tōa Dōbun Shoin agreed that steerage travel was an excessive hardship.[95] This policy suggests a view of colonial prestige in which interaction with the Chinese was acceptable within certain limits, but in ßwhich neither Japanese nor Europeans could afford to appear completely déclassé.

Beyond the policies of the Japanese company, the experiences of Japanese steamship passengers suggest some fluidity and variability in the racial order in semi-colonial China. Japanese travelers found themselves treated as colonial elites in some situations and as racialized "others" at other times. Japanese travelers were a common presence in the foreign first class of all companies' steamships in the late nineteenth and early twentieth centuries.[96] The captain in the 1879 Cheong Wan case suggested that Japanese passengers were simply outside of the category of persons with whom proximity was a problem: when pressed to explain why he had allowed two Japanese passengers to eat at the cabin table, he replied, "I could not say if they were Japanese—I did not ask them. They were not Chinese; they had not tails."[97] Without this visible mark of "John Chinaman," in other words, he inquired no further. In many other situations, Japanese were considered the nationals of a treaty power and thus members of the "foreign community": Japanese residents of Shanghai, for example, were permitted entry to the Shanghai Public Garden from which Chinese were so famously excluded.[98] Japanese steamship passengers could not always rely on such treatment. In the case of the separated European husband and Japanese wife discussed earlier, the wife was put in the Chinese first class, suggesting that the restriction of "foreign" passengers to the foreign first class did not necessarily apply to her. A Japanese woman traveling among Chinese passengers was not as much of a problem as a European doing the same or the spectacle of an interracial couple traveling together.[99] A group of Tōa Dōbun Shoin students reported a much starker example of racial exclusion in 1923. Turned away from the foreign first class on a British ship, they were told that "Orientals" (*tōyōjin*) were not allowed in the accommodation. As the author of this account explained, the students boarded the ship because the Nisshin ship by which they intended to travel was delayed. Although the writer identified the incident as an encounter with racial prejudice, he showed little solidarity with Chinese passengers receiving the same treatment, and concluded that he would patronize Japanese ships exclusively in the future.[100]

The management of the foreign first class in the China Merchants Company resembled the employment of European technical personnel on its ships. Both practices highlight the complex position of the Qing-flag company in its collaborative relations with the other conference firms, in that there were numerous pressures for it to reproduce rather than challenge prevailing practices in the shipping field. In the case of its management of its foreign first class, where it was not possible for the China Merchants Company to replicate the other firms' practices, its managers were made painfully aware of how this discrepancy fueled the impression of not only the company's but the Chinese people's deficiencies.

China Merchants' ships maintained a foreign first class set apart in amenities and price, and it was overseen by the company's predominantly

European captains. Yet because of the company's affiliation with the Qing government, it routinely offered free foreign first-class passage to officials, and thus many of the passengers in this class were Chinese. The 1896 Nagoya survey distinguished the China Merchants Company as the only firm that did not turn passengers "in Chinese dress" away from its foreign first class.[101] A slightly later Japanese survey (1903) reported that the China Merchants foreign first class was very unpopular among European travelers because the food was not to their tastes and there were too many Chinese passengers in it.[102]

It may seem logical that in a Qing-flag firm, the most expensive class of travel catered to the Qing elite, but the implicit commensurability of the conference companies meant that their practices and facilities were inevitably compared to each other. The company's first class was found wanting, and not just from the perspective of European travelers. China Merchants manager Zheng Guanying targeted the management of the company's foreign first class in his famous essay collection *Warnings to a Prosperous Age*, objecting to how it fueled rather than counteracted stereotypes of Chinese deficiency.

Zheng complained that company policy provided government officials with whom it had even the remotest connection free passage in the foreign first class and furthermore extended a free Chinese-class ticket to a friend or family member of the traveling official. These "guests," he argued, spent the duration of the journey in the saloon, where they ruined its atmosphere with their loud chatter and habit of spitting on the carpet. Such behavior, Zheng contended, was the reason that China Navigation excluded Chinese passengers from its foreign first class.[103] Implicitly, the problem he identifies is not that the company admitted Chinese passengers to this class but that it admitted too many of the wrong kind of Chinese passengers to maintain the expected atmosphere, a standard that Zheng appears to accept. The deficient conditions of the China Merchants foreign first class were visible to these other companies and in turn enabled exclusion on their ships. As much as this very text was an inspiration to later nationalists and revolutionaries, Zheng composed this critique from within the parameters of the shipping field.

Across the shipping field, the foreign first class was a space in which race and racial proximity in semi-colonial China were expressed and managed, even as they may have been unspoken or unacknowledged. This space was neither fully segregated nor open to all who wished to pay the considerable fare. Although there were variations in how the steamship companies of different nationalities approached this space, none could be said to have escaped the impact of colonial ideas of race. It was perhaps a sign of the foreign first class's exclusivity that it generated relatively little commentary from Chinese passengers and in the Chinese media. In contrast, the Chinese accommodation elicited far more critique, resistance, and interpretation.

Interpreting Steamship Space: The Chinese Accommodation as Alienated Space

Absent from the foregoing account of company practices and structural factors that shaped the social space of the steamship is an explanation of how these spaces were perceived and interpreted by those who used them. Although the possibilities for interpreting the space are only limited by the numbers of people who experienced it, there are some interpretations that appear repeatedly in travel writing or the press that provide a view into how these spaces were understood. One such interpretation, originating from literati journalists in Shanghai in the last three decades of the nineteenth century, stands out both because it was highly critical of the Chinese accommodation for its absence of social order and because it anticipated many of the key issues behind a nationalist-inspired reform of the steamship space in the late 1920s and 1930s.

The literati journalists' view can be contrasted with the foreign travelers' descriptions, which generally fit easily into the "world in miniature" interpretation of the space. For foreign passengers who wrote about their travels, the steamship space appears only to confirm their perceptions of society and the world outside the ship. The luxury, comfort, and relative isolation of their quarters reinforced the idea that the foreign passengers were separate from and more privileged than the masses of Chinese passengers. In the words of one passenger, "the voyager forgets that he is sailing up the central stream of a heathen and semi-civilized empire," and in the words of another, the luxurious quarters were a "visible sign that our lives were pitched in pleasant places."[104] One author described his own quarters as "a little niche where three or four Europeans can be accommodated, with a comfort and cleanliness upon which Englishmen will insist, as we have taught the Chinese at whatever trouble or cost."[105]

Because foreign passengers could move freely among all of the passenger classes on steamships, for them steamship travel was often an opportunity to observe Chinese passengers at close range. Foreign passengers' observations on such forays into the Chinese accommodation provided glimpses of Chinese life that tended to reinforce stereotypical vices and conditions. Isabella Bird described walking "past the Chinese cabins, where the inmates were reclining in the bliss of opium smoke, the faint, sickly smell of the drug drifting out at the open doors."[106] Japanese educator Nakano Kozan ventured below several times to observe the Chinese saloon, commenting on passengers exterminating lice in their clothing, sleeping on any available surface, and gambling intently, stopping only to dispute the results of their games. On one occasion, he was drawn by the noise and laughter coming from the Chinese saloon, and discovered a party in progress in which young female musicians were entertaining male passengers.[107] For neither observer does the visit to the Chinese accommodation furnish any unexpected information; it instead allows them to witness activities that confirm their understanding of "the Chinese." Chinese passengers without foreign first-class tickets were barred from that accommodation, so they had no opportunity to observe the foreign first class.

Contrasting sharply with the assurance in these travelers' interpretations of the steamship space was the disquiet the space produced in the writings of Chinese journalists in the *Shen bao* and other Shanghai publications in the late nineteenth century. These journalists were classically educated men who found work in Shanghai's publishing world and produced occasional essays and editorials on steamship travel between 1870 and 1900.[108] Their articles addressed a variety of topics related to travel, yet their interpretations of the steamship space were remarkably consistent over time: the steamship space continually challenged their expectations of social order. For these writers, the steamship was not so much a social space as a social vacuum, in which familiar order and lines of authority were suspended rather than enforced.

Most of these writers wrote from the perspective of a steerage passenger and did not particularly attend to the presence of foreign passengers or the stratification of passenger classes. They readily acknowledged the speed, convenience, and economy of steamship travel, but they were highly critical of conditions on board the ships. They provide detailed descriptions of the overcrowding, poor food and service, and heat and noise of travel and painstakingly identify the annoyances and crimes that passengers might encounter: thefts, swindles, and demands for extra payments or tips. Some articles implied differential treatment between Chinese and foreign passengers by noting the lack of facilities for Chinese passengers boarding and disembarking from steamships and observing that steamship crews ignored Chinese passengers in accidents.[109] In many of these pieces, the writers express the expectation that it is the responsibility of an authority—whether the steamship company or the government—to restore order to this space. They express bewilderment at the apparent lack of concern for order in this space and offer concrete suggestions for how to achieve it.

Numerous journalists observed that many of the dangers to steamship passengers were exacerbated by the permeability and anonymity of the passenger space. Thieves, touts, and other unsavory characters could board ships easily, disappear into the crowds of passengers, and disembark at the next stop.[110] Such crowded and anonymous conditions could complicate one's assessment of fellow passengers, as they were not always who they seemed to be. Editorials warned passengers to be on guard for a racket in which well-dressed thieves wandered throughout the Chinese passenger accommodation on the pretext of looking for friends.[111] Wu Jianren (1866–1910) described this type of robbery in the 1909 novel *Strange Events Witnessed over Twenty Years*, in which a thief dressed as an official nearly escapes detection.[112] Most of the articles that described the anonymity of the space urged the steamship companies to adopt effective methods of recording and supervising passengers.[113] In an 1876 article, one journalist recommended that the companies employ a system like that of the traditional Yangzi River junk *hongs*, which kept records of passengers' names and the purposes of their journeys. The junks' regular stops at Domestic Customs barriers en route allowed for greater official surveillance of passengers.[114] Although this writer acknowledges that steamship travel is far more convenient and cheaper than junk transport, he is nostalgic for the order of the earlier system.

The literati journalists also expressed alarm at how the speed with which steamships moved from port to port complicated the enforcement of Qing laws and regulations. The role of steamships in human trafficking, particularly the kidnapping of children to sell into prostitution, was addressed repeatedly in these writings. Journalists pointed out that once a kidnapper boarded a steamship with his or her victims, it was nearly impossible for the authorities from the original locality to trace them.[115] Government measures to curb the trade in women and girls required female passengers to present a pass signed by a prefect, but this measure was not enforced on Yangzi steamships.[116] The rapid removal of a person from one area of jurisdiction to another impeded other types of criminal prosecutions as well: one article cited the case of a merchant who, finding himself deeply in debt to creditors in Shanghai, simply jumped on a steamship bound upriver and was never found again.[117] For these writers, the mobility of steamships created a challenge to the enforcement of Qing laws, as they could remove criminals quickly from the scenes of their crimes (see fig. 4.4).

In the press, the journalists struggled to find explanations for the suspension of order on steamships. An 1876 *Shen bao* article speculated that the disorder of the steamship space was the result of a clash between Westerners' preference for as few rules as possible and a Chinese preference for rules for every contingency.[118] A decade later, another *Shen bao* writer rejected such an explanation. Having traveled in Europe himself, he had observed the careful enforcement of rules and regulations there that allowed large groups to travel together with ease and concluded that the chaos on steamships in China could not be attributed to European preferences or unfamiliarity with China. Instead, this writer blamed the companies, expressing outrage that they had failed to respond to repeated complaints about travel conditions in the press. He questioned why no one took responsibility for these conditions and berated the China Merchants Company for failing to respond to Chinese passengers' complaints.[119] Over time, the initial confusion with the reasons for the disorder aboard steamships gave way to a more jaded position in which these writers began to see the space as simply beyond the care or regard of anyone in a position to change it. The chaotic conditions of the Chinese accommodation and the utter failure of either state or company to address repeated

爭歸樂土
同文滬報隨報附送不准另售畫報

FIGURE 4.4 Steamships were often used to flee areas of conflict. Evacuation of Tianjin during the Boxer Uprising. *Tongwen Hu bao sui bao*, n.d. Courtesy of the Tōyō Bunko, Tokyo.

complaints and concerns made this an alienated space—not merely outside of expected structures of authority but truly beyond their reach.

Two elements of the shipping field exacerbated the alienated quality of this space: the extraterritorial status of foreign-flag ships and the ship comprador's management of the Chinese accommodation. The comprador provides the most straightforward explanation for the journalists' common complaints about their travel experiences, but the extraterritorial status of foreign-flag ships can account for the limited exercise of landed authority on steamships the journalists also perceived. Technically, ships' extraterritoriality meant that neither Qing law nor Qing officials had jurisdiction on board: the ship's interior space and all of the people on board (regardless of their individual nationalities) came under the laws of the nation under whose flag the ship sailed. In H. B. Morse's (1855–1934) words, "a British ship in Chinese waters is British soil."[120] The

Treaty of Tianjin had tempered the more extreme possibilities for ships' extraterritoriality to challenge Qing sovereignty by permitting Qing authorities to remove Qing subjects suspected of criminal activity from foreign-flag ships with a warrant from the relevant consul.[121] A similar practice governed cases in which foreign nationals committed crimes on steamships under other national flags—such as a French national committing a crime on a British ship. In such cases, the British consul had to be notified so he could formally disclaim jurisdiction and remand the offender to the French consular court.[122]

The enforcement of these rules in practice left a narrow window of time that could be exploited to evade the arresting authority. The time needed to obtain consular warrants could give those running afoul of the law in one location an opportunity to escape via steamship. Although it may not have been an everyday occurrence, there were several examples discussed in the Shanghai press. In addition to the one mentioned already, an annotated illustration in the *Dianshizhai Pictorial* told the story of a detective in Shanghai's French concession who captured a notorious thief specializing in steamship robberies. Promising to identify his accomplices, the thief led the detective to the docks, where he jumped on a departing British steamer and escaped upriver.[123] In this case, the detective did not have the time to obtain the necessary warrant before the ship was long gone. Another example of ships' extraterritoriality providing a margin of relief from local jurisdiction can be seen in a case from 1915, when Chinese officials in Hankou complained to the British consul-general that sailors and teaboys were flouting a government ban by bringing "guests" onto a British-flag ship in port to smoke opium. Although the consul-general insisted that the British shipping firms were committed to enforcing the opium ban on their ships, the ship had already served as a temporary refuge from the prohibition.[124] Extraterritoriality was probably only an occasional contributor to the disorder of the Chinese accommodation, but it may also explain the difficulties in enforcing Qing laws—like the antitrafficking measures that required a prefectural pass—on board foreign-flag steamships.

The management of the Chinese accommodation by ship compradors can account for the majority of the journalists' complaints about poor conditions and permeability and anonymity of the space. As described earlier, imperatives to maximize earnings from the passenger business were built into compradors' contracts, encouraging them to perpetuate overcrowding, minimal service, and generally poor conditions in the Chinese accommodation. Compradors had little interest in keeping careful accounts of passengers, particularly if they habitually underreported passenger earnings to the companies. Although the chaotic conditions and many of the dangers of steamship travel were directly related to the compradors' management of the space, the use of compradors alone does not explain the literati journalists' central question of why the *companies* never exercised more stewardship over the Chinese accommodation. At the very least, companies might have pressured or incentivized compradors to attend to the repeated complaints and demands of passengers.

Two aspects of compradorial management provide some insight as to why the companies maintained such a distance from the concerns of Chinese passengers. First, it was not difficult for compradors to lose control over the spaces of their ships. They collected fees from vendors, teaboys, or even thieves in exchange for the permission to ply their trades on the ship, and having paid the fees, these tradesmen often considered themselves the ships' permanent residents, resisting any attempts to control or dislodge them. In one case from 1901, China Navigation managers learned that their ships had the worst reputation for robberies on the Yangzi River and urged their compradors to take action against the thieves. The effort was a failure—the managers soon learned that the compradors had been so intimidated by the thieves' gangs on the ships that they refused to testify in court.[125] The company might apply pressure, but the comprador could not necessarily control the space. Second, the accommodation was run by a Chinese comprador who presumably catered to the needs of Chinese passengers, thus the conditions in the Chinese accommodation were easily naturalized as the "preferences" of these travelers. When foreign observers remarked on the clearly substandard conditions in the Chinese accommodation, they often attributed them to preference. In explaining how compradors packed passengers into the accommodation, for example, a China Navigation captain remarked that Chinese passengers "had a fairly thin time of it," but added: "But Chinese passengers were basically quite happy. As long as they were moving they didn't seem to object to being crowded in if they'd got a bit of security. I think they felt more secure in a crowd, but it's not the sort of thing that anybody not used to it would like. Basically I would imagine that's one of the things where we differ. We're used to spreading out and they're used to closing ranks."[126] In later years, the continued association of the conditions in this space with "Chineseness" became a point of resistance for Chinese nationalists.

The literati journalists' identification of this alienated space certainly did not represent all possible views of the Chinese accommodation. As a group, these journalists seem particularly underwhelmed by its freewheeling atmosphere and any potential for pleasure therein. From highly cultured backgrounds but traveling on steerage-level budgets, these writers perhaps did not represent most steamship passengers. Yet they had a ready platform to communicate their ideas, and their view of the Chinese accommodation as alienated space shared much with later commentaries that prompted dramatic transformations of the steamship space in the late 1920s and 1930s. In this later period, the social space of the steamship became a means through which to voice critiques of semi-colonialism and implement new visions for China. The clearest object of these reforms was not the racial stratification of the passenger space but the alienated space of the Chinese accommodation, and this alienated space was a crucial point from which the uniformity of the shipping field began to unravel.

Mohandas K. Gandhi (1869–1948) voiced a nearly identical critique of steamship accommodations in a 1917 letter to the British India Steam Navigation Company. Gandhi, recently returned to India from South Africa, presented a list of fourteen complaints about the treatment of passengers in the British India Company's deck accommodation, which like the Chinese steerage class was the least expensive of its passenger classes but the one from which it earned the most revenue.[127] Gandhi complained of overcrowding, filthy conditions, and the lack of privacy for female deck passengers, but what appeared to vex him the most was the lack of recourse for these passengers. He detailed the complete disregard of the crew members or other company employees of the needs of these passengers: no company employee on board would receive his complaints, and passengers had to bribe crew members to receive the most basic of amenities or to escape abuse at their hands.[128] For Gandhi as well as the literati journalists, the troubling feature of this space was not merely its terrible conditions but the complete lack of oversight of the space and the passengers. Both expected the ships to exercise some form of governmentality, and the source of their outrage was the evident exclusion of native passengers from it.

After the turn of the twentieth century, more explicitly nationalist interpretations of the steamship space began to address the presence of foreigners and the stratification of the passenger classes on board. In such interpretations, it is the tangible, concrete hierarchy of the passenger classes on the ship that forces the observer to confront China's national predicament and oppression. In some narratives, the recognition of the meaning of the passenger classes is depicted as a moment of conversion or awakening to the nationalist cause; some writers even depicted steamship journeys as the precise moment they literally and figuratively emerged from the provinces to be initiated into national consciousness. An example is the autobiography of Deng Xihua (Tan Shi-hua), which describes a steamship journey from Chongqing to Shanghai as the transition between his childhood in Sichuan to his life as a student in Beijing and later in the Soviet Union. In his narrative, Deng's observation of the hierarchy of passenger classes on the steamship puts his childhood experience of oppression into a larger and more systemic perspective. As a child, Deng and his family had suffered at the hands of a wealthy relative he called "Dog's Head." On the steamship, Deng finds that Dog's Head can be fitted into an even larger scheme of oppressors: "Mandarins and manufacturers traveled first class. Dog's Head and his partners traveled this way. But there was a class superior to first class—on the top decks of some of the steamers were special cabins for foreigners. Even Dog's Head would not have been allowed to go there, no matter how much money he was willing to pay."[129] Like other Chinese writers' accounts of conversion to nationalist or radical politics following an encounter with the famous (but likely apocryphal) "No Dogs or Chinese Allowed" sign in the Shanghai Public Garden, this account makes the steamship the point at which the "true" condition of the nation and the Chinese people is revealed.[130]

Neither the interpretation of the Chinese accommodation as alienated space nor the nationalist mapping of the passenger classes see the social space of the steamship as a familiar microcosm of landed world or a world in miniature. For both, the steamship space is a heterotopia, causing the observer to question their own understanding of social relations, whether through the confusion and dismay of the Shanghai journalists or the shock of the obviousness of its hierarchies to budding nationalists. In Foucault's words, the ships "expose[d] every real space."[131] In the late 1920s and 1930s, these spaces became the targets of nationalist reformers who sought to remake them along lines that corresponded to their visions of China's future.

The social space as the steamship stands as an important reminder that semi-colonial China did not stand outside of the colonial world. These ships that circulated throughout China projected through their spaces of work and travel racial categories and hierarchies that were completely continuous with those in other contexts. The world the steamship projected was perhaps not easily visible everywhere in China—but its tense and confounding relationship to landed realities made it a powerful symbol of the nation's predicament. Steamships encompassed both public spaces—open to all who could afford a ticket—and intimate, communal spaces that prioritized the maintenance of racial and social norms. Within them, racial categories and questions of proximity could be neither fully acknowledged nor fully disavowed. The world that they reflected was more that of the exclusive social spaces of foreign communities in the treaty ports, yet the steamship brought it out of such enclaves and into a larger public view, allowing the steamship space to represent China's geopolitical condition.[132]

The social space also demonstrates how foreign domination in shipping was not simply a matter of a majority of foreign flags or tonnage on the Yangzi River and coast; it also lay in the strong influence the existing modes of organization and management practices had in the shipping field as new companies joined it. The social space was shaped by the powerful position and precedence of the foreign companies and the predominance of British shipping worldwide. The case of the China Merchants Company shows that not all companies replicated British practices precisely, but the inequalities of the field made it difficult to break completely from them. In the shipping field, the conference system could operate as a disciplining force—its claim that all ships within it were interchangeable provided a disincentive for companies to innovate in their management or in the social space of their ships.

CHAPTER 5

Shipping Nationalism

The Politics and Business of Shipping in China's Early Republic, 1912–27

The early Republic (1912–27) was the period in which shipping in Chinese waters became closely intertwined with the movement for China's national independence and opposition to foreign imperialism. This shipping nationalism was not simply the adoption of nationalist rhetoric by the shipping business but a wider response to new conditions in the semi-colonial system and the shipping field. Shipping nationalism bound the political and business spheres closely together: advocates of an autonomous Chinese nation were deeply concerned by the foreign-dominated shipping business, and the new Chinese shipping entrepreneurs of this period were similarly engaged in the push for an autonomous nation.

In the early Republic, the semi-colonial order transformed as the collaboration that had long been central to the operation of the treaty system broke down. This shift was precipitated by the disintegration of a central Chinese government. The system established by the 1860 Treaty of Tianjin relied on the central government of the Qing dynasty to enforce treaty terms. After the new Republican regime passed to former Qing official and would-be emperor Yuan Shikai and the political authority subsequently splintered into the battling militarist regimes of the Warlord Era, this central indigenous authority disappeared. Although individual instances of collaboration—such as between a foreign power and a militarist regime—occurred during this period, the form of collaboration that underlay the treaty system could no longer function.

The breakdown of this collaborative mechanism had a range of effects on the semi-colonial order in China. The first was the halting of the momentum of foreign expansion into Chinese territory. As the center disintegrated, the treaty powers moved quickly to secure control over the Maritime Customs and salt revenue, guaranteeing the payment of indemnities owed to them, but they did not continue to push for new privileges and concessions in the same way they had during the last decades of the Qing dynasty. The European powers' preoccupation with World War I is often credited with diverting their attention from expansion in China, but viewed from the perspective of conditions in China itself, the pursuit of new concessions was not worthwhile if there were no reliable means of enforcing them throughout the country. The treaties remained in force and the powers treated the Beiyang regime as a de facto central government, but they did not press for any shipping concessions during this period beyond an occasional inland waters route.[1]

This suspension of foreign expansion into China might appear to be a reduction of foreign power, but the breakdown of collaboration had the further effect of magnifying the shipping privileges granted to foreigners under the treaty system. In the early Republic, there were very few state protections available to Chinese shipping. Under the previous regime, the Qing state's patronage of the China Merchants Company had ensured that the company was subject to the same conditions of mobility and taxation as the foreign firms with which it competed. With the disintegration of the central government, Chinese shipping firms were subject to taxation and military interference from multiple warlord regimes while extraterritorial privilege exempted foreign firms from these obstructions. The inequities between foreign and Chinese shipping had become more apparent and the conflict between these interests much more distinct.

A final effect of the breakdown of the earlier form of collaboration under the treaty system was the diffusion of resistance to the foreign presence throughout Chinese society. During the Qing, officials had monopolized the terms of resistance to foreign expansion, but by the early Republic this role had been extended to a much broader range of actors in Chinese society. The growing popular nationalist movement mobilized the efforts of intellectuals, workers, business elites, and at times militarist regimes. Strikes, boycotts, and other protests could force practical reductions of foreign privilege in specific cases and confrontations. At the same time, the absence of a reliable government collaborator made it more difficult to achieve treaty revision on a diplomatic level. The Beiyang government's uncertain hold on the political center severely limited its ability to advocate for the revision or revocation of existing treaty terms.

Dimensions of early Republican shipping nationalism can be viewed through four significant developments: the evolution of a discourse of shipping rights recovery as a way to articulate shipping nationalism's aspirations; the emergence of a new generation of private, Chinese-flag shipping firms on the major routes of the Yangzi and coast; the weakening effect of nationalist politics on the conference system; and the consensus among important Chinese shipping entrepreneurs of the period on the best way to develop their businesses in the service of the nation.

The discourse of shipping rights recovery (*shouhui hangquan*) framed the objectives of the anti-imperialist movement in shipping. This discourse emphasized the notion that the presence and privilege of foreign-flag shipping in Chinese waters was a violation of national sovereign rights. Rights recovery discourse originated with the elite activism of the late Qing and encompassed the ideas that the treaty clauses that granted foreign ships the right to navigate China's coastal and inland waters were violations of international law and practice, and that China was capable of meeting its own shipping needs. Although there was minimal progress toward the goals of shipping rights recovery in the early Republic, this discourse was an essential means of expressing shipping nationalism and after 1927 became an important element of the Nationalist government's program of treaty revision.

A new generation of private Chinese-flag firms became participants in coastal and river steam networks between 1912 and 1927. Some of these companies derived from late Qing inland waters shipping ventures and late Qing rights recovery projects; many were aided by the new opportunities for Chinese businesses that arose during World War I. This group of shipping firms were able to reach a size and scale that allowed them to break into the river and coastal routes that were formerly the preserve of the conference companies and compete directly against foreign firms. After World War I ended, competition between Chinese and foreign shipping interests redoubled as foreign shipping companies further extended their fleets in Chinese waters. The combination of the growth and diversity of Chinese shipping companies and the aggressive expansion of foreign companies made the conflict between Chinese and foreign interests in the shipping field far clearer than it had been in the past when Chinese interests were represented only by the China Merchants Company.

Under such conditions, nationalist politics helped Chinese ship owners resist the pressures of the conference system. Foreign firms enjoyed newly visible extraterritorial protections, but the popular nationalist movement targeted and often boycotted foreign-flag ships and shipping companies as symbols of foreign power in China. These boycotts in turn could provide unprecedented opportunities for Chinese companies to gain new market share or expand. Although the shipping conference led by the Three Companies persisted on the Yangzi and coast, such incidents made it difficult for the conference to dictate terms as it had in the past. The conference companies remained the most powerful within the network and continued to forge agreements on rates and tonnage, but the conference was no longer able to compel new firms to accept subordinate status within the organization or maintain the kind of control that it had over major shipping routes in the past.

Given these circumstances, it is not surprising that Chinese shipping entrepreneurs of the early Republic often presented themselves as nationalists. Examining the leaders of three of the most significant Chinese shipping companies of this period shows that their nationalist commitment was more than a convenient pose. All three men shared a consistent set of concerns and practices that indicates agreement over the role of enterprise in the constructions of an autonomous nation. All three companies established connections between semirural hinterland areas and treaty ports and contributed to the economic and cultural modernization of these areas. In their shipping businesses, they prioritized expansion as a means of competing with foreign firms and sought state patronage for aid in this effort. These entrepreneurs and their businesses lend some historical validity to the category "national capitalist" in describing some members of the pre-1949 bourgeoisie—a term that has been dismissed as primarily a political label—and furnish examples of individual proponents of shipping nationalism.

Shipping Rights Recovery in the Late Qing and Early Republic

In the early Republic, shipping rights recovery became the predominant means of articulating nationalist opposition to foreign domination in shipping. This discourse targeted treaty clauses that granted the ships of foreign powers the right to participate in China's coastal and inland shipping. Invoking concepts from international law, advocates argued that these clauses violated China's sovereign right to reserve coastal navigation for ships under its own flag. They also asserted the need for shipping autonomy in China: rather than depend on foreign-flag shipping, the nation had the potential to develop shipping sufficient to meet its own needs.

The discourse of shipping rights recovery emerged from the late Qing dynasty. At the founding of the China Merchants Company, Li Hongzhang and others described the company's purpose as the "recovery of profits" (*shouhui liquan*) for the Qing polity. This idea presumed that the wealth that could be taken back from competition with foreign shipping firms belonged to the dynasty. In the dynasty's last years, however, gentry, merchant, and some official activists began to agitate for the "recovery" of concessions that had been ceded to the foreign powers. These concessions were most often railway building rights or mining rights in a particular locality obtained during the treaty powers' rush for concessions after 1895. These elite activists used the terms "railway rights recovery" (*shouhui luquan*) or "mining rights recovery" (*shouhui kuangquan*) to refer to actions intended to block foreign interests from taking possession of newly obtained concessions.[2] Activists often formed their own railway and mining companies that either bought out foreign concerns or preempted their railway or mining projects with competing concerns.[3] The rights these activists worked to recover were initially to a particular parcel of land. Over time, their writings began to connect railway and mining rights and the more abstract sovereign rights of a nation struggling under foreign aggression.[4]

By the last years of the Qing dynasty, rights recovery activists' opposition to foreign expansion into Qing territory had transformed into disillusionment with the dynasty for its failure to check that expansion, and rights recovery movements became sites of anti-Qing opposition. In several provinces, railway rights recovery activists protested the government's decision to use foreign loans to finance railway construction. When the Qing Ministry of Posts and Communications tried to exert centralized control over the nation's railways in 1906, railway rights recovery groups defied its orders. In Sichuan Province, the same ministry's attempt to nationalize the Sichuan Railway in 1911 caused the activists to declare the province's independence from Qing authority.[5] In the last years of the Qing, rights recovery discourse had moved from a focus on the return of specific concessions to a more explicit defense of the need for China to resist foreign interference.

Although not as well known as efforts in railways or mining, shipping was another arena of rights recovery activism in the late Qing. Activists started new shipping companies to pursue rights recovery, either undermining foreign domination on a particular route or preventing foreign shipping from extending into a new area. Many of the late-Qing shipping rights recovery projects were closely linked to provincial railway rights recovery efforts.

One example of such a linkage was the Ning-Shao (Ningbo-Shaoxing) Steamship Company, established in 1908. This company was founded by Yu Xiaqing, a comprador for the Netherlands Bank and director of the famous Ningbo native-place association in Shanghai, the Siming Gongsuo. Yu and several of his associates were active in Zhejiang Province's railway rights recovery movement as founders and directors of the Zhejiang Railway Company, established in 1905 to prevent British construction of a rail line between Hangzhou and Ningbo.[6] The steamship company was established to provide fellow provincial sojourners in Shanghai an alternative to the shipping services of the conference companies.

Since Zhejiangese sojourners had long relied on steamship travel between Shanghai and the cities of Ningbo and Shaoxing, the Shanghai–Ningbo route was one of the most lucrative passenger routes in the steam network. Since the 1880s it had been divided between the China Navigation and China Merchants Companies, and both charged high fares. In 1906, when the French Compagnie Asiatique de Navigation tried to enter this route, fares dropped precipitously. Yu Xiaqing, acting on behalf of the Ningbo Sojourners' Association, tried to secure a promise from the companies to maintain fares at this low level, but when the French company withdrew from the route, the conference companies tripled their fares. Yu turned to the Ningbo and Shaoxing communities in Shanghai for capital to start a new steamship company. When the Ning-Shao Company began operation in 1908, the conference companies again reduced fares.[7] To ensure Ning-Shao's survival, its managers recruited more than 100 prominent Ningbo and Shaoxing merchants to form the Ning-Shao Shipping Protection Association. The association contributed funds to compensate the company for its losses in the rate war and help keep its ships on the line.[8]

Yu Xiaqing and his colleagues drew on their experience in the Zhejiang railway rights recovery movement to mobilize fellow provincials to support a new company's opposition to the conference companies. In going up against the conference firms, the new company mobilized national and provincial loyalties. Shanghai's Ningbo elites were hostile to the British company and the Guangdong-based management of the China Merchants Company, the latter for its treatment of Ningbo-based junks and Ningbonese steamship crews.[9] After 1911, the Ning-Shao Company became a permanent presence on this and other steamship routes, and Yu Xiaqing emerged as one of China's best-known shipping entrepreneurs.

Another example, the Chuanjiang ("Sichuan Rivers") Steamship Company, was established by Qing officials and Sichuanese gentry to prevent the expansion of foreign shipping onto the Upper Yangzi River. Like Ning-Shao, Chuanjiang was also related to provincial railway rights recovery efforts. In 1903, Sichuan Governor-General Xiliang (1853–1917) proposed to build a railway connecting Hankou (then emerging as China's railway hub) to Chengdu, Sichuan's provincial capital. This was to be a provincial railway financed through voluntary contributions from officials, gentry, and merchants that would also bar British, French, and U.S. companies from building railways in Sichuan.[10] News of the railway temporarily halted experiments in Upper Yangzi steam navigation, but the slow progress of railway construction soon revived interest in it.[11] When several foreign companies proposed schemes to navigate this route, Xiliang's successor, Zhao Erfeng (1845–1911), founded a steamship company to block them.[12] The Chuanjiang Company (1908) was financed with contributions from officials, merchants, and gentry, using some of the funds originally collected for the railway.[13] It pioneered the first Upper

Yangzi ship with enough cargo space to turn a profit.[14] From 1909 to 1914, this ship, the *Shutong*, was the sole steamship working between Yichang and Chongqing. Because it dramatically reduced the time needed for upriver and downriver voyages, it commanded extremely high freights. The Hankou–Chengdu railway was never completed, but the Chuanjiang Company helped keep commercial steam navigation on the Upper Yangzi under Chinese control until the early 1920s.

In the last years of the Qing dynasty, the discourse of shipping rights recovery was evident even in situations that did not result in founding a new company. The small Chinese-owned shipping firms emerging on inland routes at this time often flew foreign flags to avoid local exactions, but in areas that had been mobilized by rights recovery efforts, the reversion to a Chinese flag could be a powerful gesture. A Maritime Customs survey of shipping on the West River remarked on the sharp increase in the number of steamships flying Chinese flags after 1907, which it attributed to ship owners' desire to benefit from the popular agitation to "take back" the West River from foreign ships.[15]

Shipping rights recovery ideas even permeated the China Merchants Company. As early as 1909, China Merchants shareholders began to argue that official involvement in the company inhibited its ability to compete with foreign concerns.[16] After 1911, the company's elected board of directors resisted an effort by Yuan Shikai to place official appointees in the company. The board published a notice in the *Shen bao*, pointedly comparing Yuan's actions to the late Qing effort to nationalize the railways and describing its own efforts to keep the company independent of government control as "saving shipping rights." Yuan responded that the board was "stealing shipping rights."[17] The board prevailed in this conflict, and after four decades of "official supervision," the China Merchants Company became a private enterprise run by its shareholders.

The late Qing rights recovery movement bridged the ideas of taking back specific concessions from foreign interests and recovering sovereign rights lost through the unequal treaties. Particularly in the years after World War I, rights recovery became one of the arguments for treaty revision. Embracing Woodrow Wilson's doctrines of the self-determination of nations, diplomats and lawyers argued for the abrogation of those treaty clauses that violated China's sovereignty as an equal member of the "family of nations" in international venues such as the Paris Peace Conference

(1919) and the Washington Conference (1921–22).[18] In the context of treaty revision, shipping rights recovery advocates highlighted those treaty clauses that granted foreign ships the right to participate in China's coastal and inland shipping because such clauses violated China's sovereign right to reserve its coastal navigation for ships under its own flag. Although the Beiyang government was limited in its ability to forward this agenda through diplomatic channels, after 1916 it consistently refused to grant inland navigation rights to countries seeking treaty relations with China.[19]

Implicit in the argument for shipping rights recovery was an argument for shipping autonomy: the contention that China could fulfill its own shipping needs without foreign involvement. Since in the initial days of the Republic, Chinese-flag shipping was limited to the China Merchants Company and small inland rivers concerns, shipping autonomy was a polemical stance rather than a statement of actual capacity. Over the course of the early Republican period, the sector of private, Chinese-flag shipping expanded substantially, making shipping autonomy a question not of abstract possibility but of choosing concrete policies to support and expand Chinese-flag shipping. Both shipping rights recovery and shipping autonomy were important elements of the Nationalist government's campaign for treaty revision in 1928–31, and the discourse remained a key means of framing and articulating shipping nationalism.

Chinese and Foreign Shipping in Chinese Waters, 1912–27

One of the most evident changes within the steam network between 1911 and 1927 was the emergence of a new generation of private Chinese-flag shipping firms onto the major shipping routes of the river and coast, where they competed directly with the conference companies and other foreign companies. In the last decade of Qing rule, there had been a division of labor in which new, private Chinese-flag companies were concentrated on inland waters routes and the China Merchants Company serviced the major, conference-dominated routes. By the end of World War I, as more and more private Chinese firms entered the important routes of the Yangzi

River and coast, conflict and competition between Chinese and foreign shipping interests became a prominent feature of the shipping field.

To a limited extent, this new Chinese-flag sector can be traced to the conditions of the "Golden Age of the Chinese bourgeoisie," as explained by Marie-Claire Bergère. The Golden Age was a significant expansion of Chinese-owned businesses in many sectors of the economy between 1911–20, attributed to new opportunities brought about by World War I and minimal state involvement in Chinese business and industry. During the war, foreign businesses in China halted or reduced operations, allowing Chinese entrepreneurs to develop substitute industries at a time of increased demand for raw materials abroad and a rise in the value of silver on the world market. During the Warlord Era, there was no state attempt to guide the economy from above as the Qing dynasty had done, which allowed these entrepreneurs to pursue new opportunities without restraint. The Golden Age was primarily a phenomenon of light industry and consumer goods production, but new developments in shipping also stemmed from these conditions.[20]

At the start of World War I, many German, Austrian, British, French, and other European ships withdrew from Chinese waters for war service. The reduction of available tonnage led to a dramatic rise in freight rates, which created opportunities for Chinese companies to access new markets. Between 1911 and 1924, Chinese-flag tonnage doubled from previous levels. Chinese-owned companies entered the major coastal and riverine routes in China and overseas routes to Southeast Asia and Japan. At this time, the development of a Chinese-owned mechanical engineering industry made it possible for Chinese shipping companies to purchase and repair ships without relying on foreign shipbuilders or foreign-owned facilities in treaty ports. In addition, the development of Chinese enterprises in other areas of the economy created further demand for shipping services.[21]

Although these were undeniable gains, many of the achievements of Chinese shipping associated with Golden Age conditions were temporary. Throughout the war, some foreign companies remained active in the network and expanded with even greater force in the immediate postwar period.[22] By 1920, competition on major shipping routes was intense, and survival was an important question for new Chinese companies.

Britain remained the preeminent foreign shipping power in China during and after the war. Although China Navigation and Indo-China sent a combined thirty ships to Europe for wartime service, they were able to augment their fleets in China with captured German ships, particularly on the northern and southern coastal routes and the overseas routes to Southeast Asia, Australia, and Japan.[23] These companies' Yangzi River fleets were not suitable for wartime service, so they remained in China. After the war, between 1920 and 1926, both companies underwent major expansions, China Navigation adding a total of twenty-four new ships and Indo-China acquiring thirteen new ships.[24]

Japanese shipping in China also expanded both during the war and in the immediate postwar period. Because Japan was not directly involved in the fighting in Europe, it committed no ships to the war effort. Japanese companies profited from the withdrawal of other nations' ships from Chinese waters and a general increase in freight rates. During the war, the Nisshin Kisen Kaisha enjoyed record earnings, which it reinvested in its fleet between 1915 and 1927. It built seven new ships for the Yangzi River route and just after the conclusion of the war extended its services to the northern and southern coastal routes, matching the scope of the other conference companies.[25] Nisshin Kisen was also able to use captured German ships to open a direct line between Hankou and Osaka. The expansion of the Nisshin Kisen Kaisha paralleled the international expansion of Japanese shipping more generally, which propelled Japan from the sixth-largest world shipping power to the third. Japan's major overseas shipping lines—the Nippon Yūsen Kaisha and Osaka Shōsen Kaisha—also extended their operations on overseas lines within East Asia as well as on lines to Australia, Europe, and the United States.[26]

U.S.-flag shipping in Chinese waters grew rapidly during the war and immediate postwar periods. At the start of the war, U.S. shipping in China was at its lowest ebb, but the growth of shipbuilding, the availability of former military ships for commercial use, and government support helped it expand, replacing Germany as the third-largest foreign shipping power after Britain and Japan. The Pacific Mail Company and Dollar Line began services between the United States and China in 1916 and 1917. Also in 1917, the Standard Oil Company put ships on the Yangzi

River to distribute oil and kerosene in the Chinese interior. In the postwar period, the Dollar Line and several other small companies extended services onto the Yangzi River.[27]

The wartime conditions and the immediate expansion of foreign shipping after the war left only a narrow window for a Golden Age in Chinese shipping. For example, the China Merchants Company enjoyed a period of high profits during the war that derived from the withdrawal of foreign shipping from the coasts and overseas routes and a general relaxation of competition. Making use of these profits, the China Merchants Company added to its Yangzi fleet, more than doubling the tonnage between 1911 and 1918 and increasing its percentage of the conference companies' total tonnage from 16.2 to 21.5 percent. With the withdrawal of foreign-flag ships from routes between South China and Southeast Asia, China Merchants also profited by chartering ships to Cantonese and Fujianese merchants transporting goods to Southeast Asian ports and began to make plans for its own overseas lines.[28] The company's Southeast Asian chartering business, however, disappeared almost immediately upon the return of foreign ships to these routes around 1919, and the growth of its Yangzi fleet was soon matched by the expansions of the British and Japanese firms. Although the China Merchants Company had the largest Lower Yangzi fleet in the conference in 1925, it was unable to keep pace with the other companies in areas such as connections to overseas lines, coastal shipping, and (as we will see) Upper Yangzi shipping. For the China Merchants Company, therefore, the Golden Age provided a few important opportunities, but any advantages were largely negated by the extension of foreign shipping after the war.

For some newer Chinese companies, the small margins of time or opportunity were sufficient to gain a foothold in routes or trades where there had been little or no Chinese presence before. Even on the Yangzi River route, which saw the least "breathing space" afforded by the withdrawal of foreign ships, the World War I years were a time when new Chinese firms came into direct competition with the long-standing conference companies. These formed the basis of the new generation of Chinese shipping firms in the early Republic.

One Chinese company that was able to leverage Golden Age conditions to expand its services and compete on the Yangzi River was the Dada Shipping Group, part of a complex of industries established by scholar-turned-entrepreneur Zhang Jian (1853–1926) in the late Qing dynasty. Zhang earned a *jinshi* degree in 1894 but, disillusioned by China's defeat in the Sino-Japanese War, refused official appointments and returned to his hometown of Tongzhou in Jiangsu Province. There, he built the Dasheng cotton textile mill (est. 1899) to compete with imported cotton goods. Subsequently, Dasheng became the centerpiece of a group of industries that included salt production, ironworks, machine manufacturing, and shipping.[29] Zhang Jian entered the shipping field in 1900, purchasing a steamship to speed the movement of materials between Shanghai and Tongzhou and later raised capital to form the Dasheng Shipping Company, which provided a regular service between these places. By 1910, he had bought three new ships and renamed the company the Shanghai Dada Steamship Company, which ran its four ships between Tongzhou, Zhenjiang, and Shanghai, a route known as the "Little Yangzi" (*xiao Changjiang*). This company, along with a separate company he established in 1903 to serve inland river ports in the Subei area, formed the Dada Shipping Group. Toward the end of World War I, Dada was able to expand its Yangzi services by buying out a small British firm and by 1921 had nine ships on this route.[30] Although the Little Yangzi only overlapped slightly with the main Yangzi route dominated by the conference companies, it was a significant passenger route on which Dada remained important through the interwar years.

Another Chinese-owned company that became a significant competitor on the Yangzi under Golden Age conditions was the Sanbei Shipping Group, founded by Yu Xiaqing, the Ningbo comprador and merchant who had led the effort to found the Ning-Shao Steamship Company in 1908.[31] After resigning as general manager of Ning-Shao in 1914, Yu started his own steamship company, the Sanbei Wharf Company (Sanbei lunbu gongsi), which by 1916 ran ships between Shanghai, Ningbo, and smaller Zhejiang coastal towns, including Yu's native place of Longshan. In 1918 and 1919, he took advantage of the reduction of foreign ships and high freight rates to expand his enterprise's operations. Yu recruited fresh capital and purchased a number of large ships (over 1,000 tons) to extend Sanbei's services onto the Yangzi River, northern and southern coastal routes, and routes to Southeast Asia and Japan. He consolidated control over the former British-flag Hong'an Steamship Company, a conference affiliate on the Yangzi River between 1884 and 1909, and began running its ships under the Chinese flag.[32] He formed a joint Yangzi River service that used both Sanbei and Hong'an ships.[33] The return of foreign tonnage to China after the war and the subsequent contraction of freight rates left Yu Xiaqing overextended to the point that he asked the Beiyang government for a loan to keep the companies afloat. This loan did not materialize, and Sanbei abandoned its overseas services. It maintained service on the northern and southern coastal routes and its joint Yangzi River service with Hong'an, becoming a consistent competitor on these major domestic routes for the remainder of the Republican period.

Although Yu Xiaqing no longer held a formal position in the Ning-Shao Company after the war, he continued to maintain ties to it. Two of Ning-Shao's ships began to work the Shanghai–Hankou trade around the same time as Sanbei and Hong'an's, and they coordinated departures.[34] In 1920, Yu represented Ning-Shao, Sanbei, and Hong'an in negotiations with the conference companies, reaching an agreement with them on minimum rates for the Yangzi River.[35] Yu Xiaqing's companies were not the only Chinese firms to establish a presence on the main Yangzi line as the result of Golden Age conditions, but his were among the most significant and long-lived.

Although these newer Chinese-flag firms were able to enter major routes like the Yangzi and establish regular presences there, they remained small in comparison with the conference companies. Sanbei was the largest Chinese-flag shipping firm after the China Merchants Company, but its fleet was not even comparable, composed of older, smaller, and less sophisticated ships. A comparison of the fleets of the major firms on the Shanghai–Hankou route in 1927 can illustrate this difference in scale (see table 5.1). China Merchants, Nisshin Kisen, China Navigation, and Indo-China are roughly the same size, with Indo-China trailing slightly in number of ships and tonnage. Sanbei's and Ning-Shao's fleets are significantly smaller.

Zhang Jian's and Yu Xiaqing's companies competed with the conference companies on the Lower Yangzi route; the Upper Yangzi route between Yichang and Chongqing was yet another place in which the conflict between emerging Chinese and expanding foreign shipping interests became pronounced in the early Republic. The development of this route, however, took a somewhat different course than the Golden Age narrative suggests. By the fall of the Qing in 1911, the only steamships on

Table 5.1
Lower Yangzi (Shanghai–Hankou) Fleets, 1927

Company	Number of ships	Tonnage (g.r.t.)
China Merchants	9	27,060
Nisshin Kisen	9	25,839
China Navigation	8	22,433
Indo-China	6	20,534
Sanbei	4	8,276
Ning-Shao	2	5,007

SOURCES: Tōa Dōbunkai, *Shina shobetsu zenshi*, vol. 15, 329–30; Yonesato Monkichi, *Chōkō kō'un shi*, 6, 24–25, 30, 40–41, 51–52, 55–56.

this section of river were those of the Chuanjiang Company, started as part of the late Qing rights recovery effort. After 1911, this company was joined by several other Chinese companies that imitated the design of its ships. The Upper Yangzi was serviced by a number of small Chinese firms that enjoyed very high rates of freight because of the navigational difficulties of this section of river. Some extended further up the Yangzi from Chongqing to Yibin.[36] The potential for profit on the Upper Yangzi soon drew foreign interest: the U.S. Standard Oil and British Asiatic Petroleum Companies put specialized ships that carried oil and kerosene on the Upper Yangzi in 1917, and after the end of the war, no fewer than thirteen foreign firms entered the route, some buying up smaller Chinese concerns. Several of the new foreign-flag firms were bona fide foreign companies—the U.S. Dollar Line, French Union Franco-Chinoise de Navigation, and British Mackenzie & Company invested significant resources in building new ships for this route. Others supplied flags of convenience to Chinese companies seeking protection from the militarist conflicts in the region.[37] In 1922, China Navigation, Indo-China, and the Nisshin Kisen Kaisha entered this trade simultaneously, each putting newly built fleets on the Upper Yangzi and adding smaller ships for the Chongqing–Yibin route.[38] The route was crowded and extremely competitive.

Despite the influx of foreign companies, Chinese-owned firms remained a constant—though unstable—presence in Upper Yangzi shipping. Many of the Chinese firms owned only one or two steamships, and the roster of companies was in constant flux as ships were bought, sold, and put back on the river under different names. There were thirty-two new Upper Yangzi companies established between 1922 and 1927. Eleven flew the Chinese flag, but many, though Chinese-owned, flew foreign flags of convenience.[39]

In the late 1920s, the heavy foreign presence and the instability of Chinese-owned shipping on the Upper Yangzi attracted the concern of Liu Xiang, the military governor of Sichuan Province. With Liu's assistance, a Chinese-owned firm was able to consolidate many of these small firms to form one of the largest Chinese-owned shipping companies on the Yangzi before World War II: the Minsheng Industrial Company. Although Minsheng was formed several years too late to be the product of Golden Age conditions, it became an important competitor, first on the Upper Yangzi and eventually on the whole Yangzi River. It was founded in 1925 by a former teacher and education official named Lu Zuofu in the Jialing River (a tributary of the Yangzi) town of Hechuan, near the treaty port of Chongqing. He raised money among friends, relatives, and former colleagues to establish a shipping company that would provide passenger and cargo services between Hechuan and Chongqing. By 1929, the Minsheng Company had three steamships, which carried goods and passengers on the Jialing and other tributaries, as well as a number of small, intermediate ports on the Yangzi. It attracted Liu Xiang's attention and, with his help, began to expand into a major Yangzi River company.

Although they do not exhaust the roster of new private companies entering important shipping routes in Chinese waters at this time, the emergence of Dada, Sanbei, and Minsheng exemplifies the conditions under which a new generation of private Chinese-owned companies came into direct competition with the well-established conference companies, the majority of which flew foreign flags. Furthermore, after World War I, conditions in the shipping field made evident the struggle between Chinese- and foreign-flag shipping: precisely at the moment the new Chinese firms took their places on major routes, Japanese, British, and U.S. companies initiated yet another wave of rapid expansion into Chinese waters. Competition was intense and the new Chinese firms struggled to survive. Under these difficult conditions, nationalism and nationalist politics became an important resource for the Chinese companies.

Nationalist Politics in the Shipping Business, 1912–27

As significant as the economic conflict between foreign and Chinese shipping in the early Republic was, this conflict also had a distinctly political dimension that affected the interactions between these interests in unprecedented ways. Particularly after the beginning of the Warlord Era, foreign and Chinese shipping companies found themselves with mutually contradictory advantages and disadvantages that stemmed from the political situation of the treaty system in force within a country riven by militarist conflict and voicing nationalist aspirations. Extraterritoriality, for example, protected foreign firms from militarist interference and taxation, yet because these firms were seen to represent the treaty powers in Chinese territory, they were also the targets of nationalist protests and boycotts. Chinese companies might reap some benefit from nationalist actions against their foreign rivals, but their businesses could be easily disrupted by irregular taxation and commandeering of ships by militarist regimes. In such a context, the form of collaboration visible in the conference system of the Qing years was no longer viable. The conference survived the early Republic, remaining an institution of the shipping field, but in a much weakened form from its earlier state.

The conditions of China's Warlord Era transformed the significance of extraterritorial protection for foreign-flag ships. During the Qing dynasty, the only circumstances in which the extraterritorial protection of foreign-flag ships became an issue was when Chinese authorities or the authorities of another power needed to remove suspected criminals from a ship (in which case they needed a warrant from the relevant consul) or when court cases involving ships were prosecuted in consular courts or the Mixed Court. After the outbreak of militarist conflict in 1916, extraterritoriality furnished significant protections to foreign-flag ships. Militarist regimes, large and small, controlled different parts of the country, and each assessed its own taxes and fees. Along the Yangzi River, for example, a steamship might be stopped numerous times by different regimes, its cargo examined, and payments demanded. To prevent such interference, the treaty powers articulated the "principle of immunity from search," which interpreted foreign-flag ships' extraterritorial status to mean that they could be searched and charged duties only by agents of the Maritime Customs.[40] Therefore, foreign companies' ships could pass through militarist-controlled areas unhindered, paying duty only in the treaty ports. As battles between different militarists continued along the Yangzi and in other areas, foreign powers employed their navies to protect shipping under their flag. Naval vessels would often convoy ships under their own flag through unstable areas to prevent them from being attacked or commandeered.[41]

Chinese-flag companies, in contrast, were subject to the infinite variety of taxes and fees and the commandeering of their ships by militarist regimes, which put them at a distinct disadvantage to their foreign competitors. During militarist campaigns in the Yangzi Valley in 1924–25, Chinese river steamers remained anchored in Shanghai out of fear of interference, while foreign-flag steamers continued to run on the river. During the years of the Northern Expedition (1926–27), the businesses of Chinese firms (including that of China Merchants) were continually disrupted by the seizure or commandeering of their ships. Under such conditions, it is not surprising that some Chinese-owned firms adopted flags of convenience to obtain protection.[42] Whereas the extraterritorial status of foreign-flag ships had provided almost no competitive advantage to foreign shipping companies during the Qing dynasty, during the Warlord Era this protection had become an unmistakable privilege.

Although they could avoid interference from warlord regimes, the advantages of foreign shipping companies were checked to some degree by the rise in popular anti-imperialist protest following World War I, in which nationalist boycotts and demonstrations targeted foreign firms. Reminiscent of the Qing-period taboos that guilds organized to protest the practices of particular shipping firms, nationalist groups organized boycotts of the goods and services of particular powers (most often Britain, Japan, or both) in response to what they saw as incidents of foreign aggression against the Chinese nation. A history of the Nisshin Kisen Kaisha details each of the nine "antiforeign" boycotts that targeted its ships between World Wars I and II, noting how the intensity of boycott tactics escalated over time. Initially Chinese merchants refused to ship goods via Japanese ships, and dockworkers were mobilized to refuse to unload them, but later more explicit intimidation and violence was directed at Chinese traveling on Japanese ships, such as the stamping of their clothes with the words "slave of a defeated country" (*wangguo nu*) as they disembarked from Nisshin Kisen ships during a 1923 boycott.[43] Some large-scale nationalist demonstrations, such as those following the 1925 May Thirtieth Incident and during the Northern Expedition, brought the Yangzi River services of China Navigation, Indo-China, and Nisshin Kisen to a stop for several months at a time.[44] In the summer and fall of 1925, the crews of British and Japanese companies went on strike in sympathy with May Thirtieth protesters.[45]

In addition to nationwide protests like those of the May Thirtieth Movement, British and Japanese steamships and steamship companies were also vulnerable to boycotts arising from local incidents that stoked or played on nationalist sentiments. There were numerous incidents in which the armed guards of a foreign steamer killed protesters in a particular port or where a junk sunk in a foreign steamer's wash was interpreted as foreign aggression and resulted in an extended boycott of a company in a particular locality.[46] On the Upper Yangzi, local militarist regimes were often involved in both the precipitating incident and the maintenance of the boycott. In 1921, the Chongqing military government organized a boycott against the British-flag ship *Longmao* (of Mackenzie & Company) for sinking a junk carrying Chinese troops. The Chinese dockworkers who tried to unload the ship at Chongqing were mobbed and restrained by boycott supporters, and the protest escalated when an armed guard from a U.S. gunboat killed one of them while trying to disperse the mob.[47] One of the best-known examples was the Wanxian Incident of 1926, in which the troops of militarist Yang Sen (1884–1977) seized two China Navigation steamers at Wanxian during a dispute over the sinking of a junk. Yang's troops attacked a British gunboat and an Indo-China steamer when their crews attempted to rescue the China Navigation officers, after which the gunboat bombarded the port, killing civilians. This incident precipitated a three-year boycott of British shipping at Wanxian.[48] A British journalist reported that in 1926, all foreign-flag shipping had abandoned the routes above Chongqing as the result of boycotts and strikes.[49]

It is impossible to assess whether the disruptions suffered by British and Japanese companies from strikes and boycotts were sufficient to offset the advantages they enjoyed from extraterritorial protection, but the companies were unquestionably concerned with the damage such actions caused to their businesses and reputations. Furthermore, British diplomats believed that such incidents threatened national prestige enough to modify some policies. In 1926, the British Foreign Office decided that to secure a peaceful framework for British business in China, it would back away from the strict enforcement of treaty terms and recognize Chinese nationalist aspirations, agreeing to negotiate some revisions of the unequal treaties. One of the results of this policy shift was a restriction on the use of force in China to only those situations in which British life was threatened, which meant that naval convoys and guards could no longer routinely protect British ships.

This restriction shows how apparently chaotic conditions in China might be helpful in reducing foreign privileges. Without a reliable central government as a collaborator, British shipping faced resistance from multiple sites in Chinese society—in this case an alliance between local militarists and nationalist activists—that disrupted trade conditions enough to prompt a change in policy. Although 1926 has been interpreted as the year in which Britain gave up only minor rights and privileges while retaining important ones like extraterritoriality, these restrictions on their use of force had a very clear impact on shipping conditions.[50] British ships still enjoyed immunity from search and exemption from militarist taxation, but they could no longer be convoyed through disturbed areas by British naval vessels.

In its interference with the business of powerful British and Japanese shipping firms, the nationalist movement provided rhetorical support and at times even a boost to the businesses of emerging Chinese companies. Particularly helpful to the cause of Chinese shipping were those boycotts directed against both Britain and Japan, such as the one following the May Thirtieth Incident in 1925. Although temporary, such a boycott could provide an interval during which Chinese companies could expand market share or operations without immediate retaliation from the large foreign firms. In addition to boycotts, the longer-term National Products Movement (guohuo yundong) encouraged Chinese shippers and passengers to patronize Chinese companies. This movement, in which Chinese business leaders tried to convince Chinese consumers that it was their patriotic duty to buy Chinese products, promoted a general ethic of nationalistic consumption. Shipping companies also contended with what Karl Gerth has identified as the central problem of the National Products Movement: convincing consumers that "buying Chinese" was worth forgoing the low prices, high quality, or mystique of foreign products.[51] In the shipping field, foreign companies enjoyed reputations for efficient management and safe navigation in addition to more regular services and better connections to international shipping lines.[52] Despite the National Products Movement's ethical and political inducements to patronize Chinese shipping firms, there is little evidence that Chinese passengers and shippers abandoned the services of British and Japanese companies.

Given the increasingly clear contradictions between foreign and Chinese shipping in this period, collaboration within the shipping business was deeply affected. The shipping conference, which had survived the onslaught of new subsidized foreign tonnage between 1895 and 1911 and incorporated the Nisshin Kisen Kaisha in 1913, faced new challenges in the early Republic. Although it persisted as an institution of the shipping field and the cooperation among the original Three Companies remained relatively stable, the conference could no longer command the level of compliance it once enjoyed. The ability of a wider range of shipping companies to press for exclusive advantages at different times made it difficult to maintain conference agreements, with the result that between 1917 and 1935, the more comprehensive conference system was replaced by shorter-term rate agreements that were repeatedly violated and renegotiated. Although Republican-period participants appeared to agree that maintaining some cooperative controls on competition was desirable, they rarely hesitated to take advantage of opportunities that undermined agreements.

In 1913, the Yangzi conference agreement was arguably at the height of its power: the Three Companies had overcome the challenge of the subsidized firms, the German and French companies had withdrawn from the river, and the Nisshin Kisen Kaisha had joined the conference. Nisshin, however, was the first to withdraw from the agreement. Japanese government mandates backed the company's expansion program on the Yangzi and coast during World War I, and its leaders claimed to be unable to adjust its tonnage and services to compromise with the other companies.[53] Following Nisshin's withdrawal, the original Three Companies—China Navigation, Indo-China, and the China Merchants Company—maintained some agreements among themselves, continuing to pool their earnings according to predetermined proportions between

1917 and 1925.[54] In 1920, the Three Companies brokered an agreement on minimum rates among themselves, Nisshin, and the new Chinese firms of Sanbei/Hong'an and Ning-Shao.[55]

By the early 1920s, all of the river steamship companies—Japanese, British, and Chinese—had begun to feel the strain of the competition that resulted from their postwar expansions. At this time, enthusiasm for the controlled competition of the conference system reemerged, but a new agreement was delayed by disagreement among the Three Companies over how to respond to Nisshin's expansion. At the end of 1921, Jardine Matheson's Shanghai office reported that the Nisshin Kisen Kaisha was looking to rejoin the Yangzi conference, and the firm expressed hope that an agreement on the Yangzi would lead to one on the coast, where competition was particularly fierce.[56] Whereas Indo-China and the China Merchants welcomed the possibility of diminished competition, China Navigation saw the Japanese overture as an opportunity to attack Nisshin's new coastal services. On instructions from Swire's London office, China Navigation argued that its position as the largest payer into the existing Three Companies pool gave it power to dictate the terms of the future agreement.[57] Following this logic, the Three Companies proposed to Nisshin in 1922 that a Yangzi conference would be possible only if Nisshin agreed to restrict its routes and tonnage on the coast. When the Japanese company refused, the Three Companies dissolved the existing Yangzi rate agreement, and for the next three years raised and lowered rates to pressure the Japanese company and the new Chinese firms on the river.[58]

Conference negotiations were revived in the summer of 1924, when Butterfield & Swire's agent in Tokyo began discussions with the Nisshin Kisen Kaisha's president, surnamed Mori. Although Mori continued to express interest in a conference agreement, he also refused to limit Nisshin's coastal services, which the Japanese government had declared "a political and economic necessity."[59] By the spring of 1925, negotiations between the Three Companies and Nisshin had finally progressed to the specific proportions of a Yangzi agreement, and the correspondence among them began to refer again to the approach of the Four Companies in combating competition from new Chinese firms.[60]

In the 1920s, the new Chinese companies that had established Yangzi services during the war similarly threatened the Three Companies' ability to dictate conference terms. In the past, the Three Companies managed small-scale competitors by integrating them into the conference as affiliate members, but the Chinese firms of Sanbei/Hong'an and Ning-Shao (both represented in negotiations by Yu Xiaqing) resisted the strict limitations of affiliate membership even as they occasionally appealed to the Three Companies for rate concessions.

Yu was hardly a compliant participant in these agreements. He often challenged the terms the more established companies tried to set for the new Chinese firms. The 1920 rate agreement stipulated that Sanbei/Hong'an could only run one and Ning-Shao only two steamers on the Shanghai–Hankou route.[61] When the Three Companies decided to raise rates in 1923, they feared that the Chinese companies would try to undercut them. They dispatched China Merchants Company chairman Fu Xiao'an (1872–1940) to warn Yu Xiaqing "that if [Ning-Shao and Sanbei/Hong'an] use this increase to improve their carryings at the expense of the Three Companies, rates will revert to those now obtaining or worse."[62] Yu then made a formal request for a rate concession—permission to charge rates 10 percent lower than the new rates—a request to which the other firms agreed on condition that Sanbei/Hong'an and Ning-Shao's tonnage would not increase.[63] Over the next two years, however, Yu acquired three large, new ships for the Shanghai–Hankou route, which he did not hesitate to put on the line.[64] As the Three Companies' negotiations with Nisshin Kisen advanced in the spring of 1925, they cut rates on the Shanghai–Hankou route to pressure Yu to "come to terms," hoping to finalize a new conference agreement. When this tactic did not work, they offered a new compromise, consenting to the expansion of Sanbei /Hong'an's fleet in exchange for a promise that Yu would not add any new tonnage to the Shanghai–Hankou route for six years. Yu agreed to this and to a further condition that no "outside" firms would be allowed to use any of Sanbei/Hong'an's wharves or warehouses. This stipulation was intended to prevent any further expansion of the Chinese company's services through alliances with other Chinese shipping firms. The managers of Indo-China and China Navigation thought the tonnage permitted to Sanbei/Hong'an was excessive, but the China Merchants Company's Fu Xiao'an persuaded them to accept the agreement, because otherwise Yu might "fight indefinitely" and seek support from the Beiyang government.[65]

These compromises were rendered moot by the outbreak of boycotts and strikes against the British and Japanese companies following the May Thirtieth Incident, which shifted the balance of power among the Yangzi steamship companies yet again. During the months the boycotts remained active, Yu Xiaqing took the opportunity to add another new ship to the Lower Yangzi route and to make agreements with small Chinese firms on the Upper Yangzi to coordinate services with Sanbei/Hong'an's downriver ships.[66] With the British and Japanese companies' services stopped or slowed for the duration of the boycott, a full Yangzi River service was undoubtedly a windfall for Sanbei/Hong'an. China Navigation and Indo-China managers grumbled that Yu Xiaqing, as both president of the Shanghai General Chamber of Commerce and owner of Sanbei/Hong'an, did everything in his power to keep the strikes and boycotts against British and Japanese shipping alive in the fall of 1925.[67]

The May Thirtieth Movement also played a role in the breakdown of the conference agreement negotiated between the Three Companies and the Nisshin Kisen Kaisha. In June 1925, the China Merchants Company declined to sign the new agreement, as its leaders believed that entering into a conference with British and Japanese firms at that moment would destroy the company's reputation.[68] Despite this one nod to nationalist feeling, however, the China Merchants Company remained a consistent supporter of conference-type agreements. Months later, after the May Thirtieth fervor had died down, another set of negotiations among the Three Companies failed because China Merchants opposed a move by China Navigation to make it easier for participating companies to withdraw from agreements, citing the importance of keeping competition within the organization to a minimum.[69] For the next decade, there were a series of rate agreements concluded among the "Six Companies" of the Yangzi River (China Navigation, Indo-China, China Merchants, Nisshin, Sanbei/Hong'an, and Ning-Shao) but no full conference agreement.[70]

The different constraints and opportunities that the new political conditions furnished the steamship companies in the early Republic weakened the conference organization in Chinese waters. The organization could not command the kind of compliance it had in the past with the terms and controls it set. Nisshin's early withdrawal from the 1913 agreement because of government mandates was the result of the advancement of Japan's national shipping program, and Yu Xiaqing's casual approach to conference stipulations demonstrates his eagerness to expand his company and the opportunities furnished to a Chinese firm by nationalist boycotts of foreign companies. Although the organization was weaker, and participants had to settle for a series of rate agreements rather than a comprehensive conference agreement, all of the companies—British, Japanese, and Chinese—appeared to support the principle that some controls on competition were useful and desirable. Thus, despite Nisshin Kisen's ambivalence toward and Yu Xiaqing's resistance to conference terms, the original Three Companies continued to work closely together and maintain agreements through World War II.

In the early Republic, as political conditions magnified the contradiction between foreign and Chinese shipping, the terms of collaboration in the shipping business became more complex. The conference system had worked particularly well when it regulated the competition between the British firms and the China Merchants Company, but was far less reliable as the participants in the field became more numerous and diverse. The system was weakened by companies that would not tolerate the limits it imposed over time. The Nisshin Kisen Kaisha, with its obligations to the Japanese government, was one such example, as were new Chinese firms like Sanbei, which were willing to risk conference sanctions for a chance to expand and were unwilling to accept a permanently subordinate position. The China Merchants Company, not nearly as hungry as Sanbei, was likely the conference's most faithful supporter out of this company's need to maintain its scale and position alongside its rapidly expanding colleagues. The impetus for collaboration in the shipping business persisted, but the shipping nationalism of both China and Japan made such collaborations far less powerful.

Chinese Shipping Entrepreneurs as National Capitalists

The ubiquity of shipping nationalism in the early Republic makes it easy to imagine that those Chinese entrepreneurs who established companies that competed with foreign firms on major routes would style themselves as nationalists. Foreign shipping firms were their most formidable rivals, and any success against them could be interpreted in nationalist terms. These entrepreneurs could capitalize on antiforeign feeling as well as the disruptions that the nationalist movement brought to foreign shipping.

Furthermore, a nationalist stance could be part of an entrepreneur's public persona: presenting oneself as committed to serving the nation could attract state or elite patronage, as well as appeal to customers swayed by the ethics of nationalist consumption.[71] The benefits of such a nationalist stance might also induce some to adopt it disingenuously, such as manufacturers of items marketed as "national products" but who relied primarily on imported materials to make a profit.[72]

In the shipping field, examining enterprises like Zhang Jian's Dada Steamship Company, Yu Xiaqing's Sanbei/Hong'an Companies, and slightly later Lu Zuofu's Minsheng Industrial Company side by side reveals not a convenient nationalist pose but a set of shared principles and practices in organizing and developing their firms. These parallels suggest a set of common ideas about how such enterprises might relate to society, locality, and nation.

Chinese histories of shipping often refer to these three companies as "national capitalist shipping enterprises" (*minzu ziben hangyun ye*) and their founders as "national capitalists" (*minzu zibenjia*).[73] Although these terms might be understood as simply "indigenous" enterprises or capitalists, they are much more familiar as political labels that distinguish those members of the pre-1949 bourgeoisie who "allied with the masses" in opposing foreign imperialism and supporting China's national development from the "comprador capitalists" (*maiban zibenjia*) who allied with foreign interests and the "bureaucratic capitalists" (*guanliao zibenjia*) who allied with reactionary regimes (most often the Guomindang of the Nanjing decade).[74] At the founding of the People's Republic, these classifications indicated the acceptability of a particular enterprise or entrepreneur to the new regime.

As a historical category that describes actual members of the pre-1949 bourgeoisie or their businesses, the term has attracted far more skepticism. Marie-Claire Bergère has observed that the distinctions made between these different types of capitalists were often more apparent than real, and questioned whether a pure example of a national capitalist enterprise—one founded exclusively with Chinese capital and in opposition to foreign business—could be identified in Republican China.[75] Other historians have noted that along with a Reform era valorization of entrepreneurship in China, the term "national capitalist" has been extended to include many who earlier had been labeled "comprador" or "bureaucratic" capitalists (or other type of "class enemy") in recognition of their contributions to the modern economy.[76] Zhang Jian and Yu Xiaqing are two examples of individuals formerly labeled as "class enemies" who were rehabilitated as "national capitalists" in the Reform era.[77]

The strong commonalities among the three major Yangzi River shipping entrepreneurs of the Republican period suggest that there is some historical validity to a category of capitalist who was substantively engaged with the nationalist project. Despite their different locations in space and time, Zhang Jian's, Yu Xiaqing's, and Lu Zuofu's approaches to their shipping companies reveal a remarkably similar set of concerns and practices that suggest a shared view of the economic dimensions of nation-building. First, although all three shipping companies were eventually engaged in transport among the treaty ports in competition with conference firms, none of them originated in this sphere. All three started in the hinterlands of treaty ports—most often the founder's native place—and were designed to foster the economic development of that place, most often by facilitating communication between it and a treaty port. From these hinterland bases all developed into important shipping firms on major routes. Second, the three entrepreneurs invested in projects that modernized the social and cultural (as well as economic) life of that locality, building schools, public recreation facilities, and other modern amenities. Finally, in a process best illustrated by the careers of Yu Xiaqing and Lu Zuofu, once their companies transitioned from small local firms to those that could challenge the conference companies on major routes, these entrepreneurs prioritized rapid expansion over stable growth and sought state patronage to make it happen. The urgency with which they pursued their businesses at this stage suggests the importance they attached to working at a scale at which they could compete with foreign companies.

The shared pursuits of Zhang Jian, Yu Xiaqing, and Lu Zuofu are all the more striking because of the differences between the three men in terms of generation, location, and background. Zhang, whose entrepreneurial activities began in the late Qing, was not only a *jinshi* degree holder but the 1894 principal graduate (*zhuangyuan*). Rather than take an official post, he took the opportunity offered by Liangjiang Governor-General Zhang Zhidong to start a cotton mill in Jiangsu Province in 1895. Although official support for this project later disintegrated, Zhang went on to found the Dasheng Cotton Mill privately. Yu Xiaqing moved to Shanghai from the Ningbo area as a fifteen-year-old apprentice and later became a comprador for the Netherlands Bank. A prominent figure in Shanghai's commercial world, Yu took an active role in issues important to the Ningbo community in Shanghai in the late Qing, such as the 1898 Siming Gongsuo Cemetery affair and the Mixed Court riot of 1905, in addition to the Zhejiang railway rights recovery movement and the founding of the Ning-Shao Steamship Company. He later became the director of the Siming Gongsuo.[78] Lu Zuofu, a generation junior to Zhang and Yu, was from Hechuan County in Sichuan Province. The son of a small-scale hemp merchant, he completed an elementary school education and later taught himself a wide variety of subjects, including mathematics, classical Chinese, history, chemistry, physics, politics, and economics. Other than two brief stints of study in Shanghai, he spent most of his life prior to starting the Minsheng Company working in Sichuan as a journalist and teacher. According to his biographers, he became frustrated with his career in education when rapid turnover in militarist regimes destroyed his efforts at educational reform. He returned to his hometown to start a shipping enterprise.[79] Superficially, the three men came from different parts of China and had little in common.

Despite their different backgrounds, these men also shared some connection to the 1911 Revolution. Zhang Jian and Yu Xiaqing were active in the late Qing constitutionalist movement. Yu later joined Sun Yatsen's Revolutionary Alliance (Tongmenghui).[80] Lu Zuofu is also reported to have joined the Revolutionary Alliance as a seventeen-year-old student.[81] Zhang and Yu held official positions in the post-1911 regime: Zhang as minister of Agriculture and Commerce, and Yu in Chen Qimei's (1878–1916) administration of Shanghai.[82] Although it may be a convenient trope to explain the motivations for later actions, all three men's biographers claim that they were ultimately disappointed by the revolution, an experience that led each to think more deeply about nationalist strategies.

The men began by building shipping networks centered around their native localities. Zhang Jian's shipping companies made his native place of Nantong the hub of a network connecting the cotton-producing districts north of the Yangzi River to Nantong and Nantong to the Yangzi River ports of Zhenjiang, Nanjing, and Shanghai. The Dada Inland Rivers Shipping Company, whose ships worked on the network of inland rivers and canals north of the Yangzi, extending to the northwest as far as Yangzhou and as far north as Yancheng and Funing. These inland routes facilitated the movement of raw cotton produced in these areas to Zhang Jian's factories and linked Nantong to areas where Zhang had initiated land reclamation projects that transformed former areas of salt production into cotton fields. In 1905, he began to expand services on the Lower Yangzi through the Shanghai Dada Steamship Company, which later merged with the original Dasheng Company, running four steamships between Shanghai and Yangzhou via Nantong, Nanjing, and Zhenjiang. This shipping network was designed around the needs of Zhang Jian's cotton mills, but it also provided a transport infrastructure in an area that previously had little modern transport, linking districts that produced raw materials to the factories in Nantong and those factories to commercial cities like Shanghai.[83]

Yu Xiaqing's Sanbei Company originated in a project to improve communications between Yu Xiaqing's native place, the township of Longshan on the Zhejiang coast, other coastal towns, and Ningbo and Shanghai. The name "Sanbei" ("three north") is a reference to Longshan, which was located north of the three counties of Zhenhai, Cixi, and Yuyao. Longshan was bordered by mountains on one side and the ocean on the other, so it had few convenient transport connections to other places. In 1913, Yu constructed a bund and docks in Longshan and the following year established the Sanbei Wharf Company, which ran steamships from Longshan to other coastal towns and to Ningbo via the Yong River. Sanbei's ships connected this coastal area to the Ningbo–Shanghai steamship route served by the Ning-Shao, China Navigation, and China Merchants Companies. Yu also registered Zhenhai, in the Yong River's estuary, as an inland port so that exporters of cotton and other agricultural products from this area would not have to pay additional taxes to transport their goods to Ningbo. After he resigned as general manager of the Ning-Shao Company in 1914, Yu built the larger Sanbei Group on the basis of this local communications and trade network.[84]

Lu Zuofu's Minsheng Industrial Company likewise began as a small enterprise intended to improve troubled economic conditions in Lu's native place of Hechuan County in Sichuan. The company's first ship, the *Minsheng*, carried passengers and cargo between Hechuan on the Jialing River (a tributary of the Upper Yangzi) and the treaty port of

Chongqing. Previously, banditry and militarist conflicts had disrupted Hechuan's transport connections to the city; the new steamship service provided a swifter and safer passage to Chongqing. Because the Jialing River traversed two military garrison areas, Lu Zuofu had to negotiate with their leaders to secure the shipping route. In 1927, he established the Jialing Gorges Defense Bureau, which trained a 500-member youth corps to suppress banditry in the Jialing River counties of Hechuan, Ba, Jiangbei, and Bishan. With the shipping route secured, the Minsheng Company bought more ships and established a daily steamship service between Hechuan, Chongqing, and the Yangzi River town of Fuling. Although not a treaty port, Fuling was situated at the confluence of the Yangzi and Wu Rivers, the point from which Yunnan's and Guizhou's opium crops were distributed to downriver cities. Minsheng ships also occasionally worked on the Yangzi above Chongqing. Minsheng's shipping services forged connections between places underserved by other steamship companies and the trade center of Chongqing. In Beibei, the Jialing River town that housed his Defense Bureau, Lu Zuofu set up a group of affiliated enterprises that supported the shipping company. At first these included a machine shop, a coal mine, and an eight-kilometer railway that transported coal from the mines to the riverbank, providing an inexpensive supply of coal for the ships. Subsequently, Lu expanded the complex of enterprises in Beibei to further foster the area's economic development, adding a fabric-dyeing plant, a printing press, a coal-processing plant, a commercial orchard, and a bank. In 1930, Lu Zuofu moved Minsheng headquarters to Chongqing and began to expand its fleet and extend its services downriver on the main Yangzi line from Chongqing to Shanghai.[85]

As they built their companies, all three shipping entrepreneurs contributed to the modernization of social and cultural life in their native areas. Zhang Jian built an impressive array of educational, welfare, and cultural institutions in Nantong, as well as constructing a modern downtown area with a park, a library, a museum, and sports and entertainment facilities in addition to new roads and bridges, modern architecture, and electric lighting.[86] As Qin Shao has shown, Zhang promoted Nantong as a model city, an alternative to the Westernized modernity of the treaty ports and an "authentic" form of Chinese modernization based on local initiative, drawing curious visitors from China and abroad.[87] Yu Xiaqing's activities in Longshan were not as extensive, but he opened a telegraph office and built a light railway, a public road, a park, and schools there.[88] Lu Zuofu developed Beibei into a model city like Nantong, setting aside a percentage of Minsheng's yearly profits for the project. In addition to the industries he set up there, he established a hospital, a library, a park with a museum and a zoo, an elementary school, and Sichuan's first research institute, the West China Science Institute. Other projects included a newspaper, centers for popular education, and an "information center" where people could obtain help in settling disputes, writing letters and contracts, and searching for work.[89] Like Zhang Jian's Nantong Model, in the 1930s, the Minsheng Company promoted Beibei as a tourist destination, a place to hold academic and research conferences, and a model "planned city."[90]

There were other examples of industrial enterprises built on this model in Republican China, not least of which were the Rong brothers' cotton mills in their native Wuxi.[91] In her study of Zhang Jian's business complex, Elisabeth Köll characterizes these as "regional enterprises"—industrial operations in a hinterland setting that allowed the founder to dominate local economic development and garner political and social power in his native place.[92] The regional designation, however, may understate the significance of such enterprises' intended contributions to an autonomous national economy. Sun Yatsen had advocated connecting rural China to the more developed treaty-port economies to promote economic autarky and end imperialist domination. In this view, the entrepreneur's goal was to provide a space for economic development outside of treaty-port economies. In all three shipping companies, the local base provided an initial testing ground from which the companies extended into the treaty-port shipping network. All three entrepreneurs appear to have drawn on Sun's idea. The idea of entrepreneurs like this contributing to a "national economy" arose again in Nanjing-era economic debates when Wang Jingwei (1883–1944) argued that such entrepreneurs could be mobilized as an anti-imperialist force.[93]

All three shipping enterprises were joint-stock companies founded with local capital. Bergère's doubts about the historicity of "national capitalists" stem from her observation that modern businesses in Republican China backed exclusively by Chinese capital were extremely rare. Yet her focus on treaty port–based enterprises may have limited her view, as these hinterland-based shipping firms easily met this standard.[94] The initial locations of all three shipping enterprises in the native places of their founders helped the founders leverage local connections to develop sources of capital. Zhang Jian and Lu Zuofu relied on relatives, friends, and other associates to get their enterprises off the ground, and then widened these circles to include other local groups that would benefit from them. Local cotton cloth merchants were among Zhang Jian's initial investors.[95] Lu Zuofu purchased Minsheng's first ship before he had raised the full amount of the company's capital, using it to demonstrate the effectiveness and profitability of shipping services in the area. This gamble eventually attracted a wider group of investors from among Hechuan merchants and gentry.[96] Some accounts imply that Yu Xiaqing financed Sanbei himself with the profits he made from his many commercial endeavors in Shanghai, but like Dada and Minsheng, Sanbei was registered as a joint-stock company with an initial capital of 200,000 *yuan* divided into 100-*yuan* shares, suggesting that there were other investors from Yu's native place.[97] Further emphasizing the exclusive Chinese backing of these firms were the rules of Sanbei and Minsheng that explicitly prohibited foreign shareholding in these companies.[98]

As the shipping companies extended from their local bases onto major shipping routes, they evince further common tactics that suggest their investment in succeeding at this level. As the businesses of Sanbei and Minsheng were primarily focused on shipping, these two companies provide the best examples. Both firms prioritized the rapid expansion of their fleets to secure their places in these larger trades, going into considerable debt to achieve this goal. Both cultivated state patronage to support these expansions.

Sanbei gained its foothold in the Yangzi River and coastal trades at the end of World War I and struggled to remain on these routes through the 1920s. At the end of the war, Yu sold all of his personal real estate holdings in Shanghai to increase the company's capital to 2 million *yuan*.[99] In the early 1920s, he became famous in Shanghai for his appetite for new ships and his unorthodox methods of obtaining them. He applied for both government and bank loans to cover the costs and became known as the "King of Loans" (*jiezhai dawang*) and the "Hollow Boss" (*kongxin laoda*) for his debts, which by one account reached 5 million *yuan* by 1937. Yu developed a method of taking out a loan to buy a ship and then mortgaging the ship to a bank. Relying on his status within the Ningbo community in Shanghai and his position as comprador for the Netherlands Bank, he negotiated extended loan periods with his creditors and generated capital by selling teaboys' positions on his ships himself.[100] As one biographer wrote, nothing made Yu happier than to buy ships.[101] Although his acquisitiveness is presented almost as a personal idiosyncrasy by biographers, Sanbei was the private Chinese firm that developed the most extensive competitive services on major steamship routes before World War II.

Yu Xiaqing consistently sought financial support from the state during this period of expansion, although he never succeeded. In 1919, just six months after Sanbei had increased its capital for a second time, Yu tried to obtain a loan of 1.5 million *yuan* from the Beiyang government, secured on the fleets of the Sanbei and Hong'an Companies. He was concerned at the time that Sanbei/Hong'an would not survive the postwar expansions of the British and Japanese companies. The Ministry of Finance approved this loan, but it was canceled after a turnover of ministry personnel.[102] After 1927, Yu also sought help from Jiang Jieshi and the Nanjing regime. As the following chapter shows in greater detail, he acted as a mediator between the Shanghai shipping world and the Nanjing regime. In this role, he repeatedly requested Nanjing to issue government bonds to assist Chinese entrepreneurs in the shipping business. Later, the government approved a bond issue specifically for Sanbei, but it was withdrawn because of Yu's damaged credit. Despite many attempts, he was never able to get favorable terms for a loan from the government.[103] Although he was never secured state patronage, his actions demonstrate that he believed that the state should act as a source of support for an enterprise like his.

As Minsheng transformed from a small local concern to a competitor on major routes, Lu Zuofu found himself in a similar position. State patronage had helped Minsheng expand to the point at which it could enter the main Upper Yangzi route between Yichang and Chongqing and later extend further downriver in the early 1930s. In this case, "state patronage" consisted of an alliance between the company and the militarist Liu Xiang. Seeking greater control of the shipping coming in and out of Chongqing, Liu supported Minsheng in an effort to buy up the many small Chinese-owned companies on the Upper Yangzi, consolidating them into a single large firm. Liu offered Minsheng direct financial assistance, monopolies on certain local routes, special permission to carry opium and cash on his regime's behalf, and directed shipments of commercial cargoes and troops to the company.[104] During this process between 1930 and 1934, Minsheng had acquired the ships of twelve Chinese firms, and several officials of Liu's regime became stockholders in the Minsheng Company.

By 1935, however, Minsheng's expansion had outstripped even Liu Xiang's patronage. The company had bought larger ships and wrecks from foreign firms that made it more competitive on the main Upper Yangzi route, and it borrowed heavily to do so. Lu Zuofu himself stated that by 1935, Minsheng already carried the greatest debt burden of any enterprise in Chongqing (700,000 *yuan*). When the opportunity to purchase a failed U.S. company arose, Minsheng doubled this debt by borrowing another 700,000 *yuan* from a consortium of Shanghai banks.[105] The purchase of the U.S. firm's steamers allowed Minsheng to extend its services downriver to Shanghai, making it a significant firm on the entire Yangzi rather than one more company on the Yichang–Chongqing route. The company's relationship with Liu Xiang and its expansion process are examined in greater detail in the next chapter, but like Sanbei, Minsheng was committed enough to growth to accept militarist patronage and considerable debt to become more competitive on major routes.[106]

The histories of these three private Chinese Yangzi River steamship companies were not identical, yet there are also clear consistencies among them. All three meet the basic criteria of "national capitalist" enterprises in that they were founded with Chinese capital and formed an indigenous opposition to foreign economic power. Other shared features suggest that there may be further dimensions of that category to be discovered. All three firms enacted the idea that the national economy could be developed from places outside of the treaty ports and contribute to the modernization of hinterland areas at the same time it challenged foreign domination. The companies' rapid expansions and active courting of state patronage may well have been symptoms of Republican China's uncertain and unpredictable business climate, but given these companies' positions within the shipping business, self-preservation and profit were inseparable from advancing on foreign firms.[107] Even if one undertook the laborious task of assessing the sincerity of each entrepreneur's commitment to nationalist ideals, in the context of Republican shipping nationalism, it would be impossible to separate each company's nationalist contributions from its performance in competition with foreign firms.

The growth of these firms constituted a significant expansion of Chinese-flag shipping, transforming arguments for China's shipping autonomy from a distant possibility to a more immediate and realizable goal. When the Nationalist government came to power in 1927, it adopted shipping rights recovery discourse in its arguments for treaty revision and worked to expand Chinese shipping. Although Zhang Jian had since passed away, Yu Xiaqing and Lu Zuofu participated in Nanjing's efforts to promote these goals.

Conclusion

The transformation of the shipping field in the early Republic followed the transformation of semi-colonial relations. Collaboration under the treaty system had been the means through which the Qing dynasty had protected and preserved its sovereignty. After the dynasty's fall, the disintegration of a Chinese political center meant that this type of systemic collaboration was no longer a possibility. The shipping nationalism of the early Republic grew from the greater scope for resistance to semicolonialism afforded by these new conditions. This resistance was not necessarily coordinated or successful, but it was far more open and evident than it had been in the past and drew support from broader sections of Chinese society. In shipping, there was great conflict and opposition between foreign and Chinese interests. After World War I, a groundswell of new Chinese firms on major routes confronted the wartime and postwar expansions of established foreign shipping companies under political circumstances that magnified the extraterritorial privileges enjoyed by foreign firms. At the same time, Chinese shipping interests and entrepreneurs could draw on the resources of the larger nationalist movement to challenge the foreign firms' hold on important routes and the power of the shipping conference. The inextricable link between Chinese shipping interests and nationalist activity is underscored by the shared practices and shared views on economic development among the major Chinese shipping entrepreneurs of the period.

Another unique feature of the early Republic was that the state was almost completely absent from the shipping field. This absence was distinct from the Qing dynasty's interventionist stance (during the founding of the China Merchants Company and in the New Policies period) and it also soon changed. When the Nationalist government claimed the status of China's central government in 1927, it endeavored to bring the state back into the shipping field to guide treaty revision and support Chinese shipping. During the Nanjing decade (1927–37), the state had to confront—win over or accommodate—the force, diversity, and pervasiveness of early Republican shipping nationalism.

A comparison of shipping in China and India in this period yields not a set of distinctions between colonial and semi-colonial rule but a parallel emergence of shipping nationalism in the business and political spheres. There were differences, but the commonalities between the contexts are more striking. In India as well as in China, a postwar trade boom put capital in Indian hands, and Indian businessmen increased their participation in industrial enterprise. Within this context, new Indian-owned shipping companies began to break into India's coastal routes and some overseas trades. The most prominent of these firms was the Scindia Steam Navigation Company, founded by construction entrepreneur Walchand Hirachand (1882–1953) in 1919. Scindia directly challenged British shipping interests by putting its ships on the Bombay–London and Indian coastal routes. Like the Chinese national capitalists of a similar period, Walchand and his associates' intentions went well beyond establishing a successful business venture: they saw the company as a means to challenge British domination and build the foundation of an Indian national economy. In its early years, Scindia faced intense competition from British-controlled shipping conferences on all routes and suffered heavy losses. Its shareholders famously rejected an attractive offer by the owners of the British India Steam Navigation Company to purchase Scindia, as they agreed on the necessity of maintaining it as a national enterprise. Scindia eventually had to compromise with the shipping conferences to survive: in 1923, Walchand agreed to conference stipulations to limit the company's growth and keep off overseas routes. He called the agreement a "slave bond," but it made Scindia a member of the Coastal Conference rather than an outsider subject to aggressive conference tactics.[108] After the rise of Scindia, several other shipping companies started with Indian capital and managed by Indians joined the coastal trade. Not only was the Indian shipping sector growing, its participants shared the goal of establishing an Indian mercantile marine. In 1935, when the Coastal Conference began a rate war against new Indian firms on west coast routes, Scindia flouted the conference agreement to support the Indian companies.[109]

The activism in the shipping business was matched with political action on the part of the Indian nationalist movement. The Indian National Congress demanded "coastal reservation," employing a logic similar to shipping rights recovery: that international law and practice demanded that a nation's coastal shipping should be reserved for the ships of that nation. They also argued for shipping autonomy: Indian companies should be the basis of the country's mercantile marine. Debates over these questions were carried out in India's Legislative Assembly. For the remainder of the 1920s, nationalist legislators lobbied for a number of measures to support Indian shipping, including coastal reservation, the recognition and protection of Indian shipping interests, the training of skilled Indian mariners, and government aid for Indian shipping and shipbuilding.[110]

The struggle of the Indian legislators for coastal reservation and other shipping provisions met consistent opposition from the colonial government. A 1922–23 legislative initiative to form an Indian mercantile marine resulted in the government's appointment of a committee of British and Indian ship owners to investigate conditions in the subcontinent. Among other proposals, the committee's report recommended coastal reservation for Indian ships. Concerned that such a measure was too close to "expropriation of property and flag discrimination," the government shelved the report without acting on its central recommendations.[111] In 1928–29, another bill for coastal reservation was introduced to the Legislative Assembly, but consideration of it was postponed amid negotiations between the government and the Indian National Congress over dominion status. When the Indian National Congress decided to pursue full independence, Gandhi included coastal reservation in his "Eleven Points" (1930), a list of demands that constituted the "very simple but vital needs of India."[112] The idea reemerged in the Legislative Assembly of the

1930s until the 1935 constitution of India prohibited the passing of any laws related to it.[113]

Shipping nationalism in India was distinct from that in China in several respects. First, claims for coastal reservation and shipping autonomy were sought as concessions to be wrested from a functioning colonial state, and thus were argued in the Legislative Assembly rather than through either diplomatic channels or popular protest as required in China. A further challenge that Indian nationalists faced was the need to defend the existence of Indian nationhood. Advocates of shipping nationalism defined an Indian shipping firm as one registered in India with rupee capital in which a majority of directors and/or shareholders were Indian, yet in the Legislative Assembly, representatives of British shipping interests argued that India was not a country "separate" from the British empire and needed no mercantile marine of its own, since British ships serviced its trades and the British navy protected it.[114] Alongside these differences, however, the involvement of the shipping business in nationalist movements in China and India emerged at the same time, making a case for the importance of a commercial shipping sector—a merchant marine—to the nationalist project and connecting the shipping business to nationalist ethics and action.

CHAPTER 6

Nanjing and Chongqing

The Return of the State to Shipping, 1927–37

At the conclusion of the Northern Expedition, when the Nationalist government installed itself in Nanjing, it began to assert itself in the shipping field, an arena from which the state had been almost completely absent for several decades. Extending authority over Chinese shipping was an important part of the Nationalist government's nation-building and state-building efforts: it established control over legal and administrative structures for shipping and claimed the roles of protector of Chinese shipping and promoter of China's shipping autonomy. The new government drew on the language of shipping rights recovery to argue for the revision of the unequal treaties. Although specific measures of Nanjing's shipping program occasionally met with opposition from ship owners, they overwhelmingly welcomed its intervention, hoping that state support would allow their businesses to survive difficult economic conditions and intense competition with foreign companies. State and ship owners agreed that extensive state involvement in the shipping sector was a primary means of achieving the goals of shipping nationalism.

An obstacle to Nanjing's efforts to bring the state back into shipping was its uncertain authority in all parts of China. Although Nanjing claimed to be the central government and the treaty powers recognized it as such after its forces took Beijing in 1928, in some areas its control was challenged by militarist regimes that were nominal allies but enjoyed considerable independence. These regimes could complicate the implementation of state policy and challenge Nanjing's claims to the center.

In one case, a semi-independent militarist regime pursued its own, nearly simultaneous program of shipping rights recovery. Liu Xiang, who controlled the Upper Yangzi port of Chongqing, launched an effort to reduce the privileges of foreign shipping firms and increase the capacity of Chinese-flag shipping in his garrison area. Whereas Nanjing's shipping rights recovery program addressed shipping as a national problem linked to treaty revision and included a formal agenda developed in consultation with Shanghai-based ship owners, Liu Xiang's program derived from his more immediate need to gain better control over the revenue of Chongqing. The parallel programs underscore the concrete significance of shipping to questions of sovereignty, both local and national.

The nearly simultaneous pursuit of shipping rights recovery programs in these different contexts had paradoxical results. On one hand, the independent actions of militarist regimes like Liu Xiang's undermined Nanjing's claim to represent the central government of China. When Nanjing initiated negotiations with the powers to revise the treaties in 1930–31, the autonomy of militarist regimes led to accusations of "internal disorder" from the treaty powers, a pretext they used to defer the treaty revision process indefinitely. Although Liu Xiang's actions were not the immediate cause of this deferral, his willingness to use techniques such as strikes and boycotts against foreign shipping—techniques that Nanjing had eschewed in favor of diplomatic negotiation—unquestionably contributed to the impression of disorder.[1] On the other hand, Liu's program produced much more concrete results than Nanjing's: he achieved a practical diminishment of foreign shipping privilege in his garrison area and fostered the development of an important new Chinese-flag company, the Minsheng Industrial Company. As discussed earlier, Minsheng, with his help, grew to the point it could both compete against major foreign firms and participate in national-level debates about shipping and shipping policy. The results of Nanjing's efforts to foster shipping autonomy were not nearly as tangible: it lacked the resources to support shipping firms in substantial ways and eventually alienated many of the private firms through its exclusive patronage of the newly nationalized China Merchants Company.

Juxtaposing Nanjing's and Chongqing's interventions into the shipping field at a time when economic depression and intense competition threatened many Chinese shipping companies details the broad consensus between government and business on the need for state intervention and the impediments to achieving the goals of shipping rights recovery and shipping autonomy on a national level. The outbreak of the 1937 Sino-Japanese conflict transformed the shipping field and brought this process to a rapid close. After the war, the consensus forged during this period had a profound impact on the measures taken by the People's Republic to achieve shipping autonomy.

Nanjing: The Shipping Rights Recovery Movement

The establishment of the Nationalist government and the inauguration of its treaty revision program gave shipping rights recovery a new impetus in the late 1920s and early 1930s. A close alliance between shipping interests and the state early in the Nanjing Decade produced a more fully elaborated agenda for rights recovery. Ship owners, represented by the Shanghai Shipping Association (Shanghai hangye gonghui), mobilized in support of treaty revision and advised the government on the best methods of fostering Chinese shipping autonomy.

The Nationalist government's program of negotiated revision of the unequal treaties began after Northern Expedition forces took Beijing in June 1928 and the treaty powers recognized the government. The first problems it attempted to address were tariff autonomy and the abolition of extraterritoriality: by the end of 1928 the Foreign Ministry had concluded new tariff treaties with Britain and the United States, among other powers, through which China achieved a degree of tariff autonomy, and had signed treaties with Belgium, Denmark, Italy, Portugal, and Spain, in which these countries agreed to renounce their extraterritorial privileges when the other powers did the same. In April 1929, the Nationalist government called on all of the treaty powers to begin negotiations for the revision of extraterritoriality clauses, a process that continued until 1931.[2] In August 1929, the Guomindang's Central Political Council resolved to make the recovery of China's shipping rights a goal in the program of treaty revision.[3]

With shipping rights recovery thus incorporated into the treaty revision program, Chinese shipping interests protested what they saw as the government's subsequent conciliation of Japan during negotiations for a new Sino-Japanese commercial treaty several months later. When it became clear this treaty would not diminish Japan's shipping privileges in China, the Shanghai Shipping Association protested that the regime needed to strengthen its commitment to recovery of coastal and river navigation rights.[4] The Shanghai Shipping Association, led by Yu Xiaqing, published a statement expressing dismay at the government's appeasement of Japan, which was followed by telegrams and written protests from other Shanghai commercial organizations.[5]

The Shanghai Shipping Association's protests should be interpreted as loyal opposition rather than resistance to government efforts. Even its protests drew on the language of the Nationalist Party, referring to the success of the revolution and the "awakening" (*juewu*) of the people as well as the necessity of abolishing the unequal treaties.[6] As an institution, the Shanghai Shipping Association had also accepted the authority of the Nationalist government. Reportedly one of the five most powerful Shanghai civic organizations (*minjian tuanti*) before 1927, it was among the commercial groups that supported Jiang Jieshi as his forces entered Shanghai.[7] Later that year, Nanjing's Ministry of Communications issued regulations for shipping associations, charging them with carrying out administrative and organizational tasks on behalf of the government. These rules stipulated that the associations could be dissolved by the Ministry of Communications at any time.[8] Tasked with researching ways to develop local shipping; collecting survey data; keeping records of shipping firms and related trades; solving disputes; maintaining harbors, channels, and passenger safety; and developing effective means of competing with foreign shipping firms, these shipping associations were intended to advise the Nationalist government on shipping policy, a process in which the Shanghai Shipping Association took a leading role in the early years of the Nanjing decade.[9]

In July 1930, the Shanghai Shipping Association founded a periodical, *Shipping Monthly* (*Hangye yuekan*), that publicized the shipping rights recovery agenda. *Shipping Monthly* elaborated the developing agenda over the early years of the Nanjing decade. The inaugural issue stated that it would promote "the vanguard of shipping," emphasizing both the concern with foreign domination of shipping in Chinese waters and the need to strengthen Chinese shipping through specialized research and knowledge.[10] Addressed to the "shipping world" (*hangye jie*), *Shipping Monthly* devoted much of its space to the Nationalist government's shipping program. The inaugural issue boasted inscriptions by Jiang Jieshi and Finance Minister Song Ziwen (1894–1971) as well as an article by the director of the Ministry of Communications' Shipping Administration Department, Cai Pei (1884–1960). Through 1930 and 1931, nearly every issue contained one or more essays on shipping rights recovery.[11]

This prolonged discussion of shipping rights recovery in *Shipping Monthly* reveals a detailed and consistent set of arguments for the rendition of foreign shipping rights and the development of Chinese-flag shipping. On the political side, there were several standard arguments in circulation. Numerous articles emphasized the peculiar position of foreign shipping rights in China under international law. They traced China's loss of control over its coastal and inland shipping through the unequal treaties, arguing that this process began with the opening of the five ports under the Treaty of Nanjing and concluded with the 1898 inland navigation rules that theoretically opened all of China's inland waters to foreign navigation. Individual writers repeated the contention that these provisions contravened the general principle of international law that reserved inland and territorial waters for nationals. Since they maintained that the unequal treaties had been signed in ignorance or under coercion, they argued that to uphold them in the present was inconsistent with the climate of international cooperation and renunciation of war that followed World War I.

Most commentators also emphasized the superior position of foreign shipping—usually British and Japanese—in Chinese waters, claiming that it accounted for as much as 70–80 percent of China's modern shipping. Different writers offered varying accounts of the specific damage to Chinese sovereignty. Some stressed the vulnerabilities of China's national defenses, arguing that the entrenched presence of foreign ships, gunboats, and pilots in China's coastal and inland waters exposed strategic areas of the country to outside observation. Others argued that the large foreign presence limited the development of a merchant fleet, which made it difficult for China's merchant ships to aid in national defense as those of maritime powers like Britain and Japan did. Many writers pointed to the extraterritorial protection of foreign ships and their crews as a problem. Since extraterritoriality placed ships and crews under the jurisdiction of their own consuls rather than Chinese courts, critics claimed that disputes—such as the sinking of junks by foreign steamships—were inevitably resolved in favor of foreign interests, which in turn emboldened foreign-flag ships to carry out illegal activities, such as smuggling arms and drugs. Some went so far as to lay the responsibility for China's internal disorder at the feet of foreign shipping companies that had delivered arms to warlords. Nearly all the commentators argued that China had suffered enormous economic losses from the foreign goods that foreign ships transported to and within China as well as the freight income of foreign shipping companies.[12]

Nearly all of the solutions to the problems of foreign shipping in Chinese waters proposed in *Shipping Monthly* involved state action, and therefore assumed a strengthened state. All appear to have accepted the framework of treaty revision, but they called on the state to use different methods to rid Chinese waters of foreign tonnage once it had been achieved. Some suggested that the government buy out all foreign shipping companies, and others proposed that the government gradually restrict foreign tonnage. One writer suggested that the government should enforce a timeline for the withdrawal of foreign ships from Chinese waters that would first close inland harbors to foreign navigation, followed by major rivers, and finally the coast. Another proposed that the government prohibit the establishment of any new foreign companies and prevent existing foreign firms from expanding their fleets or replacing outdated ships. All of these proposals envisioned a future in which the Chinese state could dictate terms to foreign shipping companies.

Likewise, *Shipping Monthly*'s proposals for developing Chinese shipping autonomy imagined the state in a central role. Citing the shipping policies of other countries, writers proposed ways the government could support Chinese shipping through incentive programs, subsidies, and tax relief for shipping companies and shipbuilding facilities. They called on the government to put in place the legal and educational infrastructure necessary to develop a cadre of skilled shipping personnel. Such proposals expressed a desire for state support of shipping, but others went further, suggesting higher levels of state intervention. Some proposed the establishment of a national shipping company, arguing that such a company could overcome the problem of limited capital in the private sector and establish a Chinese presence on routes—particularly overseas routes—that would take time to become profitable. Some commentators argued that the national importance of shipping was so great that the private sector could not be relied on to develop it adequately. Some also called on the state to help coordinate efforts among existing Chinese shipping companies to improve their competitiveness with foreign firms.[13]

The shipping rights recovery agenda, as articulated in *Shipping Monthly* and other publications of the time, was formulated by the government in consultation with Chinese ship owners. The agenda revolved around a vision of the state actively intervening in the shipping field, initiating treaty revision, limiting foreign navigation, and providing aid and coordination to Chinese shipping. Given the close ties between the Nationalist government and the Shanghai Shipping Association, *Shipping Monthly* may not capture the full range of Chinese ship owners' opinions, yet the publication does make it appear as if the state's broad role was accepted and even welcomed by Chinese shipping interests.

The steps that the Nationalist government took toward shipping rights recovery between 1929 and 1931 reclaimed shipping as an area of sovereign concern. Nanjing went beyond either the Qing or the Beiyang government in establishing its authority over shipping in Chinese waters, laying the groundwork for many of the agenda's proposals. The Nationalist government first asserted control over the Maritime Customs organization, which, although technically an agency of the Chinese state, had operated with relative independence through much of the early Republic. As part of this move, it took the administration of shipping in Chinese waters away from the Maritime Customs and placed it under the authority of the Ministry of Communications. Since the mid-nineteenth century, the Maritime Customs' Marine Department had carried all of the administrative functions related to shipping—the registration and measurement of ships, maintenance of channels and navigational aids, and control of harbors and pilotage.[14] Because foreign nationals staffed the Maritime Customs, in this period many saw its administrative powers as infringing on Chinese sovereignty. Since the late Qing Ministry of Posts and Communications and the Beiyang Ministry of Communications had intended to take over these responsibilities but had never done so, Nanjing was eager to rectify the situation. In February 1929, Maritime

Customs Inspector-General Frederick Maze moved its central offices from Beijing to Nanjing.[15] In the same year, the Ministry of Communications made plans for a network of Navigation Administrative Bureaus (Hangzheng ju) in China's major ports to oversee the technical aspects of shipping administration, and in 1931 it established these bureaus in the shipping centers of Shanghai, Hankou, Tianjin, Canton, and Harbin.[16]

The Nationalist government further passed a series of laws related to shipping administration, including a maritime law, regulations for the examination of pilots, and laws on the registration of vessels in Chinese waters.[17] In October 1929, the government reopened the Wusong Navigation College to assist in the training of Chinese navigators and engineers.[18] In 1930, the Ministry of Communications announced its plans to create a national shipping company by purchasing the privately held shares of the China Merchants Company.[19] This measure would not only return the company, registered as a private firm since 1912, to "official supervision," it would set it up as the core of a state-supported national merchant fleet. This process was completed in 1933, and the company was renamed the National China Merchants Company (Guoying zhaoshangju). In recognizing shipping as an arena of paramount importance to the state and in exerting state authority over it, the Nationalist government brought China's shipping administration, laws, and policies much closer into line with international practice than its predecessors had.

Treaty revision was the key to shipping rights recovery, and the Nationalist government advanced this part of its agenda in July 1930. The Ministry of Communications drew up a program for canceling the inland navigation rules of 1898 and made plans to open negotiations with Britain and Japan.[20] Despite Nanjing's overtures to the powers, treaty revision stalled in the summer and fall of 1931, affecting not only the shipping rights recovery program but other crucial issues like the revocation of extraterritoriality. At this moment, Nanjing was facing a potential civil war as Cantonese forces rallied against Jiang Jieshi, and protests against his policy of nonresistance to Japan following the 1931 Mukden Incident reached their height. The threat of domestic instability caused the powers to withdraw from the negotiations, and they were not taken up again during the Nanjing Decade.[21] Like extraterritoriality, foreign navigation rights in China remained in force until the final abrogation of the unequal treaties in January 1943.[22]

Treaty revision had been suspended indefinitely, but Nanjing continued to build its presence in the shipping field through the 1930s. In 1933, it further refined the system of Navigation Administrative Bureaus by adding bureaus in forty-six ports, specifying the areas of each bureau's jurisdiction, and reforming the internal organization of the existing ones. The Ministry of Communications took over the adjudication of disputes arising from collisions from the Maritime Customs in 1932. In the same year, the government began the process of purchasing China Merchants Company shares. In March 1933, the Ministry of Communications held a conference for the representatives of Chinese shipping firms, which reached the resolution that cooperation among Chinese shipping interests was essential to the development of Chinese shipping. In this context, "cooperation" meant adherence to government-approved plans for dividing up routes and setting rates with the intention of diminishing competition among Chinese companies.[23]

As the Nanjing government advanced its agenda for shipping rights recovery in the late 1920s and early 1930s, it expanded the state presence in the shipping field, taking over and rationalizing earlier forms of shipping administration and in the process maximizing its claims to centrality and sovereignty. Whereas the treaty revision process halted and concrete government actions made up only a fraction of what had been proposed in the pages of *Shipping Monthly*, the indisputable change between 1927 and 1933 was an expanded state presence in the shipping field, one that had been largely in abeyance since the late Qing dynasty. Although it is difficult to confirm absolutely, there is every indication that the return of the state was welcomed by Chinese ship owners as a key aspect of shipping rights recovery. If the actions of national capitalist shipping entrepreneurs like Yu Xiaqing and Lu Zuofu are at all representative, their cultivation of state patronage suggests that they sought reliable sources of support and protection in competition with foreign companies. This apparent consensus, however, began to fray after 1933, as the government's interventions in the shipping field proved both more intrusive and more limited than what the major private shipping firms had expected.

Chongqing: Liu Xiang and Shipping Rights Recovery

Examining shipping rights recovery purely from the perspective of the putative central government at Nanjing in this period offers the impression of a singular struggle between an emerging national government and privileged foreign powers. During the Nanjing Decade, however, the shipping field was far more complex than this dualistic picture allows. Nanjing's limited territorial control and the compromises it had made with regional militarists following the Northern Expedition meant that there were plenty of places within China where Nanjing's policies could be ignored or selectively enforced, and where different rules or priorities for shipping might exist. Moving throughout the country, ships could encounter a number of different regimes, and for these regimes, shipping might pose a different set of sovereign concerns than it did for Nanjing.[24]

The Upper Yangzi River was an example: after 1926, Liu Xiang and his 21st Army controlled the port of Chongqing; by 1929, their territory included the entire stretch of the river from Chongqing to Yichang. Despite a declaration of allegiance to Jiang Jieshi at the start of the Northern Expedition, Liu ruled this area with almost complete autonomy between 1927 and 1934.[25] Thus the Upper Yangzi was controlled by Liu while the lower reaches of the river were more firmly under Nanjing's supervision. Like the Nationalist government downriver, Liu was concerned with the challenge that foreign shipping on the Upper Yangzi presented to his position in the area. Between 1929 and 1934, Liu extended his regime's authority over Upper Yangzi shipping, effectively diminishing some of the treaty privileges that gave foreign shipping companies advantages over Chinese companies and forcing foreign companies to accept the authority of his government bureaus. A little later, his regime oversaw the consolidation of Chinese shipping companies on the Upper Yangzi into a single, unified company that could compete with foreign concerns.

In the diminishment of foreign privilege and the unification and development of Chinese-flag shipping, the achievements of Liu's regime were consonant with the goals of Nanjing's shipping rights recovery program. As actions taken by a militarist regime outside of Nanjing's authority, however, Liu's efforts also helped undermine Nanjing's power to negotiate treaty revision on a national scale. Liu's shipping program emerged from immediate interests—threats to his local control—and his tactics were confrontational, an approach Nanjing had abandoned in favor of diplomacy. Nevertheless, the alternative site of resistance to the treaty system that Liu's regime represented proved capable of advancing shipping rights recovery on a practical level where diplomatic negotiations failed. Nanjing's lack of full territorial control thus had paradoxical outcomes: on one hand, its inability to bring such semi-autonomous regimes to heel undermined its claims to sovereignty and impeded the process of treaty revision; on the other hand, this weakness had the effect of multiplying the potential sites for resistance against foreign privilege across the country.

Liu Xiang's concern with foreign-flag shipping in his garrison area emerged well before the Nanjing Decade and illustrates the concrete ways foreign shipping privileges challenged sovereignty even at the local level. From the moment Liu Xiang took control of Chongqing in 1925–26, he was well aware of how the presence of foreign-flag ships complicated the extraction of revenue from the port. The key to any militarist's power was the ability to generate revenue from the territory under his control, and Chongqing, an entrepôt for goods moving through Sichuan Province and broader areas of western and southwestern China, was his hard-won prize.[26] Liu's soldiers could enforce the taxes imposed on trade by searching Chinese-flag vessels for any goods that might have evaded duty, but the principle of immunity from search—based on extraterritorial protection of foreign ships—prevented his soldiers from boarding foreign-flag vessels. The significant numbers of foreign-flag ships coming in and out of Chongqing were a serious problem for Liu because they created gaps through which goods might easily evade his taxes.

When he took the city in 1925, Liu Xiang first tried to enlist the aid of the Maritime Customs in tightening his grip over Chongqing's revenue. One of the greatest potential sources of income passing through Chongqing was the opium grown in Sichuan, Yunnan, and Guizhou Provinces. This southwestern opium made up over half of that consumed in China at the time.[27] Seeking to monopolize this flow, Liu offered the Chongqing Maritime Customs a percentage of his opium revenue in exchange for searching ships for opium cargoes without labels indicating that Liu's duties had been paid. Had the customs office cooperated, this plan would have provided a means to search both Chinese- and foreign-flag ships. Inspector-General Francis Aglen (1869–1932) refused to allow the Chongqing customs to perform these searches, since the Maritime Customs was supposed to represent the "Central Government of China" (at this time the Beiyang government), which had outlawed the opium trade. Chongqing customs staff were thus forbidden to distinguish between "labeled" and "unlabeled" opium on Liu Xiang's behalf.[28]

The following year, Liu turned to Chinese ship owners in an attempt to increase the number of Chinese-flag ships trading at Chongqing. In the summer of 1926, he "encouraged"—sometimes at gunpoint—Chinese-owned ships that had been flying foreign flags to revert to the Chinese flag.[29] These reversions increased the number of ships Liu's soldiers could search for contraband and provided a ready fleet he could requisition to transport opium downriver. As such interference was precisely what Chinese ship owners had hoped to avoid by flying foreign flags, Liu offered the inducement of allowing Chinese-flag ships to fly his military flag. Under the military flag, these ships became military transports and were thus outside of the Maritime Customs jurisdiction. As the Chongqing customs commissioner noted at the time, these ships carried goods and passengers more often than troops and military supplies.[30] Liu thus provided Chinese-flag ships at Chongqing an opportunity to evade Maritime Customs duties.

After defeating his former subordinate Yang Sen in 1929, Liu Xiang gained control of the entire Upper Yangzi shipping route between Chongqing and Yichang, and subsequently took even stronger measures to assert control over shipping. Chinese companies were rapidly losing ground to the expanding foreign firms: from the mid-1920s there was an excess of tonnage on the Upper Yangzi, and freight rates had dropped. With greater capital, superior facilities, and more reliable connections to downriver ports and overseas, foreign firms like China Navigation, Indo-China, and Nisshin Kisen had enormous advantages over the majority of Upper Yangzi Chinese firms, which generally ran only one or two ships and faced constant interference from Sichuan's militarists.[31] As small Chinese firms failed one after another, Liu Xiang was losing the fleet of Chinese-flag ships available to him. To improve the situation, he and his officials revamped the Upper Yangzi Navigation Bureau (Chuanjiang hangwu guanli chu), an agency Liu had established in 1926 to search ships for contraband, into one that had greater power over Upper Yangzi shipping.[32] They made plans to unify the small, struggling Chinese companies into a single Upper Yangzi company that could compete with the foreign firms.

Liu Xiang placed Lu Zuofu, founder of the Minsheng Industrial Company, at the helm of the reorganized Upper Yangzi Navigation Bureau. This decision was directly related to Liu's plans to consolidate the Chinese firms. When meeting with Chinese ship owners earlier that spring, Liu was frustrated with their inability to agree on a means to merge their companies and decided instead to choose a single company the regime would support to acquire the others. He and his advisors chose Minsheng for this role and put Lu Zuofu in charge of the Navigation Bureau in part to raise his profile among Chinese ship owners and in Chongqing business circles.[33]

At the time, the Minsheng Industrial Company was still in its infancy, owning three ships and working only short-distance routes around Chongqing. Yet Lu Zuofu had an excellent reputation among Liu Xiang's advisors for his work in bandit suppression along the Jialing River. Lu brought many of the young men he had trained to combat bandits with him to serve in the Navigation Bureau, where they earned praise for discipline in their work.[34]

Under Lu Zuofu's leadership, the functions of the Navigation Bureau expanded from searching ships for contraband to working to ameliorate many of the problems faced by Chinese shipping on the Upper Yangzi. Most troublesome was the harm suffered by Chinese shipping companies as the result of military interference: ships could be commandeered to carry soldiers or supplies with no reimbursement for lost passenger fares, freight, or fuel costs. Lu Zuofu convened a meeting with the representatives of militarists Liu Xiang, Liu Wenhui (1895–1976, of the 24th Army at Chengdu), and Guo Rudong (1892–1952, of the 20th Army at Fuling) in August 1929 to negotiate a process through which military leaders could request the use of merchant steamships provided they paid the cost of fuel, food, and discounted passenger fares for soldiers, and allowed the ships to load and unload en route.[35] Shipping companies had also suffered considerable losses from unruly passengers. Bandits or demobilized soldiers boarded steamships and robbed passengers or extorted money from compradors. Some passengers boarded ships without tickets and demanded to be fed. The Navigation Bureau's armed soldiers enforced order on ships and docks, searching passengers for arms and ejecting any attempting to board without a ticket.[36] The bureau also tried to ensure that ships could be loaded and unloaded smoothly in port, organizing a system of transporting passengers from steamships into the city on local boats.[37]

In the summer of 1929, Lu Zuofu announced that both foreign- and Chinese-flag ships were subject to search by the Upper Yangzi Navigation Bureau to prevent the smuggling of arms and opium.[38] The announcement directly challenged the principle of immunity from search, which invoked extraterritorial privilege precisely to protect foreign ships against search by local militarist agencies like the Navigation Bureau. For the Liu Xiang regime, the primary concern was local control. The principle of immunity from search was predicated on the principle that the Maritime Customs regularly searched foreign-flag vessels, but in summer 1929 the Chongqing branch had stopped carrying out these searches. The branch had been severely understaffed since an evacuation of foreign customs personnel in 1927 and was unable to search all vessels. From the Maritime Customs point of view, the cessation of searches was a minor procedural problem because the ships entering and leaving Chongqing could be searched in other ports.[39] For Liu Xiang, foreign-flag ships moving freely in and out of Chongqing simply meant lost revenue.

Lu Zuofu's assertion of the Navigation Bureau's authority to search foreign ships was provocative, and the first power to respond was Japan. The announcement drew immediate protests from the Japanese consul and the Nisshin Kisen Kaisha. The conflict was put to the test when on August 5, 1929, Nisshin Kisen's *Yunyang* arrived in Chongqing with a naval guard on board and refused to allow Navigation Bureau soldiers to search.[40] This show of Japanese force was met by an immediate boycott of the *Yunyang*: the laborers and boat men who loaded and unloaded ships in Chongqing harbor refused to unload goods or passengers from the ship, leaving it stranded in the middle of the river. The Japanese consul demanded that Lu Zuofu call off the boycott, but Lu denied having any power to do so. After several days of this standoff, the Japanese consul and ship's captain capitulated and allowed the Navigation Bureau soldiers to search.

In contrast to Nanjing's insistence on negotiation in treaty revision, the Liu Xiang regime had few qualms about using the "revolutionary tactic" of a boycott to pressure the Japanese. Despite Lu's protestation of innocence, he had in fact staged the boycott. Anticipating that foreign shipping companies would resist Navigation Bureau searches, he had made arrangements with the dock labor and lighter guilds in Chongqing to boycott any ship refusing inspection, promising them compensation for lost wages from Navigation Bureau funds.[41] Such a boycott was already familiar to these workers: boycotts of foreign ships at Chongqing had followed the 1925 May Thirtieth Incident and the 1926 Wanxian Incident, and were occasionally revived in subsequent years.[42] Thus, the ease with which Lu Zuofu mobilized Chongqing workers' support for the Navigation Bureau was likely the effect of earlier experience with such tactics.[43] Furthermore, the memory of earlier nationalist protests allowed Lu to shape the public perception of the issues at stake: rather than a struggle for the security of Liu Xiang's revenue, the boycott of the *Yunyang* appeared instead as a protest supporting the authority of a local agency against Japanese bullying. The *Chongqing Commercial Daily*, for example, contributed to this perception by publishing the workers' statement of support for the Navigation Bureau and praising Lu Zuofu's deft response to the Japanese consul.[44]

From the perspective of Chongqing, the showdown over the *Yunyang* was a local agency's successful challenge to foreign treaty privilege. Japan's acquiescence set a precedent that would make it difficult for other foreign companies to resist future demands for searches, thus making the principle of immunity from search inoperative on the Upper Yangzi. On the surface, it appears that a local confrontation of this kind was more effective at achieving a practical diminishment of treaty privileges than Nanjing's gradual approach to treaty revision, yet it is important to recognize that this success was achieved in the context of a broader diplomatic discussion of the principle of immunity from search.

It is striking that the Japanese stood alone against the Navigation Bureau during the *Yunyang* incident. Notably, neither the British consul nor the British shipping companies at Chongqing supported Japan's protest. The absence of British response was the result of orders from the British consul-general to the Chongqing consul to allow the Navigation Bureau to search British ships without according the practice official recognition.[45] This order resulted from an ongoing debate between British diplomats in China and the Foreign Office over the principle of immunity from search. The discussion began several months before the *Yunyang* incident, in the spring of 1929, and was precipitated by an opium suppression campaign initiated in Nanjing. At this time, the Nationalist government established Opium Suppression Bureaus in ports under its control to help enforce the ban on opium and wanted these bureaus to be able to search both foreign- and Chinese-flag ships for contraband. Although initially British Minister Miles Lampson (1880–1964) had insisted that the principle of immunity from search be upheld, the anti-opium initiative complicated the defense of the principle: while British shipping companies could guarantee that no opium had boarded their ships as part of the cargo, they could not guarantee that crew members or passengers carried no opium on their persons.[46] Eventually, Lampson conceded the point because refusing search by these bureaus might produce the perception of the British using treaty rights to obstruct the anti-opium campaign. This, he said, was a position that the British could ill afford to take politically, even if these "preventative efforts" were widely understood to be a cover for official monopolies on the opium trade.[47] As the Navigation Bureau's demands were exactly in line with those of the Opium Suppression Bureaus, the British at Chongqing were told not to resist search. It took several months, however, before Lampson announced officially (in January 1930) that "authorized prevention bureaus" could search British ships as long as they didn't interfere with legitimate business or infringe on the treaty rights of British subjects.[48]

The showdown with the Japanese and the British decision not to enforce the principle of immunity from search were instrumental in establishing the Navigation Bureau's authority, but the bureau occasionally needed to reassert this authority over the following months. The Navigation Bureau threatened boycotts against foreign shipping companies that resisted its searches. Bureau employee Chen Jinfan recalled that even months after the *Yunyang* incident, Chinese passengers and workers made preparations to boycott a U.S. ship that refused search.[49] When Japanese soldiers on board the *Changyang* forced Navigation Bureau soldiers off in the summer of 1930, the ship was boycotted and its captain and the commander of the Japanese gunboat at Chongqing had to appeal to the Navigation

Bureau to clear up the "misunderstanding," after which the bureau was permitted to search the ship.[50]

Following the *Yunyang* incident, the Navigation Bureau extended its authority over Upper Yangzi shipping in ways that went well beyond searches for contraband. It established branches at Wanxian and Yichang and inspection stations at smaller ports along the Upper Yangzi. It took on a variety of responsibilities, including surveying routes, maintaining aids to navigation, resolving disputes between Chinese and foreign merchants and shipping companies, preventing the overloading of ships, and organizing a pilots' association. The Navigation Bureau also established a travel agency and a centralized booking system for passenger tickets (*gongpiao ju*). A percentage of the proceeds from these agencies supported the bureau's work.[51]

The Navigation Bureau's organizational push also extended to the business of shipping on the Upper Yangzi. According to Lu Zuofu, the bureau negotiated an agreement among the existing steamship companies not to add any new tonnage to the Upper Yangzi route, so as to give the Chinese-flag companies an opportunity to reorganize. He also claimed that the Navigation Bureau helped maintain rates at profitable levels and implemented a system in which foreign companies paid a portion of their profits to Chinese companies that had suffered losses from military interference.[52] Although no other sources corroborate his claim that these agreements were enforced, China Navigation correspondence indicated that they were under discussion in the fall of 1929. China Navigation's agent in Chongqing reported that the Navigation Bureau intended to implement control of rates and redistribution of profits by coordinating the distribution of all Chongqing cargo. The British company opposed such an idea, but the agent suggested that the Navigation Bureau could enforce it through a government-backed boycott that he described as "a weapon against which we should all be entirely powerless."[53]

Despite shipping companies' wariness of the Navigation Bureau's expansion, many praised the greater order it brought to Upper Yangzi shipping. China Navigation credited the bureau with reducing the numbers of "undesirables" on its ships and Lu Zuofu with intervening to resolve a lingering lighter boycott against British ships at Chongqing.[54] Dong Junmin, the manager of Sanbei/Hong'an's Yichang office, acknowledged the enforcement of order on ships as being of considerable benefit to Chinese companies, and he described the leaders of the bureau as "educated youth" "without the taint of officialdom."[55]

There is no question that the Navigation Bureau's activism in Upper Yangzi shipping stemmed from Liu Xiang's concerns about control of revenue. At the same time, the steps it took to diminish the inequities between Chinese and foreign companies and strengthen Chinese shipping on the Upper Yangzi went far beyond pecuniary interest and were ideologically compatible with the shipping rights recovery agenda. Although the exact chain of events is unclear, the actions of the Navigation Bureau in the summer of 1929 appear to have attracted the attention of the downriver advocates of shipping rights recovery. In August 1929, the Shanghai Shipping Association met to discuss the problems of Upper Yangzi shipping, and then sent a delegate to Chongqing to propose that the small Chinese firms form a single company under the Chinese flag, which the gunboats of the Nationalist government could protect from rogue military interference and banditry. This proposal specified that the Chinese companies should unite under the China Merchants Company.[56] By this time, Liu Xiang's plans were well under way, but these overtures may have been an attempt to incorporate them into Nanjing's shipping rights recovery initiatives. A statement issued by the "Assembly of the Sichuan People's Movement to Recover Inland Shipping Rights" (Shouhui neihe hangquan Chuan min yundong dahui) dated October 30, 1929, shows a partial acceptance of Nanjing's goals. The document declared the organization's allegiance to the Nationalist government, support for the national shipping rights recovery program, and endorsement of the unification of Upper Yangzi steamship companies, but made no reference to the China Merchants Company.[57]

As tenuous as this relationship may seem, in later years the Navigation Bureau represented itself and its projects as part of a national shipping rights recovery program. Lu Zuofu left the bureau in January 1930 and returned to the Minsheng Company, leaving his former assistant, He Beiheng (1896–1972), in charge. From 1930 to 1931, the Navigation Bureau published its own periodical, *Star-Raft Weekly* (*Xingcha zhoukan*), which was addressed to the community of Chinese ship owners in Chongqing. It reported on the Navigation Bureau's activities and shipping conditions on the Upper Yangzi. *Star-Raft Weekly* declared that the

Navigation Bureau had obtained permission from Nanjing's Ministry of Communications to oversee shipping administration in the region in the interim preceding the formal establishment of its new Navigation Administrative Bureaus.[58] Throughout its two-year run, this periodical represented the local Navigation Bureau as reporting to and receiving orders from the Ministry of Communications, as well as publishing articles on the progress of the national shipping rights recovery program and the nationalization of the China Merchants Company.[59]

As early as 1931, the relationship between Nanjing and Chongqing appears to have foundered over questions of Sichuan's independence from the center. When the Ministry of Communications established its system of Navigation Administrative Bureaus in 1931, He Beiheng traveled to Nanjing to request that the Upper Yangzi Navigation Bureau be recognized as part of it. The ministry refused He's request.[60] Although the local Navigation Bureau had formerly declared that it would accept the authority of Nanjing's bureaus, both He and Liu Xiang opposed the ministry's plan to put Upper Yangzi shipping under the jurisdiction of its Hankou bureau. Nanjing was almost certainly wary of trying to incorporate a preexisting local agency whose activities far exceeded the scope of the Navigation Administrative Bureaus, but Nanjing's refusal did not stop the local Navigation Bureau from exercising oversight over Upper Yangzi shipping until Liu Xiang's death in 1938.

Relations between the Navigation Bureau and the Chongqing Maritime Customs also demonstrate Liu Xiang's relative independence from Nanjing. Although by 1929 the Maritime Customs was without question an agency of the Nationalist government, understaffing of its Chongqing branch allowed the Navigation Bureau to assume many of its functions, such as searching ships, overseeing pilots, and maintaining aids to navigation. In 1930, the Chongqing Customs commissioner tried to reinstate Maritime Customs procedures, undoing what he called the "irregularities" brought about by the Navigation Bureau's activism. At the time, He Beiheng agreed to cooperate with customs, "in order to show the Central Government that Sichuan is an orderly state."[61] By the following year it was clear that the Navigation Bureau had not ceded any authority to Maritime Customs. Bureau staff searched ships alongside Maritime Customs employees and shared rewards for the seizure of smuggled goods.[62] Despite the presence of central government agencies like the Maritime Customs in Sichuan and the apparent desire of the Navigation Bureau's leadership to cooperate with the Nationalist government and the shipping rights recovery program, such cooperation could not interfere with the bureau's local authority. Navigation Bureau soldiers continued to search ships on the Upper Yangzi until 1938.[63]

The complex relationship between the Navigation Bureau and the agencies of the Nationalist government mirrored Liu Xiang's ambivalence toward central authority. Throughout the Nanjing Decade, Liu's nominal loyalty to Nanjing was repeatedly belied by his independent actions. In his study of Liu's regime, Robert Kapp has argued that Liu believed that provincial problems needed to be solved before Sichuan could be integrated into the nation, which may explain the persistent unease of his alliance with Nanjing. Through the 1930s until his death in 1938, Liu drew closer to the center in some respects while maintaining his independence in others. In 1931, he offered his support to Jiang Jieshi and requested a large loan from Nanjing that he never received. In 1934, Liu again cooperated with Jiang Jieshi in campaigns against the Communists in southwest China. Although this stage of the alliance brought a greater number of central government institutions and reforms into Sichuan, the province's relations with the center remained fraught until Liu's death in 1938.[64]

Liu Xiang's use of the Navigation Bureau to exert control over Upper Yangzi shipping can be characterized as shipping rights recovery by its successes in diminishing foreign privilege and aiding Chinese-flag shipping in the area. Furthermore, Liu's efforts bear a strong resemblance to the downriver rights recovery movement in their strategy of active state intervention in the shipping field, suggesting that the "return of the state" to shipping in the Nanjing Decade was not simply an outcome of Nationalist state-building but represented a wider consensus on what was necessary to change the conditions in shipping in this period. That even for a brief time there was some coordination between the downriver movement and the Navigation Bureau indicates that both recognized the similarities of their aims and strategies.

The clear distinction that can be drawn between the Navigation Bureau's actions and Nanjing's shipping rights recovery movement was that the bureau's program originated with concerns about local control. The difference is encapsulated by the Navigation Bureau's willingness to employ confrontational tactics—the boycott of individual ships—to establish authority and enforce its policies and the challenge it continued to present to agencies of the Nationalist government, such as the Navigation Administrative Bureaus and Maritime Customs. Both aspects of the Navigation Bureau's activities undermined Nanjing's claims to represent the center: the continuation of the "revolutionary methods" that Nanjing disavowed and the persistence of competing local agencies like the Navigation Bureau on the Upper Yangzi surely contributed to the treaty powers' view that the Nationalist government did not have adequate control of the country, an argument they used to defer further negotiations for treaty revision. At the same time, Liu Xiang's efforts also demonstrate how, like the repeated conflicts that induced the British to limit the use of force in China in 1926, this fractured authority could be productive in reducing foreign privilege under the treaty system. Liu Xiang's immediate concern for control meant that he had few of the diplomatic scruples of Nanjing, and foreign shipping companies and consuls had little recourse against the independence and unpredictability of his regime's actions. It is possible to view Liu Xiang and the Navigation Bureau as yet another example of an unruly warlord undermining Nanjing's treaty revision efforts, but his independent actions also forced the issue over the principle of immunity from search, diminishing foreign shipping privilege in practical ways.

Chongqing: "Disparate Things into a Whole"

When Lu Zuofu left the Navigation Bureau in January 1930, he returned to the Minsheng Company to carry out the other large task in Liu Xiang's plan: uniting all of the small Chinese-flag shipping firms on the Upper Yangzi under a single company. For Liu, a stable Chinese-flag fleet enhanced his control over trade revenue and provided a reliable infrastructure for the transport needs of his regime. For the Minsheng Company, this process meant a rapid transformation from a small company whose three ships worked short-distance routes in the Chongqing area to a company whose fleet of forty-seven ships extended all the way down the Yangzi to Shanghai. Like the diminishment of foreign privileges by the Navigation Bureau, Minsheng's expansion had important implications for local and national contexts: it had the effect of regularizing and improving the transport infrastructure around Chongqing and throughout Sichuan Province, and it produced a company of a scale to compete with foreign firms on major routes. By 1934–35, Minsheng had become a participant in national-level shipping associations and debates within the shipping field. As a major private company working on a national scale, it contributed to the case for China's shipping autonomy.

In 1930, Lu Zuofu moved Minsheng's headquarters from Hechuan to Chongqing, where the company could benefit from the support of Liu Xiang's regime.[65] The regime funneled resources to Minsheng, providing it with funds to integrate the other shipping companies and making it difficult for the other companies to compete with it. Liu granted Minsheng monopoly rights to several shipping routes and exclusive permission to transport "special goods" (*tehuo*—opium and silver) on behalf of the regime. The Navigation Bureau also helped ensure that Minsheng's business was always good. When commercial cargoes were plentiful, the Navigation Bureau would divert shipments of valuable goods, such as salt, medicines, and mountain products, to Minsheng ships. When such cargoes were scarce, the Navigation Bureau directed troop shipments to Minsheng, so the company could at least collect the soldiers' reduced fares.[66] As Liu Xiang further pursued his goal of unifying the province in the "two Lius" war of 1932, he gave captured ships to Minsheng. That Liu Xiang also provided direct financial assistance to Minsheng is evident in the initial agreement Lu Zuofu made with Liu upon joining the Navigation Bureau in 1929: all funds loaned to Minsheng from Liu's regime would be gradually paid back.[67]

While Liu provided the backing, the task of convincing the myriad Chinese firms on the Upper Yangzi to merge with Minsheng fell to Lu Zuofu. He adopted the phrase "disparate things into a whole" (*hualing weizheng*) to describe his campaign to unite the shipping firms. In some cases, he purchased rival fleets by offering the owner the price of a new ship even if the ship's actual value had depreciated. For those owners still reluctant to sell to Minsheng, Lu proposed mergers in which he paid the original company's debts in cash, compensated the owners for the remaining value of their property in Minsheng stock, and hired all of their employees. In this way, the owners, shareholders, and employees of these shipping companies became part of Minsheng's organization.[68]

The "disparate things into a whole" campaign proceeded in distinct stages between 1930 and 1937. In October 1930 Minsheng acquired its first rival company, the Fuchuan Shipping Company, with which it organized a merger. In 1931, Minsheng focused on companies active on the Yangzi above Chongqing, acquiring seven such companies over the year. In 1932, it began to buy up small firms working on the main Upper Yangzi route between Chongqing and Yichang and incorporated six, including an Italian-flag and a British-flag firm. Although the largest fleet it acquired from any one of these companies consisted of three ships, by the end of 1932 Minsheng had twenty ships and 1,000 employees. It provided regular services on the route between Chongqing and Yibin and on the route between Chongqing and Yichang. Since it had acquired a few larger ships (over 900 tons) in the process, Minsheng ships began to make occasional trips further downriver from Yichang, sometimes as far as Shanghai.[69]

By 1933, Minsheng had completed the process of unifying most Chinese-owned firms in the area and turned its attention to building a fleet that could compete with foreign firms. Between 1933 and 1935, Minsheng concentrated on acquiring larger ships, buying several over 1,000 tons from the Italian-flag Yongqing Company and purchasing and repairing the wreck of the China Navigation Company's *Wanliu*. The new ships made Minsheng a legitimate competitor on the Chongqing–Yichang route. In 1935, following a period of intense competition with foreign firms for a share of this trade, Minsheng cemented its presence by buying the seven ships and shore properties of the American Yangtsze Rapids Steam Navigation Company. In 1936, the company built two new large ships—the *Minyuan* and the *Minben*—of 1,464 tons each. By 1937, Minsheng's fleet consisted of forty-seven ships of 20,409 tons, and it became a regular participant in the direct shipment trade between Chongqing and Shanghai (see map 6.1).[70] Although Minsheng's connections with Liu Xiang's regime were still close, at this stage the company began to look outside of Sichuan to finance its expansion. A group of Shanghai banks financed the purchase of the American Company and a loan from Song Ziwen's China Development Finance Corporation funded the building of the new ships.

One of the effects of Minsheng's unification of Chinese firms on the Upper Yangzi was the improvement of local transport infrastructure in

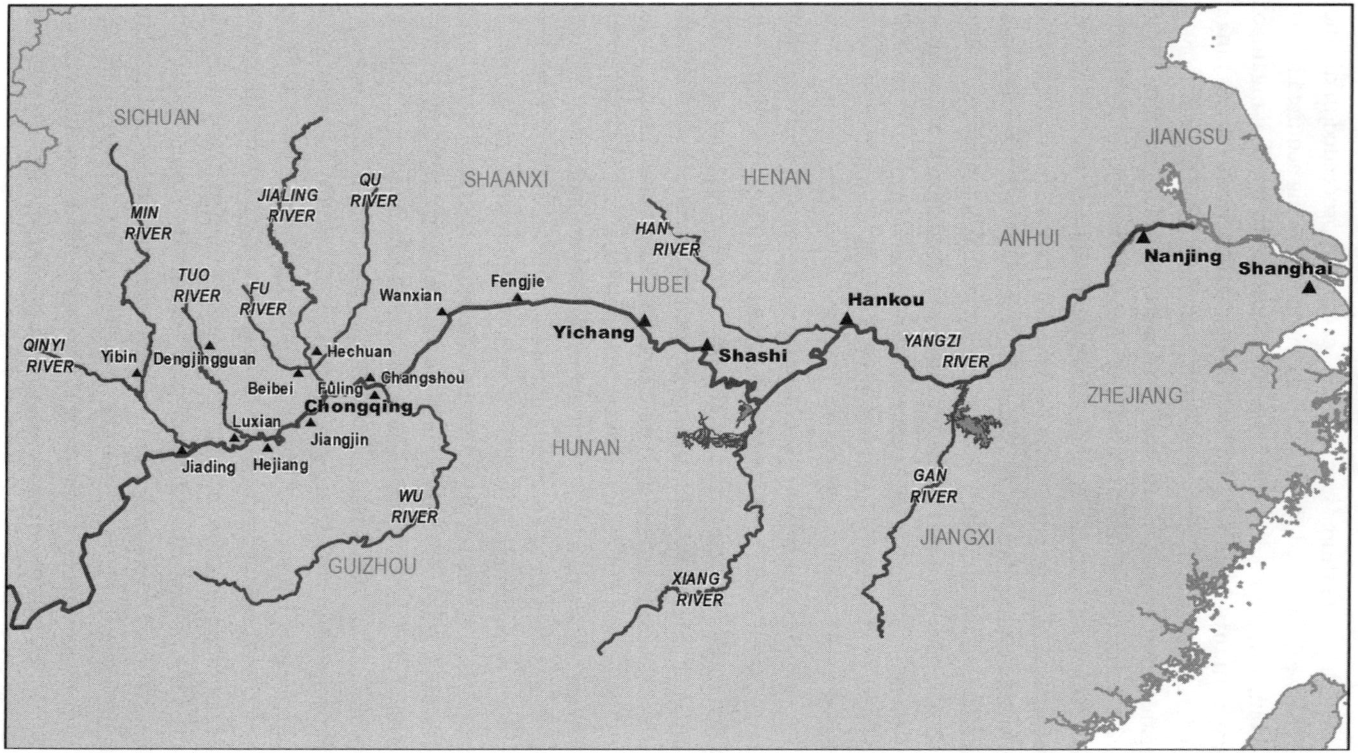

MAP 6.1 Area of Minsheng Industrial Company's Services, 1935. Adapted from Ling Yaolun, *Minsheng gongsi shi*, 57.

the Chongqing area and in ports further upriver. Minsheng organized reliable, regular passenger and cargo services in a region underserved by other modes of transport. Sichuan had few connections to roads and no railway service. Because of the navigational difficulties of the Upper Yangzi in different seasons and the poor condition of many ships, schedules had often been unpredictable. Minsheng maintained a consistent schedule on all routes. The company's control of a large fleet facilitated the scheduled services: small ships could work a tributary route in the high water season, and the Chongqing–Yichang route in the low water season when larger ships could not pass through some sections. Minsheng also tried to keep rates as stable as possible on these routes. On routes that it monopolized, the company kept its rates steady or lowered them through the 1930s. Minsheng improved passenger services, an aspect of the business that had not been important to Upper Yangzi companies in the past. It made improvements to the ships it acquired by adding safety equipment and amenities for passengers. To facilitate the movement of cargo, the company built landing stages and warehouses in all of the ports it serviced.[71] The order and coordination that Minsheng was able to effect in regional shipping would not have been possible had the field still consisted of numerous small and unstable companies.

As the company's presence on the Chongqing–Yichang route grew, Lu Zuofu tried to mediate between local concerns and the large foreign companies. In particular, he tried to steady the fluctuations in freight and passenger rates that resulted from the intense competition on this route by proposing rate agreements among the companies. Lu defended such agreements by arguing that stable rates benefited both shipper and ship owner, but the foreign firms did not always respond to his overtures. As the British companies and Nisshin Kisen expanded their services on this route at different points throughout the 1930s, they were less interested in binding agreements and tended to raise and lower rates at their own convenience.[72]

By 1937, Minsheng had become an important company in Yangzi River shipping, but its profile was different from those of the other major Yangzi firms. First, in contrast to China Navigation, Indo-China, Nisshin, China Merchants, and Sanbei/Hong'an, it was based in Chongqing rather than Shanghai. Its strengths derived from that location. Minsheng nearly monopolized shipping on the Yangzi tributaries around

Chongqing and the "upper section" of the Yangzi between Chongqing and Yibin. On the ultracompetitive Chongqing–Yichang route, where it was up against foreign companies, one estimate says that it controlled 60 percent of the trade by 1936. Although it did extend downriver to Shanghai, its downriver services never matched those of the major Yangzi companies. Minsheng participated primarily in the direct shipment trade between Chongqing and Shanghai, which transported the products of southwestern China (tong oil, raw silk, pig bristles, medicines, tobacco, tea, and mountain products) directly to Shanghai for export and brought goods such as cotton thread, petroleum, and metals from Shanghai directly to Chongqing. Its role in this trade was considerable—by 1936 it employed fifteen ships in and controlled one-third of it—but the company played very little role in the port-to-port traffic on the Lower and Middle Yangzi and offered no connections to coastal or overseas services. In 1937, with forty-seven ships, it had the largest fleet on the Yangzi River, but since many of these ships were smaller vessels designed for Upper Yangzi navigation, its tonnage was smaller than any of the other major companies.[73] In comparison to a company like Sanbei/Hong'an, which generally tried to match the services offered by the original conference firms, Minsheng had some distinct strengths, but its services were not nearly as comprehensive.

Despite this distinct profile, the mid-1930s propelled the company and Lu Zuofu from regional to national significance. This change was partially the result of Minsheng's growth: as it began to offer more downriver services, it built offices in Shanghai and thus had more contact with government and business in areas firmly under Nationalist control. It was also the result of the 1934 alliance between Liu Xiang and Jiang Jieshi against the Communists, after which there were more Nationalist government institutions and networks active in Chongqing.[74] At this time, Minsheng registered with the Nationalist government's Enterprise Bureau, became a member of the Shanghai Shipping Association, and negotiated a through-service agreement with the National China Merchants Company, although the agreement was ultimately unsuccessful. Lu Zuofu offered advice and assistance to New Life Movement leaders and published in national-level journals like *L'Impartial* (*Dagong bao*).[75]

Minsheng is considered not just a national capitalist firm but also a private (*minying*) company. This account of the company's growth, particularly its close ties with Liu Xiang's regime, may call this characterization into question. Both the China Merchants Company under Qing rule and the National China Merchants Company under the Nationalist government are usually classified as bureaucratic capital for their close relationships with government regimes, and it is worth asking whether Minsheng also fits in this category. Minsheng's case draws attention to the arbitrary criteria by which such categories have been applied, but it ultimately should be considered a private company in the Republican era. Liu Xiang's support of Minsheng through special concessions and monopolies was very similar to Qing support of the China Merchants Company, but quite different from Nanjing's relationship to the National China Merchants Company, which was state-owned and supervised by the Ministry of Communications. Although Minsheng received aid from Liu Xiang, it was a joint-stock company whose shares were privately held, and its rules ensured that the decision-making power in the company rested with its general manager, Lu Zuofu.

The definition is further complicated when we consider that both officials of Sichuan militarist regimes and the Nationalist government held shares in Minsheng, but the company was consistent in maintaining the independence of its leadership. Shareholding was a significant means through which Minsheng cemented ties with others, and prominent officials and businessmen held stock in the company or served on its board of directors. Militarists Liu Xiang, Liu Wenhui, and Yang Sen held shares, and the 21st Army officials Liu Hangchen (1896–1975), He Beiheng, and Tang Kangzhi were on its board of directors. In the mid-1930s, many with close ties to Nanjing such as Du Yuesheng (1888–1951), Song Ziwen, and Song's father-in-law also became board members or shareholders.[76] The company's rules, however, prevented any individual or single group of shareholders from obtaining a controlling share. The rules limited the voting power of large shareholders, and the board of directors were elected rather than included based on the number of shares they owned. Furthermore, the board of directors' role was primarily advisory: it oversaw company policy, but executive power remained with Lu Zuofu as general manager.[77] Minsheng accepted assistance from governments and actively cultivated their patronage, but unlike the National China Merchants Company, it was not owned or supervised by either Liu Xiang or the Nationalist regime.

The consolidation of Chinese-flag shipping on the Upper Yangzi under Minsheng and its expansion into a major Yangzi company progressed from a project to benefit Liu Xiang's regime to one of wider national significance. It provided Liu's regime with a reliable fleet and shipping infrastructure and eventually made Minsheng an important competitor on the Yangzi and a major private firm participating in the national-level debates on shipping rights recovery and shipping policy in this period. Arguably, however, its most important contribution to the national cause was that Minsheng's Upper Yangzi shipping infrastructure was well developed when Jiang Jieshi and the Nationalist government retreated to Chongqing in 1938 as the Japanese army advanced up the Yangzi River. Minsheng's large fleet, well suited to Upper Yangzi navigation, provided a crucial lifeline for the regime during wartime. Lu Zuofu became assistant minister of Communications and distinguished himself through his solutions to numerous thorny problems of transport and logistics. Although like other Chinese shipping firms the Minsheng Company suffered losses during the war, the war gave the company opportunities to build its fleet and services and plan for an extensive postwar expansion.

Nanjing: State and Private in Chinese Shipping, 1933–37

As the relationship between Liu Xiang's regime and the Minsheng Company attests, close cooperation between the state and Chinese-flag shipping was seen as the primary means of counteracting foreign dominance in the shipping field. In laying out the shipping rights recovery agenda between 1930 and 1932, the periodical *Shipping Monthly* consistently advocated for a central role for the state in fostering the growth of Chinese merchant shipping that drew on the model of the Japanese government's support of its national fleet. The proposals in these pages included state subsidies for companies to enlarge their fleets, financial programs to help increase the capital of small-scale ship owners, and support for companies to develop new routes and trades. Many proposals called for the nationalization of a major shipping firm as a necessary step to develop overseas services under the Chinese flag. In these discussions, state support was most often envisioned as a resource available to state and private firms to maximize the possibility of achieving shipping autonomy.

In Nanjing between 1933 and 1937, the Nationalist government increased its involvement in the shipping business, going beyond the legal and administrative frameworks it had established in earlier years. In many respects, its involvement adhered closely to the shipping rights recovery agenda, particularly in its decision to nationalize the China Merchants Company, a process completed in 1933. It also initiated programs designed to help Chinese shipping by reducing competition among Chinese firms. Despite rhetorical appeals to the shipping nationalism of the period, the realities of Nanjing's involvement in the shipping business resulted in the alienation of the private shipping firms. The assistance it offered was extremely limited and most of it was channeled to the National China Merchants Company alone. The private firms were excluded from this support and were subject to increasing demands from Nanjing in the name of promoting national shipping, from contributions to accepting controls on the conduct of their businesses. By the eve of the Second Sino-Japanese War, the private firms had lost faith in the idea that the Nationalist government would improve conditions for all Chinese-flag companies.

A key point in this gradual disillusionment of the private firms was the nationalization of the China Merchants Company, as the new National China Merchants Company was where the state chose to concentrate its resources. The 1933 nationalization was the culmination of a series of government interventions in the once private company's affairs that began as early as 1927. These interventions were directed at corruption and mismanagement within the company and progressively increased state supervision and control over the firm. In 1927, Jiang Jieshi issued an order to "investigate and organize" (*qingcha zhengli*) the China Merchants Company, allegedly to save the company from bankruptcy.[78] There was a political intent behind this investigation as well: Fu Xiao'an, the company's managing director, was close to Sun Chuanfang, the militarist in control of Shanghai prior to Jiang's conquest. Fu had refused the Nationalist demand of a 10 million *yuan* loan, after which Jiang Jieshi ordered his arrest for the crime of financing warlords. Fu fled, and the Nationalists placed the company under the supervision of the Ministry of

Communications.[79] The following year, the ministry dissolved the company's board of directors and demanded another reorganization led by ministry official Zhao Tieqiao (1886–1930). Zhao's measures were opposed by shareholders and his superiors in the ministry, and his assassination at the entrance to the China Merchants Company offices in July 1930 was attributed to this opposition.[80] The revelation of another financial scandal involving the company's general manager and the assistant minister of Communications in 1931 prompted the full nationalization of the company. The government purchased all of its privately held stock at 10 percent of its value. By August 1933, the company was fully state-owned.[81]

The nationalization process provides glimpses into the complex and fraught history of the China Merchants Company and its relations with the government, but the nationalization of this company was not at all controversial within a shipping rights recovery framework. China Merchants had the longest history, largest fleet, and best potential to develop overseas services of any Chinese company and was thus the natural choice for nationalization.[82] After 1933, however, the company remained something of a battleground for different interests. In that year, the government appointed Liu Hongsheng (1888–1956) to be China Merchants' new general manager and charged him with thoroughly reforming its business practices. Liu was an English-speaking businessman familiar with Western management techniques and the founder of the successful China Match Company.[83] Liu tried to rationalize the China Merchants Company's management structure and promote professionalization and expertise in the company. Like earlier attempts at reorganization, however, this program met with resistance from the military, the underworld, and factions within the Nationalist government. After the Ministry of Communications limited his power as general manager, Liu resigned from the post in February 1936. His successor, Cai Zengji (b. 1890), had a closer relationship with the Ministry of Communications. Cai was also charged with reforming the company's management, but his efforts, like implementing the New Life Movement within the company, aligned closely with ministry interests.[84]

State control of the National China Merchants Company increased between 1933 and 1937, but the levels of state aid offered to it over this period were much lower than expected. The government offered the company some direct financial assistance, such as helping it clear debts and recover mortgaged dock properties in 1933. Company leaders, however, had hoped for more sustained aid to solve persistent problems such as a heavy debt burden and outdated fleet. The Nationalist government did not provide this degree of support. During his tenure, Liu Hongsheng made repeated requests for direct government aid to reduce the company's debt, but the government offered only further loans and China Merchants had to borrow more to manage its debt.[85] The company shelved an ambitious shipbuilding program that would have replaced outdated ships and added oceangoing vessels to its fleet since the additional loans that the government offered as aid could not approach its actual cost. In the end, the company had to lease ships to update its fleet.[86] Although company leaders were disappointed in the level of government support, nationalization did improve the company's financial health generally and strengthened its position in the shipping field: after 1933 the China Merchants enjoyed better earnings and a larger share of major trades than it had since World War I.[87]

As inadequate as government support to the National China Merchants Company may have been, from the perspective of the private shipping firms of the Shanghai Shipping Association, China Merchants was the sole recipient of aid that should have been distributed to all companies. In 1933—a time of trade depression, when many private firms were struggling—the government initiated a through land-and-water service linking steamship lines to China's railway network.[88] When the Shanghai Shipping Association learned that the service was intended as a monopoly for the National China Merchants Company, private firms petitioned and later applied to participate. In 1934, the Ministry of Communications approved the participation of nine private firms, including Sanbei/Hong'an, Ning-Shao, and Dada, and required them to coordinate services with the National China Merchants Company through a joint office. Yu Xiaqing, representing the private firms, and Liu Hongsheng of National China Merchants began negotiations for administering this office. When these negotiations extended into 1935, the Railway Ministry stepped in to demand a resolution, and National China Merchants arranged to carry out the service by itself, cutting out the private firms.[89]

The private shipping firms faced additional disappointments in their relationship with the Nationalist government. At a time when many such firms were facing bankruptcy, Nanjing denied the Shanghai Shipping

Association's request to issue government bonds for the shipping industry. A shipping bond issue had been approved by the government in 1930, but the Finance Ministry delayed it because of insufficient funds. In 1935, it denied the request again. In 1936, Nanjing further failed to respond to a petition from private firms to halt the required yearly contributions they made to the Wusong Merchant Marine Academy. They argued that these contributions had become burdensome for companies in financial straits.[90]

At the same time the private firms were excluded from the through land-and-water service and denied the state aid they hoped for, the Ministry of Communications pressured them to join the China Shipping Cooperative (Zhongguo hangye hezuo she), an organization intended to aid Chinese shipping by reducing competition among firms. As initially proposed, the cooperative would lease all ships and shore properties from the shipping firms, collect all freight and passenger earnings, and distribute profits among its participants. The cooperative could dictate the tonnage on all routes; members who wanted to expand their fleets needed its approval. Member companies wishing to sell their ships were required to sell to the cooperative. It resembled a very restrictive conference agreement for Chinese firms, but it went further to promise aid to member companies and assist in establishing a Chinese-flag presence on overseas routes.[91] In 1934, the Ministry of Communications formed a committee composed of representatives from the Shanghai Shipping Association and the National China Merchants Company to organize it under the ministry's supervision. By January 1935, the committee had drafted rules and elected representatives—five from the National China Merchants Company (including Liu Hongsheng) and six from the Shanghai Shipping Association (including Yu Xiaqing)—to serve on its board of directors.[92] In October 1935, the representatives of the private shipping companies resigned, complaining of conflict on the board and that private companies' concerns were not taken seriously.[93] Thereafter, the cooperative was "established in name only."[94]

One reason for the breakdown of the cooperative may have been the conclusion of a conference agreement among the six companies on the Yangzi River at about the same time. Negotiations among China Navigation, Indo-China, Nisshin Kisen, China Merchants, Sanbei/Hong'an, and Ning-Shao for a new working agreement had begun as early as 1930 but foundered during the Yangzi shipping depression in the mid-1930s. The companies finalized an agreement in the summer of 1935, just as an excellent harvest began to improve trade conditions.[95] Although the relationship between the conclusion of this agreement and the failure of the cooperative is not clear, the participation of the National China Merchants Company and two major private firms in the conference agreement suggests that these Chinese firms had greater faith in the power of the conference to control competition among the major companies than in Nanjing to protect Chinese firms from foreign competition.

A year later, the Ministry of Communications introduced more coercive measures to entice Chinese shipping companies to participate in a cooperative system.[96] At the end of 1936, the ministry issued a new set of regulations that it called a cooperative method (*hezuo banfa*) rather than a cooperative (*hezuo she*). These regulations stipulated that all ships registered with the ministry had to enter into working agreements that set passenger fares, freight rates, and schedules on their routes as well as divided profits equally among the participants. Companies that refused to participate would have their licenses revoked by the ministry.[97] Although there is little indication that these regulations were enforced in the months prior to the outbreak of the Second Sino-Japanese War, they suggest that the Nationalist government was intent on establishing an organization that would coordinate the business of the Chinese firms.

The 1933–37 period in Nanjing suggests that the Nationalist government lacked the resources and may have lacked the intention or will to fulfill the role of state patron envisioned in the pages of *Shipping Monthly*, supporting both private firms and a nationalized company. This interval was only four years long, and the rapid shift into wartime conditions in 1937 make it difficult to judge how the situation might have evolved under more stable conditions. In this short span, the National China Merchants Company was disappointed in the level of support it received, and the private shipping firms had lost faith that the Nationalist government would help them. Along with the regime's prior failures in treaty revision, the shipping autonomy agenda was almost completely unfulfilled by the beginning of the war. More significant than Nanjing's inadequacies, however, was the clear consensus that state involvement in the shipping business was essential to achieving shipping autonomy. This was a conviction shared by the Nationalist government, shipping firms (national and private), and semi-independent militarists like Liu Xiang. This consensus continued to inform shipping debates, plans, and policies after World War II and into the early People's Republic.

Conclusion

A final comparison between Nanjing and Chongqing confirms the ideas shared between them and highlights some of the difficulties Nanjing faced in implementing its plans. Nanjing's Ministry of Communications and Liu Xiang saw intervention in the shipping business as a means to bolster Chinese-flag shipping against foreign competition, and both attempted to organize it to diminish competition among Chinese firms. Although it was a much more explicit policy in Chongqing, both regimes chose to support a single firm to lead the charge rather than offering broad support to the industry. Liu Xiang's program was initiated earlier and achieved a notable level of completion, whereas Nanjing's did not. Liu had the advantage of a more defined and localized context and a small, new, and well-managed firm through which to carry out his program. The Minsheng Company could only grow through its alliance with Liu Xiang, and although it almost certainly encountered resistance to its "disparate things into a whole" campaign, this resistance did not disrupt the campaign. In contrast, Nanjing worked on a national level, backing China's oldest and largest shipping company that had often come under suspicion for corruption and in which many different groups had a stake. Furthermore, the private Chinese firms that Nanjing tried to organize into cooperatives were larger, more complex, and better organized than the small and unstable Chinese firms consolidated under Minsheng in Chongqing. Without question Nanjing had the more complicated task, but Liu Xiang's success indicated that it may not have been impossible, if given adequate time and resources.

The significance of shipping autonomy was that it represented the full decolonization of Chinese waters. Once the treaty clauses were rescinded and Chinese-flag shipping developed enough to meet all of China's needs, there would be no place for foreign ships on China's rivers and coasts. The state assumed the central, active role in most visions of this decolonization process, not only during the Nanjing Decade but at the founding of the People's Republic as well. In 1949, the unequal treaties had already been abrogated, and the new regime declared coastal reservation for Chinese ships. Foreign shipping companies retreated from mainland China by 1953–54.[98] As the new People's Republic of China struggled to fulfill the nation's shipping needs, it worked closely with the shipping business, moving quickly to set up private–state partnerships (*gong-si heying*) with previously private firms. Although such partnerships can be interpreted as first steps toward the expropriation of private property under a socialist regime, ship owners like Lu Zuofu saw them as very much in the interest of their businesses and Chinese shipping autonomy. In 1950, Zhou Enlai persuaded Lu to return to mainland China from Hong Kong with the promise of state support for the Minsheng Company. Subsequently, Lu helped to promote the idea of private–state partnerships; Minsheng was one of the very first companies to undergo the process.[99]

The centrality of the state in achieving shipping autonomy is also visible in India's decolonization process. In India, under British rule, nationalist legislators continued to call for coastal reservation and invoked the example of Japan to argue for state support of Indian shipping and shipbuilding.[100] Before World War II, such appeals to the colonial state were not successful. After Independence (1947), the Indian government established coastal reservation for Indian ships, forcing foreign companies out of Indian waters by 1952. Furthermore, like in China, the postcolonial government also sought to build state–private partnerships with existing Indian firms. In India, these were called shipping corporations, for which the state provided 51 percent of the capital and the original firm or the public owned the remainder. Not all shipping companies welcomed this initiative, but those that had struggled through the 1920s and 1930s, like Scindia, participated actively. Between 1956 and 1961, the formerly public–private shipping corporations became a single public sector enterprise: the Shipping Corporation of India.[101] The principal difference between the Indian and Chinese context by the late 1950s was that the

Shipping Corporation of India operated alongside private shipping firms, whereas in China both the public–private and the remaining private firms were amalgamated into fully state-run shipping companies by 1956.[102]

Given the importance of socialist or socialist-influenced modes of development in China and India at this time, it would be easy to dismiss these post-Liberation/post-Independence shipping regimes as the outcomes of an ideology hostile to enterprise. Yet the history of shipping nationalism in both places in the 1920s and 1930s and the close connections between shipping and semi-colonialism/colonialism suggests that the shipping regimes enjoyed far more support from enterprise than such a view would allow. In China's Nanjing Decade, enterprise's calls to the state and the state's efforts to respond should be viewed as a mode of imagining decolonization that continued through the first decades of the People's Republic.

CHAPTER 7

The "New Steamship"

Transformations of Social Space, 1925–37

In his 1923 essay "Various Notes on Ocean Travel," writer Zhu Ziqing (1898–1948) offered a distinctive critique of the social space of the steamship. He joked that when boarding a ship from Shanghai to Ningbo, he was more apprehensive about the dirty conditions he expected in the Chinese accommodation than he was by the news that the ship had recently endured a pirate attack. He wrote:

> This was a British company's ship, and the filth on board was nearly enough to sully the colors of the British flag. But, the British say, what of it? The ship is really for Chinese, and filth is freedom for the Chinese. Why should the British bother with it? When British people ride the steamship, they can ride in foreign first class. What does it look like? Chinese travelers in second or third class are not allowed to go up there, so therefore it must be good.[1]

Going well beyond a description of the poor conditions in the Chinese quarters, Zhu pointed to their frustrating immutability and the inexorable logic by which the "British company" in question deflected responsibility for this accommodation by suggesting that its conditions were what Chinese passengers preferred. In the foreign first class, by inference, good conditions prevailed because Chinese travelers were excluded for the most part. The clear racial hierarchy of steamship classes was thus justified by a seemingly natural realm of native predilection, making the hierarchy difficult to challenge. Zhu named this situation, calling the ship "the 'imperialism' ship," emphasizing the neologism through his use of quotation marks (*"diguozhuyi" de chuan*).[2]

Zhu's critique was more penetrating than the bewilderment nineteenth-century journalists expressed over the "alienated space" of the Chinese accommodation or the more standard nationalist reading of the stratifications of the steamship as a concretization of China's predicament. His essay mocked the very rationality that lay behind the racial divisions on the steamship. In doing so, the essay anticipated an important shift in the conception of the social space of the steamship that took place in the late 1920s and 1930s. From the 1860s through this time, the social space of the steamship made the racial ideologies of colonialism readily visible in China, articulated through various practices of exclusion, the justification of racial distinction through a discourse of racial competencies, and anxieties about "position" and proximity between colonial elites and subject peoples. There were variations among companies of different nationalities, but British, Japanese, and Chinese companies all participated in maintaining and reproducing this distinct social space. In the late 1920s and 1930s, the lineaments of this space came under sharp attack, and the uniformity produced by the shipping field's shared practices began to unravel.

Chinese nationalism was the most significant motivating force behind these changes. Chinese and foreign companies began to modify the social spaces of their ships in this period, and at times, these changes were prompted by considerations of cost, efficiency, or control. Even these factors were affected by the wide preoccupation with nationalism in Chinese society. Rather than being a uniform ideology, this nationalism came from a variety of sources that included the nation-building efforts of the Nanjing regime, the specific vision of Minsheng founder Lu Zuofu, and the heightened nationalist consciousness and sensitivities of Chinese publics. The intersection of these multiple nationalisms within the shipping field brought the tacit structures that underlay the social space of the steamship under closer scrutiny and lent greater urgency to their reform. By 1937 the social space of the steamship was no longer a relic of collaboration as much as an arena of contestation within the shipping field in which the conceptions of Chineseness, modernity, and nationhood were at stake.

Nearly every element that characterized the earlier social space became a target of transformation in the late 1920s and 1930s. One of the first things to change was the racial and technical hierarchy that had characterized steamship crews. In the late 1920s, the rigid boundary that separated European and Japanese technical personnel from Chinese crew members began to blur, with increasing numbers of Chinese assuming positions requiring technical expertise. The Nationalist government's promulgation of the legal and educational measures necessary to develop and certify a cadre of skilled Chinese mariners was an important driver for this change. At the same time, the Chinese labor movement attacked steamship companies' use of labor recruiters to hire crews, a practice that had contributed to the rigidity of the distinction between foreign technical personnel and Chinese workers. The racial hierarchies of steamship crews were not entirely eradicated in this period, but they were challenged by these new conditions.

In the 1930s, a crisis experienced by numerous steamship companies caused some to reconsider the management practices at the root of disorderly conditions in the Chinese accommodation. *Shen bao* journalists in the nineteenth century had complained that the expected lines of authority and responsibility were suspended in this space; in the mid-1930s the chaos it generated threatened to overwhelm the entire ship. At the center of this crisis were the passenger attendants known as teaboys, who purchased the right to work for tips from a ship's comprador. On many ships, financially pressed compradors had sold so many teaboy positions that the teaboys could not make a living from tips and resorted to means such as extortion and smuggling to generate income. Teaboys violently resisted attempts to reduce their numbers or control their activities. The teaboy crisis affected foreign and Chinese companies, and in attempting to solve it, many questioned the enduring and nearly universal practice of using compradors to manage the Chinese accommodation. In the solutions adopted by steamship companies to address the teaboy crisis, Chinese and foreign companies diverged. Overall, Chinese companies were willing to reorganize their management structures to eliminate compradors, allowing the companies to exert greater control over this space, while many foreign companies hesitated to adopt such extreme measures. The novel management structure was pioneered by the Minsheng Company and later extended to other Chinese firms with the aid of the Nationalist government's New Life Movement (Xin shenghuo yundong). For many Chinese firms, this solution brought teaboys under control and eradicated the fraught "alienated space" that the Chinese accommodation so long represented.

Steamship companies were increasingly aware of passengers' nationalist sensitivities and were keen to respond by modifying various aspects of the passenger accommodation. As the accommodation was a key means through which the company represented itself to the public and competed with other firms, many companies made changes that attempted to create a contemporary image, distancing themselves from the more exclusionary practices of the past. In this context as well, Minsheng's effort to reimagine the passenger accommodation of its steamships was the most distinctive. From 1933 onward, Minsheng's new passenger spaces articulated a critique of prevailing practice in the shipping field and used the attractive spaces of its ships as didactic tools to reinforce a nationalist message and mold new forms of "modern" behavior for the traveling public.

By 1937 the uniform, characteristic social space of the earlier period had been replaced by multiple "new steamships," displaying different degrees and types of change. The competition among companies, particularly the heightened competition between Chinese and foreign companies in this period, made the transformations of social space all the more visible, with each company vying for favor and creating new benchmarks for comparison. Within this variation, however, Minsheng's "new steamship" stood out as a particularly cogent nationalist critique of the preexisting steamship space. In redesigning and redefining the social space, it made a clear case for Chinese expertise and competency; by doing so, it disrupted the frustratingly rigid racial associations Zhu Ziqing identified in his essay. Treaty revision and shipping autonomy were means to overcome foreign domination in the political and economic spheres of shipping. The "new steamship" was a means of questioning and dismantling the colonial culture and categories transmitted by the steamship's social space.

Blurring Lines of Race and Skill on Steamships

The characteristic feature of the organization of work aboard steamships in the nineteenth and early twentieth centuries had been the racial and technical stratification of the crew. Foreigners—Europeans and

Japanese—were employed in technically skilled positions such as captains and engineers, and Chinese were employed in the less skilled positions such as sailors and stokers. The racial divide in steamship crews was perpetuated by the absence of training and certification procedures in China, as well as the idea affecting consumers (including Chinese consumers) and the insurance business that ships commanded by foreigners were safer. Furthermore, companies' use of labor recruiters to hire Chinese crews seasonally inhibited mobility out of the common ranks of the crew. For the nineteenth and most of the early twentieth century, the China Merchants Company had conformed to this hierarchy, the outcome of the domination of the shipping field by nations with more developed shipping industries. Company leaders were aware of the problems of dependence on costly foreign personnel, but they feared insurance and other difficulties if they tried to change these conditions. Small-scale Chinese companies willing to hire unlicensed Chinese mariners for officers' and engineers' positions provided some challenge to the hierarchy, but it prevailed in most of the major steamship companies through the late 1920s. After 1929, however, Chinese seamen began to move into highly skilled positions across the field. The clearest cause for this change was the Nationalist government's effort to develop a cadre of skilled Chinese mariners to promote shipping autonomy, but a combination of other factors, such as the activism of the Chinese labor movement, the nationalist commitments of some ship owners, concerns with public relations, and the economic pressures of the Depression era, also contributed to it. These changes did not completely eradicate racial and technical hierarchies on steamship crews but within a brief span of time afforded far greater opportunities for technically trained or skilled Chinese in the shipping field than before.

The Nationalist government's development of legal and educational systems to certify Chinese steamship officers and engineers was a major change that helped give Chinese access to technically skilled positions across the shipping field. Although the Qing Ministry of Posts and Communications of the New Policies period (1901–11) and the Beiyang government's Ministry of Communications claimed authority over Chinese merchant shipping, neither had established certification measures. As part of its shipping rights recovery program, the Nationalist government committed itself to the "cultivation of shipping talent" (*peiyang hangye rencai*) to promote China's shipping autonomy.[3] In 1929, it established regulations for the certification of seamen, offering licenses to those with formal navigational or engineering training and those with practical experience on steamships. It opened the Wusong Mercantile Marine College, which offered courses in navigation and engineering.[4] The Ministry of Communications made further plans to "cultivate shipping talent" by establishing training schools in Hankou, Tianjin, Canton, and Harbin, setting up special courses for experienced seamen without formal education and sending students abroad to study navigation, engineering, and shipping management.[5]

The immediate impact of this program was that it provided formal credentials to Chinese mariners with prior experience. Although the major steamship companies employed almost no Chinese captains or engineers before 1929, smaller Chinese firms did offer these positions to Chinese who claimed some experience. In the early decades of the twentieth century, the Maritime Customs Marine Department tried to regulate the increasing numbers of Chinese acting as masters and engineers in the absence of a formal certification process, but these officials only had the authority to detain ships whose captains or engineers posed an obvious danger.[6] According to statistics from the Ministry of Communications, the vast majority of Chinese mariners who were certified in the first five years of the program (1929–34) received their certification based on prior experience rather than formal training.[7] In 1934, even after the Wusong Mercantile Marine College had graduated its first classes, only 10 out of 230 seamen certified that year had degrees from educational institutions, while the remainder listed prior experience as a qualification.[8] Furthermore, most certifications were granted for coast and river navigation, rather than overseas or short distance navigation, suggesting that the new process was predominantly providing credentials to men who had already been working in the field.[9]

These certification processes were implemented alongside a concerted effort to hire Chinese mariners in Chinese-flag companies. The case of the China Merchants Company shows how nationalism and cost were compatible motivations. After 1927, the China Merchants Company broke with its long history of employing mostly Europeans as officers and engineers, replacing them with Chinese seamen. The cost of paying high salaries to European employees had been a controversial topic within the company since the 1890s, and the precarious financial position of the China Merchants Company in the early years of the Nanjing Decade provided an incentive to recruit Chinese personnel. Equally significant, however, was the China Merchants Company's deepening ties to the Nationalist government. Even before its full nationalization in 1933, both the government and advocates of shipping nationalism viewed China Merchants as a "national" concern that should lead the charge for shipping autonomy. Thus when it came under the supervision of Nanjing's Ministry of Communications in 1927, it began to give preference to graduates of the Wusong Mercantile Marine College and the company's own school of navigation for captain's and engineer's positions.[10]

The replacement of foreign personnel within the company with Chinese was completed in less than a decade: two 1936 surveys of the National China Merchants Company's fleet show that all captains', officers', and engineers' positions were held by Chinese, with the exception of one foreign captain and one foreign engineer in the Yangzi fleet, and one foreign captain and two foreign engineers in the coastal fleet. A 1936 survey of graduates of the Wusong Mercantile Marine College showed the National China Merchants Company to be their largest employer.[11] Almost all of the Chinese technical personnel entered the company after 1927.[12]

The company's program of hiring Chinese personnel was matched with a simultaneous effort to induce foreign personnel to leave the company. A complaint from the British consul-general in Shanghai to the Foreign Office stated that there were 170 British, Norwegian, and Russian employees in the company in spring 1928 but that the company was two months behind in the payment of their salaries. In what the consul-general reported as a deliberate measure to force foreign employees out, the company was only paying back salaries to those who resigned.[13] In 1930, the China Merchants also stopped paying for European employees' home leaves and ceased making payments to retired officers' pensions.[14] The company offered the explanation that the "special rights [of Europeans] automatically lapsed" when the company "converted to a state enterprise in 1928," and claimed, "it would not be right for foreign officers to be treated any differently than Chinese officers."[15]

By the mid-1930s, private Chinese shipping firms were also employing mostly Chinese as officers and engineers. Sanbei had only two foreign captains in its coastal fleet and hired several Wusong graduates.[16]

The Minsheng Company made the recruitment of Chinese for skilled positions a component of its nationalist mission. Lu Zuofu described actively seeking Chinese trained in navigation and engineering from universities and technical institutes within China and abroad and offering these employees higher salaries than those paid to managers.[17] By 1936, Minsheng was the second-largest employer of Wusong Mercantile Marine College graduates after the China Merchants Company.[18] Minsheng also recruited employees with practical experience in Upper Yangzi navigation, calling these employees "local experts" (*tu zhuanjia*). Several Minsheng captains started out as Upper Yangzi pilots, and several of its engineers began their careers as mechanics.[19] Private steamship firms like these had an additional stake in hiring Chinese mariners since the government mandated that they provide yearly support to the Wusong Mercantile Marine College.[20]

In the 1930s, the British companies also began to hire more skilled Chinese, usually as petty officers and assistant engineers. Cost was an important factor for the British as well, as these companies were spending far more for technical personnel than were their competitors. The Nisshin Kisen Kaisha continued to reserve its skilled positions for Japanese nationals alone, but this company paid them much less—30 percent less in one estimate—than the British firms paid their European employees.[21] Chinese mariners commanded far lower salaries and fewer benefits than Europeans, so hiring Chinese in junior technical positions was a means to bring the British companies' costs down. Furthermore, in the charged political environment of the late 1920s and 1930s, company leaders believed that employing Chinese in more visible positions would improve the companies' images.[22]

The certification of Chinese mariners and their expanded opportunities for employment in the late 1920s and 1930s disrupted the formerly rigid hierarchies of race and skill in steamship crews but did not eradicate them altogether. Within this brief period of rapid change, the association of the mostly highly skilled work with foreigners persisted. Not only did the British and Japanese companies reserve all or most skilled positions for their own nationals and/or Europeans, even Chinese companies committed to hiring Chinese navigators retained small numbers of foreign personnel.[23] In 1929, the Nationalist government required all foreign officers working on Chinese-owned ships to obtain Chinese certifications. Statistics from 1934 on these foreign navigators show that their numbers were small but their ranks remained high: of nine Norwegians, eight were captains and one was a chief engineer, and of seven Britons, four were captains and three were chief engineers.[24] The association of foreign captains and engineers with safe navigation remained active, despite the growing numbers of Chinese in skilled positions: as late as 1931 some insurance companies still insisted that Upper Yangzi ships be commanded by Europeans.[25]

Ministry of Communications statistics on Chinese-certified foreign seamen also show the changing composition of this group. A large majority of non-Chinese holding Chinese certifications—133 out of a total of 178—were Russians.[26] Because Russian refugees in China at this time were stateless, a Chinese certification was likely the only one available to them. The statistics on these Russian seamen indicate that the majority occupied junior ranks: eleven captains, seventy-four first or second mates, and forty-eight assistant engineers. Some may have had prior education or training, but many earned certificates based on experience. Russians served on strike-breaking crews for foreign companies during the May Thirtieth Movement and other nationalist actions.[27] Most were refugees rather than recruits from abroad, and the salaries they commanded were closer to those paid to Chinese than to those paid to experienced European navigators. Their percentage of the 1,960 Chinese certifications granted by 1934 was small but substantial enough to suggest that some employment was available to foreign seamen who did not fit the older profile of a highly skilled and well-compensated European navigator.

The Nationalist government's implementation of certification procedures was one significant change that began to erode the formerly rigid division between foreign technical personnel and Chinese crew on steamships, but labor activism also played a part in this transformation. From the early 1920s, the labor movement in China began to demand better compensation and working conditions for Chinese seamen, and along with these demands targeted the customary recruitment practices that had kept members of the Chinese crew in subordinate positions. The General Industrial Federation of Chinese Seamen was founded in 1921 by bringing together sailors' mutual aid societies that had participated in the general strike of the 1919 May Fourth Movement. Like other labor organizations of the time, this one was built on existing native-place ties: the Shanghai branch of the Seamen's Union was made up of members of the Yanying Society of stokers and mechanics, and the Jun'an Seamen's Guild, both of which were organizations of Ningbonese steamship workers.[28] In the 1920s, the union was led by Zhu Baoting, a Ningbonese sailor and Communist Party member. In the early 1920s, the Seamen's Union participated in a wave of militant labor struggles along with other Communist-backed unions. In January 1922, the Seamen's Union famously declared a strike against overseas shipping companies in Hong Kong, which other Chinese workers in Hong Kong joined in sympathy. Several months later, the Hong Kong and Canton branches of the Seamen's Union helped organize a strike of Yangzi River seamen.[29]

In addition to significant wage increases for the workers, the strikers demanded that the companies stop using brokers to recruit steamship crews and turn this task over to the Seamen's Union. Brokers were seen as exploitative for charging workers for their positions, collecting their wages, and keeping them in debt, and the union claimed it could deliver better qualified crews.[30] Eliminating these brokers or labor recruiters was a common goal of the Chinese labor movement in other sectors as well as in seamen's labor struggles worldwide. Seamen's unions in India and Europe also called for the eradication of brokers to improve working conditions.[31] In China as elsewhere, seamen's unions were not entirely successful in replacing brokers with union representation, but through the 1920s, the Seamen's Union continuously brought the needs and aspirations of Chinese crew members to the attention of steamship company management. In the past, management had had no incentive to address the conditions faced by these workers.

After 1927, the politics of the Seamen's Union became more conservative, although it continued to be involved in labor disputes involving steamship workers. The Communist leadership of the union was purged in this year and its strike activity diminished. The Canton branch was said to be affiliated with the Guomindang left wing, and was more active in labor disputes. Between 1927 and 1934, the Shanghai branch of the Seamen's Union was led by Yu Xiaqing. Although he was prominent in Shanghai's Ningbo community, from which the majority of steamship crew members hailed, Yu was also the owner of Sanbei and leader of the Shanghai Shipping Association, and thus not likely to be an ideal labor advocate. In 1934, Jiang Jieshi further tightened Nationalist Party control of this union, putting it under the leadership of General Yang Hu

(1889–1966), the Shanghai garrison commander.[32] Despite this conservative turn in leadership, however, the Canton and Shanghai branches of the union remained important checks on the power of steamship companies to dictate terms to the crews. Seamen's gains from the labor movement were perhaps not dramatic, but by the early 1930s there were fissures in the earlier regimes of labor recruitment that had prevented them from rising in the ranks. A significant proportion of the certified Chinese seamen in *Shipping Monthly*'s 1934 survey listed their background as that of a sailor or other steamship crew member, suggesting that they had found ways to gain the experience necessary to be certified as captains or engineers.[33]

The Nationalist government's establishment of certification procedures for Chinese mariners and shipping companies' subsequent questioning of the cost of employing foreign personnel were important changes that prompted the rapid infusion of Chinese mariners into captain's, officer's, and engineer's positions in the late 1920s and early 1930s. Equally significant was the companies' growing sensitivity to the image projected by the social space of their ships to the public within the political context of Republican China. As a result, numerous companies began to depart from the previously uniform practices of the shipping field. In the hiring of skilled personnel, national identity had become a source of division among the companies. Chinese firms with explicit nationalist commitments, such as the China Merchants and Minsheng Companies, were especially vigilant about filling high-ranking positions with skilled Chinese, and many other Chinese firms did the same. Although they retained their senior European staff, the British firms tried to avoid appearing "too British" by hiring Chinese mariners for junior positions. These divergences in the social space became evident not just in hiring but also in the management and passenger spaces of the ships.

The Teaboy Crisis, 1930–37

Zhu Ziqing's critique of the "imperialism" ship had touched on a key problem of the Chinese accommodation: it remained outside the control of any specific authority but was firmly associated with Chineseness and Chinese preferences. In the early 1930s, this space became increasingly chaotic, to the point that it challenged steamship companies' control over their own ships. The usual disorder was brought to intolerable levels by the aggressive and unruly behavior of the stewards in the Chinese accommodation—called teaboys. Teaboys were not part of the crew (and thus not subject to the authority of captains and officers), nor were they company employees. Their behavior was a problem because companies had little control over public perceptions of their ships and could not guarantee the safety of passengers or the legality of the ships' actions. The problematic behavior of the teaboys was the result of the use of compradors to oversee the cargo and passenger businesses of each ship. Solutions to this teaboy crisis would thus demand significant changes to the way steamship companies were organized and managed. Solving the crisis in either the long or the short term required change, and different companies came up with different solutions.[34]

The teaboy crisis signified more than simply a call for change within the steamship business. The solutions adopted for it provide another instance of the divergence among foreign and Chinese firms in the organization and management of their ships' social spaces, and the disappearance of the past uniformity within the shipping field. Influenced by nationalist ideas and with the assistance of the Nationalist government's New Life Movement, many Chinese companies undertook much more thorough reorganizations of their ships and management. British companies, which suffered from the teaboy crisis as much as the Chinese firms, were far more reluctant to take such drastic measures. The difference between their approaches went back to the problem of the Chinese accommodation that Zhu Ziqing raised. The teaboy crisis exacerbated the conditions of dirt, chaos, and danger that were associated with the Chinese accommodation on steamships and, more significantly, with Chinese cultural preferences. The teaboys themselves provided an unmistakable spectacle of the John Chinaman stereotype. As much as the colonial critique of John Chinaman focused on issues like bodily deportment and hygiene, its target was Chinese indiscipline, ungovernability, and ultimately inability to govern. For Chinese nationalists, such a visible confirmation of this stereotype was increasingly insupportable. Several companies attempted to solve the teaboy problem, and Lu Zuofu's reform of the teaboy system in Minsheng Company in 1933–34 was the most successful. His methods were later adopted by Jiang Jieshi's New Life

Movement, which moved against the teaboys across the Chinese shipping field in 1935. The urgency that nationalism lent this reform strongly distinguished the Chinese from the foreign firms.

Teaboys had worked on steamships in China since steam's earliest days, but the crisis of the 1930s stemmed from intense economic pressures on well-established management practices. As discussed in chapter 4, ship comprador contracts required compradors to take on risk, obligating them to remit a certain amount of money to the company after each voyage and cover their own costs. Compradors notoriously resorted to extraordinary measures to maximize earnings, such as overcrowding the Chinese passenger accommodation and underreporting passenger numbers to the company.[35] Hiring teaboys was another means through which compradors supplemented their income. Teaboys were nominally members of the comprador's staff but received no regular pay. They were expected to earn a living from tips, a privilege for which they paid the ship's comprador a sizable down payment and a percentage of the tips they collected on each voyage. The cause of the teaboy crisis of the 1930s was compradors selling far more teaboy positions than their ships could accommodate. At the time of the crisis, some ships carried one teaboy per passenger, and some ships carried as many as 500 in total.[36] Such conditions made it extremely difficult for teaboys to earn a reasonable living on the ships, with the result that their behavior became increasingly aggressive and unruly.

Chinese steamship passengers had complained of poor service and forceful demands for tips from teaboys since the 1870s, but in the early 1930s, travelers began to report incidents of abuse and extortion.[37] Teaboys embarrassed or humiliated passengers: one recalled a teaboy who cursed at him and threw his money on the ground because he was not satisfied with the tip offered.[38] Teaboys had also developed new means of extracting money from passengers: since it was so common for compradors to sell more tickets than there were berths on the ship, teaboys would occupy the berths and cede them to passengers in exchange for a fee. Although the ticket price was supposed to include the use of a berth, the "berth money" teaboys demanded was as much as the cost of another ticket. Passengers unable to pay would have to sleep on the cabin floor, the deck, the hallway, or the cargo hold. Some teaboys demanded fees for the use of rice bowls, chopsticks, and water bottles, all of which were supposed to be provided to passengers free of charge.[39] Steamship company management became concerned about reports of teaboys forcing these payments from even the poorest passengers.[40]

The numbers of teaboys on steamships in the 1930s threatened to overwhelm the ship's space and undercut the companies' control of their ships. As members of the comprador's staff, teaboys were not on the ship's articles, which meant they were not subject to the authority of the captain and officers. As their numbers exploded, many engaged in illegal means of generating income, such as smuggling goods or opium on board. Because they had no authority over the teaboys crowding their ships, captains could not guarantee that their ships were free from contraband.[41] One Yangzi River captain was assaulted for trying to remove "hangers-on" suspected of smuggling from his ship.[42]

The teaboy crisis was most acute on the ships of the China Navigation and China Merchants companies. The terms of comprador contracts in both of these companies placed considerable financial pressure on their ship compradors, requiring them to cover the expenses of the cargo business with the proceeds from the passenger business. In 1930–31, both companies tried to improve earnings by revising their comprador contracts and replacing some of their compradors with new men. In the process, they discovered that the teaboys hired by the original comprador would not leave the ship. The company saw them as members of the comprador's staff, but the teaboys argued that they had already invested a substantial down payment and a regular percentage of their earnings in their positions and thus had paid for the right to work aboard a particular ship. The companies were unwilling to provide compensation, so hundreds of teaboys remained on China Navigation and China Merchants ships, obstructing reform efforts.[43]

In 1932 and 1933 China Navigation and China Merchants attempted to remove teaboys from their fleets by force, using armed guards and police. These attempts brought strikes against the companies by branches of the Seamen's Union claiming to represent the teaboys. Both companies expected support from the Nationalist government in resolving the strikes and the teaboy problem more generally, but found that it was not forthcoming at this time.

Public outcry against teaboys on China Navigation ships reached a climax in the fall of 1932, as many Shanghai residents fled upriver to escape the Japanese bombing of Zhabei. China Navigation received numerous complaints that teaboys extorted money from refugees, in some cases intimidating them into parting with their life savings.[44] The company tried to pressure its compradors to evict the teaboys, but the compradors threatened to resign. It also tried to use ships' officers to supervise teaboys, but the teaboys ignored their orders.[45] China Navigation managers were aware that forcibly removing teaboys from their ships would result in a strike or boycott against the company in support of the teaboys' right to work, but the company decided to take its chances and evict the teaboys from a single ship, the *Woosung*, and replace them with a new staff of paid stewards.[46] One night in January 1933, when the *Woosung* was docked at Shanghai, armed guards boarded the ship and dragged the sleeping teaboys off. Police blocked the teaboys from forcing their way back onto the ship at Shanghai and ports upriver.[47]

Although the Seamen's Union objected immediately to China Navigation's experiment, the company found that the *Woosung*'s profits increased and passengers praised the improvements in service.[48] The experiment revealed the extent of compradors' financial dependence on teaboys: a comprador could no longer meet his expenses after the loss of the ship's teaboys, and his salary had to be increased.[49] The Shanghai branch of the Seamen's Union was satisfied with the company's promise to recruit its paid stewards from among the better behaved *Woosung* teaboys, but the Canton branch formed a "*Woosung* Tragedy Support Committee" that initiated a strike against the China Navigation Company in June 1933.[50]

China Navigation believed it could weather the strike because it had the support of passengers, other steamship firms, and the Nationalist government in attempting to resolve the crisis.[51] In the summer of 1933, representatives of China Navigation and the other Yangzi River steamship lines met with representatives of the teaboys, the Shanghai branch of the Seamen's Union, and General Yang Hu to negotiate an agreement under which all steamship companies could reduce the numbers of teaboys on their ships and exert greater control over them. The meeting concluded with a detailed plan: compradors would no longer be allowed to collect payments from teaboys, and teaboys would not be allowed to ask for tips. Instead, the companies would raise ticket prices 15–20 percent to pay teaboys regular wages. Companies would also be allowed to reduce teaboy numbers quickly by discharging those with infectious diseases and paying off known troublemakers.[52] As the steamship companies had received assurances of General Yang's support for this agreement, they expected government help in enforcing the new conditions.[53]

As the strike against China Navigation wore on through the fall of 1933, support for this settlement disintegrated. The Nationalist government withdrew, a change that some attributed to the Guomindang left wing's accusation that Nanjing was supporting the interests of foreign companies over those of Chinese workers.[54] Some within China Navigation blamed Yu Xiaqing, who was head of the Shanghai Seamen's Union and owner of rival steamship firm Sanbei/Hong'an. They claimed Yu was using the union to block the settlement because he had collected large deposits from teaboys himself to finance new ships for Sanbei, and any plan that involved paying teaboys or refunding their deposits would put him in desperate straits.[55] Moreover, China Navigation did not have the full support of other foreign steamship companies: Nisshin's teaboy problems were not nearly as severe, and Indo-China was engaged in negotiations with the Canton Seamen's Union over a different labor dispute.[56] There was little prospect of a general resolution for the teaboy crisis among these different interests. In November 1933, after more than five months of strike activity, China Navigation settled the strike on its own with a large cash payment and the reinstatement of some of the original *Woosung* teaboys.[57] The company asked the working teaboys to wear uniforms, carry identification, and follow the orders of the captain and officers, but it decided to suspend any further initiatives to address the teaboy crisis until a Chinese company took the lead.[58]

The newly reorganized National China Merchants Company, under general manager Liu Hongsheng, took up the issue of teaboys late in 1933 as China Navigation abandoned its efforts. Charged with improving management and curbing abuses within the company, Liu planned to reform the use of ship compradors, taking the passenger business out of their hands and subjecting them and their staffs to the captain's authority. Under this new system, teaboys would be paid wages.[59] Liu found his reforms nearly impossible to implement because he could not remove uncooperative compradors and teaboys from China Merchants ships. He found that comprador positions had been passed down through several generations of the same family, and in many cases these families had influential connections. Often, the man who held the title of comprador had never ventured onto the ship and had little control over the subordinates who ran its day-to-day business. When Liu tried to dismiss teaboys found guilty of misconduct, the Seamen's Union organized a strike against the China Merchants Company.[60]

Facing the compradors' and teaboys' recalcitrance and the union's opposition, Liu sought support from allies in the Nationalist government. Although his former classmate, Finance Minister Song Ziwen, endorsed his efforts, he encountered resistance to his reforms from other parts of the government. In the end, he received no government help in settling the strike. A China Navigation Company report described his frustration:

> Lieu's [Liu Hongsheng's] view is that the Government have so far, either deliberately or through actual ignorance of conditions, either shelved or ignored the gravity of the teaboy issue, which he himself considers a matter of the first importance, realising that without a settlement of it, real control, and consequently efficiency of management, cannot be achieved; and he is determined to force the Government to face the problem they have hitherto shirked.[61]

Liu and the China Merchants board of directors threatened to resign if they did not get assistance from the government in removing compradors and teaboys from the ships. It was not until two years later, when the New Life Movement took up the teaboy problem in 1935, that Liu got the help he expected.

As the China Navigation and China Merchants companies conceded defeat in their attempts to solve the teaboy crisis, it was becoming increasingly evident that the Minsheng Company had found a solution. Passengers reported that on Minsheng ships, which in 1933–34 were just beginning to extend services from the Upper Yangzi to downriver ports, the teaboys' numbers were carefully controlled and they did not demand tips. Minsheng teaboys wore uniforms and provided excellent service, ranging from helping passengers with luggage to introducing them to the ship's amenities and sights of historical or scenic interest en route. On many Minsheng ships, teaboys served as the ship's security force, carrying out armed searches for weapons or bandits.[62]

The distinct profile of Minsheng teaboys was the product of the company's particular system of organization and management, one that had been implemented in stages as Minsheng consolidated the Chinese-owned companies on the Upper Yangzi and began to expand downriver. This system was very different from the prevailing practices in the other companies because Lu Zuofu had designed it as a response to what he perceived as the problems of the shipping field when he founded Minsheng in 1925. In that year, Lu and his associates surveyed the mostly small-scale Chinese-owned shipping firms in the Chongqing area. Anxious to recruit investors for Minsheng at a time when shipping was seen as an extremely volatile business, Lu looked for ways to address the sources of that instability.[63]

Lu rejected the strategy—common throughout the steam shipping business from the largest to the smallest companies—of contracting out the management of different aspects of the business to middlemen who assumed some of the risk. The strategy was evident in the largest firms' use of compradors, but was even more extreme among the small Chinese firms Lu surveyed. Chinese firms in the Chongqing area used what they called the "three responsibility" (*sanbao*) system on their ships, in which they not only contracted out the ship's passenger and cargo business but also recruited their captains and engineers on a similar basis.[64] Captains, engineers, and compradors all received small salaries out of which they covered all costs of their area of responsibility (including subordinates' wages, supplies, and repairs), assumed the risk if funds fell short, and profited if they were able to generate income. This system was a cheap and convenient way for small companies to manage their fleets without having to invest in a large staff, but it intensified many of the problems associated with the comprador system in the larger steamship firms.

Lu Zuofu's critique of the three responsibility system was that it pitted the interests of the employees against those of the company. Ship owners were most likely to hire the person offering the best returns on the lowest salary, rather than the one with the best skills or qualifications. The system gave compradors every incentive to smuggle cargo, carry passengers without tickets, and take bribes without regard for the company's reputation. Captains and engineers might skimp on staff, supplies, and repairs, thereby risking the safety of the ship. All three were likely to keep their subordinates' wages low and collect deposits from them, which could compromise control over the staffs. Lu Zuofu observed that the three responsibility system created independent factions on board a ship rather than a single chain of command, and each faction had cause to pursue its own gain rather than work for the benefit of the company. He further objected that if employees could not work in the interest of the company, they would have no ability to work in the interests of society or the Chinese nation.[65] In later writings, Lu described the use of compradors as a way for foreigners to exploit a particularly Chinese "every man for himself" mentality.[66]

In the Minsheng Company, Lu replaced this system with a vertically integrated corporate hierarchy in which every worker was a salaried company employee. In its overall structure, authority was centered on the company's general manager (Lu Zuofu), below which level there were specific departments—general affairs, marine, cargo, and accounting—further broken down into divisions. Division managers reported to department managers, who reported to the general manager. This hierarchy extended to the ships: rather than ship compradors, Minsheng ships carried salaried "business managers" who remitted all funds to the company's main office. Even the lowest level of employees, such as teaboys, received wages and reported to supervisors—the ships' business managers.[67] Minsheng implemented this system as it incorporated the Chinese firms in the Chongqing area. In 1933, Lu Zuofu declared that while the comprador system remained a problem for other foreign and Chinese shipping companies, "it is only our company that has decisively sought out methods and forcefully rectified [this system], and we have finally seen our efforts succeed."[68]

Minsheng teaboys were unique not just because they were paid but because they were carefully recruited, trained, and supervised. The company recruited low-level employees such as sailors, stokers, office workers, and teaboys through open examinations rather than through personal introductions or labor recruiters. To be eligible for the examination, a prospective employee had to be between the ages of eighteen and twenty-five, be a graduate of elementary or middle school (or equivalent), be free of addictions and communicable diseases, and present a letter of guarantee.[69] The examination included written tests of Chinese, arithmetic, English, record-keeping, and "general knowledge" plus a physical examination, psychological examination, and personal interview.[70] The requirements and exam content demanded a younger and much better-educated worker than teaboys in other companies. Company leaders wanted to hire "educated youth" because they saw them as easier to train and less likely to indulge in pastimes that could interfere with their work, such as gambling, smoking opium, or visiting prostitutes. The examinations were competitive: between 1932 and 1935, the company held them three or four times a year to recruit different types of workers. The acceptance rate rarely exceeded 20 percent and was often far lower.[71]

If hired, teaboys and other entry-level workers had to complete two months of training before taking up their positions. The company produced manuals such as *Essential Information for Teaboys* (*Chafang xu zhi*) that introduced job requirements and company expectations and tested employees on them at the end of the training period (see figure 7.1). All workers—even office workers—studied the basics of navigation and ship safety so that they would be familiar with the demands of the shipping business. Military drills and the use of weapons were also part of the training process, which allowed teaboys to act as both stewards and security forces on the ships. All new employees were trained in the "Minsheng spirit" (*Minsheng jingshen*) of active and dutiful service to the company and Chinese nation.[72]

On the job, Minsheng teaboys were subject to company supervision and discipline and also had opportunities to advance within the company. Minsheng had a system of rewards and punishments to encourage workers to follow company rules. Rewards ranged from a commendation to a promotion, and punishments ranged from a "recorded error" to dismissal. This system allowed the company to weed out those who were not amenable to its practices and continue the training of all workers.[73] It held competitions, designated model workers (publishing their profiles in the company magazine, *New World*), and carried out campaigns to improve service and economy—such as maintaining the cleanliness of ships or conserving fuel.[74] During a campaign to improve the service provided to passengers in 1933, Lu Zuofu cited the paid *Woosung* stewards and the performance of service workers in other companies and industries as models.[75]

Workers could earn raises through good performance of their jobs or through a high score on occasional, voluntary tests of Chinese, English, math, general knowledge, and fire prevention skills.[76] The company developed training programs that would allow workers in low-level jobs to advance to higher positions. Sailors could train to become helmsmen, stokers to become assistant engineers, cargo handlers to become hold

FIGURE 7.1 Minsheng Company Teaboy Reading *Essential Information for Teaboys* (*Chafang xu zhi*) *Minsheng shiye gongsi shi yi zhounian jinian kan*, 1937. Courtesy of Minsheng gongsi, Chongqing.

supervisors, and accountants to become business managers. Even teaboys had the opportunity to advance to the ship manager's staff. Particularly able employees were recommended for apprenticeships and special training courses.[77]

As Minsheng expanded and became a more visible presence on the Yangzi River, the degree of discipline and order on their ships became the envy of the field. The captain of a China Navigation ship recalled: "When times were bad and passengers scarce, it was a depressing sight to see a Ming [Minsheng] ship pass with only a handful of men in uniform, including the cooks, standing on deck; then later to pass a ship under a foreign flag with its lower decks a teeming mass of people, the great majority of whom would be unpaid hangers-on."[78] Press accounts from the time indicate that Minsheng's novel practices attracted attention and favorable comparisons to other companies, both Chinese and foreign.[79]

Minsheng's organization and management was unprecedented in the shipping field, but not entirely original in the business world. In the 1920s, other industries that had used compradors began to replace them with professional managers.[80] Liu Hongsheng's reform of the China Merchants Company was comparable in its effort to replace compradors with managers and bring ships under the company's control. What set Minsheng apart was its ability to implement a novel organization with very little opposition or resistance. In this, the Chongqing-based firm had some distinct advantages over its Shanghai-based competitors: it was a new company, so it did not have a long management history to overturn or workers with long histories in the firm. Minsheng also enjoyed a close relationship with military governor Liu Xiang and could count on his support. In the late 1920s, Liu had driven both Nationalist and Communist labor organizers out of Chongqing, so Minsheng did not have to contend with labor unions in the way the downriver companies had.[81]

The impact of Minsheng's reorganization of the ship within the steam shipping field was tremendous. As a Chinese company that had succeeded in ordering its ships where others had failed, Minsheng disrupted the once immutable association of onboard chaos and filth with Chinese preferences. If, as Zhu Ziqing had suggested in his essay, it had seemed impossible to challenge the idea that "filth is freedom" for the Chinese when the Chinese accommodation was in disarray and Chinese passengers were excluded from the foreign accommodation, the appearance of Minsheng's disciplined teaboys and orderly ships dramatically challenged this assumption. More than a victory for the Minsheng Company itself, it provided a demonstration of the nationalist potential of new forms of management in a field in which Chinese and foreign firms were in close competition.

The nationalist significance of Minsheng's management techniques was affirmed by the leaders of Jiang Jieshi's New Life Movement, who adopted them as the template for solving the teaboy crisis on Chinese ships in spring 1935. Inaugurated the previous year, the New Life Movement was intended to be a mass movement to transform Chinese society, a moral regeneration of the Chinese people that would make them into "new citizens" committed to the nation.[82] The movement is best known for its campaigns to improve standards of hygiene and civility in public and private life. Although criticized for its authoritarian style and seemingly trivial preoccupation with rectifying bad habits such as spitting or leaving clothes unbuttoned in public, it was an attempt to redress the perceived Chinese deficiencies of hygiene and behavior that reinforced the John Chinaman stereotype. In this frame, the clean habits and bodily discipline of the Chinese people would demonstrate China's ability to govern itself.[83]

Teaboys were a natural target of the New Life Movement, offering a veritable spectacle of indiscipline and ungovernability. On most ships, teaboys were fractious and uncivil, ragged and suffering from disease, and well beyond the authority of captain or company. The New Life Movement wanted to do more than exhort teaboys to behave better; it wanted to transform the structural conditions that underlay the teaboy crisis and integrate these men into the collectives of company and nation. Minsheng's methods provided a model, and the New Life Movement provided support and sometimes muscle to other Chinese steamship companies to transform along these lines.

In spring 1935, New Life Movement leaders traveled to Shanghai and met with the heads of Chinese shipping firms (such as Liu Hongsheng, Yu Xiaqing, and Lu Zuofu) and with General Yang Hu to discuss how to use the movement's resources to address the teaboy problem. New Life organizers voiced their approval of Lu Zuofu's methods of selecting, managing, and training teaboys as "very concrete and in line with the spirit" of their movement. They made recommendations that were based on Minsheng's policies, including the abolition of the comprador system, the selection of employees through examinations, the provision of systems of advancement, and training in specific work skills and general knowledge of national defense, economy, and shipping.[84] New Life further advocated that steamship companies adopt methods of job evaluation, rewards and punishments for performance, and extra learning opportunities to develop work as well as artistic and athletic skills.[85] Later that year, the Ministry of Communications ordered the National China Merchants Company and private Chinese shipping firms to implement the New Life Movement's recommendations on board their ships.[86]

The ministry's order was ambitious, because it demanded the thorough reorganization of most Chinese shipping companies. The National China Merchants Company began later in 1935 by reforming a single ship, the *Xin Jiangtian*. This ship worked the Shanghai–Ningbo route and carried 564 teaboys even though it required 170 at most. The company planned to dismiss half of the teaboys and make the other half paid employees, receiving a salary of sixteen *yuan* a month and a five *yuan* per month food subsidy. New Life Movement personnel helped the China Merchants Company secure an agreement with the Seamen's Union not to obstruct the teaboys' dismissal.[87] Even with this assurance, the company found it had to pay the dismissed teaboys the equivalent of several months' wages to keep them off the ships.[88] The remaining *Xin Jiangtian* teaboys were sent in groups to a "New Life Training Center" on the China Merchants Company's wharf in Pudong. There, New Life Movement personnel provided two months of military and job training, during which they were instructed on improving their service, politeness, and hygiene. After two months, the trained teaboys returned to the ship and a new group arrived at the center.[89]

Following the experiment on the *Xin Jiangtian*, the China Merchants Company took measures to reduce teaboy numbers throughout its fleet. Each ship held a lottery in which teaboys holding lucky tickets became paid employees and those without were dismissed with a small cash payment.[90] Like the *Xin Jiangtian* experiment, each teaboy who retained his position underwent two months of training by New Life Movement instructors. In addition, inspectors from the New Life Movement staff were stationed on China Merchants ships to aid in the enforcement of the changes and new standards of behavior.[91] Teaboys who resisted could be conscripted into the army.[92]

The New Life Movement provided the external support the previous attempt to address the crisis had lacked, and it set in motion a longer process of bringing ships and teaboys under the China Merchants Company's control. In February 1936, Liu Hongsheng's successor, Cai Zengji, tried to replace ship compradors on Yangzi steamers with salaried pursers. Like Liu before him, Cai found it nearly impossible to get rid of the existing compradors, and eventually he reappointed them under new terms, renaming them "business managers."[93] An inspection report from later that year warned that since so many of the old compradors remained in these positions, the company needed to be vigilant against the reappearance of old abuses. The same report stated that most ships still carried excessive numbers of teaboys, many of them older than the maximum age of fifty stipulated in the company's rules, and suggested that all teaboys over sixty-five be required to resign.[94] The China Merchants Company continued to try to regulate teaboys' behavior, promulgating rules that prohibited practices such as demanding tips, selling berths, boarding passengers without tickets, smuggling, stealing, and offending officers or passengers. Teaboys could be fined for failing to wear uniforms, ignoring orders, disturbing passengers with loud talk, and sleeping outside of their allotted places.[95] In July 1937, the company announced new procedures for hiring teaboys that made literacy a prerequisite and dropped the term "teaboy," replacing it with "server" (*qinwu sheng*) to refer to these workers.[96]

As difficult as reforming existing practices was, many private steamship firms also requested the New Life Movement's aid in carrying out similar programs on their ships. Teaboys of the Dada and Datong steamship companies began their training in December 1935, and other private firms invited New Life inspectors onto their ships. Provincial New Life groups carried out reforms on ships on inland waters routes, and the leadership planned to extend their program to municipal shipping companies in Shanghai.[97] It is unlikely that all Chinese shipping companies undertook to transform in this way, but a significant number accepted the assistance of the New Life Movement to begin the process.

The reform of steamship companies' organization along the lines of the Minsheng model was a measure that set Chinese shipping companies apart from foreign companies in this period. The China Navigation Company had suffered from the teaboy crisis and already expended time and resources trying to ameliorate it, but it balked at adopting these methods to solve the problem. China Navigation managers were impressed with the results they saw from the collaboration between the China Merchants and the New Life Movement, but they rejected the ideas of paying teaboys regular wages and compensating dismissed ones. They were concerned that the generosity of the wages and food allowances for China Merchants teaboys would lead to similar demands from their own workers. They speculated that the China Merchants Company was able to afford these because it was receiving subsidies from the Nationalist government.[98] China Navigation was willing to pay to solve its teaboy problem but was not willing to make a long-term investment in these workers. In 1937, the company made a deal with General Yang Hu to dismiss teaboys found unfit for service or guilty of misconduct. To secure support, the company made payments to Yang, several branches of the Seamen's Union, and the Ministry of Foreign Affairs and the Ministry of Communications. Even as company managers admitted that this was only a temporary solution to the problem, the company still refused to put teaboys on its payroll. It also continued to use ship compradors to run its cargo and passenger businesses.[99]

For the British companies, bringing their ships under closer control was desirable, but for many Chinese firms, the New Life Movement, and the Nationalist government, the persistence of the teaboy problem was intolerable. Teaboys' behavior embodied the John Chinaman stereotype, and their overrunning and overwhelming of ships in the mid-1930s presented a spectacle of Chinese indiscipline and ungovernability. Although the British firms might see it as a limited problem to be weighed against other costs, Lu Zuofu had demonstrated that teaboys could be reinvented as well-disciplined, contributing members of the company and the nation. Minsheng's measures were not simple to adopt, but the government and state and private shipping firms embarked on the process to bring their ships under control and transform the negative image of Chineseness that teaboys exhibited. The parallel management practices of the steamship companies that had determined the social space of the steamship in the past had diverged clearly along national lines.

Reconceiving Passenger Space, 1930–37

The passenger accommodation was another aspect of the steamship's social space that was increasingly questioned and transformed in late 1920s and 1930s China. Many companies sought to distance themselves from the earlier organization of the passenger space or provide new alternatives to it, particularly for Chinese passengers. The companies responded to both Chinese nationalist sensibilities and the more exacting demands of Chinese consumers who had numerous steamship lines from which to choose. Passenger accommodation was yet another space in which the approaches of the steamship companies diverged, as they adopted different measures and implemented different degrees of change. In this arena, once again the Minsheng Company provided the most evident rupture with past practice, offering a thoroughly revamped passenger experience aboard its ships. In doing so, Minsheng did not simply redesign the physical space, it reimagined the passenger as someone who could be transformed by his or her experience of the ship.

In the late 1920s, some companies tried to meet consumer demands and acknowledge nationalist feeling by distancing their passenger accommodation from past associations. As the China Merchants Company came under Ministry of Communications supervision in 1928, for instance, it changed the nomenclature of its passenger classes in response to "numerous requests from customers." The company abandoned the standard Chinese terms for passenger classes that had been used throughout the shipping field in the past. It changed the older, more descriptive names—"saloon," "mandarin class," "cabin class," and "steerage"—to a more straightforward ranking: "special class" (*tedeng cang*), "first class" (*toudeng cang*), "second class" (*erdeng cang*), and "third class" (*sandeng cang*).[100] The next year, China Navigation decided to remove the term "Chinese" from the English names of the three classes previously designated as such in its advertisements and publications.[101]

The sense among the companies that the existing passenger arrangements had become outdated was confirmed by British companies adding a new class for Chinese passengers in the early 1930s. They called this new class "intermediate saloon" and designed it to provide Chinese passengers a higher level of service and luxury than the preexisting Chinese first class (or mandarin class). It was called "intermediate," however, because it remained distinct from the foreign first class (or saloon). The new class was partly a response to the teaboy crisis: run by the captain and staffed by stewards rather than coming under the ship comprador's authority, it removed elite Chinese travelers from the melee of the regular Chinese accommodation. Indo-China's advertisements for the new class in 1931 and 1932 emphasized service: it was for the convenience of "China's gentlemen and merchants" (*Zhongguo de shen-shang*), provided private cabins, offered a choice of Chinese or Western food, and provided service "like that in Western accommodation"—no tipping required.[102] A review of this class in the Chinese magazine *China Traveler* (*Luxing zazhi*) praised it as significantly more orderly and comfortable than the Chinese first class but noted that the companies had downgraded the quality of the older class by altering the ships to accommodate the new one, making it barely distinguishable from second class.[103]

Correspondence among China Navigation Company managers in 1929 reveals the debates and decisions that went into creating the intermediate saloon class. The managers acknowledged increased demand from Chinese passengers for luxury accommodation. They also acknowledged that the political climate in China demanded the eradication of distinctions between "foreign" and "Chinese" accommodation, particularly in the most expensive classes. Yet they hesitated to combine the old "foreign" and "Chinese" first classes into a single class. One of the obstacles was the steep price difference between the two, which they questioned whether Chinese passengers would be willing to pay.[104] More significant was their lingering concern about proximity between foreign and Chinese passengers, which they articulated, characteristically, as a problem of *Chinese* travelers' preferences:

> In the event of the combined foreign/Chinese first class being adopted, it is the idea that tickets be purchased through our office on personal application, so that the standard of cleanliness, etc., be kept up. This would seriously affect the whole system on which this business is being worked by hotels, and would be most unpopular with passengers who prefer to book their accommodation through brokers and would resent any interference with this.[105]

The passage reveals the company's intention to monitor which Chinese passengers could travel in this class by requiring them to apply in person, ensuring "cleanliness, etc." presumably by excluding some applicants. But it quickly shifts its focus to anticipating Chinese passengers' objections to booking tickets in a new way.

This correspondence shows that the new intermediate saloon class was the compromise that permitted the company to address the new demands of Chinese travelers while postponing deliberations on the question of whether foreign and Chinese first classes should be combined. By offering better accommodation to Chinese travelers at only a slightly higher cost, the intermediate saloon provided "a better chance for a decision at some future date as to the possibilities of being able to combine the two classes."[106] The China Navigation managers perceived the need for change, but they were reluctant to abandon the older organization of the passenger space completely.

The Minsheng Company, by contrast, had no investment in the previous arrangement of passenger space. As it had done in the management of its ships, Minsheng made a point of rejecting the standard practices of the shipping field in its passenger business and accommodation. The company's general approach to passengers originated with Lu Zuofu's survey of Chongqing shipping companies in 1925. He observed that these companies prioritized their cargo business well above passenger services, and because the availability of cargo determined their shipping schedules, passengers were often delayed as ships waited in port. Lu Zuofu planned to use passenger services as a means to distinguish Minsheng from the other companies and profit from it. From its earliest days, Minsheng committed to a predictable schedule to benefit passengers.[107]

Lu Zuofu's writings provide some insight into the experiences on other companies' ships, against which Minsheng constructed its passenger accommodation and services. His *Travels to the Northeast* (1930), for example, recorded his impressions of a trip to Qingdao, Dalian, and other coastal cities, and he criticized the privileges that foreign passengers enjoyed on steamships in different parts of China. Lu described preferential treatment given to foreigners traveling alongside Chinese passengers. Entering a crowded third-class cabin on one voyage, Lu and his companions placed their baggage in an empty space in the center. Several Russian passengers arrived a few moments later and pushed the luggage aside. A teaboy explained to Lu that the center of the third-class cabin was reserved for such foreign passengers. Since there was no other available space in the cabin, he and his party had to settle in the cargo hold. Lu objected to the idea that the Russians had paid the same fare as the Chinese passengers in third class but were accorded special privileges as foreigners. He commented that such an experience should increase Chinese passengers' appreciation of Chinese-owned steamship companies.[108] The text records Lu's disapproval of the stratification of passenger classes on steamships more generally. He and his companions traveled third class throughout the trip, but when he had an opportunity to explore different parts of a ship, he was perplexed by how far superior the conditions in second class were to those in third class and was annoyed that he was not even allowed to enter the saloon accommodation. For a difference in price of only a few *yuan* or a few tens of *yuan*, he wrote, "both heaven and hell can be found on a steamship, partitioned only by cabins and decks."[109] These specific incidents and observations may not have informed Minsheng policy, but they reflect some of the key values embodied in the company's passenger accommodation. Minsheng ships never provided any spaces specifically designated for foreign passengers. They worked to minimize the differences between passenger classes: the company's larger ships offered the full range of saloon and first-, second-, and third-class accommodation, and tried to provide good service and amenities in all of them.

Minsheng's approach to its passenger accommodation is explicated in greater detail in descriptions of its 1933 campaign to improve passenger services in the company magazine, *New World*. Initiated after Minsheng had consolidated the Chinese companies on the Upper Yangzi, the campaign targeted services and amenities in all classes of travel. In its most concrete measures, it tried to redress the most common complaints of travelers. For instance, the company established a system to ensure that every Minsheng passenger was guaranteed a berth, limiting ticket sales to the precise numbers of berths on each ship, and requiring staff to wire the numbers of still-empty berths ahead to the next port. Raising ticket prices slightly, Minsheng also tried to improve the quality of its food and replaced washrooms with baths with running water in all classes.[110] In the third-class accommodation, in which berths were arrayed in an open cabin, the company designated sections to be curtained off to provide privacy for female travelers.[111] As part of the campaign, Minsheng teaboys were required to improve the precision, hygiene, and attitude with which they performed their regular tasks as well as to offer new services to passengers. Teaboys and other staff were trained to answer questions about the ship, the shipping business, and the Minsheng Company as well as points of interest and scenery en route.[112] They learned to provide local travel information to passengers, such as standard fees for sampans, hotels, and porters at all ports along the route.[113]

The campaign also sought to improve entertainment and recreation on board Minsheng ships. Campaign literature specified luxury ocean-liners as models, since these ships had extensive amenities such as tennis courts, swimming pools, libraries, musical entertainment, and wireless radio. Although confined to the small spaces of an Upper Yangzi steamship, Minsheng endeavored to supply entertainments to alleviate the boredom of long journeys. Each ship had books and magazines in a lending library, and managers distributed a daily news digest compiled from wire services. Ships stocked musical instruments and games that passengers could borrow.[114]

An additional campaign goal was to develop the Sichuan economy through tourism, bringing both money and modernity to the province and diminishing its economic crisis.[115] Minsheng promoted travel itineraries that included destinations like Mount Emei, the Yangzi Gorges, and the Ziliujing salt wells as well as Beibei, the Jialing River town developed by Lu Zuofu.[116] The company promoted Beibei as a destination for those interested in it as a model town, providing tours of its modern hospital, parks, libraries, and elementary school.[117]

The campaign's changes to Minsheng ships resulted in increased popularity among Chinese passengers: one manager claimed that Chinese passengers were willing to wait several days in port for the chance to travel in Minsheng ships.[118] The experience was unprecedented, particularly for third-class passengers. Even in this least expensive class, passengers enjoyed reserved berths, bathing facilities, responsive service, and entertainments provided by the company. The company's effort to equalize the service and amenities in the different passenger classes may have been almost too successful: a 1934 analysis of the campaign results in *New World* reported that most of the company's passenger income came from third-class passengers. Although the author acknowledged that difficult economic conditions in Sichuan may have accounted for the popularity of third-class travel, he also expressed concern that the improved facilities in third class had removed passengers' incentive to pay more for their accommodation. Rather than reinstitute distinctions in conditions among classes, he suggested lowering the prices of saloon and first-class tickets to make them more accessible.[119]

Minsheng Company literature states clearly that the company's ships were intended to do more than simply attract passengers with quality service and amenities: they were also intended to be didactic tools that shaped passengers' behavior and expectations. The ship's entertainment facilities were intended to provide alternatives to what company officials saw as the ubiquitous but objectionable pastimes of opium smoking and gambling on steamships.[120] The company's publication *Essential Information for Passengers* (*Chengke xuzhi*) had a title parallel to Minsheng's employee training manuals and introduced passengers to the rules of the ship and the services available on board. It provided detailed instructions for passenger behavior, exhorting them to not occupy berths other than their own, to maintain public order, to refrain from disturbing others' sleep, and to eat meals only at prescribed times. It also encouraged passengers to take advantage of the ship's services and amenities, inviting them to use the ship's stock of medicines if they fell sick, borrow books and magazines, and buy snacks, fruit, and coffee from the ship's "consumption cooperative" (*xiaofei hezuo she*). It detailed services that teaboys could provide: drawing water for baths, making appointments with the ship's barber for a haircut or shave, arranging for laundry, and picking up medicines, books, or games from the office. Passengers were encouraged to report any bad service to the manager.[121] Although some introduction to the novel services and amenities on Minsheng ships was undoubtedly necessary, the manual also depicts a more closely regulated and supervised travel experience than the chaotic and freewheeling one associated with the Chinese accommodation on other companies' ships.

The Minsheng Company did not hesitate to use its distinctive ships to communicate political ideas, such as opposition to Japanese expansion in China or support for nationalistic consumption. Teaboys were trained to discuss with passengers the necessity of resisting Japanese aggression and consuming Chinese products.[122] The sheets on each passenger berth were printed with the slogan "Do not forget the great peril of our country, even in your dreams."[123] The company used the didactic potential of its well-run ships to advance its nationalist message.

A travel narrative published in a 1933 issue of *New World* communicates the intended experience of a Minsheng ship. Ostensibly written by a middle school student, Chen Jiming, it describes his journey home to Sichuan from school in Shanghai for the summer vacation. Chen extolled the superior accommodations and service aboard Minsheng ships, contrasting it with his experiences on other ships. He praised its quality food, polite service, and orderly accommodations when elsewhere he had spent about twice the price of his ticket in "berth money," eaten terrible food, and endured rude treatment by teaboys. He mentioned the new baths on Minsheng ships as an especially welcome addition for travel in the summer heat. Beyond this comparison, the narrative also made an argument for the practical and political attractions of Minsheng ships for students in particular, explaining in detail how to obtain a 20 percent student discount on direct voyages from Shanghai to Chongqing. He contended that Minsheng ships were a natural choice for patriotic students since "we young students are not like cold-blooded animals or shameless merchants"—who would travel on foreign ships rather than Chinese. Chen's account describes how the voyage transformed his classmates' behavior. He writes that although there were some who could afford to travel in first or second class, they "broke out of their 'young master', 'princeling', and 'dandy' habits and came back and forth to visit their friends in the third-class cabin," suggesting that the openness of the Minsheng passenger accommodation allowed student camaraderie to overcome class divisions.[124] This narrative was clearly company-approved advertising, but it provides a very clear encapsulation of the company's intentions in reforming its passenger accommodation: the service and amenities would attract passengers, but the travel experience would also teach them new ways of interacting and reinforce the bonds between them.

In a context in which many companies were attempting to modify or update their passenger spaces, the Minsheng Company completely reimagined the relationship between the Chinese passenger and the steamship company. In contrast to the Chinese accommodation of the earlier configuration of passenger space, in which Chinese passengers were at the mercy of ship compradors and thus beyond the company's authority, Minsheng's passengers were fully integrated into the company's and each ship's organization. Minsheng's guarantee of a berth to all passengers in all classes of course responded to a long-standing passenger complaint exacerbated by the teaboy crisis, but it required that the ship's management count and account for each passenger. Furthermore, passengers were encouraged to seek help from and interact with Minsheng staff, especially the teaboys. In turn, teaboys were trained to act as the key point of contact between the company and the public, providing services, travel information, and information about the company. In Minsheng's focus on passenger service and its goal to improve the Sichuan economy through tourism, it acknowledged their economic value and potential contribution of passengers. Ultimately, the dignifying of Chinese passengers on Minsheng ships was a means to attract them and a means of persuading them to adopt the values promoted by the company, ranging from the choice of more wholesome entertainments on board to the ethics of nationalist consumption.

By the mid-1930s, the uniform, characteristic social space of the steamship in Chinese waters in evidence at earlier times had disappeared. From the late 1920s onward, Chinese and foreign companies had begun to question and modify that space in response to new opportunities, crises, and the changing demands of passengers. The factors that had underlay the uniform social space, such as the preference for foreign technical personnel, contracting the Chinese accommodation to compradors, and providing separate accommodation for foreigners and Chinese, were now very much under question, with different companies arriving at different solutions. Rather than one characteristic social space of the steamship, there were now many alternatives.

In a political climate characterized not only by Chinese nationalism but also by nationalist nation-building, Chinese steamship companies began to take more extreme and often costly measures to distance their companies from this earlier social space. Such departures dispelled the prior mode of collaboration in which the China Merchants Company reproduced the characteristic social space and its associations. Under these new conditions, a significantly larger group of Chinese shipping firms was not nearly as bound by the false symmetry of the shipping conference. With the infrastructure, exhortation, and occasional support provided by the Nationalist government, Chinese firms prioritized the transformation of this space.

Within this broader context of change in the shipping field, Minsheng's "new steamship" stands out as the sharpest rejoinder to the earlier organization of steamship space. The spaces of this new steamship challenged nearly every element of the earlier space: the rigid racial lines in steamship crews, contracting out the Chinese accommodation, and the implicit racial segregation of classes. In focusing on hiring skilled Chinese, rejecting the use of ship compradors, integrating teaboys into the company, and leveling disparities in amenities and service among passenger classes, Minsheng's new steamship reformulated rather than modified earlier practices. In doing so, the company made spaces that had previously showcased Chinese deficiencies into models of expertise and order, making an argument for Chinese competencies against the seemingly immutable associations visible on other ships. Minsheng's new steamship made a clear case for Chinese competencies, whether through its employment of exclusively Chinese technical personnel, its disciplined workforce, or its well-ordered and comfortable ships.

As chapter 4 argued, for Chinese observers the steamship had rarely reflected familiar or expected social relations and had more often forced a questioning of those expectations. Minsheng's "new steamship" took the steamship's unstable relationship with outer reality in a new direction, creating instead an idealized space of aspiration. In Foucault's words, it was a "heterotopia of compensation," a projection of a future Chinese nation that was orderly, disciplined, unified, and incontrovertibly modern.[125] Furthermore, Minsheng's new steamship did not just reflect these ideals, it also provided a means to arrive at them through the persuasion and transformation of all those who partook of the space.

The new steamship was a microcosm of the Minsheng Company. Both ship and company were ethical communities intent on transforming society and nation. Many of Lu Zuofu's writings place the company on a continuum that encompassed the individual, society, and the Chinese nation, in which change in one area benefited all. Improving employees' thinking, knowledge, skills, and physiques were conceived as contributions to society and nation.[126] Such arguments merged the Republican-era interest in forms of training with the Confucian idea that the moral cultivation of the self leads to the ordering of the family and state.[127] Lu also emphasized that work performed for the company was central to this larger project: the value of one's work was far greater than the compensation one received for it, and the surplus value could be dedicated to the improvement of society.[128] Thus, to be an employee in the Minsheng Company meant to be constantly reminded of the greater impact of one's daily work, stressing its contribution to a wider community and ultimately to the Chinese nation.

Lu and other company leaders encouraged employees to identify with the company and downplay class divisions. Company policies were designed to prevent the development of an exclusive executive culture. Managers were to "remain close" to the workers through group activities and mutual assistance. Each year, managers, even high-level ones, were required to inspect conditions at different levels of the company and talk to workers, becoming familiar with each ship, dock, harbor, and factory. The company also impressed on upper management the need to act as role models, and held them to the same standards as workers in terms of job performance and behavior: managers were required to wear the same uniforms as workers—a version of the Sun Yatsen suit—and were not allowed to use company funds for banquets or company cars for private business. Lu Zuofu, as general manager, particularly cultivated an image of himself as adhering to these principles: he attended all company meetings, ate the same food as the workers, and collected a lower salary that most of the ship captains. Despite having founded Minsheng, Lu did not own any company stock. He lived off his salary alone. Nor did he accept personal gifts: anything he received he donated to the company.[129]

Further cultivating identification with the company was the encouragement of communication among employees at all levels. In 1932, Minsheng adopted a method called "democratic management" (*minzhu guanli*) to facilitate communications between management and workers. "Democratic management" referred to a schedule of company-wide meetings intended to improve workers' and managers' understanding of one another's working conditions as well as to increase employees' understanding of the company's business in general. Minsheng's intensive meeting culture also provided a platform from which the company could carry out campaigns. The most extensive of these was the national salvation campaign following the Japanese takeover of Manchuria.[130] On the first anniversary of this incident, Minsheng employees passed a resolution that patriotic activity was a necessary part of employment in the company, and that all employees and their families would refuse to serve Japanese customers, buy or sell any Japanese products, and break off friendships with those with connections to Japanese.[131]

As the Minsheng Company grew, it developed policies intended to shape employees' lives beyond their work. Lu Zuofu expounded an idea of "group life" (*jituan shenghuo*) in a 1934 issue of *New World*. He claimed that the idea of "group life"—in which each person relies on the group and the group relies on each person—had always existed within the Chinese family system, as families relied on all members to compete with other families in society. In the modern world, he argued, the company was better equipped than the family to mediate between the individual and society to preserve China's national autonomy. The elements of group life were "work," "learning," and "leisure," all of which the Minsheng Company sought to provide for its employees.[132] The company organized lectures, reading groups, sports matches, clubs, and other entertainments to foster the employees' identification with the group. Like on the ships, these activities also scripted sanctioned behavior: when in port, in place of an evening on the town, seamen were encouraged to participate in them (see figure 7.2).[133] In the late 1930s, the company further developed a system of benefits designed to foster group life that included housing for single workers, medical care, pensions, vacation time, food subsidies, and a cooperative store.[134] In 1937, it was planning to build Minsheng "New Villages" (*Minsheng Xincun*)—company communities in Yichang, Hankou, and Shanghai that would provide apartments, dining halls, schools, cooperative stores, hospitals, sports fields, libraries, and auditoriums. Minsheng raised the funds and bought land to build these New Villages, but their construction was interrupted by the war.[135]

The Minsheng Company was thus a social space comparable to a Minsheng ship: both were designed to counteract perceived deficiencies in society, promote identification with a group, and diminish signs of class difference. Both were attractive, modern spaces, but ones that made considerable disciplinary and biopolitical demands of their denizens: company employees and steamship passengers were expected to imbibe the company's ideas and standards of behavior. Together, the two spaces

FIGURE 7.2 Minsheng Company Sailors' Singing Group. *Minsheng shiye gongsi shi yi zhounian jinian kan*, 1937. Courtesy of Minsheng gongsi, Chongqing.

evince a consistent approach to fostering change within Chinese society, distinguished by the effort to secure a role for a company or other economic institution in the ethical continuum of self, society, and polity.

Within the shipping field, the Minsheng Company was extraordinary, proposing novel solutions to problems most steamship companies struggled with. Minsheng's approach was deeply ingrained in the milieu of Republican-era business and culture, with precedents and counterparts in many other contexts. Lu Zuofu began his career as an educator, and the influence of Republican educational models on Minsheng Company culture is unmistakable. As a young man, Lu studied with Huang Yanpei (1878–1965), founder of the Chinese Society for Vocational Education, and later sought his advice on bringing education and industry together.[136] Lu's methods of training employees with a combination of job, military, and ethical training while offering opportunities to advance their learning were similar to models of citizenship training used in Republican-era schools and organizations like the Chinese Scouts.[137] The pedagogical emphasis in the Minsheng Company is also comparable to the Nationalist and Communist Parties' commitments to political tutelage, in which "awakened" political instructors were empowered to rule and discipline the not-yet-awakened until they reached the desired state of consciousness.[138] In the 1930s, Lu Zuofu had no formal affiliation with either party, but Minsheng practices speak to the currency of this idea as a means of fostering social and political change.[139]

Minsheng's management structure was based on Frederick Taylor's (1856–1915) ideas of scientific management, particularly in its vertical structures of authority, careful selection of employees, focus on training, and incentives for employee performance. These ideas were well known in China of the 1920s and 1930s. Chinese industrialists saw scientific management as a means for companies facing militant labor activism and foreign competition to increase productivity, improve relations between labor and capital, and offer new incentives to workers. Sun Yatsen had linked scientific management's benefits to nationalism, arguing that industrial development was an important solution to China's problems, but that Chinese industry needed to promote nationalism and social harmony along with industrial growth, reconciling the interests of workers and employers.[140] The adoption of scientific management ideas in China was part of an international movement for industrial efficiency and workplace reform ongoing in the United States, Europe, and Japan as well.[141]

Lu Zuofu's fostering of group life by creating communities that included housing, facilities, and leisure activities was also a familiar practice of Chinese entrepreneurs of the 1920s and 1930s. At the Shenxin Cotton Mills, Rong Zongjing made similar provisions for workers that included housing, dining halls, medical care, and activities.[142] Intriguingly similar to Minsheng culture was that of the Bank of China under Zhang Gongquan (1889–1979). In the late 1920s and 1930s, the Bank of China also created communities in which employees resided with their immediate families in compounds. The bank presented itself as an enterprise whose purpose went beyond profit, emphasized modern expertise, trained its employees in the proper "spirit" of work, and expected its workers to devote time to self-improvement, including learning and teaching others. Like Lu Zuofu, Zhang Gongquan cultivated an image of the general manager as a personal and ethical exemplar and involved the bank in the Rural Reconstruction Movement.[143] Wen-hsin Yeh and others have argued that these and other Republican enterprise communities anticipated the work units (*danwei*) of the People's Republic.[144]

What distinguished Minsheng among these Republican enterprises was its unequivocal political mission. Yeh interprets Zhang Gongquan's enterprise community at the Bank of China as expressive of a modern urban culture and as a means of inculcating corporate discipline in its employees.[145] Marie-Claire Bergère sees such practices as a "Confucian paternalism" that bridged traditional social relations and emerging industrial relations.[146] Such objectives are visible in Minsheng's company and community, yet the company's self-presentation in its publications and Lu Zuofu's writings made constant reference to the nation. Victory in the nationalist struggle was always cited as the ultimate goal of any individual or company effort.[147] It is not difficult to imagine that many enterprise or business leaders might adopt such a stance, but the company's very cogent riposte to the racial associations in the social space of the steamship suggests a far more robust engagement with the political and cultural impact of semi-colonialism in China.

In the new steamship, Lu Zuofu and Minsheng responded to an image of Chinese deficiency produced by a mode of accumulation that relied on the absolute minimum investment of steamship companies—Chinese or foreign—in their Chinese employees and Chinese passengers. Under these conditions, the deployment of modern but well-known management techniques allowed him to produce the ordered and disciplined new steamship, which was not only a corrective to the racialized deficiencies associated with the steamship's social space but also a means of surpassing foreign companies by demonstrating the ability of a Chinese company to manage its ships in ways that foreign companies could not. This strategy was more than one-upsmanship directed at the foreign firms, it was also a demonstration to other Chinese companies that this particular form of modernity could dismantle the authority of the foreign-derived models of social space within the shipping field.

Lu's new steamship further challenged the racial associations of the steamship space not by dismantling racial categories but by insisting on their impermanence. He addressed this issue in a 1934 article on training in *Dagong bao*, arguing that there were no innate differences between "the white race" (*baizhong ren*) and "the yellow race" (*huangzhong ren*) or between Chinese and Japanese. The differences lay instead in how each group was trained to act and behave in society. Even these differences in behavior, however, were relative and historically conditioned. He contended that had China not been subject to imperialism, there would be little need for the Chinese to change their social behavior, but the reality of this oppression made such change urgently necessary. He then explained a concept of training that consisted of a process of breaking deeply engrained and embodied habits.[148] Whereas Lu's focus on Chinese bodies and Chinese competencies is a response to the John Chinaman discourse, his point is that both body and competence are ultimately malleable. This idea was evident in his exhortations to Minsheng teaboys. He told a class of trainees, "you do not have to have a high nose in order to do [this correctly]," and warned them that they could not afford to relax their efforts. Following Japan's occupation of Manchuria, Lu Zuofu urged Minsheng teaboys to express their patriotic vigilance by doing their jobs perfectly, so as to "triumph over Japanese teaboys." Helping passengers with luggage, providing them with towels, and adding rice to their bowls would aid this greater cause, as would teaboys trimming their fingernails, keeping their thumbs out of passengers' rice bowls, touching only the middle sections of chopsticks, and washing dishes with boiled water.[149] In both examples, even the most minor skills help overcome the disparities between races and nations. What Zhu Ziqing called "imperialism" in his essay on the steamship was not the existence of racial associations but their apparent immutability, and Lu's insistence on the adaptability of bodies and minds responded precisely to this point.

Lu's company and his new steamship were unapologetically modernizing projects—which can be seen from the company's constant evocation of the "new"—the publication *New World*, the company's New Villages—to the streamlined design of the company's logo (see figure 7.3). Lu Zuofu's new steamship shared some elements with Sun Yatsen's declaration that "building a new state is like building a new steamship" in the *Three Principles of the People*. If Sun imagined reengineering a ship's machinery, transforming its inner workings to make it the "fastest and largest new steamship in the world," Lu's "new steamship" was also a feat of reengineering that focused on the spaces, human relationships, and associations on board. Although both shared the intention of surpassing existing standards, Lu's was actually implemented in the 1930s shipping field, among companies of different nationalities that faced many

FIGURE 7.3 Advertisement for the Minsheng Company. The company's logo is imposed on the image of the ship at the top, with the characters "min sheng" printed in an abstract style and read right to left. *Luxing zazhi* 11:5 (May 1937). Courtesy of Minsheng gongsi, Chongqing.

of the same problems on their ships. By reformulating the space and the people within it, Lu demonstrated a Chinese competency to solve problems that others could not and furnished a model for other Chinese companies to do the same.

CONCLUSION

Decolonizing the Steamship Network, 1937–56

From the first European ships transporting Chinese merchant cargoes along the coast in the years between the Opium Wars, shipping was central to the foreign presence in China and China's relationship to nineteenth- and twentieth-century European expansionism. For Europeans, shipping provided an entrée into the Qing dynasty: it was a service in high enough demand to justify flouting the restrictions of the trade system. After 1860, the once informal coasting trade was recognized and regulated within the treaty system, becoming synonymous with the network of open treaty ports that were increasingly connected by steam rather than sail. Qing officials worked to limit the scope of foreign navigation in Chinese waters, but this network continued to grow over the latter years of the dynasty, becoming denser along existing routes and extending into new areas. The steam network was a key transport infrastructure in late Qing and Republican China. The many tendrils of this initial foreign expansion extended into various arenas of Sino–foreign interaction and Chinese life.

This book's project has been to use the multifaceted arena of steam navigation to reflect on China's experience of Western and Japanese imperialism in the nineteenth and twentieth centuries. Based on a reading of the term "semi-colonialism," which places equal emphasis on the specificity of China's experience and its comparability and continuity with various aspects of colonialism, the book highlights the particularity of China's semi-colonial formation and its links to colonial contexts and wider global processes. Comparisons with similar facets of steam navigation in British India have sharpened the accounts of particularity, continuity, and the interrelated histories of each place.

The most basic case for the distinctiveness of China's semi-colonial formation is the margin of sovereignty and autonomy left to Chinese governments under it. The trajectories of the steam transport network and the steamship business in China reveal numerous cases where the exercise of this sovereignty was significant. At the same time, these cases show that a characteristic dynamic of this formation was not simply the existence of Chinese sovereignty under the treaty system but its enactment through collaborative mechanisms such as the treaty system and the shipping conference. These mechanisms depended on Qing sovereignty and limited it. Comparing the formation of the steam network and the steam shipping business in China and India in the 1860s and 1870s shows that sovereignty was not negligible: the steam network in China was much sparser and less malleable than that in India, and the government-sponsored China Merchants Steam Navigation Company maintained a merchant fleet under Chinese flags, whereas British shipping quickly overwhelmed indigenous shipping enterprise in India. Nevertheless, within the collaborative mechanism, these assertions of Qing sovereignty did not constitute unqualified resistance. These collaborations were undertaken under significant imbalances of power, and despite the importance they granted to indigenous sovereignty, the collaborations ultimately forwarded the expansionist project. By the last years of the Qing dynasty, the steam networks and foreign shipping privileges had grown substantially, and British shipping companies had readily overtaken the China Merchants Company. The new shipping powers that sought entry to Chinese waters at the turn of the twentieth century—Japanese, German, and French—saw the British firms, rather than the China Merchants Company, as their main opponents.

While recognizing the specificity of China's semi-colonial formation, it is vital that we do not assume the consequences of this formation were entirely different from those associated with "full" colonies or that China was insulated from or unaffected by the wider hegemonic projects of colonialism. The specific dynamics of semi-colonialism were always informed by the possibility of colonization. The expansionist agenda of the China Hands was predicated on the possibility or expectation of full colonial rule in China, usually based on the example of British India. As much as the British Foreign Office and British officials in China worked to manage the ambitions of the China Hands, they never disavowed or discounted these desires, regularly returning to the China Hands' agenda to formulate new demands for treaty (and extra-treaty) negotiations. The hope of colonization and the example of British India propelled the process of expanding foreign shipping privileges in Chinese waters.

The social space of the steamship shows the impact of colonial conceptions of race in China. This case evinces direct continuities with the practices of colonial regimes—such as the conflation of race and skill and similar racialized hierarchies visible in the technical departments of the government of India—as well as the wider reach of colonialism "unbounded" in the parallel hierarchies of work and anxieties about social intimacy across races that characterized European shipping in many parts of the world. Steam navigation provides a very specific context in which to view this phenomenon, but it should not be dismissed as trivial or epiphenomenal. Limited numbers of workers and passengers in China may have been involved in the social space of the steamship in Chinese waters, but it elicited a powerful response from those who witnessed it. A ship's space rendered its presumptive governmentality and social order unmistakably concrete. Steamship travel quickly ceased to be a new experience in nineteenth-century China, but it continued to be a personally significant one encountered as people left home for larger cities or abroad or moved from place to place within China. The personal importance of the experience may account for the galvanizing effect of steamship travel on those critical of the order it represented: in 1917, Mohandas Gandhi's response to the deck accommodation on Indian coastal steamships was nearly the same as Chinese literati journalists' to the steerage class in Chinese waters. In the 1930s, Lu Zuofu's thorough critique and reworking of this space spoke of his profound dissatisfaction with the social relations and view of Chineseness projected by the space. The alacrity with which Minsheng's model transformation of the social space was taken up by the New Life Movement and other steamship companies in China suggests the urgency felt by many at the time to realign the equations of race and competence that space projected. Like Sun Yatsen's "new steamship," Lu Zuofu's ordering of a fully Chinese ship went well beyond a claim to equivalence: it asserted a superior competence—greater efficiency, modernity, and cohesion—than could be seen anywhere else in the shipping field.

The intertwined histories of China and India in the nineteenth and early twentieth centuries suggest the necessity of moving beyond comparisons of these contexts as individual examples of semi-colony and colony to consider how they were implicated in global processes extending beyond their borders. The rise of British shipping in the mid-nineteenth century was a globalizing force. China and India played distinct roles within it: colonial state-building in India in the 1860s abetted Britain's rise as the world center of shipping, finance, and insurance and helped make British enterprises the center of the communications revolution of the 1860s and 1870s. The arrival of powerful British shipping firms into Chinese waters in the 1870s and 1880s was an outcome of these developments and a further contribution to Britain's global shipping power. In India and China, British shipping enterprises supported by British capital and shipbuilding superseded local ventures that relied on indigenous capital and participation. The precise contours of domination in each context were different: the British India Steam Navigation Company supplanted all but a few competing steamship enterprises, and the British companies in China divided the trade with the China Merchants Company and eventually the Nisshin Kisen Kaisha—but in both places British firms could draw on superior worldwide resources to buttress their position. The colonial state in India and the semi-colonial order in China participated in this process, but British shipping enjoyed a reach that extended far beyond these contexts.

The nationalist responses to shipping regimes in China and India, particularly after World War I, underscore the significance of the global link between the two contexts. The perception of the problem and the solutions proposed for it in both places were strikingly similar, despite obvious differences in circumstances. Alliances of indigenous ship owners and political parties sought the reservation of coastal and inland shipping for their own ships based on the principle that this was a right due a nation under international law. At the same time, nationalists sought to develop and expand indigenous shipping to eradicate arguments that foreign participation was necessary to meet the country's shipping needs. In China, the indigenous shipping sector was larger and had a longer history, and nationalist arguments were addressed to different sources of power in each case (the Legislative Assembly in India versus foreign diplomats in China), but the basic issues and solutions were similar. In both places, this struggle persisted through the 1920s and 1930s, remaining unresolved through the end of World War II, and was revived after the war as part of these countries' pursuit of decolonization.

The processes of decolonizing shipping in China and India were also very similar. After Indian Independence was declared in 1947, the new government established coastal reservation, removed foreign shipping companies by 1952, and established shipping corporations in which the state partnered with private shipping firms to support them. In China, decolonization proceeded in a more piecemeal fashion, beginning with the abrogation of the unequal treaties in 1943 and complicated by the devastations of the Second Sino-Japanese and Civil Wars.[1] It was completed in the 1950s under the new People's Republic, with the final exclusion of foreign shipping and an alliance between private shipping firms and the state to ensure shipping autonomy. The strong parallels between China's and India's nationalist movements in shipping suggest that in this period the differences between semi-colony and colony were less significant than their shared adversaries.

This book does not propose a comprehensive model of semi-colonialism. Because steam navigation was just one element of the semi-colonial order, it provides instead a specific case that can highlight significant elements of this order to be considered alongside others studied and yet-to-be studied, such as treaty port communities and governance, the Maritime Customs, extraterritoriality, trade and business systems, and cultural and religious missions. In addition to the perspective on Chinese sovereignty that it provides, a further element that steam navigation illuminates is the significance of particular powers in the semi-colonial formation. The steam networks, as well as the steam shipping business, were almost entirely the preserve of Great Britain until it was joined by Japan after 1895. This view is in tension with the common argument that one of the key distinguishing features of semi-colonialism was that China was subject to the domination of multiple treaty powers instead of a single colonizing power. For some, that multiplicity complicates comparisons between semi- and "full" colonialism. Yet as steam navigation shows, the presence of multiple powers in China need not excessively complicate or palliate the exercise of domination there. The goal should be to understand the powers' uneven investments and interests, and consequently the very different roles that each might have played in the semi-colonial formation of the nineteenth and twentieth centuries.

The year 1937 provides a natural endpoint for this study, since the outbreak of the Second Sino-Japanese War significantly transformed the shipping networks and active shipping enterprises in Chinese waters. Its final conclusion, however, must extend into the 1950s to demonstrate both the significance of the wartime period and the gradual and uneven quality of the decolonization process. The outbreak of war in eastern and central China in 1937 disrupted the workings of the treaty system, shipping networks, and shipping business in a way that on the surface brought much of the shipping system that began with the 1860 Treaty of Tianjin to an end. However dramatically transformed these conditions were, Chinese aspirations to shipping autonomy remained intact and vital throughout the war, and the struggle to achieve it extended into the early years of the People's Republic.

As the Second Sino-Japanese War began in July 1937, Japan and China became enemy combatants in Chinese territory and their respective ships were enemy property, vulnerable to stoppage and attack in areas under the other's control. The Japanese seized many of the northern coastal ports and advanced up the Yangzi River in the late summer of 1937, prompting the Nationalist government's retreat from Nanjing to Wuhan, and then to its eventual wartime capital of Chongqing in 1938. As the Japanese captured several of the southern coastal ports in the next year, most of the coastal and Yangzi shipping routes lay within Japanese-occupied territory. In August 1939, the Japanese government amalgamated the Nisshin Kisen Kaisha and the China-based services of the Nippon Yūsen Kaisha, Osaka Shōsen Kaisha, and other Japanese companies into a new national policy company, the Tōa Kaiun Kaisha (East Asia Shipping Company), intended to promote Japanese control of shipping in occupied China.[2] The first years of the war scattered many Chinese fleets: some ships were captured, others commandeered. Some sought safety in Hong Kong. The small number of ships suitable to navigate the Upper Yangzi River followed the Nationalist government to Chongqing.

Great Britain's neutrality in the Sino-Japanese conflict before 1941 allowed British ships to traverse occupied and unoccupied China, giving the British firms some unique opportunities. China Navigation and Indo-China could continue to run their businesses on the Yangzi and coast, at times convoyed by Japanese naval ships through areas of conflict.[3] In the early years of the war, they extended some aid to Chinese interests: China Navigation ships transported Chinese refugees sponsored by native-place associations and charitable organizations, established a cargo service between Shanghai and Tongzhou in cooperation with the Dada Steamship Company, and carried some factory equipment upriver for the Nationalist government.[4] As the war went on, the British companies earned high profits from their passenger businesses, since there were few Chinese ships sailing and British ships offered greater security. The China Navigation Company used the opportunity to bring its Chinese passenger business under the direct control of its offices and finally out of the hands of its ship compradors.[5] British neutrality ended after the Japanese attacks on Pearl Harbor (1941), when most of the British companies' offices in China ceased operations and staff members were detained by the Japanese. Although the British firms maintained offices in Chongqing throughout the war, many of their ships and shore facilities were taken over by the Japanese after 1941.[6]

Chinese shipping companies were hardest hit by wartime conditions, but some found opportunities that proved beneficial. The Lower Yangzi and coastal fleets of the China Merchants and Sanbei Companies sustained heavy losses, their ships attacked and commandeered to carry soldiers and munitions.[7] The China Merchants Company's coastal business ceased in 1937–38, and its newest and largest ships were sent to Hong Kong. Before the fall of Wuhan, the China Merchants continued to make some use of its river fleet—by some accounts repainted in the British companies' colors—but after the company retreated with the Nationalist government to Chongqing, it all but stopped operations because its remaining ships were not appropriate for Upper Yangzi navigation.[8]

Yu Xiaqing, Sanbei's owner, chose to remain in Shanghai for the first years of the war, navigating the occupied city's dangers and possibilities. Sanbei had lost over half of its fleet in the first months of the war, but with 40,000 tons left in Shanghai, Yu entered into an agreement with an Italian merchant through which his ships could fly the Italian flag. This was a great advantage because Italy was an Axis power, and Italian ships could pass in and out of the harbor of Japanese-occupied Shanghai. Yu used the fleet to import rice from Rangoon and Saigon into Shanghai's concessions, which were awash in war refugees and in desperate need of food. As a result, Yu is said to have finally cleared his fabled debt and made a fortune of five million *yuan*. Yu's success and high profile in Shanghai society, however, attracted the attention of the Wang Jingwei regime, which pressured him to collaborate with the Japanese. Fearing assassination, Yu left Shanghai for Chongqing in spring 1941. The remainder of Sanbei's fleet was useless on the Upper Yangzi, but Yu purchased several small motor ships in Chongqing that kept the shipping company going as he diversified into the land transport business and the importation of much-needed trucks from Burma into China. He died of an illness in Chongqing in 1945.[9]

The Nationalist government's retreat to Chongqing in 1938 made Upper Yangzi shipping one of the wartime capital's main transport lifelines. Railways and highways had fallen into Japanese hands and were cut off. Southwest China, an important conduit for goods and supplies to Chongqing, had few roads, and difficulties in obtaining gasoline kept land transport through this region limited. The importance of Upper Yangzi shipping put Lu Zuofu's Minsheng Company at the center of wartime transport because its entire fleet was designed to navigate this part of the river. In fall 1938, Lu Zuofu was appointed assistant minister of communications and personally oversaw the transport of factory machinery, schools, cultural facilities, government offices, and hospitals from downriver cities that had collected at Yichang, awaiting shipment through the Yangzi gorges. In the same year, Jiang Jieshi ordered that the company's ships be taken over by the military for troop transport, but Lu parried this attempt at a takeover by agreeing to prioritize military transport above the company's other business and providing its services to the military at reduced prices.[10] Over the course of the war, Minsheng facilitated the shipment of food to troops on the front lines, opened new shipping routes on the Upper Yangzi tributaries, and coordinated transfers of goods and equipment between air and river ships in China's southwestern region.[11] Despite the many difficult conditions and losses of ships the company endured during the war, it was overall a time of rapid growth for Minsheng. The company bought ships at low prices and made use of the experts in navigation, engineering, and management who had migrated to Chongqing.[12] By the end of the war, the Minsheng fleet had grown from forty-six ships of 18,718 tons to eighty-four ships at 25,781 tons.[13]

In January 1943, Britain and the United States abrogated their unequal treaties with China in recognition of its participation in the Allied cause. With this action, the treaty clauses that had provided a legal basis for foreign-flag shipping in China's coastal waters were rescinded, and the treaty-based "rights recovery" sought by nationalists in the 1920s and 1930s was achieved, at least on paper. Although treaty revision had been a central demand of Republican shipping nationalism, the ongoing war made it difficult for Chinese shipping firms or the Nationalist government to do more than imagine and make plans to realize the nation's shipping autonomy after its end.

The goal of shipping autonomy, however, was very much on the mind of Lu Zuofu, even before the abrogation of the treaties. As early as 1938, Lu Zuofu was planning Minsheng's postwar expansion. He published a detailed plan in *New World* that described restoring Minsheng services along the Yangzi River and initiating new services on the northern and southern coast as well as an overseas line to Japan and Southeast Asia. Lu's hope was that by offering these comprehensive services, Minsheng could capture some of the market share previously held by the British and Japanese firms, dissuading them from returning to China after the war. Believing that the company would need a loan from abroad to build the ships for such an ambitious program of expansion, Lu set to work publicizing his cause. In 1943, he used the occasion of a trade conference in New York to travel through the United States and Canada in search of a lender. By early 1945, he obtained the promise of a loan from the Canadian government to build eighteen ships in Canadian shipyards.[14] Although he had big plans for Minsheng, Lu was also closely involved in discussions with the Nationalist government about postwar reconstruction. In these discussions, his concern with shipping autonomy was evident. He advocated for government aid to Chinese shipping firms as well as government coordination of their services to minimize competition and ensure that Chinese firms could meet the demand for shipping in the immediate postwar period.[15]

After the Japanese surrender, the China Merchants Company also began to restore its prewar services and extend onto new routes. Like Minsheng, it intended to offer comprehensive services on the Yangzi River and coast and establish its own overseas lines to Japan and Southeast Asia. The company's headquarters returned to Shanghai from Chongqing in

October 1945. Soon thereafter, it received 143 ships from the Nationalist government that had belonged to Japanese companies and the shipping organizations of puppet regimes, a gift that tripled the size of the China Merchants' prewar fleet.[16] The Nationalist government's support of the China Merchants Company in the immediate postwar period replicated many of the tensions within the shipping business during the Nanjing Decade: private firms had hoped that the state would offer support to all Chinese shipping firms, but the most valuable aid was channeled to China Merchants. Despite Lu Zuofu's sterling record of wartime service, Minsheng did not received the aid it had anticipated, and the government did not make the effort that Lu had envisioned to oversee and coordinate Chinese shipping companies in the immediate postwar period.[17]

Anxieties about the reconstruction process put the Nationalist government at odds with Chinese shipping interests—including the China Merchants Company—over the question of shipping autonomy. The government feared that there were simply not enough ships to meet the country's needs as soldiers were demobilized and relief goods needed distribution throughout the country.[18] Unlike the Chinese shipping firms, the government was open to the idea of bringing foreign-flag ships back to China—even temporarily—to relieve these immediate requirements. Furthermore, the British companies and British officials were interested in returning to Chinese waters: the 1943 Sino-British treaty included several clauses that could have been interpreted to provide a legal basis for the return of British shipping to China after the war.[19] The Nationalist government agreed to allow British ships to return to China's rivers and coast to ship relief goods in 1945–46, but the Shanghai Shipping Association and Seamen's Union protested the decision, demanding that the government maintain navigation rights for the Chinese alone. Minsheng, China Merchants, and Dada, among other Chinese firms, protested that their fleets were large enough to complete the distribution and criticized the Nationalists for failing to support Chinese shipping. The British companies were deterred from resuming operations in China immediately but hoped that a new trade treaty might allow them to return. The negotiations for this treaty began in 1946 but stalled over the issue of navigating Chinese waters. In the same year, the Nationalist government signed a treaty with the United States that allowed U.S. ships to navigate China's rivers and coasts. This treaty was met with protests from Chinese shipping organizations and boycotts organized against U.S. ships in Chinese ports.[20]

British shipping did not return to Chinese waters after the war, although British shipping interests continued to lobby for a return. A British delegation visited China in 1947, urging it not to "clos[e] itself in," which prompted yet another surge of protest by Chinese shipping interests. In the late 1940s, the China Navigation and Indo-China Companies moved their remaining operations from the Chinese mainland to Hong Kong. The shipping companies' offices were followed by the offices of managing agents Butterfield & Swire and Jardine, Matheson & Company in 1953–54, after which these firms continued to be involved in shipping, transport, and other businesses in other parts of East and Southeast Asia.[21]

The outbreak of the civil war between Nationalists and Communists in 1946 further complicated the pursuit of shipping autonomy. Under these wartime conditions, ships could be requisitioned, and companies suffered from hyperinflation, struggling to pay for fuel and salaries. The progress of the war also cut off vital shipping routes: in 1948, for example, Minsheng's Yangzi River and northern coast services were disrupted by the fighting, and the company had little choice but to move its offices to Hong Kong and concentrate on its overseas lines. The Communist victory in October 1949 precipitated yet another realignment within Chinese shipping: Jiang Jieshi took the best of the China Merchants fleet with him to Taiwan. Lu Zuofu, who was in Hong Kong, had to decide between an invitation from Jiang to go to Taiwan and from Zhou Enlai to return to mainland China.

In early 1950, Lu Zuofu and the Minsheng fleet returned to mainland China. By February 1952, Lu was dead, having committed suicide as the Five-Anti campaign progressed in the Minsheng Company in Chongqing. This tragic end, however, should not completely overshadow the long-desired opportunity that the government of the People's Republic offered to Lu when requesting his return: a central role for him and the Minsheng Company in a newly autonomous Chinese shipping sector. Communist leaders intent on economic reconstruction were anxious for both Lu, with his expertise, and the Minsheng fleet to return to the mainland because many of the country's largest ships had accompanied Jiang Jieshi to Taiwan. They offered Minsheng direct support, using state funds to pay off the company's Canadian loan and the sizable domestic debt it had accrued during its postwar expansion. Lu served as a member of the First National People's Political Consultative Committee and on the Southwest Military Commission. He became a spokesperson for the idea of joint public–private management of enterprises (*gong-si heying*), promoting Minsheng as a model private firm undergoing this process. In the first years of the People's Republic, the Communist leadership offered Lu the precise conditions he had long advocated as essential to achieving shipping autonomy: an uncompromising rejection of foreign shipping in Chinese waters and state support of existing shipping companies to fulfill the country's shipping needs.

In the very first years of the People's Republic, shipping in Chinese waters was thus finally decolonized along the lines imagined during the Republican period. The particular form that shipping business took at that time, however, turned out to be temporary: the Five-Anti campaign itself was part of the Communist Party's more general shift away from the ideas of New Democracy and a mixed economy toward greater concerns with security and state control of economy and society. By 1956, Minsheng and all remaining private shipping companies in China were amalgamated into state-run shipping firms.[22] Once domestic shipping was brought under state control, in 1961 the government established the China Ocean Shipping Company (COSCO), a state-run enterprise focused on the sustained development of overseas shipping, suggesting that although the government may have moved away from views of decolonization like Lu Zuofu's, its semi-colonial shipping history continued to inform its development priorities.[23]

Shipping enterprises continue to be important economic movers in the Reform era. Although the best of the China Merchants fleet was taken to Taiwan in 1949 and the ships remaining on the mainland were absorbed into state-run companies, the Hong Kong branch of the China Merchants Company continued to operate from that port under the supervision of Beijing's Ministry of Communications. This enterprise was one of the first to invest in the Shenzhen Special Economic Zone in the late 1970s. Now the China Merchants Group (Zhaoshangju jituan), it oversees a number of subsidiaries that include shipping, banking, and industrial ventures in Shenzhen.[24] Lu Zuofu's son, Lu Guoji, revived the Minsheng Company in Chongqing in 1984, making it one of the very first private businesses established in the Reform period. It now operates shipping services on the Yangzi River and on international lines. The priority placed on developing China as an international shipping power also continued into the Reform period: by the early 2010s, China had the third largest merchant fleet in the world. It also has a system of modern ports and is the world's largest shipbuilder.[25] COSCO, now a public company, still owns four-fifths of China's international fleet.[26] The era of the steamship and the treaty system is long gone, but shipping remains a significant part of China's global presence.

List of Chinese and Japanese Characters

Anqing 安慶

baizhong ren 白種人
ban fengjian 半封建
ban zhimindi 半殖民地
bang 幫
baoguan hang 報關行
baoxiao 報效
Beibei 北碚

Cai Pei 蔡培
Cai Zengji 蔡增基
Chafang xu zhi 茶房須知
chafang 茶房
Changde 常德
changguan 常關
Changjiang 長江
chaohui 朝會
Chen Qimei 陳其美
Chen Yüchang (Choping) 陳裕昌
Chengke xuzhi 乘客須知
Chuandong daotai 川東道臺
Chuanjiang hangwu guanli chu 川江航務管理處
Chuanjiang Steamship Company 川江輪船公司
chuanzhang zeren zhi 船長責任制
Cixi 慈溪

da canjian cang 大餐間艙
Dada Steamship Company 大達輪埠公司
Dagong bao 大公報
dai ryokō 大旅行
danwei 單位
Danyang 丹陽
Datong Steamship Company 大通輪船公司
Dianshizhai Pictorial 點石齋畫報
"diguozhuyi" de chuan "帝國主義" 的船
Ding Richang 丁日昌
Du Yuesheng 杜月笙

erdeng cang 二等艙

fang cang 房艙
Fu Xiao'an 傅筱庵
Fuchuan Steamship Company 福川輪船公司
fugu 附股
Fuling 涪陵
Funing 阜寧

gaikokujin shōtō 外國人上等
Gelaohui 哥老會
gongpiao ju 公票局
gong-si heying 公私合營
guan cang 官艙

guandu shangban 官督商辦
Guangzhao huiguan 廣肇會館
guanliao zibenjia 官僚資本家
Guanwen 官文
Guo Rudong 郭汝棟
Guohuo yundong 國貨運動
Guoying zhaoshang ju 國營招商局

haiguan 海關
Han Suyin 韓素音
hangye jie 航業界
Hangye yuekan 航業月刊
Hangzheng ju 航政局
Hanyang Ironworks 漢陽鐵廠
He Beiheng 何北衡
Hechuan 合川
hezuo banfa 合作辦法
hezuo she 合作社
Ho Tung (Robert) 何東
Hong'an Steamship Company 鴻安輪船公司
hualing weizheng 化零爲整
Huang Yanpei 黄炎培
huangzhong ren 黄種人
Huashang maiyong yangshang huolun xiaban dengchuan xiang zhangcheng 華商買用洋商火輪狭搬等船詳章程
Hukou 湖口

Jialing River 嘉陵江
jian shou liquan 漸收利權
Jiang Jieshi 蔣介石
jianshe shiye 建設實業
jiezhai dawang 借債大王
jinshi 進士
jituan shenghuo 集團生活
Jiujiang 九江
juewu 覺悟
Jun'an Seamen's Guild 均安公所

kai xiandai sixiang 開現代思想
Kaiping Mines 開平煤礦
kokusaku kaisha 國策會社
Kōnan Kisen Kaisha 湖南汽船會社
kongxin laoda 空心老大

Li Boyuan 李伯元
Li Hongzhang 李鴻章
lijin 釐金
liquan 利權
Liu Bingzhang 劉秉璋
Liu Hangchen 劉航琛
Liu Hongsheng 劉鴻生
Liu Mingchuan 劉銘傳
Liu Tieyun 劉鐵雲
Liu Wenhui 劉文輝
Liu Xiang 劉湘
Longshan 龍山
Lu Zuofu 盧作孚
Lunchuan zhaoshang ju 輪船招商局
Luxikou 鹿溪口
Luxing zazhi 旅行雜誌

maiban 買辦
maiban zibenjia 買辦資本家
minjian tuanti 民間團體
Minsheng jingshen 民生精神
Minsheng shiye gongsi 民生實業公司
Minsheng xincun 民生新村
minying 民營
minzhu guanli 民主管理
minzu ziben hangyun ye 民族資本航運業
minzu zibenjia 民族資本家

Nakano Kozan 中野孤山
Nantong 南通
neidi 內地
Neihe lunchuan zhaoshang ju 內河輪船招商局
Ning-Shao Steamship Company 寧紹輪船公司
Nippon Yūsen Kaisha 日本郵船會社
Nisshin Kisen Kaisha 日清汽船會社
Niuzhuang 牛庄

Ōsaka Shōsen Kaisha 大阪商船會社

peiyang hangye rencai 培養航業人才
Pingxiang Coal Mines 萍鄉煤礦

qingcha zhengli 清查整理
qinwu sheng 勤務生
Qiying 耆英

Renhe Insurance Company 仁和保險公司
Rong Zongjing 榮宗敬
Ronglu 榮祿

san gongsi 三公司
sanbao 三包
Sanbei lunbu gongsi 三北輪埠公司
sandeng cang 三等艙
shachuan 沙船
Shanghai hangye gonghui 上海航業公會
Shangwu chu 商務處
shangzhan 商戰
Shantou 汕頭
Shashi 沙市
Shen bao 申報
Sheng Xuanhuai 盛宣懷
shinshi 紳士
shiye jiuguo 實業救國
shouhui hangquan 收回航權
shouhui kuangquan 收回礦權
shouhui luquan 收回路權
Shouhui neihe hangquan Chuan min yundong dahui 收回内河航權川民運動大會
Shuishou xu zhi 水手須知
Siming Gongsuo 四明公所
Song Jin 宋晉
Song Ziwen 宋子文
Sun Yatsen 孫中山

Tang Tingshu 唐廷樞
tedeng cang 特等艙
tehuo 特貨
Tōa Dōbun Shoin 東亞同文書院
Tōa Kaiun Kaisha 東亞海運會社
tong cang 通艙
Tongmao Ironworks 同茂鐵廠
Tongmenghui 同盟會
Tongzhou 通州
toudeng cang 頭等艙
tōyōjin 東洋人
tu zhuanjia 土專家

Waiwu bu 外務部
Wang Jingwei 汪精衛
Wang Wenshao 王文韶
wangguo nu 亡國奴
Wanxian 萬縣
Wu Jianren 吳趼人
Wu River 烏江
Wu Tang 吳棠
Wu Tingfang 伍廷芳
Wuhu 蕪湖
Wusong shangchuan zhuanke xuexiao 吳淞商船專科學校
Wuxue 武穴

Xiangtan 湘潭
xiao Changjiang 小長江
Xiliang 錫良
Xin shenghuo yundong 新生活運動
Xin Shijie 新世界
Xingcha zhoukan 星槎周刊
Xu Run 徐潤

Yancheng 鹽城
Yang Hu 楊虎
Yang Sen 楊森
yangwu 洋務
yanjiang 沿江
Yanying Society 炎盈社
Yibin 宜賓
Yichang 宜昌
Yixin 奕訢
yōjin shōtō 洋人上等
Yong River 甬江
Yongqing Company 永慶公司
Youchuan bu 郵傳部
Yu Xiaqing 虞洽卿
yuan 元
Yuan Shikai 袁世凱
Yuezhou 岳州
Yuhang 渝行
Yülu 裕祿

yundong 運動
Yuyao 余姚

Zeng Guofan 曾國藩
Zhang Gongquan 張公權
Zhang Jian 張謇
Zhang Zhidong 張之洞
Zhao Erfeng 趙爾豐
Zhao Tieqiao 趙鐵橋
Zhaoshang ju jituan 招商局集團
Zheng Guanying 鄭官應
Zhenhai 鎮海
Zhenjiang 鎮江
Zhongguo de shen-shang 中國的紳商
Zhongguo hangye hezuo she 中國航業合作社
Zhu Baoting 朱寶庭
Zhu Qi'ang 朱其昂
Zhu Ziqing 朱自清
zhuangyuan 狀元
Zongli geguo shiwu *yamen* (Zongli *yamen*) 總理各國事務衙門 (總理衙門)
Zuo Zongtang 左宗棠

Abbreviations in Notes

CBYWSM: *Chouban yiwu shimo: Tongzhi* [Complete Account of the Management of Barbarian Affairs: Tongzhi Reign]. Reprint of 1930 Beiping edition in *Xu xiu siku quanshu*, vols. 418–21. Shanghai: Shanghai guji chuban she.

CMC: Maritime Customs Archives, Second Historical Archives, Nanjing, China.

HFD: Zhongyang yanjiu yuan jindaishi yanjiu suo [Academia Sinica Institute of Modern History], ed. *Haifang dang: shen: goumai chuanxiao* [Archives of Maritime Defense, Part I: Purchase of Ships], vol. 2. Taipei: Zhongyang yanjiu yuan jindaishi yanjiu suo, 1957.

HYYK: *Hangye yuekan* [Shipping Monthly]. Shanghai, 1930–37.

IMC Decennial: China. Imperial Maritime Customs. *Decennial Reports on Trade, Navigation, Industries, etc. of the Ports open to Foreign Commerce in China*. Shanghai: Inspectorate of Customs, Statistical Department, 1882–1920.

IMC Reports on Trade: China. Imperial Maritime Customs. *Reports on Trade at the Treaty Ports in China. 1861–1875*. Shanghai: Imperial Maritime Customs Statistical Department, 1861–75.

IUP-BPP: Irish University Press Area Studies Series of British Parliamentary Papers: China. Shannon: Irish University Press, 1971.

JMA: Jardine, Matheson & Company Archives. Cambridge University. Cambridge, UK.

JSS: John Swire & Sons Archives. School of Oriental and African Studies. London, UK.

JTS-HZB: China. Jiaotong bu [Ministry of Communications]. Jiaotong shi bianzuan weiyuanhui [Editorial Committee of the History of Communications]. *Jiaotong shi: hangzheng bian* [History of Communications: Shipping Administration]. Nanjing: n.p., 1931.

NCH: *North China Herald*. Shanghai, 1870–1941.

OSK: Ōsaka Shōsen Kabushiki Kaisha. *Shinkoku Chōkō unsōgyō genkō* [Conditions in China's Yangzi River Shipping Business]. Ōsaka: Ōsaka Shōsen Kaisha, 1900.

PRO-FO: Foreign Office Correspondence. Public Record Office. Kew Gardens, UK.

YWYD: Zhongguo shixue hui [China History Association], eds. *Yangwu yundong* [The Western Affairs Movement], vol. 6. Shanghai: Shanghai renmin chuban she, 1961.

Zhaoshang ju dang'an: Zhaoshang ju lunchuan gufen youxian gongsi dang'an [Archives of the China Merchants Steam Navigation Company, Ltd.], 1872–1949. Second Historical Archives, Nanjing, China.

ZLY-IMH: Zongli Yamen Archives. Institute of Modern History. Academia Sinica. Taipei, Taiwan.

Notes

Introduction

1. Sun Yatsen, *San Min Chu I*, 139.
2. Kirby, "Engineering China," 138–39.
3. Liu T'ieh-yun, *Travels of Lao Can*, 7–11.
4. Foucault, "Governmentality," 208–9.
5. The historiographical debates on imperialism in China are reviewed in Cohen, *Discovering History in China*, chaps. 1–3, and Osterhammel, "Semi-Colonialism and Informal Empire," 292–95.
6. Osterhammel, "Semi-Colonialism and Informal Empire," 296; Lenin, *Imperialism*, 79.
7. Dirlik, *Revolution and History*, 69–90; Wang Ya'nan, *Ban fengjian ban zhimindi*. In this work, Wang echoes Lenin's understanding of semi-colonialism as a transitional phase on the way to colonialism, as seen through his repeated description of China as "a semi-colony, approaching a colony" (*ban zhimindi, nai zhi zhimindi*).
8. Sun Yatsen, *San Min Chu I*, 10; Rogaski, *Hygienic Modernity*, 11–13; Goodman and Goodman, *Twentieth Century Colonialism and China*, 3–7.
9. The term "informal empire" is perhaps semi-colonialism's closest competitor for a phrase that captures the situation of China under the treaties. Unlike informal empire, which derives from the historiography of the British empire, semi-colonialism does not demand a focus on the investments or institutions of a single power but is broad enough to address the domination of multiple powers (Gallagher and Robinson, "Imperialism of Free Trade"; Duus, Myers, and Peattie, *Japanese Informal Empire*; Osterhammel, "Semi-Colonialism and Informal Empire," 297–309).
10. Barlow, "Colonialism," 400.
11. Ibid., 373–411.
12. Shu-mei Shih, *Lure of the Modern*, 35–37.
13. Goodman, "Improvisations," 916. Her particular target are those scholars associated with the journal *positions* who describe modern Chinese history and culture as "colonial modernity."

14. Goodman, "Improvisations," 918–20. Another work that emphasizes the distinct effects of semi-colonial rule is Hershatter, "The Subaltern Talks Back," 103–30.

15. Hevia, *English Lessons*, 13–14, 347–48.

16. Ibid., 26.

17. Rey Chow, *Writing Diaspora*, 7–8; Lydia H. Liu, *Clash of Empires*; Rogaski, *Hygienic Modernity*, 301.

18. Frederick Cooper, *Colonialism in Question*, 14–15.

19. Ibid., 4, 52. Recently scholars involved in colonial studies have called for a move beyond this focus on the colony toward a more diverse, comparative history of "imperial formations" that includes non-European and early modern forms of empire, as well as contexts in which partial sovereignty existed in varying degrees (Stoler, McGranahan, and Perdue, *Imperial Formations*, 10–14).

20. Zheng Wang, *Never Forget National Humiliation*.

21. Previous scholarship on shipping in China has tended to focus on business competition, entrepreneurship, or bureaucratic involvement in Chinese shipping enterprises. On competition, see K.-C. Liu, *Anglo-American Steamship Rivalry*, and Marriner and Hyde, *Senior John Samuel Swire*. On entrepreneurship, see Feuerwerker, *China's Early Industrialization*. More recent work that has focused on the role of the Qing bureaucracy in the development of the China Merchants Steam Navigation Company includes Chi-kong Lai, "Li Hung-chang and Modern Enterprise," and Yi Li, *Chinese Bureaucratic Culture*.

22. Osterhammel, *Colonialism*, 63–64.

23. Osterhammel, "Semi-Colonialism and Informal Empire," 305–7; Duus, Myers, and Peattie, *Japanese Informal Empire*, xviii.

24. Wang Ya'nan, *Ban fengjian ban zhimindi*, 1 and passim.

25. Robinson, "Non-European Foundations," 130–31, 136. Robinson discusses white colonists in Australia, New Zealand, Canada, and South Africa; indigenous participants in the institutions of colonial rule—such as Indian sepoys in the armies of the British Raj—and indigenous elites such as "Ottoman rayahs, Levantine traders, Chinese mandarins, Indian Brahmins, and African chiefs" who were the partners of the "free trade imperialism" of the 1820s–1870s.

26. Ibid., 131–33.

27. Ibid., 137. Jurgen Osterhammel has done the most to think through Robinson's notion of collaboration in China's history of imperialism. In "Semi-Colonialism and Informal Empire," he attributes collaboration to compradors and compradorial mechanisms as well as to Republican-era rulers such as Yuan Shikai and individual militarists who exchanged control of resources for the support of foreign regimes. He exempts the Qing state from charges of collaboration, arguing instead that Chinese governments upheld a continuous tradition of "official *resistance*" to foreign expansion (304–6). In later work, however, he includes the Qing's involvement in the treaty system as evidence of a collaborative patron–client relationship (Osterhammel, *Colonialism*, 65).

28. Hevia, *English Lessons*, chap. 5; Lydia H. Liu, *Clash of Empires*, chap. 2.

29. Mary Wright, *Last Stand of Chinese Conservatism*, 24, 67; Pelcovits, *Old China Hands*, 4.

30. Osterhammel, "China," 647–48.

31. Fan Baichuan, *Zhongguo lunchuan hangyun ye*, 287–88, 293; Chen Chao, "Qijia hetong," 643–44.

32. See Stoler, *Carnal Knowledge and Imperial Power*, chap. 4.

33. Bickers and Henriot, *New Frontiers*, 256–57; Bickers, *Britain in China*, chap. 3.

34. Bickers and Wasserstrom, "'Dogs and Chinese Not Admitted,'" 446; Ye Xiaoqing, "Shanghai before Nationalism."

35. Murphey, "Treaty Ports," 65; Pye, "How China's Nationalism Was Shanghaied," 113. Osterhammel refers to this view as the "marginality argument" ("Semi-Colonialism and Informal Empire," 293–94).

36. Fitzgerald, *Awakening China*, 104.

37. Duara, *Rescuing History from the Nation*, provides an extensive cultural comparison.

38. Bickers, "Britain and China, and India," 58; Bickers, *Britain in China*, 76–77; Hevia, *English Lessons*, 348.

Chapter 1. Sovereign Concerns

1. Quoted in Michie, *Englishman in China*, 207.

2. This transformation happened quickly within the network of Chinese coastal and Yangzi ports, although sailing ships remained important in overseas trades into the 1880s. See Graham, "Ascendancy of the Sailing Ship."

3. Mary Wright, *Last Stand of Chinese Conservatism*, 23–24; Pelcovits, *Old China Hands*, 4–5.

4. Fairbank, *Trade and Diplomacy*, 313–15; Stanley Wright, *Hart and the Chinese Customs*, 202.

5. Michie, *Englishman in China*, 218; Stanley Wright, *China's Struggle for Tariff Autonomy*, 190; IUP-BPP vol. 33, 451.

6. Fairbank, *Trade and Diplomacy*, chap. 17; Stanley Wright, *Hart and the Chinese Customs*, 202–3.

7. Fairbank, *Trade and Diplomacy*, 337.

8. Stanley Wright, *China's Struggle for Tariff Autonomy*, 191–92.

9. Fairbank, *Trade and Diplomacy*, 317–19.

10. Stanley Wright, *China's Struggle for Tariff Autonomy*, 189.

11. Fairbank, *Trade and Diplomacy*, 317–19; Stanley Wright, *China's Struggle for Tariff Autonomy*, 193–95.

12. Stanley Wright, *China's Struggle for Tariff Autonomy*, 191.

13. Morse, *International Relations*, vol. II, 154; Stanley Wright, *China's Struggle for Tariff Autonomy*, 192–93.

14. Stanley Wright, *China's Struggle for Tariff Autonomy*, 195.

15. This book uses "Treaty of Tianjin" to refer to the provisions of both the 1858 Treaty of Tianjin and the 1860 Peking Convention.

16. Hevia, *English Lessons*, 69.

17. Banno, *China and the West*, 15; Mary Wright, *Last Stand of Chinese Conservatism*, 22–23; Stanley Wright, *Hart and the Chinese Customs*, 134.

18. Banno, *China and the West.*

19. Mary Wright, *Last Stand of Chinese Conservatism*; Ting-yee Kuo and Kwang-ching Liu, "Self-Strengthening: The Pursuit of Western Technology," 491–500.

20. Stanley Wright, *Hart and the Chinese Customs*, 133–34.

21. Ibid., 152. See the description of Hart's role in Osterhammel, "Britain and China," 156.

22. Stanley Wright, *Hart and the Chinese Customs*, 204–6, and *China's Struggle for Tariff Autonomy*, 198–99; Dean, *China and Great Britain*, 62–63, 74–77.

23. Stanley Wright, *Hart and the Chinese Customs*, 207.

24. Dean, *China and Great Britain*, 31.

25. Fan Baichuan, *Zhongguo lunchuan hangyun ye*, 120; Fairbank, *Trade and Diplomacy*, 168; Michie, *Englishman in China*, 216–17.

26. IUP-BPP vol. 6, 101–2; vol. 9, 379.

27. Dean, *China and Great Britain*, 29–31; Stanley Wright, *China's Struggle for Tariff Autonomy*, 207.

28. Dean, *China and Great Britain*, 34.

29. IUP-BPP vol. 32, 73.

30. Dean, *China and Great Britain*, 33–34; Stanley Wright, *China's Struggle for Tariff Autonomy*, 208–9.

31. Michie, *Englishman in China*, 225.

32. Fan Baichuan, *Zhongguo lunchuan hangyun ye*, 124; Blue, "European Navigation," 110.

33. IUP-BPP vol. 32, 89–91.

34. IUP-BPP vol. 33, 451.

35. IUP-BPP vol. 32, 89–91; Dean, *China and Great Britain*, 111; Stanley Wright, *China's Struggle for Tariff Autonomy*, 209–10.

36. Dean, *China and Great Britain*, 122.

37. NCH 13 Dec. 1862, 198.

38. NCH 13 Dec. 1862, 198.

39. NCH 21 Mar. 1863, 48. Records of Qing enforcement of the ban on trading at nontreaty places can be found in ZLY-IMH 01-31-1 (1–5).

40. IUP-BPP vol. 32, 446, 493–94.

41. Ibid., 493–94.

42. NCH 25 Apr. 1863.

43. Stanley Wright, *Hart and the Chinese Customs*, 203, and *China's Struggle for Tariff Autonomy*, 191.

44. IUP-BPP vol. 7, 177–78.

45. K.-C. Liu, *Anglo-American Steamship Rivalry*, 153–54.

46. Robert Hart's memorial on the regulation of Chinese purchases mentions this prohibition. HFD: Robert Hart, Tongzhi 4/8/16 (5 Oct. 1865), 828. This practice originated in the 1850s, when British and U.S. consuls began issuing "sailing letters" to Chinese-owned ships that afforded them protection under foreign flags. Initiated by Hong Kong Governor John Bowring (1792–1872) as a measure to keep trade at Hong Kong and Canton moving despite coastal piracy and Taiping insurgency, these "sailing letters" allowed Chinese-owned ships to claim the protection of a foreign national flag for a period of a year. Bowring argued that the measure was necessary because the Qing regime was not

providing protection to its own ships, yet consuls also profited by collecting steep fees for the purchase of a registration. The lorcha *Arrow*, whose boarding by Qing officials precipitated the Second Opium War, was owned by a Hong Kong Chinese and had been registered under sailing letters as a British ship (Morse, *International Relations,* vol. I, 409–10, 409 n. 40).

47. Hao, *Commercial Revolution*, 246–50.

48. Ibid., 258; Lai, "Li Hung-chang and Modern Enterprise," 219.

49. Yi Li, *Chinese Bureaucratic Culture*, 73–74, 80.

50. In these discussions, the debate centered on how to define a ship as "Chinese." For some officials, ownership and registration by a Qing subject was enough. For others, the ship needed to have no foreign passengers and crew aboard to be granted the same mobility as junks. HFD: Zuo Zongtang to Zongli *yamen*, Tongzhi 4/run 5/21 (13 Jul. 1865), 821–22; HFD: Li Hongzhang to Zongli *yamen*, Tongzhi 3/9/6 (14 Apr. 1864), 809.

51. HFD: Li Hongzhang to Zongli *yamen*, Tongzhi 4/11/25 (11 Jan. 1866), 835. Also see Yi Li, *Chinese Bureaucratic Culture*, 88–89; Fan Baichuan, *Zhongguo lunchuan hangyun ye*, 187–90.

52. Fan Baichuan, *Zhongguo lunchuan hangyun ye*, 190.

53. JTS-HZB, 146.

54. Fan Baichuan, *Zhongguo lunchuan hangyun ye*, 190; Zhu Yin'gui, *Guojia ganyu jingji*, 44.

55. Fan Baichuan, *Zhongguo lunchuan hangyun ye*, 170–77; Rawski, *Economic Growth in Prewar China*, 189.

56. K.-C. Liu, *Anglo-American Steamship Rivalry*, 54.

57. IUP-BPP vol. 7, 112–13, vol. 8, 324–27, vol. 9, 17–18.

58. IUP-BPP vol. 6, 225.

59. Ibid., 63–64; IUP-BPP vol. 6, 408, 494, vol. 8, 37–38.

60. NCH 7 Jul. 1866, 106.

61. K.-C. Liu, *Anglo-American Steamship Rivalry*, 88–90; IMC Reports on Trade, Shanghai, 1871–72, 91; NCH 8 Nov. 1870, 336, 16 Jun. 1871, 25 Oct. 1871, 810, 28 Mar. 1872, 242.

62. Yi Li, *Chinese Bureaucratic Culture*, 81–83; Stanley Wright, *Hart and the Chinese Customs*, 1–2, 204–6.

63. Mary Wright, *Last Stand of Chinese Conservatism*, 24; Pelcovits, *Old China Hands*, 4; Dean, *China and Great Britain*, 9.

64. Pelcovits, *Old China Hands*, chap. 1.

65. Ibid., 1–5.

66. Mary Wright, *Last Stand of Chinese Conservatism*, 67.

67. Adas, *Machines as the Measure of Men*, 231–33.

68. ZLY-IMH 01-13-9 (1) Li Hongzhang to Zongli *yamen* Tongzhi 4/8/17 (11 May 1865); ZLY-IMH 01-13-9 (2) French Minister to Zongli *yamen* Tongzhi 5/8/20 (20 Jun. 1866).

69. Pelcovits, *Old China Hands*, 26–27.

70. ZLY-IMH 01-31-12(8) Tongzhi 5 (1866).

71. NCH 2 Jun. 1866, 86.

72. The *North China Herald* article described Li's concerns about traffic as a "morbid fear of collisions," yet collisions between steamships and junks were more of an admin-

istrative headache for the Zongli *yamen* than a frightening spectacle. In the 1860s, the Zongli *yamen* adjudicated cases of collisions on the Yangzi River and elsewhere on almost a daily basis, requiring lengthy negotiations over compensation for loss of life or property (ZLY-IMH 01-16-6 to 01-16-9).

73. ZLY-IMH 01-13-9(1) Li Hongzhang to Zongli *yamen* Tongzhi 4/8/17 (11 May 1865).

74. Biggerstaff, "Secret Correspondence of 1867–8," 122–36.

75. Pelcovits, *Old China Hands*, 33–41.

76. NCH 9 Mar. 1867, 39.

77. Stanley Wright, *China's Struggle for Tariff Autonomy*, 234; NCH 12 Oct. 1867, 296, 9 Nov. 1867, 343.

78. NCH 25 Oct. 1867, 320.

79. CBYWSM 50, Zongli *yamen* to various officials, Tongzhi 6/1/12 (16 Feb. 1867), 33b–34a.

80. CBYWSM 55, Li Hongzhang to Zongli *yamen*, Tongzhi 6/12/6 (31 Dec. 1867), 14a–b; 53 Shen Baozhen Tongzhi 6/11/21 (16 Dec. 1867), 5b–6a; 52 Ruilin Tongzhi 6/11/15 (10 Dec. 1867), 20b; 51 Zuo Zongtang Tongzhi 6/10/25 (20 Nov. 1867), 22a; 52 Li Hanzhang, Tongzhi 6/11/21 (16 Dec. 1867), 34a.

81. NCH 22 Jun. 1867; NCH 5 Jun. 1868, 273; CBYWSM 50 Zongli *yamen* to various officials Tongzhi 6/1/12 (16 Feb. 1867), 33b–34a.

82. CBYWSM 51, Zuo Zongtang Tongzhi 6/10/25 (20 Nov. 1867), 22a; 55 Wu Tang Tongzhi 6/12/3 (28 Dec. 1867), 3b–4a; 56 Guanwen Tongzhi 6/12/22 (16 Jan. 1868), 13a–b. See also Yi Li, *Chinese Bureaucratic Culture*, 86.

83. Pelcovits, *Old China Hands*, 53, 71.

84. Ibid., 84.

85. Lydia H. Liu, *Clash of Empires*, 110–11.

86. In its most scholarly guise, the argument that Qing officials opposed Western technologies conflates this opposition with an ideological antiforeign stance based on a deep commitment to Chinese cultural traditions. This argument is most often associated with the late Qing Grand Secretary Woren and others who criticized Western Affairs officials' attempts to adapt foreign technologies for the benefit of the dynasty. Unlike the Western Affairs officials, however, these critics were not involved in the daily management of these technologies. Hao and Wang, "Changing Chinese Views," 172–76.

87. Stanley Wright, *Hart and the Chinese Customs*, 403; Yi Li, *Chinese Bureaucratic Culture*, 79–121; Lu Shiqiang, *Zaoqi de lunchuan jingying*.

88. For example, Cohen, *Discovering History in China*, 57–96; Barlow, "Colonialism's Career," 373–411; Waley-Cohen, *Sextants of Beijing*.

89. Mary Wright, *Last Stand of Chinese Conservatism*, 67; Pelcovits, *Old China Hands*, 104–5.

90. Despite the dangers of the Three Gorges area, junks had routinely shipped goods through it since the Han dynasty. Van Slyke, *Yangtze*, 19; Smith, "Commerce, Agriculture, and Core Formation."

91. Blakiston, *Five Months on the Yang-tsze*, 84, 129, 211, 302; Thomas Cooper, *Travels of a Pioneer*, 8, 100–101.

92. IUP-BPP vol. 22, 118–21.

93. Pelcovits, *Old China Hands*, 108.

94. Ibid., 106–8.

95. Britain annexed lower Burma in 1852. Blue, "Land and River Routes," 162. On the range of proposals for overland routes between Burma and China between 1864 and 1898, see IUP-BPP vol. 41.

96. Stanley Wright, *China's Struggle for Tariff Autonomy*, 261.

97. IUP-BPP vol. 22, 120–21; Pelcovits, *Old China Hands*, 105–6.

98. IUP-BPP vol. 11, 296, 534.

99. Pelcovits, *Old China Hands*, 126; ZLY-IMH 01-21-31 (2–3); PRO-FO 228/591 Hankow, 29 Mar. 1877.

100. Stanley Wright, *China's Struggle for Tariff Autonomy*, 264. This codification of the translation of the term can be compared to the provision of the Treaty of Tianjin that fixed the translation of the term *yi* as "barbarian" (Lydia H. Liu, *Clash of Empires*, 33–34; Hevia, *English Lessons*, 57–58). A different view of these types of translated terms is Cassel, *Grounds of Judgment*, 79–80.

101. Pelcovits, *Old China Hands*, 126.

102. Wyman, "Ambiguities of Chinese Antiforeignism."

103. H. B. Morse Papers, May–Aug. 1886; PRO-FO 228/852, Ichang, 1886–87; JMA Hankow I, #1931; JSS I 15 Dec. 1886.

104. Little, *Through the Yang-tse Gorges*, 4–5.

105. Stanley Wright, *Hart and the Chinese Customs*, 608–9; PRO-FO 405/51, "Memorandum on the Question of the Navigation of the Upper Yangtze" (1890); Blue, "Land and River Routes," 171.

106. Nie Baozhang, *Jindai hangyun shi ziliao, 1840–1895*, vol. 1, 420.

107. Ibid., 420. Discussion of local resistance and unrest related to Little's voyage can be found in PRO-FO 228/1031; PRO-FO 228/852 Ichang 24 Oct. 1887, 228/864 Ichang, 1888; Sasaki Masaya, *Shimmatsu no haigai undō*, 169–71.

108. PRO-FO 228/864 Ichang 15 Dec. 1888. On the sale of Little's ship, see Stanley Wright, *Hart and the Chinese Customs*, 610, and PRO-FO 405/51.

109. Stanley Wright, *Hart and the Chinese Customs*, 610.

110. Nie Baozhang, *Jindai hangyun shi ziliao 1840–1895*, vol. 1, 418.

111. Ibid., 418–20.

112. NCH 9 Nov. 1867, 343.

113. Pelcovits, *Old China Hands*, chaps. 7–8; Morse, *International Relations*, vol. III, 109–20.

114. Fan Baichuan, *Zhongguo lunchuan hangyun ye*, 318–19.

115. Stanley Wright, *Hart and the Chinese Customs*, 701, and *China's Struggle for Tariff Autonomy*, 338.

116. Stanley Wright, *Hart and the Chinese Customs*, 700.

117. Ibid., 760–61.

118. Stanley Wright, *China's Struggle for Tariff Autonomy*, 378.

119. NCH 9 Nov. 1867, 343.

120. PRO-FO 228/2301, 23 Jan. 1905, 228/2302, 25 May 1905, 29 Jun. 1905, 10 Jul. 1905, 22 Aug. 1905.

121. Stanley Wright, *Hart and the Chinese Customs*, 761.

122. Stanley Wright, *China's Struggle for Tariff Autonomy*, 377–78; IMC Decennial, 1912–1921, Changsha, 280, Hankow, 309, Kiukiang, 332, Wuhu, 347.

123. Even after the dynasty's demise, the principle that new inland routes required the approval of Maritime Customs and central and provincial authorities remained unchanged.

124. Fan Baichuan, *Zhongguo lunchuan hangyun ye*, 300–302.

125. Ibid., 320.

126. Ibid., 427.

127. Stanley Wright, *Hart and the Chinese Customs*, 761, and *China's Struggle for Tariff Autonomy*, 377–78.

128. Yang Tianhong, *Kou'an kaifang yu shehui biange*, 70–74, 124–32.

129. Bickers, "Good Work for China," 32–35.

130. Where new treaty ports were opened, it was most often on the initiative of Republican authorities in conjunction with the Maritime Customs for the purpose of facilitating connections between steamship and rail transport. Yang Tianhong, *Kou'an kaifang*, 394–97.

131. For example, Bickers, *Britain in China*; Bickers and Henriot, *New Frontiers*; Rogaski, *Hygienic Modernity*; Meng, *Shanghai and the Edges of Empires*; Wasserstrom, *Global Shanghai*.

132. Feuerwerker, *Chinese Economy*, 56.

133. The point that treaty ports had a significant impact on their hinterlands has been made in Pomeranz, *Making of a Hinterland*, and Bun, "Mapping the Hinterland."

134. IMC Decennial 1882–1891, Wuhu, 239–53.

135. Honig, *Creating Chinese Ethnicity*, 86–87; Perry, *Shanghai on Strike*, 53–54; IMC Decennial 1882–1891, Wuhu, 240. For reports on migrant labor at other Yangzi treaty ports, see IMC Decennial 1902–11, Hankow, 363, Shanghai, 24; PRO-FO 22/1291 Shashi, 1898; Gaimushō Archives, 5.3.2–15, 4 Jul. 1899.

136. Reinhardt, "Treaty Ports as Shipping Infrastructure."

137. Ray, "Asian Capital," 455–75.

138. Pope, "British Steamshipping," 4–7, 19.

139. Blake, *B.I. Centenary*, 72.

140. Pope, "British Steamshipping," 12.

141. Ibid., 11.

142. Munro, *Maritime Enterprise and Empire*, 46.

143. Ibid., 37–50; Pope, "British Steamshipping," 9.

144. Munro, *Maritime Enterprise and Empire*, 51.

145. Blake, *B.I. Centenary*, 71.

146. Ibid., 52, 73. Pope, "British Steamshipping," 9. The Indian Railway was also the product of a similar alliance between the government of India and British enterprise. Excepting the 1870s, during which the government built railways itself, railway building in India between 1849 and 1914 was accomplished by private companies subsidized by the East India Company and later by the government of India. Headrick, *Tentacles of Progress*, 49–81.

147. Harcourt, "British Oceanic Mail Contracts," 41.

148. NCH 3 Nov. 1866, 174.

Chapter 2. Aligning Capital and Flag

1. NCH 18 Jan. 1877, 49.

2. On the development of trading firms, see Greenberg, *British Trade*, 144–85; Geoffrey Jones, *Merchants to Multinationals*, 32–33; Hao, *Commercial Revolution*, 22–33; Lockwood, *Augustine Heard and Company*, 6–7.

3. Haviland, "American Steam Navigation, Part I," 160–61, 167–68, "American Steam Navigation Part IV," 299; Hao, *Commercial Revolution*, 196; Michie, *Englishman in China*, 216–17.

4. NCH 12 Dec. 1862; IUP-BPP vol. 6, 184; K.-C. Liu, *Anglo-American Steamship Rivalry*, 10.

5. Haviland, "American Steam Navigation, Part III," 43.

6. Hao, *Commercial Revolution*, 246–47.

7. K.-C. Liu, *Anglo-American Steamship Rivalry*, 72, 78–81; Wang Jingyu, "Huashang fugu huodong," 40–43.

8. K.-C. Liu, *Anglo-American Steamship Rivalry*, 19.

9. Ibid., 25–29, 32.

10. Ibid., 38–39, 54.

11. Ibid., 44, 48, 65–66.

12. Ibid., 55–56, 72.

13. Ibid., 71–72.

14. Ibid., 78; Hao, *Commercial Revolution*, 248.

15. K.-C. Liu, *Anglo-American Steamship Rivalry*, 141.

16. Wang Jingyu, "Huashang fugu huodong"; Hao, *Commercial Revolution*, 245.

17. Hao, *Commercial Revolution*, 258; Lai, "Li Hung-chang and Modern Enterprise," 219.

18. Fan Baichuan, *Zhongguo lunchuan hangyun ye*, 190.

19. HFD, Li Hongzhang to Zongli *yamen*, Tongzhi 11/11/24 (25 Dec. 1872), 919.

20. Ibid., 919.

21. K.-C. Liu, *Anglo-American Steamship Rivalry*, 32.

22. Ibid., 33, 100–101.

23. Faure, *China and Capitalism*, 52–53.

24. K.-C. Liu, *Anglo-American Steamship Rivalry*, 141–43; Hao, *Commercial Revolution*, 249.

25. Headrick, *Tentacles of Progress*, 25–27, 42–44.

26. Ibid., 27; IUP-BPP vol. 9, 379.

27. Hyde, *Far Eastern Trade*, 22–23.

28. Haviland, "American Steam Navigation, Part VII," 62; K.-C. Liu, *Anglo-American Steamship Rivalry*, 96.

29. Lockwood, *Augustine Heard and Company*, 104; NCH 11 Jan. 1872, 21.

30. Hao, *Commercial Revolution*, 163–64; Lockwood, *Augustine Heard and Company*, 103, 107–8; Eiichi Motono, "The 'Traffic Revolution,'" 86–89; Osterhammel, "British Business in China," 192; Le Fevour, *Western Enterprise*, 138–39; Geoffrey Jones, *Merchants to Multinationals*, 45–47, 48–51.

31. K.-C. Liu, *Anglo-American Steamship Rivalry*, 88–90.

32. IMC *Reports on Trade*, 1871–72, Chinkiang, 91; NCH 8 Nov. 1870, 336, 16 Jul. 1871, 439, 25 Oct. 1871, 810, 28 Mar. 1872, 242.

33. K.-C. Liu, *Anglo-American Steamship Rivalry*, 86–87; NCH 8 Nov. 1870, 336.

34. NCH 8 Nov. 1870, 336.

35. Hinton, *Grain Tribute System*, 16–33; Yung Wing, *My Life*, 171; Yi Li, *Chinese Bureaucratic Culture*, 84–89, 98–101; Lu Shiqiang, *Zaoqi de lunchuan jingying*, 121–84.

36. Marriner and Hyde, *Senior John Samuel Swire*, 38–39. In 1868 the partnership between Swire and Butterfield ended, leaving the firm of Butterfield & Swire under the control of John Swire & Sons. The trading firm kept its original name.

37. Geoffrey Jones, *Merchants to Multinationals*, 35–36; Marriner and Hyde, *Senior John Samuel Swire*, 58–61.

38. Marriner and Hyde, *Senior John Samuel Swire*, 60; K.-C. Liu, *Anglo-American Steamship Rivalry*, 117; Geoffrey Jones, *Merchants to Multinationals*, 37, 241–43.

39. Geoffrey Jones, *Merchants to Multinationals*, 51.

40. Marriner and Hyde, *Senior John Samuel Swire*, 62; K.-C. Liu, *Anglo-American Steamship Rivalry*, 122–34.

41. K.-C. Liu, *Anglo-American Steamship Rivalry*, 126.

42. Ibid., 130–31.

43. NCH 12 Jul. 1873.

44. YWYD Li Hongzhang, Tongzhi 11/11/23 (24 Dec. 1872), 5–6.

45. Hao and Wang, "Changing Chinese Views," 190–91; Yi Li, *Chinese Bureaucratic Culture*, 68–69. The term *shangzhan* is often associated with the late nineteenth-century writings of the "scholarly comprador" Zheng Guanying. Zheng's later use of the term was a criticism of enterprises like China Merchants Company, as he argued that merchants needed freedom from state supervision to carry out commercial warfare effectively. Guo Wu, *Zheng Guanying*, 42, 48, 133, 188.

46. YWYD Li Hongzhang, Tongzhi 11/11/23 (24 Dec. 1872), 6. See also HFD Li Hongzhang to Zongli *yamen*, Tongzhi 11/11/24 (25 Dec. 1872), 920. In later memorials concerning China Merchants Company, the idea of recovering *liquan* is consistently invoked through the phrases *jian shou liquan*, *wan liquan*, *shouhui liquan*, and so on. See YWYD Chen Lanbin, Guangxu 2/10/24 (9 Dec. 1876), 10, Shen Baozhen Guangxu 2/11/27 (11 Jan. 1877), 14, Liu Kunyi Guangxu 7/1/15 (13 Feb. 1881), 41.

47. Hao and Wang, "Changing Chinese Views," 190–91.

48. HFD Li Hongzhang to Zongli *yamen*, Tongzhi 11/11/24 (25 Dec. 1872), 923. A later (1873) version of the company's rules stipulated that Chinese could not invest on behalf of foreigners or allow foreigners to gain stock in the company (JTS-HZB, 144).

49. HFD Li Hongzhang to Zongli *yamen*, Tongzhi 11/11/24 (25 Dec. 1872), 920.

50. Ibid., 919–20.

51. On the structure of *guandu shangban* enterprises, see K.-C. Liu, "British-Chinese Steamship Rivalry," 54; Lai, "Li Hung-chang and Modern Enterprise," 218; and Feuerwerker, *China's Early Industrialization*, 8–12, 22–26.

52. On Zhu Qi'ang's role, see Li Hongzhang Memorial Tongzhi 11/11/23 YWYD, 6; Hao, *Comprador*, 139; Feuerwerker, *China's Early Industrialization*, 108–10; Yi Li, *Chinese Bureaucratic Culture*, 124–27.

53. Feuerwerker, *China's Early Industrialization*, 110–11; Yi Li, *Chinese Bureaucratic Culture*, 129–30; Wang Jingyu, "Huashang fugu huodong," 46.

54. Fan Baichuan, *Zhongguo lunchuan hangyun ye*, 260; Hao, *Commercial Revolution*, 199–200; Lai, "Li Hung-chang and Modern Enterprise," 221.

55. Fan Baichuan, *Zhongguo lunchuan hangyun ye*, 261; Zhang Houquan, *Zhaoshang ju shi*, 50.

56. Feuerwerker, *China's Early Industrialization*, 125–26.

57. K.-C. Liu, "British-Chinese Steamship Rivalry" 56; Wang Jingyu, "Huashang fugu huodong," 73.

58. Fan Baichuan, *Zhongguo lunchuan hangyun ye*, 260; K.-C. Liu, "Steamship Enterprise," 439–43.

59. NCH 2 Jan. 1873.

60. Yi Li, *Chinese Bureaucratic Culture*, 124; Hao, *Commercial Revolution*, 202.

61. JTS-HZB, 147.

62. NCH 12 Apr. 1877, 370–74.

63. K.-C. Liu, "British-Chinese Steamship Rivalry," 55–60.

64. Ibid., 58–61.

65. NCH 18 Jan. 1877, 49.

66. NCH 28 Apr. 1877, 426.

67. K.-C. Liu, "Steamship Enterprise," 443.

68. Feuerwerker, *China's Early Industrialization*, 170–72.

69. Fan Baichuan, *Zhongguo lunchuan hangyun ye*, 300–302.

70. Feuerwerker, *China's Early Industrialization*, 28–29, 172.

71. Lai, "Li Hung-chang and Modern Enterprise," 237.

72. K.-C. Liu, "British-Chinese Steamship Rivalry," 56–57, 60; K.-C. Liu, "Steamship Enterprise," 440; Feuerwerker, *China's Early Industrialization*, 126.

73. K.-C. Liu, "British-Chinese Steamship Rivalry," 62–63.

74. Feuerwerker, *China's Early Industrialization*, 126; NCH 5 Apr. 1877, 345.

75. Wang Jingyu, "Huashang fugu huodong," 73.

76. Feuerwerker, *China's Early Industrialization*, 127–30; Fan Baichuan, *Zhongguo lunchuan hangyun ye*, 255–56.

77. Faure, *China and Capitalism*, 52–53; Wang Jingyu, "Huashang fugu huodong," 69.

78. Hao, *Commercial Revolution*, 251; K.-C. Liu, "Steamship Enterprise," 439.

79. K.-C. Liu, "British-Chinese Steamship Rivalry," 65.

80. Ibid., 65; K.-C. Liu, "Steamship Enterprise," 239.

81. Keswick, *Thistle and the Jade*, 142.

82. K.-C. Liu, "Steamship Enterprise," 239.

83. K.-C. Liu, "British-Chinese Steamship Rivalry," 65.

84. Marriner and Hyde, *Senior John Samuel Swire*, 61.

85. As chapter 3 will show, in the two cases in which foreign-flag companies supported by Chinese merchant capital operated within the steam network, these companies played a decidedly subordinate role to the Three Companies. Wang Jingyu, "Huashang fugu huodong," 48; Hao, *Commercial Revolution*, 251.

86. Wang Jingyu, "Huashang fugu huodong," 39–40, 46, 69; Hao, *Commercial Revolution*, 250. Both Wang and Hao depict Chinese merchant investments in foreign

shipping firms as increasing over this period because of developments such as the decision to make Shanghai a British port of registry in 1875 and British steamship companies' acceptance of commercial laws concerning limited liability. The shipping companies they cite as evidence of increased share affiliation, however, provided in-port services (such as the Cooperative Cargo Boat Company of Shanghai or the Taku Tug and Lighter Company of Tianjin) and did not operate within the treaty-port steam network.

87. Headrick, *Tentacles of Progress*, 44.

88. In the days of sail, there were Bombay-based Parsi and other ship owners involved in overseas trade to China, Africa, and the Middle East and on the Indian Ocean. There were Indian-owned and joint-venture steamship companies that worked India's west coast and routes between Bombay, Calcutta, and China with some success. Rao, *Short History of Indian Shipping*, 46–47, 54; Munro, *Maritime Enterprise and Empire*, 45.

89. Historians of Indian shipping point to the rise of the British India Steam Navigation Company as merely a latter chapter in a longer history in which British policies undermined Indian shipping and shipbuilding, forcing the subcontinent into a state of "dependency" on British technology, skill, and enterprise for maritime transport. Going back to the days of the East India Company, these historians point to parliamentary acts of the 1810s–30s that undermined a thriving Indian shipbuilding industry by discouraging British owners from buying Indian-built ships and excluding these ships from trade with Europe. Broeze, "Underdevelopment and Dependency," 429–57.

90. Munro, *Maritime Enterprise and Empire*, 68, 145; Broeze, "Underdevelopment and Dependency," 444.

91. Munro, *Maritime Enterprise and Empire*, 122–25.

92. Ibid., 126–27.

93. Ibid., 128, 140.

94. Ibid., 133–34.

95. Blake, *B.I. Centenary*, 19–20; Munro, *Maritime Enterprise and Empire*, 40.

96. Nayar, *State and Market in India's Shipping*, 44.

Chapter 3. The Shipping Conference as Collaboration, 1882–1913

1. John S. Swire to T. H. Ismay, 28 Mar. 1883. Quoted in Marriner and Hyde, *Senior John Samuel Swire*, 83.

2. Cafruny, *Ruling the Waves*, 53–57.

3. The British companies participating in the Far East Conference were the Peninsular & Oriental Company, the Ocean Steamship Company, the Glen, Castle, and Shire Lines and the ships of Gellatly, Hankey & Sewell, Norris & Joyner, and Shaw, Williams & Company. Marriner and Hyde, *Senior John Samuel Swire*, 160–61.

4. Cafruny, *Ruling the Waves*, 54. On the rationales for international shipping conferences and their practices, see ibid., 52–57; Marriner and Hyde, *Senior John Samuel Swire*, chaps. 8–9; Headrick, *Tentacles of Progress*, 35–38; Wray, *Mitsubishi and the N.Y.K.*, 308–13.

5. K.-C. Liu, "British-Chinese Steamship Rivalry," 42–47, 72–73, 79; Marriner and Hyde, *Senior John Samuel Swire*, 62.

6. K.-C. Liu, "British-Chinese Steamship Rivalry," 133–34.
7. Marriner and Hyde, *Senior John Samuel Swire*, 135–41.
8. Ibid., 73; K.-C. Liu, "British-Chinese Steamship Rivalry," 68.
9. Marriner and Hyde, *Senior John Samuel Swire*, 83–85.
10. OSK, 20.
11. Nagoya shōgyō kaigisho, *Shinkoku shinkai kōjō shōgyō*, 127; OSK, 21–22.
12. Wray, *Mitsubishi and the N.Y.K.*, 313.
13. Ibid., 351; Tōa Dōbun Shoin, *Shina keizai zensho*, vol. 3, 343.
14. OSK, 20.
15. NCH 6 Jul. 1889, 1.
16. Tōa Dōbun Shoin, *Shina keizai zensho*, vol. 2, 495, and vol. 3, 342; Fan Baichuan, *Zhongguo lunchuan hangyun ye*, 209–10; Nie Baozhang, *Jindai hangyun shi ziliao 1840–1895*, vol. 2, 1421.
17. NCH 18 Jul. 1890, 73.
18. Marriner and Hyde, *Senior John Samuel Swire*, 86–88; Zhang, Chen, and Yao, *Swire Group*, 86, 111.
19. Cafruny, *Ruling the Waves*, 49–50, 52–53.
20. Marriner and Hyde, *Senior John Samuel Swire*, 183.
21. Ibid., 182; Cafruny, *Ruling the Waves*, 56.
22. Marriner and Hyde, *Senior John Samuel Swire*, 183.
23. Cafruny, *Ruling the Waves*, 55–56; Headrick, *Tentacles of Progress*, 38.
24. NCH 6 Jul. 1889, 1–2.
25. NCH 25 Jun. 1886, 657.
26. NCH 1 Aug. 1890, 121.
27. IMC Decennial 1882–91, Wuhu, 257–61.
28. Ibid.; IMC Decennial 1882–91, Kiukiang, 219–20.
29. Morse, *Gilds of China*, 55–56.
30. K.-C. Liu, *Anglo-American Steamship Rivalry*, 147–48; Morse, *Gilds of China*, 23.
31. In 1884, McBain, a conference affiliate, tried to set up an exclusive relationship with the Shantou Guild when it organized a taboo against the China Navigation Company in protest of conference policies. JSS In 25 Jul. 1884, 5 Nov. 1884, 26 Nov. 1884.
32. JSS In 30 Nov. 1888.
33. Fan Baichuan, *Zhongguo lunchuan hangyun ye*, 287–88, 293.
34. Chen Chao, "Qijia hetong," 643–44.
35. K.-C. Liu, "Steamship Enterprise," 450–51.
36. Ibid., 447–48, 451; K.-C. Liu, "British-Chinese Steamship Rivalry," 64; Marriner and Hyde, *Senior John Samuel Swire*, 84–85.
37. K.-C. Liu, "Steamship Enterprise," 446–47.
38. Feuerwerker, *China's Early Industrialization*, 182–83; Y. Zhu, *Guojia ganyu jingji*, 115–18; Lai, "Li Hung-chang and Modern Enterprise," 238.
39. Marriner and Hyde, *Senior John Samuel Swire*, 111–12; Geoffrey Jones, *Merchants to Multinationals*, 72.
40. Marriner and Hyde, *Senior John Samuel Swire*, 90.
41. Geoffrey Jones, *Merchants to Multinationals*, 41.
42. Ibid., 33.

43. Ibid.

44. Marriner and Hyde, *Senior John Samuel Swire*, 124–29; Geoffrey Jones, *Merchants to Multinationals*, 72.

45. Yi Li, *Chinese Bureaucratic Culture*, 179–80; Zhang Houquan, *Zhaoshang ju shi*, 59.

46. K.-C. Liu, "British-Chinese Steamship Rivalry," 69.

47. Fan Baichuan, *Zhongguo lunchuan hangyun ye*, 297–98.

48. Zhang Houquan, *Zhaoshang ju shi*, 59–64.

49. Ibid., 162.

50. Ibid., 79–81, 174–75.

51. Carlson, *Kaiping Mines*, 7–8, 24–26. Kaiping's output of coal was never great enough to meet demand, and coal continued to be imported into China from Britain, Australia, and Japan (Tim Wright, *Coal Mining*, 51–52).

52. Feuerwerker, *China's Early Industrialization*, 214–15.

53. Dick and Kentwell, *Beancaker to Boxboat*, 191–205.

54. Zhang Houquan, *Zhaoshang ju shi*, 190–91, 249.

55. Most China Navigation ships were built by Scott & Company in Greenock. Indo-China occasionally built ships in British-owned shipyards in Shanghai, but most of its fleet was built in England or Scotland. After the turn of the twentieth century, these firms began to rely more on British-owned shipbuilding facilities in China (Dick and Kentwell, *Beancaker to Boxboat*, 25–38, 77–98).

56. Jiang Tianfeng, *Changjiang hangyun shi*, 297–300.

57. Broeze, "Underdevelopment and Dependency," 432–41; Pope, "British Steamshipping," 13.

58. Zhang Houquan, *Zhaoshang ju shi*, 115.

59. Yi Li, *Chinese Bureaucratic Culture*, 24–26.

60. Ibid., 182, 246–47; Lai, "Li Hung-chang and Modern Enterprise," 234–35.

61. Feuerwerker, *China's Early Industrialization*, 115–16; Lai, "Li Hung-chang and Modern Enterprise," 236–37.

62. K.-C. Liu, "Steamship Enterprise," 451.

63. Li Zhigang, "Zhaoshang ju jingying guanli," 100.

64. The Upper Yangzi route was not incorporated into the conference agreement until 1897. IMC Decennial, 1882–91, Ichang, 142, 184; JSS In 24 Dec. 1889–8 Jul. 1892.

65. Tajima Shigeji, *Yōsukō kisengyō chōsa hōkoku*, 35.

66. Feuerwerker, *China's Early Industrialization*, 145–46.

67. Cafruny, *Ruling the Waves*, 52–61.

68. Marriner and Hyde, *Senior John Samuel Swire*, 161.

69. Pelcovits, *Old China Hands*, chaps. 7–8.

70. Wray, *Mitsubishi and the N.Y.K.*, 289, 306–7; Zhu Yin'gui, *Jindai lunchuan hangyun ye*, 62.

71. Wray, *Mitsubishi and the N.Y.K.*, 46.

72. Zhu Yin'gui, *Jindai lunchuan hangyun ye*, 66–67; Fan Baichuan, *Zhongguo lunchuan hangyun ye*, 347–48.

73. Wray, *Mitsubishi and the N.Y.K.*, 341, 344.

74. Ibid., 348–52; Zhu Yin'gui, *Jindai lunchuan hangyun ye*, 71.

75. Zhu Yin'gui, *Jindai lunchuan hangyun ye*, 69–70.

76. Before 1895, several overseas lines to China received subsidies, such as a monthly mail service and a North German Lloyd line to Hong Kong initiated in 1886. Francis Jones, "German Challenge to British Shipping," 154–58.

77. Fan Baichuan, *Zhongguo lunchuan hangyun ye*, 348–49; also see Wray, *Mitsubishi and the N.Y.K.*, 348.

78. Francis Jones, "German Challenge to British Shipping," 157–58.

79. OSK, 20–22.

80. Tōa Dōbun Shoin, *Shina keizai zensho*, vol. 3, 364.

81. IMC Decennial 1892–1901, Ichang, 184.

82. Wray, *Mitsubishi and the N.Y.K.*, 348; Zhang, Chen, and Yao, *Swire Group*, 127.

83. IMC Decennial, 1902–11, Kiukiang, 367.

84. Fan Baichuan, *Zhongguo lunchuan hangyun ye*, 350–51; NCH 21 Aug. 1903, 401. The French Compagnie Asiatique de Navigation recruited some Chinese shareholders.

85. Zhu Yin'gui, *Jindai lunchuan hangyun ye*, 71; NCH 21 Aug. 1903, 401.

86. Wray, *Mitsubishi and the N.Y.K.*, 386.

87. NCH 29 Jun. 1906, 769.

88. Nisshin Kisen Kaisha, *Kankō jijō*, 53–59.

89. Tōa Dōbun Shoin, *Shina keizai zensho*, vol. 3, 384.

90. Ibid., 363.

91. Wray, *Mitsubishi and the N.Y.K.*, 353.

92. Zhang, Chen, and Yao, *Swire Group*, 129–33.

93. IMC Decennial 1902–11, Kiukiang, 367–68.

94. Reinhardt, "Treaty Ports as Shipping Infrastructure," 111–13.

95. The merger provided some space for Chinese investment in the Nisshin Kisen Kaisha. Its rules specified that Qing subjects could own up to 20 percent of the company's shares. If there were Chinese shareholders in Nisshin, they owned significantly less than this figure because the Nippon Yūsen Kaisha and Osaka Shōsen Kaisha owned a combined 89.9 percent of the shares (Wray, *Mitsubishi and the N.Y.K.*, 388, 396; Nisshin Kisen Kaisha, *Sanjū nenshi*, 299).

96. Zhu Yin'gui, *Jindai lunchuan hangyun ye*, 73; Nisshin Kisen Kaisha, *Sanjū nenshi*, 55–68; Wray, *Mitsubishi and the N.Y.K.*, 388.

97. Kokaze Hidemasa, *Teikokushugi ka no Nihon kai'un*, 278–83.

98. Wray, *Mitsubishi and the N.Y.K.*, 34, 223; Wray, "Japan's Big-Three Service Enterprises," 40; Zhu Yin'gui, *Jindai lunchuan hangyun ye*, 73.

99. Zhu Ying'ui, *Jindai lunchuan hangyun ye*, 73.

100. Wray, *Mitsubishi and the N.Y.K.*, 390–93.

101. Zhu Yin'gui, *Jindai lunchuan hangyun ye*, 75; Fan Baichuan, *Zhongguo lunchuan hangyun ye*, 353–55.

102. Zhang, Chen, and Yao, *Swire Group*, 134.

103. Zhu Yin'gui, *Jindai lunchuan hangyun ye*, 74; Wray, *Mitsubishi and the N.Y.K.*, 393–94.

104. Wray, *Mitsubishi and the N.Y.K.*, 393–94.

105. Wray, "Japan's Big-Three Service Enterprises," 53.

106. Zhang, Chen, and Yao, *Swire Group*, 145.

107. Nisshin Kisen Kaisha, *Kankō jijō*, 53–59.

108. Wray, *Mitsubishi and the N.Y.K.*, 391.

109. Zhang Houquan, *Zhaoshang ju shi*, 230; Tōa Dōbun Shoin, *Shina keizai zensho*, vol. 3, 384–87; Nisshin Kisen Kaisha, *Kankō jijō*, 57.

110. Fan Baichuan, *Zhongguo lunchuan hangyun ye*, 431–32; JTS-HZB, 216–17; Tōa Dōbun Shoin, *Shina keizai zensho*, vol. 3, 403–4.

111. Tōa Dōbun Shoin, *Shina keizai zensho*, vol. 3, 343–44; Nisshin Kisen Kaisha, *Kankō jijō*, 55–57.

112. Zhang Houquan, *Zhaoshang ju shi*, 226; Dick and Kentwell, *Beancaker to Boxboat*, 199–200.

113. Nisshin Kisen Kaisha, *Kankō jijō*, 57.

114. Zhang, Chen, and Yao, *Swire Group*, 144.

115. Zhu Yin'gui, *Guojia ganyu jingji*, 129, 134–37; Chen Chao, "Qijia hetong," 645; Zhang Houquan, *Zhaoshang ju shi*, 233.

116. Lai, "Li Hung-chang and Modern Enterprise," 238; Chen Chao, "Qijia hetong," 646; Feuerwerker, *China's Early Industrialization*, 173; Zhu Yin'gui, *Guojia ganyu jingji*, 130–31.

117. Zhu Yin'gui, *Guojia ganyu jingji*, 131–33.

118. Feuerwerker, *China's Early Industrialization*, 177.

119. Ibid., 181–82; Zhu Yin'gui, *Guojia ganyu jingji*, 120–21, 124–28.

120. Fan Baichuan, *Zhongguo lunchuan hangyun ye*, 320–22.

121. Ibid., 324, 431–32, 457; see also Zhu Yin'gui, *Jindai lunchuan hangyun ye*, 13, and Tōa Dōbun Shoin, *Shina keizai zensho*, vol. 3, 385, 387, 396, 399.

122. Zhu Yin'gui, *Jindai lunchuan hangyun ye*, 12–13. Fan Baichuan, *Zhongguo lunchuan hangyun ye*, 322–23, 339, 427–28.

123. See Kirby, "China Unincorporated."

124. Feuerwerker, *China's Early Industrialization*, 120–21, 160–68.

125. Munro, *Maritime Enterprise and Empire*, 141–42. This company was backed by T. H. Ismay and W. Imrie of the White Star Line, who were also shareholders in the China Navigation Company.

126. Ibid., 312–14.

127. Rao, *Short History of Indian Shipping*, 68.

128. Ibid., 67–70; Broeze, "Underdevelopment and Dependency," 444–45.

129. Wray, *Mitsubishi and the N.Y.K.*, 295–300.

130. Rao, *Short History of Indian Shipping*, 73–74.

131. Ibid., 71–73.

132. Ray, *Entrepreneurship and Industry in India*, 18–30.

Chapter 4. The Steamship as Social Space, 1860–1925

1. Fox, *Ocean Railway*, 197; Hunter, *Steamboats on the Western Rivers*, 391.
2. Foucault, "Of Other Spaces," 3, 7.
3. Cochran, *Encountering Chinese Networks*, 2.

4. Feuerwerker, *China's Early Industrialization*, 11.
5. Geoffrey Jones, *Merchants to Multinationals*, 212.
6. Ibid., 206; Jiang Yongsheng, "Ri-Qing gaikuang," 24.
7. Geoffrey Jones, *Merchants to Multinationals*, 164, 172.
8. Ibid., 207–8, 242–43.
9. Ibid., 213.
10. Feuerwerker, *China's Early Industrialization*, 107; Yi Li, *Chinese Bureaucratic Culture*, 132.
11. Jiang Yongsheng, "Ri-Qing gaikuang," 24.
12. On different types of compradors, see Sha Weikai, *Zhongguo maiban zhi*, 25–32; Negishi Tadashi, *Baiben seido no kenkyū*, 196–203; Tōa Dōbun Shoin, *Shina keizai zensho*, vol. 2, 356–64; Tajima Shigeji, *Yōsukō kisengyō*, 35–36.
13. Hao, *Comprador*, 32, 74–76, 92.
14. Compradors were common in banking and insurance firms from the 1860s, and in the 1890s companies such as the British-American Tobacco Company and the Standard Oil Company also relied on them to market products and oversee interregional distribution in China. Cochran, *Big Business in China*, 28–29, and *Encountering Chinese Networks*, 20–31, 55–57.
15. Zhang Houquan, *Zhaoshang ju shi*, 92–96.
16. Ibid., 90–92.
17. Sources such as OSK; Tajima Shigeji, *Yōsukō kisengyō*; Nagoya shōgyō kaigisho, *Shinkoku shinkai kōjō shōgyō*; Shanghai Tōa Dōbun Shoin, *Shinkoku shōgyō kanshū*; and Tōa Dōbun Shoin, *Shina keizai zensho* are Japanese surveys and reports that examine the practices in the shipping business around the turn of the twentieth century.
18. Zhang Houquan, *Zhaoshang ju shi*, 96, 191, 247–48.
19. Balachandran, "Conflicts in International Maritime Labour Market," 74–75.
20. For conditions of captains' employment, see JSS I 21 Sep. 1872, 6 Jun. 1874, 20 Feb. 1890.
21. Zhongguo haiyuan gonghui, *Zhongguo haiyuan gongren yundong*, 10–11; Jiang Tianfeng, *Changjiang hangyun shi*, 188–97.
22. This type of system of recruiting labor was not exclusive to the shipping field but was a common way of recruiting dock and factory labor in Shanghai and other large cities. Hershatter, *Workers of Tianjin*, 140–44; Honig, *Sisters and Strangers*, 79–87; Perry, *Shanghai on Strike*, 53.
23. Crews for particular steamship routes tended to be hired from a specific port: Tianjin for the northern coastal route, Canton for the southern coastal route, and Shanghai for the Yangzi River route. Wu Ling and Zhao Bizhen, *Zuijin Yangzi jiang*, 27; Zhongguo haiyuan gonghui, *Zhongguo haiyuan gongren yundong*, 11.
24. Cook, *Lion and the Dragon*, 72–73.
25. Youchuanbu erci tongjibiao, 1908, reprinted in Zhu Yin'gui, *Guojia ganyu jingji*, 195–97.
26. Nie Baozhang, *Jindai hangyun shi ziliao 1840–1895*, vol. 2, 1227–28.
27. JSS I 19 Jan. 1872.

28. NCH 15 Mar. 1877, 258–59. When U.S. ships returned to Chinese waters in force in the 1920s, there were similar problems in enforcing this law. Grover, *American Merchant Ships*, 49–50.

29. Zhang Houquan, *Zhaoshangju shi*, 93–97, 181–90.

30. JTS-HZB, 146; Wang Guang, *Zhongguo shuiyun zhi*, 202–3.

31. Zhang Houquan, *Zhaoshangju shi*, 79–81, 174–75. Renhe and another insurance business started by Xu Run in 1878 maintained a relationship to the China Merchants Company but never attained the capacity to insure the company's fleet.

32. Ibid., 96; Zhu Yin'gui, *Guojia ganyu jingji*, 201.

33. Zhang Houquan, *Zhaoshangju shi*, 353–64.

34. Ibid., 353–54, 446.

35. Qing naval academies included the school attached to the Fuzhou Arsenal (est. 1861) and a group of academies established by Li Hongzhang in the 1880s. Wei Qizhang, *Wan Qing haijun*, 177–82; Rawlinson, *China's Struggle*, 154–56.

36. In 1912, the early Republican government established a school to train merchant mariners, the Wusong Merchant Marine Training School (Wusong shangchuan zhuanke xuexiao). It closed in 1915 due to financial problems and the difficulties its graduates experienced finding employment and opportunities for practical training. Jiang Tianfeng, *Changjiang hangyun shi*, 302; Wang Jianping, *Hangquan wenti*, 101; Wang Guang, *Hangye yu hangquan*, 139.

37. The marine department of the Maritime Customs tried to regulate the increasing numbers of Chinese acting as masters and engineers in the absence of a formal certification process by detaining ships whose captains or engineers posed an obvious danger. This practice was an unauthorized extension of Maritime Customs powers. Marine Department officials were not allowed to test Chinese mariners because such tests might be interpreted as a form of certification; they instead tried to determine whether the experience claimed by the acting captain or engineer was appropriate to the vessel. CMC 679/21057, 5 Mar. 1918.

38. Chamberlain, *Foreign Flags*, 20.

39. Zhu Yin'gui, *Guojia ganyu jingji*, 174–76.

40. Ibid., 185–91.

41. Zhang Houquan, *Zhaoshang ju shi*, 353.

42. Chamberlain, *Foreign Flags*, 19–20.

43. Broeze, "Muscles of Empire," 46.

44. Balachandran, "International Maritime Labour Market," 74–76; Broeze, "Muscles of Empire," 44–45; Bernstein, *Steamboats on the Ganges*, 116, 127–28; Balachandran, "Recruitment and Control," 1–18.

45. Headrick, *Tentacles of Progress*, 321–24, 369.

46. K.-C. Liu, *Anglo-American Steamship Rivalry*, 88–89; IMC Reports on Trade 1869, 41, 1870, 22; Tajima Shigeji, *Yōsukō kisengyō*, 45.

47. Maritime Customs commissioners reported just over 10,000 steamship passengers coming in and out of Zhenjiang in 1868, and just under 10,000 traveling through Hankou in 1870 (IMC Reports on Trade, Chinkiang, 1868, Hankow, 1870). A review of passenger lists in the *North China Daily News* shows a steady growth in the numbers of Chinese passengers reported between 1872 and 1923. The heaviest passenger traffic was

on the Yangzi River and Shanghai–Ningbo routes. Numbers of Chinese passengers are reported intermittently in the *North China Daily News* "arrivals" list between the 1870s and 1900s—150–400 Chinese passengers on Yangzi River or Ningbo–Shanghai steamers, with smaller numbers (around 100) of passengers reported coming from Tianjin to Shanghai or Hong Kong to Shanghai (*North China Daily News* 1872–1915 *passim.*). By 1931, China Navigation planned to build steamships accommodating 1,000 passengers to serve the 2.1 million people traveling on the Middle and Lower Yangzi routes. JSS III 27 Feb. 1931.

48. JSS III 15 Feb. 1872; OSK, 11; Nagoya shōgyō kaigisho, *Shinkoku shinkai kōjō shōgyō*, 127.

49. JSS III Feb. 1928.

50. OSK, 11. Steamship designs in other contexts likewise arrayed their passenger classes to put some at the advantage of light, air, and distance from the noise and heat of the engine (Howarth and Howarth, *Story of P&O*, 67).

51. Geil, *Yankee on the Yangtze*, 13.

52. Shanghai shangye chuxu yinhang luxing bu, *You chuan xu zhi*, 10–12.

53. OSK, 50–51; JSS II 21 Jul. 1922.

54. Sha Weikai, *Zhongguo maiban zhi*, 28–30; Negishi Tadashi, *Baiben seido no kenkyū*, 200–201; Tōa Dōbun Shoin, *Shina keizai zensho*, vol. 2, 361–63; Tajima Shigeji, *Yōsukō kisengyō*, 39.

55. *Shen bao*, 30 Jun. 1888; Zheng Guohan, *Shu cheng riji*, 2b–3a; Shu Xincheng, *Shu you xinying*, 7–14; Guo Moruo, "Chu chu Kuimen," 325.

56. Sha Weikai, *Zhongguo maiban zhi*, 29. There are numerous complaints of compradors falsifying returns to the companies, some of which suggest that ship captains were aware of and perhaps complicit in this practice, for example, JSS I 13 May 1874; JSS I 5 Oct. 1910.

57. *Shen bao*, 30 Jun. 1888.

58. Cook, *Lion and Dragon*, 132–33; *Hangsheng* 12:12 (Dec. 1930), 45–46.

59. For example, *Shen bao*, 5 Nov. 1873.

60. Ge Yuanxi, *Hu you zaji*, 21; *Shen bao*, 5 Nov. 1873, 18 Sep. 1879, 6 Jun. 1880.

61. Gill, *River of Golden Sand*, 45.

62. Percival, *Land of the Dragon*, 2–3; Bird, *Yangtze Valley and Beyond*, 56.

63. Fitkin, *Great River*, 7; Torrible, *Yangtsze Reminiscences*, 2–3. In their emphasis on luxury in the highest class of accommodation, steamships in China were very like their counterparts in the United States, on the transatlantic route, or in the Peninsular & Oriental Company. Often called "floating palaces" or "moving hotels," the first class tried to impress with richly decorated surroundings and an overabundance of food. Fox, *Ocean Railway*, 197; Hunter, *Steamboats on the Western Rivers*, 390; Howarth and Howarth, *Story of P&O*, 62.

64. *North China Daily News*, Jul. 1872–Nov. 1923 *passim*.

65. Cook, *Lion and Dragon*, 84; Percival, *Land of the Dragon*, 82–83.

66. Bird, *Yangtze Valley and Beyond*, 83.

67. JSS I 15 Feb. 1872; Nagoya shōgyō kaigisho, *Shinkoku shinkai kōjō shōgyō*, 127; OSK, 11.

68. *North China Daily News*, 4 Jan. 1877, 2 Jun. 1881, 14 Mar. 1884, 26 Sep. 1891.

69. Nagoya shōgyō kaigisho, *Shinkoku shinkai kōjō shōgyō*, 127.

70. Han Suyin, *Crippled Tree*, 278–80.

71. Bickers, *Britain in China*, 94.

72. Ibid., 174.

73. Torrible, *Yangtsze Reminiscences*, 3; Cook, *Lion and Dragon*, 131–32.

74. Nagoya shōgyō kaigisho, *Shinkoku shinkai kōjō shōgyō*, 127.

75. See the Cheong Wan case detailed later in this chapter. NCH 24 Jun. 1879, 626–27.

76. OSK, 11.

77. Bird, *Yangzi Valley and Beyond*, 83; Torrible, *Yangtsze Reminiscences*, 2–3.

78. Li Boyuan, *Modern Times*, 441–42.

79. Fitzgerald, *Awakening China*, 10–12.

80. An emphasis on dress as an indicator of nationality or cultural affinity may have owed something to the Qing dynasty's insistence on forms of dress and hairstyle as markers of allegiance. In the 1850s, Qing officials argued that citizenship was more accurately determined by "hairstyle and dress" than by birthplace (Waley-Cohen, *Sextants of Beijing*, 152; Fairbank, *Trade and Diplomacy*, 216–17). Later, the rules of the Shanghai Public Garden urged Japanese to dress in Western or Japanese clothing so they would not be mistaken for Chinese and denied entrance to the park (Bickers and Wasserstrom, "'Dogs and Chinese Not Admitted,'" 458, 462).

81. See Rogaski, *Hygienic Modernity*, 133.

82. Stoler, *Carnal Knowledge and Imperial Power*, 84; Ballhatchet, *Race, Sex, and Class*, 110.

83. JSS I 13 Jun. 1900.

84. Bickers, *Britain in China*, 97–98.

85. Han Suyin, *Crippled Tree*, 278–80.

86. Shu Xincheng, *Shu you xinying*, 8.

87. An account of the trial is published in NCH 24 Jun. 1879, 626–27. All references to the trial are taken from this report. I am grateful to Pär Cassel for drawing my attention to this case.

88. Thampi, *Indians in China*, 76, 80–106.

89. Fox, *Ocean Railway*, 200.

90. Torrible, *Yangtsze Reminiscences*, 3.

91. Tōa Dōbun Shoin, *Kinsei gyokushin*, 583.

92. Jiang Yongsheng, "Ri-Qing gaikuang," 26.

93. The "big trips" (*dai ryokō*) were investigative field trips taken by graduating students of the Tōa Dōbun Shoin to different areas of China. In addition to the official compendia of the results of these investigations, the students published travelogues of their journeys (Reynolds, "Training Young China Hands," 241–42; Fogel, *Literature of Travel*, 184–87). On travel in the Chinese first class, see Tōa Dōbun Shoin, *Kohan sōtei*, 3, *Moku'u shippū*, 197, *Fūsan ushuku*, 2–3, 70, *Sokuseki: Dai ryokō kinenshi*, 158.

94. Peattie, "Japanese Treaty Port Settlements," 171–72, 187, 193.

95. Nagoya shōgyō kaigisho, *Shinkoku shinkai kōjō shōgyō*, 131; Tōa Dōbun Shoin, *Moku'u shippū*, 196, *Koketsu ryūgan*, 106.

96. Nakano Kozan, *Shina tairiku*, 12; He Boxin, *Ba sheng luxing*, 37.

97. NCH 24 Jun. 1879, 626–27.

98. Bickers and Wasserstrom, "'Dogs and Chinese Not Admitted,'" 458.

99. In his account of the British settler community's "sexual taboo," Robert Bickers mentions that marriage to a Japanese or white Russian was slightly more acceptable than marriage to a Chinese. Bickers, *Britain in China*, 98.

100. Tōa Dōbun Shoin, *Kinsei gyokushin*, 583.

101. Nagoya shōgyō kaigisho, *Shinkoku shinkai kōjō shōgyō*, 127.

102. OSK, 68–69.

103. Zheng Guanying, "Shengshi weiyan," 636–37.

104. NCH 10 Oct. 1872, 301; Percival, *Land of the Dragon*, 83.

105. Knollys, *English Life in China*, 115.

106. Bird, *Yangtze Valley and Beyond*, 83.

107. Nakano Kozan, *Shina tairiku*, 15, 52–53.

108. On the editorial perspectives of Shanghai's literati journalists, see Mittler, *Newspaper for China?*

109. *Shen bao*, 14 Feb. 1884, 25 Mar. 1891; Cassel, *Grounds of Judgment*, 164–70.

110. *Shen bao*, 29 Apr. 1876, 18 Sep. 1876.

111. Ge Yuanxi, *Hu you zaji*, 21.

112. In Wu's telling, the occupants of the Chinese first-class cabins are awoken one night by a man shouting that he had been robbed. As a crowd gathered around him, the man accused the occupant of the neighboring cabin of the theft. The crowd disputed the charge since the accused was dressed as an expectant official. In the end, the official was revealed to have numerous items of his fellow passengers' clothing in his possession, and the accuser's property was discovered with shadowy accomplices in steerage. The incident was a late-Qing fictional dig at officialdom, but it also shows how the passengers' reliance on appearances nearly deceives them completely. Wu Jianren, *Ershi nian mudu*, 7–9.

113. *Shen bao*, 29 Apr. 1876, 18 Sep. 1876, 6 Jun. 1880, 1 Feb. 1888, 3 Feb. 1888, 30 Jun. 1888.

114. *Shen bao*, 29 Apr. 1876.

115. *Shen bao*, 19 Jul. 1894; *Dianshizhai huabao* 1: yi, 36.

116. *Shen bao*, 19 Jul. 1894. Qing officials in the southeastern ports of Taipei and Beihai enlisted the aid of Maritime Customs inspectors to prevent a trade in women and girls from these ports. H. B. Morse Papers, Tamsui 7 Jul. 1894 and Pakhoi 5 Aug. 1898.

117. *Shen bao*, 29 Apr. 1876, 18 Sep. 1876.

118. *Shen bao*, 29 Apr. 1876.

119. *Shen bao*, 30 Jun. 1888.

120. Prior to the First Opium War, European ships in Canton were sites from which arguments for extraterritoriality were formulated. Cases such as that of the British-flag *Lady Hughes* (1784) and the U.S.-flag *Emily* (1821), in which Qing officials tried and executed members of these ships' crews for crimes committed in China, provided the justification for this treaty provision. The 1843 Treaty of the Bogue (Britain) established the interiors of foreign-flag ships as spaces of extraterritorial jurisdiction, in which all persons and goods on board were subject to British law. This provision was justified as

an extension of the "law of the high seas," in which the laws of the ship's country of origin apply within the space of the ship itself when the ship is at sea. Morse, *International Relations*, vol. 1, 425.

121. PRO-FO 228/4012, 25 Sep. 1929.

122. Morse, *International Relations*, vol. 2, 130.

123. *Dianshizhai huabao*, pao 6 (1892), 48. See also Ye Xiaoqing, *Dianshizhai Pictorial*, 170.

124. *Hubei jiaoshe shu zhaiyao*, 30a. The temporary sanctuary from Chinese authority that steamships provided was also significant when authority on land was contested. In the days following the 1911 Wuchang Uprising, Jardine, Matheson's agent at Hankou persuaded the firm's comprador and his staff to remain in the city by offering to house them and their families aboard the steamer *Changwo*. The comprador subsequently arranged for eighty of his friends to join him on the ship, paying the company $2,000 to accommodate them for a week (JMA J 18/1, 15 Oct. 1911). Commercial steamships were also used to either sequester or evacuate the foreign residents of the Yangzi treaty ports during a series of antiforeign riots along the Yangzi in 1891. In this case, the ships may have acted as adjuncts to the naval fleets of the various powers, called in to protect foreign lives and property, or simply provided an effective barrier between foreign residents and the rioters (IMC Decennial 1882–91, Wuhu, 261 and Hankow, 167).

125. JSS I 20 Mar. 1901.

126. Cook, *Lion and Dragon*, 132.

127. Blake, *B.I. Centenary*, 65–67.

128. Gandhi, "Letter to Secretary," 474–76.

129. Tan Shi-hua, *Chinese Testament*, 188.

130. Bickers and Wasserstrom, "'Dogs and Chinese Not Admitted,'" 454. Another example of a nationalist conversion inspired by steamship travel is Lu Guoji, *Wo de fuqin Lu Zuofu*, 22.

131. Foucault, "Of Other Spaces," 6.

132. Bickers, *Britain in China*, chap. 3.

Chapter 5. Shipping Nationalism

1. Jurgen Osterhammel shows that during the Warlord Era, no central authority could be held responsible for a local incident in the same way the Qing had been for the Margary incident or Boxer Rebellion. Consular authorities had difficulty ensuring punishment for Chinese who attacked or threatened foreigners, and court sentences against Chinese in debt to foreigners were often ignored (Osterhammel, "China," 647–48). One of the key reasons for the maintenance of the Beiyang government as a fictive center was that the Maritime Customs, whose revenue was completely pledged to the service of foreign loans to meet China's indemnity payments, maintained indemnity and loan payments through the Beiyang government (Hall, *Chinese Maritime Customs*, 30, 35). Although a few new treaty ports were opened, it was most often on the initiative of the Republican regime for the purpose of facilitating connections between steamship and rail transport (Yang Tianhong, *Kou'an kaifang*, 394–97).

2. Tim Wright, *Coal Mining*, 120–25; Esherick, *Reform and Revolution*, 82–84; Rankin, "Nationalistic Contestation," 321–22.

3. Rankin, "Nationalistic Contestation," 317.

4. Ibid., 339.

5. Ibid., 317–18.

6. Ibid., 321–22; Rankin, *Elite Activism*, 253, 268.

7. Fan Baichuan, *Zhongguo lunchuan hangyun ye*, 412–13; JTS-HZB, 375–76.

8. Bryna Goodman, *Native Place, City, and Nation*, 140.

9. Ibid., 140–41; Fan Baichuan, *Zhongguo lunchuan hangyun ye*, 412–13; Zhu Yin'gui, *Jindai lunchuan hangyun ye*, 18.

10. DesForges, *Hsi-liang*, 63.

11. Rankin, "Nationalistic Contestation," 323–24; Blue, "Land and River Routes," 171–73; Little, *Through the Yang-tse Gorges*, 287–300; IMC Decennial, 1892–1901, Ichang, 180.

12. CMC 679/1030; Waiwu bu Archives, 02-06-7(4), 02-06-5(1), 02-06-5 (2); Deng Xiaoqin, *Chuanjiang hangyun jianshi*, 93.

13. Wei Yingtao and Zhou Yong, *Chongqing kaibu shi*, 63–64; Deng Xiaoqin, *Chuanjiang hangyun jianshi*, 94–95; DesForges, *Hsi-liang*, 63.

14. Cornell Plant, the Maritime Customs' Upper Yangzi River inspector and the captain who had piloted Archibald Little's steamship in 1898, designed a ship composed of a powerful steam tug pulling a cargo flat. This design solved the persistent problem of ensuring that a ship had adequate power to navigate the rapids, was of light enough draft to pass over the shoals, and had enough cargo space to earn freight. Deng Xiaoqin, *Chuanjiang hangyun jianshi*, 93; CMC 679/1027.

15. Zhu Yin'gui, *Jindai lunchuan hangyun ye*, 16–17.

16. Zhang Houquan, *Zhaoshang ju shi*, 268–71.

17. Ibid., 293.

18. Fung, *Diplomacy of Imperial Retreat*, 14–21.

19. Bau, *Foreign Navigation in Chinese Waters*, 21–22.

20. Bergère, *Golden Age*, chap. 2.

21. Zhu Yin'gui, *Jindai lunchuan hangyun ye*, 21–27; Fan Baichuan, *Zhongguo lunchuan hangyun ye*, 468–70.

22. Zhu Yin'gui, *Jindai lunchuan hangyun ye*, 82.

23. Ibid., 87–88.

24. For lists of both companies' fleets in 1927, see Yonesato Monkichi, *Chōkō kō'un shi*, 5–15, 29–36.

25. Ibid., 51–54.

26. Zhu Yin'gui, *Jindai lunchuan hangyun ye*, 91–94; Fan Baichuan, *Zhongguo lunchuan hangyun ye*, 556–60.

27. Zhu Yin'gui, *Jindai lunchuan hangyun ye*, 84; Fan Baichuan, *Zhongguo lunchuan hangyun ye*, 567–72.

28. Zhang Houquan, *Zhaoshang ju shi*, 309–10; Zhang, Chen, and Yao, *Swire Group*, 157–58.

29. Shao, "Space, Time, and Politics," 101.

30. Jiang Tianfeng, *Changjiang hangyun shi*, 220–23. On the formation of the Dada Companies, see also JTS-HZB, 319–21, and Köll, *Cotton Mill to Business Empire*, 260–61.

31. The Sanbei Group consisted of four companies: the Sanbei Wharf Company, the Hong'an Steamship Company, the Ningxing Steamship Company (which ran a single ship on the coast), and the Hongsheng Dock and Warehouse Company. On its formation, see JTS-HZB, 391–97; Yonesato Monkichi, *Chōkō kō'un shi*, 37–40; Jiang Tianfeng, *Changjiang hangyun shi*, 248–51; Fan Baichuan, *Zhongguo lunchuan hangyun ye*, 479–81.

32. The original Hong'an Company ceased operations in 1909 and Yu Xiaqing and his associates acquired control of it as early as that year. They kept it under the British flag for the next ten years, however, since Hong'an's docks and shore properties were located in the British concessions in the treaty ports and the company would have run into difficulties using these sites if it had adopted a different flag. In 1918, Yu successfully petitioned the Beiyang government to obtain the leases to the shore properties owned by the German firm of Melchers & Company, former agents for the North German Lloyd Company. That there was still interpower rivalry over dock facilities is demonstrated by the fact that the British consul-general at Hankou recommended that Jardine, Matheson & Company apply for the sites. With access to these docking sites and warehouses, Yu was able to make Hong'an a fully Chinese-owned company by buying out the remaining British-owned stock. Yonesato Monkichi, *Chōkō kō'un shi*, 37–38; JMA J23/1 30 Jan. 1919.

33. Yonesato Monkichi, *Chōkō kō'un shi*, 39–40.

34. Ibid., 55–58; Jiang Tianfeng, *Changjiang hangyun shi*, 249.

35. JMA J18/25 13 Jan. 1922, 30 Mar. 1922, 19 May 1922.

36. Fan Baichuan, *Zhongguo lunchuan hangyun ye*, 487; Tōa Dōbunkai, *Shina shōbetsu zenshi*, vol. 5, 401–8.

37. Yonesato Monkichi, *Chōkō kō'un shi*, 70.

38. Ibid., 84–85.

39. Ibid., 73–80.

40. Descriptions of the principle of immunity from search can be found in PRO-FO 228/4012, 21 Jan. 1929 and 18 Mar. 1929.

41. Chamberlain, *Foreign Flags*, 20.

42. Ibid., 17–19.

43. Nisshin Kisen Kaisha, *Sanjū nenshi*, 393–96; Gerth, *China Made*, 131, 161.

44. Nisshin Kisen Kaisha, *Sanjū nenshi*, 397, 399; Woodhead, *Yangtsze and its Problems*, 39.

45. On the progress of the strike, see JMA J18/31 and J18/32 20 Aug. 1925 and 7 Oct. 1925.

46. Gerth, *China Made*, 165, 175–76.

47. Fearing similar actions against their own ships, the China Navigation Company issued rules to ships' captains, urging them to maintain good relations with the junk population on the Upper Yangzi as "the existence of a good feeling may be a very material advantage in the event of a ship being in difficulty at any time." JSS III 7 Nov. 1921.

48. Kapp, *Szechwan and the Chinese Republic*, 76; Woodhead, *Yangtsze and its Problems*, 35–36.

49. Woodhead, *Yangtsze and its Problems*, 75.

50. Fung, *Diplomacy of Imperial Retreat*, chap. 7; Woodhead, *Yangtsze and its Problems*, 39–40, 76.

51. Gerth, *China Made*, 19.

52. Woodhead, *Yangtsze and its Problems*, 76.

53. Wray, "Japan's Big-Three Service Enterprises," 53.

54. JMA J18/19 24 Sep. 1920, J18/46 2 Nov. 1932. There was one agreement among the Three Companies active from 1917 to 1919 and another from 1920 to 1925.

55. JMA J18/25 13 Jan. 1922.

56. JMA J18/23 S/O Shanghai-Hongkong 12 Dec. 1921.

57. JMA J18/25 8 Feb. 1922, 23 Feb. 1922, 2 Mar. 1922; Nie Baozhang and Zhu Yin'gui, *Jindai hangyun shi ziliao 1895–1927*, vol. 1, 473–74.

58. JMA J18/25 11 May 1922, 19 May 1922, 30 Jun. 1922, 6 Jul. 1922, 14 Jul. 1922, 3 Aug. 1922, 15 Sep. 1922, J18/27 3 May 1923, 21 Jun. 1923, J18/29 5 Jun. 1924.

59. JMA J18/30 5 Aug. 1924, 25 Jul. 1924, J18/31 9 Jan. 1925, 24 Dec. 1924.

60. JMA J18/31 17 Apr. 1925, 24 Apr. 1925, 21 May 1925.

61. JMA J18/25 19 May 1922, also J18/31 30 Apr. 1925.

62. JMA J18/27 21 Jun. 1923.

63. JMA J18/30 20 Nov. 1924.

64. JMA J-30 5 Nov. 1924; JTS-HZB, 392–93; Yonesato Monkichi, *Chōkō kō'un shi*, 41.

65. JMA J18/31 30 Apr. 1925, 7 May 1925, 21 May 1925.

66. JMA J18/32 5 Nov. 1925; Yonesato Monkichi, *Chōkō kō'un shi*, 41.

67. JMA J18/32 7 Oct. 1925, 23 Dec. 1925.

68. JMA J18/32 24 Jul. 1925.

69. JMA J18/34 16 Apr. 1926, 7 May 1926, 3 Jun. 1926, J18/33 6 Jul. 1926.

70. JMA J18/35 20 May 1927, J18/48 15 Dec. 1933, J18/49 26 Jul. 1935.

71. Yeh, "Huang Yanpei," 26, and *Shanghai Splendor*, 28.

72. Gerth, *China Made*, 348.

73. Fan Baichuan, *Zhongguo lunchuan hangyun ye*; Zhu Yin'gui, *Jindai lunchuan hangyun ye*.

74. Bergère, *Golden Age*, 3–4.

75. Ibid., 49, 243.

76. Gerth, *China Made*, 336–37; Tim Wright, "Spiritual Heritage of Chinese Capitalism."

77. Köll, *Cotton Mill to Business Empire*, 25; Ding Richu and Du Yuncheng, "Yu Xiaqing jianlun," 145–66.

78. Bryna Goodman, *Native Place, City, and Nation*, 168, 189, 193–94, 205–6.

79. Lu Guoji, *Wo de fuqin Lu Zuofu*, chaps. 1–10.

80. Bergère, *Golden Age*, 193–94.

81. Lu Guoji, *Wo de fuqin Lu Zuofu*, 14.

82. Bryna Goodman, *Native Place, City, and Nation*, 207–8.

83. Jiang Tianfeng, *Changjiang hangyun shi*, 220–23; JTS-HZB, 319–21.

84. Jiang Tianfeng, *Changjiang hangyun shi*, 248–51; JTS-HZB, 391–97; Ding Richu and Du Yuncheng, "Yu Xiaqing jianlun," 149; Fang Teng, "Yu Xiaqing lun," 66.

85. Lu Zuofu, "Yizhuang candan jingying de shiye," 545–48; Zheng Dongqin, "Minsheng gongsi chuanye jieduan," 1–3; Tong Shaosheng, "Minsheng lunchuan gongsi jilue," 85–87 and "Huiyi Minsheng lunchuan gongsi," 149; Ling Yaolun, *Minsheng gongsi shi*, 22–29.

86. Shao, *Culturing Modernity*, chap. 2.

87. Ibid., 5; Köll, *Cotton Mill to Business Empire*, chap. 7.

88. Fang Teng, "Yu Xiaqing lun," 66; Negishi Tadashi, *Baiben seido no kenkyū*, 306.

89. Lu Zuofu described his activities in Beibei as part of the Rural Reconstruction Movement (xiangcun jianshe yundong) undertaken in different parts of China after 1927 as the Nanjing regime, provincial governments, and independent militarist governments became concerned about China's rural sector. Lu Zuofu's development of Beibei can be distinguished from well-known Rural Reconstruction projects such as James Yen's in Ding County (Hebei Province) and Liang Shuming's in Zouping County (Shandong Province) in that it was focused on industrial enterprises rather than agriculture. It was similar to Zhang Jian's Nantong model. In his own essay "Rural Reconstruction," Lu emphasized the importance of economic reconstruction through industry, modern transport, local defense, and improved hygiene (Lu Zuofu, "Xiangcun jianshe"; Ling Yaolun, *Minsheng gongsi shi*, 21–22; and Liu Chonglai, "Lu Zuofu xiangcun jianshe," 122–28; Alitto, *Last Confucian*; Hayford, *To the People*). A preliminary comparison between the ideas of Zhang Jian and Lu Zuofu is Yan Xuexi, "Lu Zuofu he Zhang Jian," 112–31.

90. Zheng Bicheng, *Sichuan dao you*.

91. Köll, *Cotton Mill to Business Empire*, 286–87; Cochran, *Encountering Chinese Networks*, 117–21.

92. Köll, *Cotton Mill to Business Empire*, 11–12.

93. Zanasi, *Saving the Nation*, 4.

94. Bergère, *Golden Age*, 49, 243.

95. Köll, *Cotton Mill to Business Empire*, 65–66.

96. Lu Zuofu, "Yizhuang candan jingying de shiye," 546. On the early financing and organization of the Minsheng Company, see Zheng Dongqin, "Minsheng gongsi chuanye jieduan," 3.

97. Fang Teng, "Yu Xiaqing lun," 66; JTS-HZB, 395; Jiang Tianfeng, *Changjiang hangyun shi*, 250.

98. Minsheng gongsi yanjiushi dang'an 147, 19; Jiang Tianfeng, *Changjiang hangyun shi*, 250; Yonesato Monkichi, *Chōkō kō'un shi*, 37–38; JTS-HZB, 397.

99. Fang Teng, "Yu Xiaqing lun," 66.

100. Jiang Tianfeng, *Changjiang hangyun shi*, 249–51; Ding Richu and Du Yuncheng, "Yu Xiaqing jianlun," 152.

101. Fang Teng, "Yu Xiaqing lun," 67.

102. JTS-HZB, 395–96.

103. Fang Teng, "Yu Xiaqing lun," 67.

104. Tong Shaosheng, "Huiyi Minsheng lunchuan gongsi," 149–50; Ling Yaolun, *Minsheng gongsi shi*, 32.

105. Lu Zuofu, "Yizhuang candan jingying de shiye," 551–52.

106. Shipping was not as central to Zhang Jian's Dasheng Mills complex, but Zhang appears to have had a similar relationship to expansion and debt. After World War I, the complex was deeply in debt as the result of the overexpansion of its factories, land reclamation companies, and other local projects. Zhang acknowledged his willingness to go into debt to achieve his business ambitions. Eventually the enterprise went bankrupt and its creditor-banks became involved in its management (Köll, *Cotton Mill to Business Empire,* chap. 6; Shao, *Culturing Modernity*, 202).

107. See Bergère, *Capitalismes et capitalistes*, 125.

108. Rao, *Short History of Indian Shipping*, 79–86.

109. Ibid., 86, 89–90.

110. See Headrick, *Tentacles of Progress*, 369–71; Rao, *Short History of Indian Shipping*, 91–92.

111. Rao, *Short History of Indian Shipping*, 102–5.

112. Ibid., 118.

113. Ibid., 121.

114. Ibid., 98.

Chapter 6. Nanjing and Chongqing

1. One of the most dramatic cases of militarist resistance undermining treaty revision was the 1931 revolt of two north China militarists, which, along with the Japanese annexation of Manchuria, brought an abrupt end to Nanjing's negotiations with Britain to end extraterritoriality. Fung, *Diplomacy of Imperial Retreat*, 165–66, 236.

2. Fung, *Diplomacy of Imperial Retreat*, 156–64 and chap. 10.

3. Otte, "Shipping Policy, Part II," 486, 488.

4. Ibid., 487. This organization's statement objected to the use of the term "mutuality" for navigation rights in the new Sino-Japanese treaty. Rather than Japan relinquishing its right to navigate China's coastal and inland waters, the treaty extended to Chinese ships the right to navigate Japanese waters. Ship owners regarded this as an empty gesture that simply maintained the status quo, since Japanese ships would continue to enjoy their well-entrenched position in Chinese waters, while the nascent Chinese shipping industry would have little chance of breaking into trades in Japanese waters already well served by Japanese companies. Zhu Huisen, *Hangzheng shiliao,* 1055–58.

5. Wang Jianping, *Hangquan wenti*, 105–7. On Yu Xiaqing's involvement with the Shanghai Shipping Association, see Fang Teng, "Yu Xiaqing lun," 67; Ding Richu and Du Yuncheng, "Yu Xiaqing jianlun," 160.

6. Zhu Huisen, *Hangzheng shiliao*, 1055–66; Wang Jianping, *Hangquan wenti*, 106–7.

7. Coble, *Shanghai Capitalists*, 30; Fewsmith, *Party, State, and Local Elites*, 117.

8. Zhu Huisen, *Hangzheng shiliao*, 1–4.

9. The relationship between these shipping associations and the government had precedents in the late Qing and early Republic. The Shanghai Shipping Association was a Nanjing decade iteration of local shipping associations dating from the late Qing that

carried out administrative and organizational functions on behalf of government ministries. JTB–HZB, 103–18. For an account of the interpenetration of state and society in organizations such as these in the Nanjing Decade, see Bryna Goodman, *Native Place, City, and Nation*, 291–304.

10. HYYK 1:1 (Jul. 1930), 1.

11. HYYK 1:1 (Jul. 1930), 1:2 (Aug. 1930), 1:3 (Sep. 1930), 1:4 (Oct. 1930), 1:5 (Dec. 1930), 1:6 (Jun. 1931), 1:7 (Jul. 1931), 1:8 (Aug. 1931), 1:10 (Oct. 1931), 1:11 (Nov. 1931).

12. Pieces that include some or all of the arguments of this type are Lu Huajin, "Yan'an ji neihe"; HYYK 1:2 (Aug. 1930), 1–5; HYYK 1:3 (Sep. 1930), 10–16; HYYK 1:4 (Oct. 1930), 18–38; HYYK 1:4 (Oct. 1930), 39–43; HYYK 1:6 (Jun. 1931), 23–28; Zhu Huisen, *Hangzheng shiliao*, 1058–66; Wang Jianping, *Hangquan wenti*, 92–95; Bau, *Foreign Navigation*, 20–21; Wang Guang, *Hangye yu hangquan*, 176–77.

13. Such solutions are proposed in Bau, *Foreign Navigation*, 25–27; Wang Jianping, *Hangquan wenti*, 96–104; Wang Guang, *Hangye yu hangquan*, 135–56; Lu Huajin, "Yan'an ji neihe"; HYYK 1:3 (Sep. 1930), 10–16.

14. Stanley Wright, *Hart and the Chinese Customs*, 295–316. In the late 1860s when the Maritime Customs Marine Department was established, Robert Hart proposed that it should oversee navigational, harbor, and pilotage affairs. He believed that incorporating these functions into the Maritime Customs would be more efficient than setting up separate organizations to handle them. The late Qing Ministry of Posts and Communications and the Beiyang Ministry of Communications intended for their shipping departments to take over these functions. In the case of the Beiyang government, the plans were shelved because of strong objections from Maritime Customs authorities. Wang Guang, *Zhongguo shuiyun zhi*, 178; Jiang Tianfeng, *Changjiang hangyun shi*, 399–400; Chu, *China's Postal*, 113.

15. Brunero, *Britain's Imperial Cornerstone*, 98–99.

16. Wang Guang, *Shuiyun zhi*, 279; Jiang Tianfeng, *Changjiang hangyun shi*, 406–7.

17. Bau, *Foreign Navigation*, 28.

18. Ibid., 28–29.

19. Otte, "Shipping Policy, Part II," 488, 500.

20. Ibid., 489.

21. Fung, *Diplomacy of Imperial Retreat*, 236–38.

22. There were two minor changes: first that foreign shipping interests operating in Chinese waters had to submit their vessels for survey to Chinese inspectors at the Navigation Administrative Bureaus (rather than at the Maritime Customs) as of July 1931 (Chu, *China's Postal*, 141–42). The second was the 1929 decision against enforcing the principle of immunity from search, addressed in greater detail later in this chapter.

23. Chu, *China's Postal*, 115–16, 125–26, 147.

24. This section has been revised from Reinhardt, "'Decolonisation' on the Periphery."

25. Kapp, *Szechwan and the Chinese Republic*, 7.

26. Ibid., 39, 42.

27. Baumler, "Playing with Fire," 48.

28. CMC 679 (1) 32046, 9 Sep. 1925 and 10 Sep. 1925.

29. CMC 679 (1) 32046, 9 Sep. 1926.

30. Ibid. A later complaint that these ships were conducting trade under the military flag is CMC 679 (1) 32047, 22 Jan. 1927.

31. Descriptions of the crisis in Upper Yangzi shipping can be found in *Xingcha zhoukan* 1 (Jun. 1930), 4–10, 6 (5 Jul. 1930), 1–7; HYYK 2:5–6 (1932), 1–7; Zhu Huisen, *Hangzheng shiliao*, 1058–66.

32. I have used Upper Yangzi Navigation Bureau as the translation of Chuanjiang hangwu guanli chu because the English-language sources that refer to it use that name (e.g., JSS, CMC). It should not be confused with the Nationalist government's Navigation Administrative Bureaus (Hangzheng ju), which in some sources are referred to as navigation bureaus as well.

33. Zhang Jin, *Quanli, chongtu yu biange*, 268–69; Liu Hangchen, *Rong mu ban sheng*, 174–76; Tong Shaosheng, "Minsheng lunchuan gongsi jieduan," 85–86 and "Huiyi Minsheng lunchuan gongsi," 149.

34. Ling Yaolun, *Minsheng gongsi shi*, 29. See also JSS III 2/8 Box 89, 13 Sep. 1929. Swire's representative in Chongqing wrote that "Lu replaced the old ragged Navigation Bureau soldiers with orderly cadets from his school near Lung Wan T'ung. These men undoubtedly set a new standard for discipline in the harbour."

35. Ling Yaolun, *Minsheng gongsi shi*, 27–28; Lu Guoji, *Wo de fuqin Lu Zuofu*, 100; Lu Zuofu, "Yizhuang candan jingying de shiye," 548. The exact process is spelled out in *Xingcha zhoukan* 6 (5 Jul. 1930), 19–23.

36. HYYK 2:5–6 (1932), 6; *Xingcha zhoukan* 6 (5 Jul. 1930), 6–7.

37. *Xingcha zhoukan* 6 (5 Jul. 1930), 23–27.

38. Lu Guoji, *Wo de fuqin Lu Zuofu*, 94.

39. CMC 679 (1) 32047, 8 Feb. 1927, 18 Apr. 1927, 7 Sep. 1927.

40. Liu Hangchen, *Rong mu ban sheng*, 177.

41. Ling Yaolun, *Minsheng gongsi shi*, 31.

42. One initiated in May 1929 cited the nonsettlement of the Wanxian Incident as its cause, but the British companies suspected that it was supported by the Upper Yangzi Freight Conference as a way to diminish the intense competition Chinese companies faced from British companies' system of through shipments. JSS III 2/8 Box 89 1929, 10 May 1929, 17 May 1929, 24 May 1929, 12 Jul. 1929.

43. By 1929, Liu Xiang had driven out the Communist and Guomindang labor organizers who had mobilized dockworkers for boycotts in 1925 and 1926, but these protest tactics were still familiar to the workers, because boycotts organized by Chinese shipping interests persisted after this time. Kapp, *Szechwan and the Chinese Republic*, 78–80; Remer, *Study of Chinese Boycotts*, 98, 100; JSS III 2/8 Box 89 1929, 10 May 1929, 17 May 1929. On the mobilizing power of repeated boycotts, see Gerth, *China Made*, 168.

44. *Chongqing shangwu ribao* 9 Aug. 1929, 1.

45. JSS III 2/8 Box 89 1929, 12 Sep. 1929.

46. PRO-FO 228/4012, 18 Mar. 1928 (Lampson to Foreign Office); 228/4224, 4 Apr. 1930 (Chongqing Consul to Lampson); 228/3833, 15 Jun. 1928 (Lampson to Hankou Consul); 228/4012 21 Jan. 1929, 18 Mar. 1929.

47. PRO-FO 228/4012, 22 Jan. 1929, 13 May 1929 (Lampson to Foreign Office).

48. PRO-FO 228/4224, 1 Jan. 1930 (British Legation to consuls). The decision not to enforce the principle of immunity from search was consistent with general British

policy toward Chinese nationalism after 1926: the relinquishment of minor treaty rights and privileges to protect the most important ones, such as the extraterritoriality of British subjects. Along with this policy came the necessity of British business interests to compromise with local conditions rather than rely on consuls and gunboats to enforce their treaty rights. See Fung, *Diplomacy of Imperial Retreat*, 8; Osterhammel, "China," 655.

49. Chen Jinfan, "Changjiang yandu zousi jianwen," 565.

50. *Xingcha zhoukan* 8 (19 Jul. 1930), 5–7.

51. *Xingcha zhoukan* 23 (1 Nov. 1930), 8–11.

52. Lu Zuofu, "Yizhuang candan jingying de shiye," 548.

53. JSS III 2/8 Box 89 1929, 13 Sep. 1929.

54. Ibid.

55. HYYK 2:5–6 (1932), 6.

56. Wang Jianping, *Hangquan wenti*, 11–115. See also translation of an article from *Dazhong Hua ribao*, 16 Aug. 1929, enclosed in JSS III 2/8 Box 89 1929, 13 Sep. 1929.

57. Zhu Huisen, *Hangzheng shiliao*, 1058–66.

58. *Xingcha zhoukan* 7 (12 Jul. 1930), 12.

59. On the Navigation Bureau's correspondence and interactions with Nanjing's Ministry of Communications, see *Xingcha zhoukan* 1 (1 Jun. 1930), 17–19, 21 (18 Oct. 1930), 6–7, 22 (25 Oct. 1930), 5–6; 29 (13 Dec. 1930), 4–6, 40 (14 Mar. 1931), 1–2, 41 (21 Mar. 1931), 1–2, 42 (28 Mar. 1931), 1–5; 43 (4 Apr. 1931), 1–4. The periodical also published specific articles dealing with the national problem of shipping rights recovery, such as 16 (13 Sep. 1930), 4–6, 21 (18 Oct. 1930), 15–18, 37 (14 Feb. 1931), 6–8, 44 (11 Apr. 1931), 16–21. Many of these articles were likely reprinted from other periodicals.

60. CMC 679 (1), 32051, 22 Apr. 1931, 28 Oct. 1931.

61. CMC 679 (1), 32050, 27 Jun. 1930.

62. CMC 679 (1), 32051, 24 Sep. 1931 and 4 Apr. 1934.

63. Chen Jinfan, "Chanjiang yandu zousi jianwen," 558. Clashes between the Ministry of Communications hierarchy of shipping administrative bureaus and local bodies that had exercised oversight over shipping occurred elsewhere in Sichuan and Hubei Provinces. These local agencies had been established in the interests of local finance and often performed functions that overlapped with those of the Maritime Customs or the Navigation Administrative Bureaus: registering ships, issuing permits, adjudicating shipping disputes, and maintaining standards of safety (Jiang Tianfeng, *Changjiang hangyun shi*, 402–5).

64. Kapp, *Szechwan and the Chinese Republic*, 82–83, 133.

65. Lu Zuofu, "Yizhuang candan jingying de shiye," 549.

66. Tong Shaosheng, "Huiyi Minsheng lunchuan gongsi," 149–50; Ling Yaolun, *Minsheng gongsi shi*, 32.

67. Ling Yaolun, *Minsheng gongsi shi*, 29, 37–38.

68. Ibid., 32–33.

69. Ibid., 33–35.

70. Ibid., 33–34, 50.

71. Ibid., 34–37, 59–63.

72. Ibid., 43, 45–46.

73. Ibid., 48–50, 56.

74. Kapp, *Szechwan and the Chinese Republic*, 96.

75. Zhang Shouguang, *Lu Zuofu nianpu changbian*, vol. 1, 419, 442–44, 499; Jiang Tianfeng, *Changjiang hangyun shi*, 341–42.

76. Ling Yaolun, *Minsheng gongsi shi*, 83. Zhang Jin has argued that shares in the company were distributed broadly enough that the 21st Army and its administrative officials could not obtain a controlling interest in Minsheng (*Quanli, chongtu yu biange*, 274–5). Song Ziwen and his father-in-law became members of the board in 1933–34 when Minsheng made a deal with Song's China Development Finance Corporation. Song's company had made plans to build a railway between Chongqing and Chengdu, using new steamships to transport the railway materials upriver. To keep this new tonnage off the route, Minsheng agreed to ship railway materials and personnel at low rates and the China Development Finance Corporation loaned Minsheng 1.6 million *yuan* to build new ships (Ling Yaolun, *Minsheng gongsi shi*, 38–39).

77. Ling Yaolun, *Minsheng gongsi shi*, 82–85, 101–3. Anyone owning more than eleven shares only received a one-share vote for every two shares over eleven, and anyone owning more than thirty shares was limited to a twenty-share vote. Zheng Dongqin, who served as chairman of the board from 1930 to 1949, owned only seven shares in the Minsheng Company.

78. From 1923 onward, China Merchants experienced annual deficits of 1.25 million *yuan* and was forced to mortgage some of its properties to get cash for working expenses. It had endured commandeering and demands for cash contributions during the battles of the Northern Expedition. Chu, *China's Postal*, 123–24; Jiang Tianfeng, *Changjiang hangyun shi*, 335.

79. Fewsmith, *Party, State, and Local Elites*, 118–19; Coble, *Shanghai Capitalists*, 32–33; Jiang Tianfeng, *Changjiang hangyun shi*, 329. The report of the Committee of Inquiry on the China Merchants Company was published in 1927: Zhang Renjie, *Guomin zhengfu qingcha zhengli*.

80. Jiang Tianfeng, *Changjiang hangyun shi*, 331–32; Zhu Yin'gui, *Jiandai lunchuan hangyun ye*, 44; Zhang Houquan, *Zhaoshang ju shi*, 380–84. Zhao's reform efforts are recorded in *Zhaoshangju zong guanlichu huibao*. Zhao's investigations exposed the so-called Three Big Cases (*San da'an*) of corruption in the China Merchants Company, one of which was Li Guojie's role in the affiliated Jiyu Property Company. Zhao's investigation led to Li's removal from Jiyu and Jiyu's formal incorporation into the China Merchants Company (Li Gufan, *Zhaoshang ju san da'an*).

81. Zhu Yin'gui, *Jiandai lunchuan hangyun ye*, 41; Chu, *China's Postal*, 125, Zhang Houquan, *Zhaoshang ju shi*, 403–8.

82. For example, Wang Guang, *Hangye yu hangquan*, 140–43, 147–50; Wang Jianping, *Hangquan wenti*, 100–103; 119.

83. Chu, *China's Postal*, 126; Cochran, *Encountering Chinese Networks*, 150–51.

84. Jiang Tianfeng, *Changjiang hangyun shi*, 333–35; Zhang Houquan, *Zhaoshang ju shi*, 408–13.

85. Zhu Yin'gui, *Jiandai lunchuan hangyun ye*, 44; Chu, *China's Postal*, 127.

86. Jiang Tianfeng, *Changjiang hangyun shi*, 335–36.

87. Ibid., 336–37; Zhang Houquan, *Zhaoshang ju shi*, 414–26.
88. Zhang, Chen, and Yao, *Swire Group*, 191.
89. HYYK 3:10 (Feb. 1936), 15; Jiang Tianfeng, *Changjiang hangyun shi*, 336–37.
90. HYYK 3:10 (Feb. 1936), 15.
91. HYYK 3:2 (Jun. 1935), 5–7.
92. Ibid., 6–11.
93. HYYK 3:10 (Feb. 1936), 13.
94. Ibid.; HYYK 3:3 (Jul. 1935), 1–2.
95. Zhang, Chen, and Yao, *Swire Group*, 191–94; *Hangye nianjian* (1935), 13; JMA J 18/49, 26 Jul. 1935. Jardine, Matheson & Company correspondence reported that even the Three Companies had a difficult time adhering to the rates they had agreed on during 1933. Indo-China and China Navigation contemplated privately pooling their businesses, as well as decreasing rates even further to force the Chinese and Japanese companies to come to an agreement (JMA J18/48, 29 Jun. 1933, 29 Jul. 1933, 13 Dec. 1933).
96. Chu, *China's Postal*, 140.
97. Ibid., 140; HYYK 4:6 (Jan. 1937), 6.
98. Zhang, Chen, and Yao, *Swire Group*, 254–78, 284–86.
99. Wang Guang, *Zhongguo hangye shi*, 82–83; Ling Yaolun, *Minsheng gongsi shi*, 402–26.
100. Rao, *Short History of Indian Shipping*, 94.
101. Ibid., 150–52.
102. Wang Guang, *Zhongguo hangye shi*, 82–83; Ling Yaolun, *Minsheng gongsi shi*, 402–26.

Chapter 7. The "New Steamship"

1. Zhu Ziqing, "Haixing zaji," 104.
2. Ibid., 104.
3. Bau, *Foreign Navigation*, 28–29; Wang Jianping, *Hangquan wenti*, 101; Wang Guang, *Hangye yu hangquan*, 139–40.
4. Chu, *China's Postal*, 145. The establishment of the Wusong Merchant Marine College was in fact the revival of the Wusong Merchant Marine Training School (*Wusong shangchuan zhuanke xuexiao*) set up by the early Republican government in 1912.
5. *Jiaotong bu tongji nianbao* 1930, 267–68; Wang Guang, *Hangye yu hangquan*, 140.
6. CMC 679/21057, 5 Mar. 1918.
7. *Jiaotong bu tongji nianbao*, 1930, 272, 1931, 280, 1932, 326, 1934, 324–25; Chu, *China's Postal*, 146.
8. HYYK 2:11 (1 Mar. 1934), 1–18, HYYK 2:12 (1 Sep. 1934), 27–51.
9. *Jiaotong bu tongji nianbao*, 1934, 329.
10. Jiang Tianfeng, *Changjiang hangyun shi*, 333–34; Zhang Houquan, *Zhaoshang ju shi*, 353–54, 408–13, 446. This school is mentioned in Wang Jianping, *Hangquan wenti*, 101, but said to offer only a very basic level of education and training.
11. *Hangye nianjian* (1936), 69–82.

12. Zhaoshang ju dang'an, 468/403, 1936; HYYK 4:1 (Aug. 1936), 1–12.
13. PRO-FO 228/3834, 1 May 1928, 9 May 1928.
14. PRO-FO 228/4225, 4 Apr. 1930.
15. PRO-FO 228/4225, 2 Dec. 1930.
16. HYYK 4:1 (Aug. 1936), 1–12; *Hangye nianjian* (1936), 69–82.
17. Ling Yaolun, *Minsheng gongsi shi*, 116–17; Lu Zuofu, "Yizhuang candan jingying de shiye," 552–53. A 1937 commemorative volume on Minsheng lists one Italian and one British employee, but does not specify what type of work they did in the company. *Minsheng gongsi jinian kan*, 174.
18. *Hangye nianjian* (1936), 69–82.
19. Lu Zuofu, "Yizhuang candan jingying de shiye," 552–53; Ling Yaolun, *Minsheng gongsi shi*, 116–17.
20. HYYK 3:10 (15 Feb. 1936), 11–16, 15.
21. JSS III 2 Box 87, 4 Nov. 1927.
22. Bickers, *Britain in China*, 177–88.
23. HYYK 4:1 (Aug. 1936), 1–12.
24. *Jiaotong bu tongji nianbao* 1934, 327–29.
25. Chamberlain, *Foreign Flags*, 20.
26. PRO-FO 228/4226, 25 Jun. 1930.
27. Ristaino, "Russian Diaspora Community," 192–210.
28. Chesneaux, *Chinese Labor Movement*, 122.
29. Ibid., 180–84, 194; Ming K. Chan, "Labor and Empire."
30. JSS III 11 Aug. 1922, 1 Sep. 1922, 25 Jun. 1923; Chesneaux, *Chinese Labor Movement*, 180–84.
31. Broeze, "Muscles of Empire," 48–58; Balachandran, "International Maritime Labor Market," 94–95.
32. Susan Mann Jones, "Ningpo *pang*," 86; JSS III 2/16 Box 97, 13 Apr. 1934.
33. HYYK 2:11 (Mar. 1934), 1–18; HYYK 2:12 (Sep. 1934), 27–51.
34. An earlier version of this section was published as Reinhardt, "Lu Zuofu and the Teaboy."
35. Sha Weikai, *Zhongguo maiban zhi*, 29. There are numerous complaints of compradors falsifying returns to the companies, most of which suggest that the ship captain was aware of and perhaps complicit in this practice. JSS I 13 May 1874, 5 Oct. 1910.
36. Cook, *Lion and the Dragon*, 133.
37. Editorials from the *Shen bao* complained about teaboys' behavior as early as the 1870s, for example, *Shen bao*, 5 Nov. 1873.
38. *Xin shijie* 2 (20 Aug. 1932), 18–32.
39. Cook, *Lion and the Dragon*, 132; HYYK 1:4 (1 Oct. 1930), 1–14.
40. HYYK 1:4 (Oct. 1930), 39–42.
41. PRO-FO 228/4012, 22 Jan. 1929, 13 May 1929.
42. JSS III 18 Dec. 1936.
43. JSS III 24 Oct. 1930, 9 Dec. 1932; Swire Group Archives, C-5-8-10, 13 Nov. 1931; Jiang Tianfeng, *Changjiang hangyun shi*, 333–34; Zhang Houquan, *Zhaoshang ju shi*, 408–13.

44. JSS Misc. 1 Jul. 1933.
45. JSS III 9 Dec. 1932.
46. JSS III 19 Dec. 1932.
47. JSS Misc. 30 Mar. 1933.
48. JSS III 19 Dec. 1932.
49. JSS III 17 Feb. 1933.
50. JSS Misc. 30 Mar. 1933; JSS Misc. 1 Aug. 1933.
51. JSS III 13 Jul. 1933; JSS Misc. 1 Aug. 1933.
52. JSS III 8 Aug. 1933.
53. JSS III 13 Jul. 1933.
54. JSS III 1 Sep. 1933, 16 Sep. 1933.
55. JSS III 13 Apr. 1934.
56. Chūgoku tsūshinsha, *Baiben seido*, 34; Jiang Yongsheng, "Ri-Qing gaikuang," 24–25; *Xin shijie* 2 (20 Aug. 1932). Nisshin's ship compradors were not expected to cover the costs of the cargo business with the earnings of the passenger business and thus did not depend as heavily on teaboys as a source of income. The company did not have the same problem of excessive numbers of teaboys on its ships. Those on Nisshin ships were not paid, but they received free meals and were not allowed to demand tips. On Indo-China's labor dispute, see JMA J18/47, 7 Jun. 1933, 13 Jun. 1933, 19 Jun. 1933, 29 Jun. 1933; J18/48, 13 Jul. 1933.
57. JSS Misc. 15 Nov. 1933.
58. JSS III 13 Apr. 1934.
59. On Liu Hongsheng's reforms, see Zhu Yin'gui, *Jindai lunchuan hangyun ye*, 46; Zhang Houquan, *Zhaoshang ju shi*, 410–11; Jiang Tianfeng, *Changjiang hangyun shi*, 333–34.
60. JSS III 1 Sep. 1933; JSS III 24 Aug. 1934.
61. JSS III 1 Sep. 1933.
62. *Xin shijie* 47 (1 Jun. 1934).
63. Ling Yaolun, *Minsheng gongsi shi*, 97.
64. Lu Zuofu, "Yizhuang candan jingying de shiye," 552.
65. Ibid.; *Minsheng gongsi jinian kan*, 99–100.
66. Lu Zuofu, "Minsheng gongsi ba zhou nian jinian," 253.
67. Sherman Cochran defines a corporate hierarchy as "clear departmental boundaries, clean lines of authority, detailed reporting mechanisms, and formal reporting procedures." Cochran, *Encountering Chinese Networks*, 2. Ling Yaolun, *Minsheng gongsi shi*, 98, 103–10.
68. Lu Zuofu, "Minsheng gongsi ba zhou nian jinian," 253.
69. *Xin shijie* 51 (1 Aug. 1934).
70. *Xin shijie* 22 (16 May 1933).
71. *Minsheng gongsi jinian kan*, 195–230.
72. Ibid., 111, 116.
73. Ling Yaolun, *Minsheng gongsi shi*, 119.
74. *Minsheng gongsi jinian kan*, 101–2.
75. Lu Zuofu, "Gao chafang," 235–36.

76. Ling Yaolun, *Minsheng gongsi shi*, 138–40.

77. *Xin shijie* 51 (1 Aug. 1934); *Minsheng gongsi jinian kan*, 101.

78. Torrible, *Yangtze Reminiscences*, 16. The name "Minsheng" was often romanized as Ming Sung.

79. HYYK 3:1 (1 May 1935), 7–8.

80. Cochran, *Encountering Chinese Networks*, 82–85; Duus, Myers, and Peattie, *Japanese Informal Empire in China*, 8; Bickers, *Britain in China*, 183. Some Japanese firms had tried to replace compradors as early as the turn of the twentieth century, but had found this change costly and difficult (Tōa Dōbun Shoin, *Shina keizai zensho*, vol. 2, 370–81).

81. Kapp, *Szechwan and the Chinese Republic*, 78–80.

82. Dirlik, "Ideological Foundations," 945–46.

83. Fitzgerald, *Awakening China*, 105.

84. *Xinyun dao bao* 4 and 5 (April 1937), 68–81; Zhang Shouguang, *Lu Zuofu nianpu changbian*, vol. 1, 499.

85. *Hangye nianjian* (1935), 8–10.

86. HYYK 3:2 (Jun. 1935), 8.

87. JSS III 21 Jun. 1935, 28 Jun. 1935; HYYK 3:3 (15 Jul. 1935), 13.

88. Chu, *China's Postal*, 135.

89. HYYK 3:5 (Sep. 1935), 1–3.

90. Ibid.

91. JSS III 16 Oct. 1936; see also Chu, *China's Postal*, 135–36.

92. Chu, *China's Postal*, 135–36.

93. Ibid., 133–34; Zhu Huisen, *Hangzheng shiliao*, 771–79.

94. Zhaoshang ju dang'an, 468/403.

95. Zhu Huisen, *Hangzheng shiliao*, 769–71.

96. Ibid., 790–99.

97. *Xinyun dao bao* 4–5 (Apr. 1937), 68–81.

98. JSS III 21 Jun. 1935, 28 Jun. 1935.

99. JSS III 23 Apr. 1937; JSS Misc. 25 Feb. 1938; JSS III 26 Aug. 1938; Torrible, *Yangtze Reminiscences*, 19.

100. Lunchuan zhaoshang zongju, *Lu hang zhi you*, 25–26.

101. JSS III 30 Aug. 1929.

102. *Luxing zazhi* 1931, 1932.

103. *Luxing zazhi* (May 1932), 25–26.

104. Ibid.

105. JSS III 11 Jan. 1929.

106. Ibid.

107. Lu Zuofu, "Yizhuang candan jingying de shiye," 545.

108. Lu Zuofu, *Dongbei youji*, 108. The memoir of Lu Zuofu's son Lu Guoji, *My Father, Lu Zuofu* (1984), describes Lu's first journey out of Sichuan, to Shanghai in 1914. Like in other memoirs of the time, Lu's journey out of the provinces is depicted as an important moment in his nationalist awakening: he also disliked that the best travel conditions and services were reserved for foreigners and only the wealthiest Chinese. Perhaps for good

measure, the memoir also depicts Lu's anger in encountering the "No Dogs and Chinese Allowed" sign upon arrival in Shanghai (Lu Guoji, *Wo de fuqin Lu Zuofu*, 22).

109. Lu Zuofu, *Dongbei youji*, quoted in Ling Yaolun, *Minsheng gongsi shi*, 40.

110. *Xin shijie* 17 (3 Mar. 1933), 1–3.

111. Minsheng shiye gufen youxian gongsi, *Chengke xu zhi*; *Xin shijie* 54 (16 Sep. 1934), 12–15.

112. *Xin shijie* 17 (3 Mar. 1933), 1–3.

113. Minsheng shiye gufen youxian gongsi, *Chengke xu zhi*, 1–20.

114. *Xin shijie* 17 (3 Mar. 1933), 1–3.

115. Zheng Bicheng, *Sichuan dao you*, 3–4.

116. *Xin shijie* 61 (1/1/1935), 2–5.

117. Numerous travelers visited Beibei by invitation of the Minsheng Company or in support of Lu Zuofu's reconstruction efforts. *Luxing zazhi* 7:3 (Mar. 1933), 17–21; He Boxin, *Basheng luxing wenjian lu*, 8–10; Chen Youqin, *Chuan you manji*, 12; Huang Yanpei, *Shu dao*, 6–7; Hu Xiansuan, *Shu you za gan*, 1–4.

118. Tong Shaosheng, "Huiyi Minsheng lunchuan gongsi," 154.

119. *Xin shijie* 54 (16 Sep. 1934), 12–15.

120. *Xin shijie* 17 (3 Mar. 1933), 1–3.

121. Minsheng shiye gufen youxian gongsi, *Chengke xuzhi*, 1–20.

122. Lu Zuofu, "Gao chafang," 235–36.

123. Ling Yaolun, *Minsheng gongsi shi*, 41.

124. *Xin shijie* 29 (1 Sep. 1933), 21–25.

125. Foucault, "Of Other Spaces," 3.

126. *Minsheng gongsi jinian kan*, 102.

127. For example, "The Great Learning" (*Daxue*) excerpted in Wing-tsit Chan, *Sourcebook in Chinese Philosophy*, 85.

128. Lu Zuofu, "Chao geren chenggong," 412.

129. Ling Yaolun, *Minsheng gongsi shi*, 131–32.

130. Ibid., 124–25.

131. Tong Shaosheng, "Huiyi Minsheng lunchuan gongsi," 152.

132. Lu Zuofu, "Shehui shenghuo yu jituan shenghuo," 311.

133. *Xin shijie* 51 (1 Aug. 1934).

134. Ling Yaolun, *Minsheng gongsi shi*, 142, 153.

135. *Xin shijie* (5 Jan. 1937), 14–16; Ling Yaolun, *Minsheng gongsi shi*, 151.

136. Yeh, "Huang Yanpei," 35–36; Lu Guoji, *Wo de fuqin Lu Zuofu*, 26, 45.

137. Culp, *Articulating Citizenship*, 163–64.

138. Fitzgerald, *Awakening China*, 78–79.

139. In 1938, Lu formally joined the Guomindang, but only after he had been appointed assistant minister of Communications in Chongqing by Jiang Jieshi (*Xinmin bao* [Chongqing], 27 Jun. 1938).

140. Bergère, *Golden Age*, 209–13.

141. Morgan, "Scientific Management in China." Companies such as the Rong family's Shenxin No. 3 Cotton Mill, the Kangyuan Can Factory, Yongtai Silk Filature, and Shanghai Huasheng Electrical Company and Commercial Press were known

to have experimented with scientific management techniques. Under Kong Xiangxi, the Nationalist government minister for Industry and Commerce, a Chinese Scientific Management Association was established as a research and activist group, and its members included Liu Hongsheng and Rong Zongjing.

142. Frazier, *Making of the Chinese Industrial Workplace*, 27–28, 57–59; Cochran, *Encountering Chinese Networks*, 70–116, 132–33. See also Yeh, "Corporate Space, Communal Time," and Bergère, *Capitalismes et capitalistes*, 115–17.

143. Yeh, *Shanghai Splendor*, 94–98.

144. Ibid., 99. See also Lu and Perry, *Danwei*, and Bian, *Making of the State Enterprise System*.

145. Yeh, *Shanghai Splendor*, 82, 86.

146. Bergère, *Capitalismes et capitalistes*, 117.

147. Close counterparts to Lu Zuofu and Minsheng in these political and moral aspects of enterprise were the father-and-son team Song Chuandian and Song Feiqing of the Dongya Corporation. Sheehan, *Industrial Eden*.

148. Lu Zuofu, "Zhongguo de genben wenti," 294–98.

149. Lu Zuofu, "Gao chafang," 235–36.

Conclusion

1. Howlett, "'Decolonisation' in China," 224.

2. Coble, *China's Capitalists*, 54. JSS 8 April 1938 includes a clipping from the *Asahi Shinbun* that describes plans for this "giant company."

3. JSS 31 Dec. 1937; JMA 18/51 14 Jan. 1938.

4. JSS 1 Oct. 1937, 15 Oct. 1937, 12 Nov. 1937.

5. JSS 8 Apr. 1938, 20 May 1938, 15 Jul. 1938, 26 Aug. 1938.

6. Zhang, Chen, and Yao, *Swire Group*, 203.

7. Wang Guang, *Zhongguo hangye shi*, 68.

8. Ibid., 68–69; JSS 12 Nov. 1937.

9. Ding Richu and Du Yuncheng, "Yu Xiaqing jianlun," 164–65; Wang Guang, *Zhongguo hangye shi*, 69; Wang Guang, *Zhongguo shuiyun zhi*, 60.

10. Ling Yaolun, *Minsheng gongsi shi*, 174.

11. Ibid., 189–201.

12. Wang Guang, *Zhongguo hangye shi*, 69–70; Wang Guang, *Zhongguo shuiyun zhi*, 60–61; Jiang Tianfeng, *Changjiang hangyun shi*, 483–91; T. H. Sun, "Lu Tso-fu."

13. Ling Yaolun, *Minsheng gongsi shi*, 202–3.

14. Ibid., 328–29.

15. Lu Zuofu, "Lun Zhongguo zhanhou jianshe."

16. Wang Guang, *Zhongguo hangye shi*, 82.

17. Huang Shaozhou, "Zhaoshang ju yu Minsheng gongsi," 272–73.

18. Zhang, Chen, and Yao, *Swire Group*, 255.

19. Ibid., 250–52, 271.

20. Ling Yaolun and Xiong Pu, *Lu Zuofu wenji (zengding ben)*, 514.

21. Zhang, Chen, and Yao, *Swire Group*, 254–78, 284–86.

22. Wang Guang, *Zhongguo hangye shi*, 82–83; Ling Yaolun, *Minsheng gongsi shi*, 402–26.

23. Dooley, "Great Leap Outward," 56.

24. Vogel, *One Step Ahead in China*, 130–33.

25. Dooley, "Great Leap Outward," 58, 72.

26. Ibid., 57.

Works Cited

Adas, Michael. *Machines as the Measure of Men: Science, Technology, and Ideologies of Western Dominance.* Ithaca, NY: Cornell University Press, 1989.
Alitto, Guy S. *The Last Confucian: Liang Shu-ming and the Chinese Dilemma of Modernity.* 2nd ed. Berkeley: University of California Press, 1986.

Balachandran, G. "Conflicts in the International Maritime Labour Market: British and India Seamen, Employers, and the State, 1890–1939." *Indian Economic and Social History Review* 39:1 (2002): 71–100.
———. "Recruitment and Control of Indian Seamen: Calcutta, 1880–1935." *International Journal of Maritime History* 9:1 (June 1997): 1–18.
Ballhatchet, Kenneth. *Race, Sex, and Class under the Raj: Imperial Attitudes and Policies and their Critics, 1793–1905.* London: Weidenfeld and Nicolson, 1980.
Banno, Masataka. *China and the West, 1858–1861: The Origins of the Tsungli Yamen.* Cambridge, MA: Harvard University Press, 1964.
Barlow, Tani E. "Colonialism's Career in Postwar China Studies." In *Formations of Colonial Modernity in East Asia*, ed. Tani E. Barlow, 373–411. Durham, NC: Duke University Press, 1997.
Bau, Mingchien Joshua. *Foreign Navigation in Chinese Waters.* Shanghai: China Institute of Pacific Relations, 1931.
Baumler, Alan. "Playing with Fire: The Nationalist Government and Popular Anti-Opium Agitation in 1927–1928." *Republican China* 21:1 (Nov. 1995): 43–91.
Bergère, Marie Claire. *Capitalismes et capitalistes en Chine: Des origines a nos jours* [Capitalisms and Capitalists in China: Origins to Today]. Paris: Perrin, 2007.
———. *The Golden Age of the Chinese Bourgeoisie.* Trans. Janet Lloyd. Cambridge: Cambridge University Press, 1989.
Bernstein, Henry T. *Steamboats on the Ganges: An Exploration in the History of India's Modernization through Science and Technology.* Bombay: Orient Longmans, 1960.

Bian, Morris L. *The Making of the State Enterprise System in Modern China: The Dynamics of Institutional Change.* Cambridge, MA: Harvard University Press, 2005.

Bickers, Robert. "Britain and China, and India." In *Britain and China*, ed. Bickers and Howlett, 58–83.

———. *Britain in China: Community, Culture, and Colonialism, 1900–1949.* Manchester: Manchester University Press, 1999.

———. "'Good Work for China in Every Possible Direction': The Foreign Inspectorate of the Chinese Maritime Customs, 1854–1950." In *Twentieth Century Colonialism and China*, ed. Goodman and Goodman, 25–36.

Bickers, Robert, and Christian Henriot, eds. *New Frontiers: Imperialism's New Communities in East Asia, 1842–1953.* Manchester: Manchester University Press, 2000.

Bickers, Robert, and Jonathan J. Howlett, eds. *Britain and China, 1840–1970: Empire, Finance, and War.* Abingdon, Oxon: Routledge, 2016.

Bickers, Robert, and Isabella Jackson, eds. *Treaty Ports in Modern China: Law, Land, and Power.* Abingdon, Oxon: Routledge, 2016.

Bickers, Robert, and Jeffrey Wasserstrom. "Shanghai's 'Dogs and Chinese Not Admitted' Sign: Legend, History, and Contemporary Symbol." *China Quarterly* (Jun. 1995): 444–66.

Biggerstaff, Knight. "The Secret Correspondence of 1867–8: Views of Leading Chinese Statesmen Regarding the Further Opening of China to Western Influence." *Journal of Modern History* 22:2 (June 1950): 122–36.

Bird, Isabella. *The Yangtze Valley and Beyond.* London: John Murray, 1899.

Blake, George. *B.I. Centenary.* London: Collins, 1956.

Blakiston, Thomas W. *Five Months on the Yang-tsze; with a Narrative of the Exploration of its Upper Waters, and Notices of the Present Rebellions in China.* London: John Murray, 1862.

Blue, A. D. "European Navigation on the Yangtse." *Journal of the Hong Kong Branch of the Royal Asiatic Society* 3 (1963): 107–30.

———. "Land and River Routes to Western China." *Journal of the Hong Kong Branch of the Royal Asiatic Society* 16 (1976): 162–78.

Broeze, Frank. "The Muscles of Empire—Indian Seamen and the Raj, 1919–1939." *Indian Economic and Social History Review* 18:1 (1981): 43–67.

———. "Underdevelopment and Dependency: Maritime India under the Raj." *Modern Asian Studies* 18:3 (May 1984): 429–57.

Brunero, Donna. *Britain's Imperial Cornerstone in China: The Maritime Customs Service, 1854–1949.* New York: Routledge, 2006.

Bun, Kwan Man. "Mapping the Hinterland: Treaty Ports and Regional Analysis in Modern China." In *Remapping China: Fissures in Historical Terrain*, ed. Gail Hershatter et al., 181–93. Stanford, CA: Stanford University Press, 1996.

Cafruny, Alan W. *Ruling the Waves: The Political Economy of International Shipping.* Berkeley: University of California Press, 1987.

Carlson, Ellsworth C. *The Kaiping Mines, 1877–1912.* 2nd ed. Cambridge, MA: East Asian Research Center, Harvard University, 1971.

Cassel, Pär Kristoffer. *Grounds of Judgment: Extraterritoriality and Imperial Power in Nineteenth-Century China and Japan*. Oxford: Oxford University Press, 2012.

Chamberlain, J. P. *Foreign Flags in China's Internal Navigation.* New York: American Council, Institute of Pacific Relations, 1931.

Chan, Ming K. "Labor and Empire: The Chinese Labor Movement in the Canton Delta, 1895–1927." Ph.D. diss., Stanford University, 1975.

Chan, Wing-tsit. *A Sourcebook in Chinese Philosophy*. Princeton, NJ: Princeton University Press, 1963.

Chen, Chao. "Cong qijia hetong kan lunchuan zhaoshang ju yu waiguo ziben de guanxi" (Examining the China Merchants Company's Relationship to Foreign Capital from the Conference Agreement). In *Zhaoshang ju yu jindai Zhongguo yanjiu* (Studies of the China Merchants Company and Modern China), ed. Yi Huili, 625–50. Beijing: Zhongguo shehui kexue chuban she, 2005.

Chen Jinfan. "Changjiang yandu zousi jianwen" (A Simple Look at Opium Smuggling on the Yangzi River). In *Sichuan wenshi ziliao jicui*, vol. 6. Chengdu: Sichuan renmin chuban she, 1996.

Chen Youqin. *Chuan you manji* (Leisurely Notes on Travel to Sichuan). Shanghai: Zhonghua shuju, 1934.

Chesneaux, Jean. *The Chinese Labor Movement, 1919–1927*. Trans. H. M. Wright. Stanford, CA: Stanford University Press, 1968.

China, Imperial Maritime Customs. *Decennial Reports on Trade, Navigation, Industries, etc. of the Ports open to Foreign Commerce in China.* Shanghai: Inspectorate of Customs, Statistical Department, 1882–1920.

———. *Reports on Trade at the Treaty Ports in China. 1861–1875*. Shanghai: Imperial Maritime Customs Statistical Department, 1861–75.

China, Jiaotong bu (Ministry of Communications), Jiaotong shi bianzuan weiyuanhui (Editorial Committee of the History of Communications). *Jiaotong shi: hangzheng bian* (History of Communications: Shipping Administration). Nanjing: N.p., 1931.

———. *Jiaotong bu tongji nianbao* (Yearly Report of Ministry of Communications Statisics). Nanjing: N.p., 1930–34.

Chongqing shangwu ribao (Chongqing Commercial Daily), 1929.

Chouban yiwu shimo: Tongzhi (Complete Account of the Management of Barbarian Affairs: Tongzhi Reign). Reprint of 1930 Beiping edition in *Xu xiu siku quanshu*, vols. 418–21. Shanghai: Shanghai guji chuban she.

Chow, Rey. *Writing Diaspora: Tactics of Intervention in Contemporary Cultural Studies.* Bloomington: University of Indiana Press, 1993.

Chu, Chia-hua. *China's Postal and Other Communications Services*. London: Kegan Paul, 1937.

Chūgoku tsūshinsha (China News Agency). *Botsuraku ni chokumen seru baiben seido* (The Comprador System Facing Collapse). N.p., 1936.

Coble, Parks M. *China's Capitalists in Japan's New Order: The Occupied Lower Yangzi, 1937–1945*. Berkeley: University of California Press, 2003.

———. *The Shanghai Capitalists and the Nationalist Government, 1927–1937*. Cambridge, MA: Council on East Asian Studies, Harvard University, 1980.

Cochran, Sherman. *Big Business in China: Sino-Foreign Rivalry in the Cigarette Industry, 1890–1930*. Cambridge, MA: Harvard University Press, 1980.

———. *Encountering Chinese Networks: Western, Japanese, and Chinese Corporations in China, 1880–1937*. Berkeley: University of California Press, 2000.

Cohen, Paul A. *Discovering History in China: American Historical Writing on the Recent Chinese Past*. New York: Columbia University Press, 1984.

Cook, Christopher. *The Lion and the Dragon: British Voices from the China Coast*. London: Elm Tree Books, 1985.

Cooper, Frederick. *Colonialism in Question: Theory, Knowledge, History*. Berkeley: University of California Press, 2005.

Cooper, Thomas T. *Travels of a Pioneer of Commerce in Pigtail and Petticoats: or, an Overland Journey from China Towards India*. 1871. Reprint, New York: Arno Press, 1967.

Culp, Robert. *Articulating Citizenship: Civic Education and Student Politics in Southeastern China, 1912–1940*. Cambridge, MA: Harvard University Asia Center, 2007.

Dean, Britten. *China and Great Britain: The Diplomacy of Commercial Relations, 1860–1864*. Cambridge, MA: East Asian Research Center, Harvard University, 1974.

Deng Xiaoqin. *Jindai Chuanjiang hangyun jianshi* (A Concise History of Modern Upper Yangzi Shipping). Chongqing: Difangshi ziliao congkan, 1940.

DesForges, Roger V. *Hsi-liang and the Chinese National Revolution*. New Haven, CT: Yale University Press, 1973.

Dianshizhai huabao (Dianshizhai Pictorial). Guangzhou: Renmin chuban she, 1983.

Dick, H. W., and S. A. Kentwell. *Beancaker to Boxboat: Steamship Companies in Chinese Waters*. Canberra: Nautical Association of Australia, 1988.

Ding Richu and Du Yuncheng. "Yu Xiaqing jianlun" (A Brief Discussion of Yu Xiaqing). *Lishi yanjiu* 3 (1981): 145–66.

Dirlik, Arif. "The Ideological Foundations of the New Life Movement: A Study in Counterrevolution." *Journal of Asian Studies* 34:4 (Aug. 1975): 945–80.

———. *Revolution and History: The Origins of Marxist Historiography in China, 1919–1937*. Berkeley: University of California Press, 1978.

Dooley, Howard J. "The Great Leap Outward: China's Maritime Renaissance." *Journal of East Asian Affairs* 26:1 (Spring/Summer 2012): 53–76.

Duara, Prasenjit. *Rescuing History from the Nation: Questioning Narratives of Modern China*. Chicago: University of Chicago Press, 1995.

Duus, Peter, Ramon H. Myers, and Mark R. Peattie, eds. *The Japanese Informal Empire in China, 1895–1937*. Princeton, NJ: Princeton University Press, 1989.

Elvin, Mark, and William Skinner, eds. *The Chinese City between Two Worlds*. Stanford, CA: Stanford University Press, 1974.

Esherick, Joseph. *Reform and Revolution in China: The 1911 Revolution in Hunan and Hubei*. Berkeley: University of California Press, 1976.

Fairbank, John King. *Trade and Diplomacy on the China Coast: The Opening of the Treaty Ports, 1842–1854*. Cambridge, MA: Harvard University Press, 1953.

Fan Baichuan. *Zhongguo lunchuan hangyun ye de xingqi* (The Rise of China's Steam Shipping Business). Chengdu: Sichuan renmin chubanshe, 1985.

Fang Teng. "Yu Xiaqing lun" (On Yu Xiaqing). *Zazhi yuekan* (Monthly Miscellany) 12:2–4 (1943).

Faure, David. *China and Capitalism: A History of Business Enterprise in Modern China*. Hong Kong: Hong Kong University Press, 2006.

Feuerwerker, Albert. *China's Early Industrialization: Sheng Hsuan-huai and Mandarin Enterprise*. Cambridge, MA: Harvard University Press, 1958.

———. *The Chinese Economy, 1870–1949*. Ann Arbor: Center for Chinese Studies, University of Michigan, 1995.

———. "The Foreign Presence in China." In *Cambridge History of China, Volume 12: Republican China, 1912–1949, Part I*, 128–207. Cambridge: Cambridge University Press, 1983.

Fewsmith, Joseph. *Party, State, and Local Elites in Republican China: Merchant Organizations and Politics in Shanghai, 1890–1930*. Honolulu: University of Hawaii Press, 1985.

Fitkin, Gretchen Mae. *The Great River: The Story of a Voyage on the Yangtze Kiang*. Shanghai: North China Daily News and Herald (Kelly and Walsh), 1922.

Fitzgerald, John. *Awakening China: Politics, Culture, and Class in the Nationalist Revolution*. Stanford, CA: Stanford University Press, 1996.

Fogel, Joshua A. *The Literature of Travel in the Japanese Rediscovery of China, 1862–1945*. Stanford, CA: Stanford University Press, 1996.

Foreign Office Correspondence. Public Record Office. Kew Gardens, UK.

Foucault, Michel. "Governmentality." In *Essential Works of Foucault 1954–1984: Power, Volume 3*, ed. James D. Faubion, 201–22. New York: New Press, 1994.

———. "Of Other Spaces" (1967): Heterotopias. http://foucault.info/documents/heteroTopia/foucault.heteroTopia.en.html.

Fox, Stephen. *The Ocean Railway: Isambard Kingdom Brunel, Samuel Cunard, and the Revolutionary World of the Great Atlantic Steamships*. London: Harper Perennial, 2003.

Frazier, Mark W. *The Making of the Chinese Industrial Workplace: State, Revolution, and Labor Management*. Cambridge: Cambridge University Press, 2002.

Fung, Edmund S. K. *The Diplomacy of Imperial Retreat: Britain's South China Policy, 1924–1931*. Hong Kong: Oxford University Press, 1991.

Gaimushō [Japanese Foreign Ministry] Archives. Tokyo, Japan.

Gallagher, John, and Ronald Robinson. "The Imperialism of Free Trade." *Economic History Review* 6:1 (Aug. 1953): 1–15.

Gandhi, Mohandas K. "Letter to Secretary, Passengers' Grievances Committee, Rangoon (July 25, 1917)." *The Collected Works of Mahatma Gandhi*, vol. 15, 474–76. Delhi: Publications Division, Ministry of Information and Broadcasting, Government of India, 1958–.

Ge Yuanxi. *Hu you zaji*. (1876). Shanghai: Shanghai guji chubanshe, 1989.

Geil, William Edgar. A *Yankee on the Yangtze*. New York: Armstrong and Son, 1904.

Gerth, Karl. *China Made: Consumer Culture and the Creation of the Nation*. Cambridge, MA: Harvard University Asia Center, 2003.

Gill, Captain William. *The River of Golden Sand: Being the Narrative of a Journey through China and Eastern Tibet to Burmah*. London: John Murray, 1883.

Gongzhong dang (Unpublished Palace Memorials). Palace Museum Library. Taipei, Taiwan.

Goodman, Bryna. "Improvisations on a Semicolonial Theme, or How to Read a Celebration of Transnational Urban Community." *Journal of Asian Studies* 59:4 (Nov. 2000): 889–926.

———. *Native Place, City, and Nation: Regional Networks and Identities in Shanghai, 1853–1937*. Berkeley: University of California Press, 1995.

Goodman, Bryna, and David S. G. Goodman, eds. *Twentieth Century Colonialism and China: Localities, the Everyday, and the World*. Abingdon, Oxon: Routledge, 2012.

Graham, Gerald S. "The Ascendancy of the Sailing Ship, 1850–85." *Economic History Review* New Series 9:1 (1956): 74–88.

Greenberg, Michael. *British Trade and the Opening of China, 1800–42*. Cambridge: Cambridge University Press, 1951.

Grover, David. *American Merchant Ships on the Yangtze, 1920–1941*. Westport, CT: Praeger, 1992.

Guo Moruo. "Chu chu Kuimen" (Emerging from Kui Gate). In *Guo Moruo quanji* (The Complete Works of Guo Moruo). Beijing: Kexue chuban she, 1992.

Guomin zhengfu qingcha zhengli Zhaoshang ju weiyuan hui baogao shu (Report of the Nationalist Government Committee to Investigate and Reorganize the China Merchants Steam Navigation Company). Preface by Zhang Renjie. [Nanjing]: N.p., 1927.

Guoying zhaoshangju qishiwu zhounian jinian kan (Commemoration of the 75th Anniversary of the National China Merchants Steam Navigation Company). Preface by Yu Dawei. [Nanjing], 1947.

Hall, B. Foster. *The Chinese Maritime Customs: An International Service, 1854–1950*. Greenwich: National Maritime Museum, 1977.

Han Suyin. *The Crippled Tree*. New York: Putnam's Sons, 1965.

Hangsheng (Voice of Shipping). Shanghai, 1930.

Hangye nianjian (Shipping Yearbook). Shanghai, 1935–36.

Hangye yuekan (Shipping Monthly). Shanghai, 1930–37.

Hao, Yen-p'ing. *The Commercial Revolution in Nineteenth-Century China: The Rise of Sino-Western Mercantile Capitalism*. Berkeley: University of California Press, 1986.

———. *The Comprador in Nineteenth Century China: A Bridge Between East and West*. Cambridge, MA: Harvard University Press, 1970.

Hao, Yen-p'ing, and Erh-min Wang. "Changing Chinese Views of Western Relations, 1840–1895." In *Cambridge History of China, Volume 11: Late Ch'ing, 1800–1911, Part 2*, ed. John K. Fairbank and K. C. Liu, 142–201. Cambridge: Cambridge University Press, 1978.

Harcourt, Freda. "British Oceanic Mail Contracts in the Age of Steam, 1838–1914." In *The World of Shipping*, ed. David M. Williams, 33–50. Aldershot: Ashgate, 1997.

Haviland, Edward Kenneth. "American Steam Navigation in China, 1845–1878." Parts I–VII *American Neptune*; Part I 16:3 (Jul. 1956): 157–79; Part II 16:4 (Oct. 1956): 243–69; Part III 17:1 (Jan. 1957): 38–64; Part IV 17:2 (Apr. 1957): 134–51; Part V 17:3 (Jul. 1957): 212–30; Part VI 17:4 (Oct. 1957): 298–314; Part VII 18:1 (Jan.1958): 59–65.
Hayford, Charles. *To the People: James Yen and Village China*. New York: Columbia University Press, 1990.
Headrick, Daniel. *The Tentacles of Progress: Technology Transfer in the Age of Imperialism, 1850–1940*. New York: Oxford University Press, 1988.
He Boxin. *Ba sheng luxing wenjian lu* (Record of Things Seen and Heard Traveling through Eight Provinces). Chongqing: Kaiming shudian, 1935.
Hershatter, Gail. "The Subaltern Talks Back: Reflections on Subaltern Theory and Chinese History." *positions* 1:1 (1993): 103–30.
———. *The Workers of Tianjin, 1900–1949*. Stanford, CA: Stanford University Press, 1986.
Hevia, James L. *English Lessons: The Pedagogy of Imperialism in Nineteenth-Century China*. Durham, NC: Duke University Press, 2003.
Hinton, Harold C. *The Grain Tribute System of China, 1845–1911*. Cambridge, MA: Harvard University Press, 1956.
Hobson, J. A. *Imperialism, A Study*. London: J. Nisbet, 1902.
Honig, Emily. *Creating Chinese Ethnicity: Subei People in Shanghai, 1850–1980*. New Haven, CT: Yale University Press, 1992.
———. *Sisters and Strangers: Women in the Shanghai Cotton Mills, 1919–1949*. Stanford, CA: Stanford University Press, 1986.
Howarth, David, and Stephen Howarth. *The Story of P&O: The Peninsular and Oriental Steam Navigation Company*. London: Weidenfeld and Nicolson, 1986.
Howlett, Jonathan J. "'Decolonisation' in China, 1949–1959." In *Britain and China, 1840–1970*, ed. Bickers and Howlett, 222–41.
Hu Xiansuan. *Shu you za gan* (Various Impressions of Travels in Sichuan). N.p.: [Minfu gongsi], n.d.
Huang Shaozhou. "Zhaoshang ju yu Minsheng gongsi de mingzheng andou" (The Open Strife and Veiled Rivalry between the China Merchants and Minsheng Companies). In *Lu Zuofu zhuisi lu* (Recollections of Lu Zuofu), ed. Ling Yaolun and Zhou Yonglin, 269–76. Chongqing: Chongqing chubanshe, 2001.
Huang Yanpei. *Shu dao* (A Guide to Sichuan). Shanghai: Kaiming shudian, 1936.
Hubei jiaoshe shu zhaiyao (Abstracts of Foreign Affairs Incidents in Hubei Province). N.p., 1915.
Hunter, Louis C. *Steamboats on the Western Rivers: An Economic and Technological History*. New York: Dover, 1949, 1993.
Hyde, Francis E. *Far Eastern Trade, 1860–1914*. London: A. and C. Black, 1973.

Irish University Press Area Studies Series of British Parliamentary Papers: China. Shannon: Irish University Press, 1971.

Jardine, Matheson & Company Archives. Cambridge University. Cambridge.
Jardine, Matheson & Company. *The China Shipping Manual*. Shanghai: Willow Pattern Press, 1937.

Jiang Tianfeng, ed. *Changjiang hangyun shi: jindai bufen* (History of Yangzi River Shipping: The Modern Period). Beijing: Renmin jiaotong chubanshe, 1992.

Jiaotong bu (Ministry of Communications) Archives. Second Historical Archives. Nanjing, China.

Jiang Yongsheng. "Ri-Qing qichuan zhushi huishe gaikuang" (Conditions in the Nisshin Kisen Kaisha). *Wenshi ziliao xuanji* vol. 49, 1981.

John Swire & Sons Archives. School of Oriental and African Studies. London.

John Swire & Sons Archives. Swire House, London.

Jones, Francis. "The German Challenge to British Shipping, 1885–1914." *Mariner's Mirror* 76:2 (1990): 151–67.

Jones, Geoffrey. *Merchants to Multinationals: British Trading Companies in the Nineteenth and Twentieth Centuries.* Oxford: Oxford University Press, 2000.

Jones, Susan Mann. "The Ningbo *pang* and Financial Power at Shanghai." In *The Chinese City between Two Worlds*, ed. Elvin and Skinner, 73–96.

Kapp, Robert A. *Szechwan and the Chinese Republic: Provincial Militarism and Central Power, 1911–1938.* New Haven, CT: Yale University Press, 1973.

Keswick, Maggie, ed. *The Thistle and the Jade: A Celebration of 150 Years of Jardine, Matheson, and Co.* Octopus Books, 1982.

Kirby, William C. "China Unincorporated: Company Law and Business Enterprise in Twentieth-Century China." *Journal of Asian Studies* 54:1 (Feb. 1995): 43–64.

———. "Engineering China: Birth of the Developmental State, 1928–1937." In *Becoming Chinese: Passages to Modernity and Beyond*, ed. Wen-hsin Yeh, 137–60. Berkeley: University of California Press, 2001.

Knollys, Major Henry. *English Life in China.* London: Smith, Elder, 1885.

Kokaze Hidemasa. *Teikokushugi ka no Nihon kai'un* (Japanese Shipping under Imperialism). Tokyo: Yamagawa, 1995.

Köll, Elisabeth. *From Cotton Mill to Business Empire: The Emergence of Regional Enterprises in Modern China.* Cambridge, MA: Harvard University Asia Center, 2003.

Kuo, Ting-yee, and Kwang-ching Liu. "Self-Strengthening: The Pursuit of Western Technology." In the *Cambridge History of China. Volume 10: Late Ch'ing, Part I*, 491–542. Cambridge: Cambridge University Press, 1978.

Lai, Chi-kong. "Li Hung-chang and Modern Enterprise: The China Merchants' Company, 1872–1885." In *Li Hung-chang and China's Early Modernization*, ed. Samuel C. Chu and Kwang-ching Liu. Armonk, NY: M.E. Sharpe, 1994.

Le Fevour, Edward. *Western Enterprise in Late Ch'ing China: A Selective Survey of Jardine, Matheson & Company's Operations, 1842–1895.* Cambridge, MA: East Asian Resource Center, Harvard University, 1968.

Lenin, V. I. *Imperialism: The Highest Stage of Capitalism.* New York: International, 1939.

Li Boyuan. *Modern Times: A Brief History of Enlightenment* (1905). Trans. Douglas Lancashire. Hong Kong: Research Center for Translation, Chinese University of Hong Kong, 1996.

Li Gufan. *Zhaoshangju san da'an* (The Three Great Cases of the China Merchants Company). Shanghai: Xiandai shuju, 1933.

Li, Yi. *Chinese Bureaucratic Culture and its Influence on the Nineteenth-Century Steamship Operation, 1864–1885: The Bureau for Recruiting Merchants.* Lewiston, NY: Edwin Mellen Press, 2001.

Li Zhigang (Lai Chi-kong). "Lunchuan zhaoshang ju jingying guanli wenti, 1872–1901" (Problems in the Management of the China Merchants Company). *Zhongyang yanjiu yuan Jindaishi yanjiusuo jikan* 19 (1990): 67–105.

Ling Yaolun, ed. *Minsheng gongsi shi* (A History of the Minsheng Company). Beijing: Renmin jiaotong chubanshe, 1990.

Ling Yaolun, and Xiong Pu, eds. *Lu Zuofu wenji* (Collected Works of Lu Zuofu). Beijing: Beijing daxue chuban she, 1999.

———, eds. *Lu Zuofu wenji, zengding ben* [Collected Works of Lu Zuofu, expanded edition]. Beijing: Beijing daxue chuban she, 2012.

Little, Archibald. *Through the Yang-tse Gorges or Trade and Travel in Western China.* London: Sampson Low, Marston, Searle, & Rivington, 1888.

Liu Chonglai. "Lun Lu Zuofu xiangcun jianshe zhi lu" (On Lu Zuofu's Approach to Rural Reconstruction). *Xinan shifan daxue xuebao* 4 (1998): 122–28.

Liu Hangchen. *Rong mu ban sheng* (Half a Life in the Inner Circle). Taibei xian Yonghe zhen: Wenhai chuban she, 1978.

Liu, Kwang-Ching. *Anglo-American Steamship Rivalry in China, 1862–1874.* Cambridge, MA: Harvard University Press, 1962.

———. "British-Chinese Steamship Rivalry in China, 1873–85." In *The Economic Development of China and Japan*, ed. C. D. Cowan, 49–78. New York: Praeger, 1964.

———. "Steamship Enterprise in Nineteenth-Century China." *Journal of Asian Studies* 18:4 (Nov. 1959): 435–55.

Liu, Lydia H. *The Clash of Empires: The Invention of China in Modern World Making.* Cambridge, MA: Harvard University Press, 2004.

Liu T'ieh-yun. *The Travels of Lao Can.* Trans. Harold Shadick. New York: Columbia University Press, 1990.

Lockwood, Stephen C. *Augustine Heard and Company, 1858–1862: American Merchants in China.* Cambridge, MA: East Asian Research Center, Harvard University, 1971.

Lu Guoji. *Wo de fuqin Lu Zuofu* (My Father, Lu Zuofu). Chengdu: Sichuan renmin chuban she, 1993.

Lu Huajin. "Yan'an ji neihe neigang hang xing quan wenti" (Issues in Shipping Rights on the Coasts, Inland Rivers, and Inland Ports). *Dongfang zazhi* (Eastern Miscellany) 26:16 (25 Aug. 1929): 23–35.

Lu Shiqiang. *Zhongguo zaoqi de lunchuan jingying* (China's Early Management of Steamships). Taipei: Zhongyang yanjiu yuan jindaishi yanjiu suo, 1976.

Lu, Xiaobo, and Elizabeth Perry, eds. *Danwei: The Changing Chinese Workplace in Historical and Comparative Perspective.* Armonk, NY: M. E. Sharpe, 1997.

Lu Zuofu. "Chao geren chenggong de shiye, chao zhuanqian zhuyi de shengyi" (An Enterprise that Goes beyond Individual Success, A Business that Goes beyond Earning Money). (1936). In Ling Yaolun and Xiong Pu, *Lu Zuofu wenji* (1999), 411–13.

———. *Dongbei youji* (Travels to the Northeast). Chongqing: [Chuanjiang hangwu guanli chu], 1930; 1931.

———. "Gao chafang" (To the Teaboys). (1933). In Ling Yaolun and Xiong Pu, *Lu Zuofu wenji* (1999), 235–36.

———. "Lun Zhongguo zhanhou jianshe" (On China's Postwar Reconstruction). (1946). In Ling Yaolun and Xiong Pu, *Lu Zuofu wenji* (1999), 598–626.

———. "Shehui shenghuo yu jituan shenghuo" (Social Life and Group Life). (1934). In Ling Yaolun and Xiong Pu, *Lu Zuofu wenji* (1999), 308–11.

———. "Xiangcun jianshe" (Rural Reconstruction). (1930). In Ling Yaolun and Xiong Pu, *Lu Zuofu wenji* (1999), 86–101.

———. "Yizhuang candan jingying de shiye—Minsheng shiye gongsi" (An Enterprise Dismally Managed—the Minsheng Industrial Company). (1943). In Ling Yaolun and Xiong Pu, *Lu Zuofu wenji* (1999), 544–69.

———. "Zai Minsheng gongsi ba zhou nian jinian da hui shang de kai hui ci" (Opening Address at the Eighth Anniversary of the Minsheng Company). (1933). In Ling Yaolun and Xiong Pu, *Lu Zuofu wenji* (1999), 252–58.

———. "Zhongguo de genben wenti shi ren de xunlian" (China's Basic Problem Is the Training of People). (1934). In Ling Yaolun and Xiong Pu, *Lu Zuofu wenji* (1999), 294–98.

Lunchuan zhaoshang ju (China Merchants Steam Navigation Company). *Chenke bianlan* (Guide for Passengers). Shanghai: Lunchuan zhaoshang ju, 1929.

———. *Lu hang zhi you* (The Ship Traveler's Friend). Shanghai: Lunchuan zhaoshang ju, 1928.

———. *Zhaoshang ju zong guanlichu huibao* (Report of the China Merchants Company's Office of General Management). Shanghai: Lunchuan zhaoshang ju, 1929.

Luxing zazhi (The China Traveler). Shanghai: Zhongguo luxing she, 1927–52.

Maritime Customs Archives. Second Historical Archives. Nanjing, China.

Marriner, Sheila, and Francis E. Hyde. *The Senior John Samuel Swire: Management in Far Eastern Shipping Trades*. Liverpool: Liverpool University Press, 1967.

Meng Yue. *Shanghai and the Edges of Empires*. Minneapolis: University of Minnesota Press, 2006.

Michie, Alexander. *The Englishman in China during the Victorian Era, as Illustrated in the Career of Sir Rutherford Alcock*. Reprint: Taipei, Ch'eng-wen, 1966.

Minsheng gongsi yanjiushi dang'an (Archives of the Minsheng Company's Historical Research Section). Minsheng gongsi, Chongqing, China.

Minsheng shiye gongsi shi yi zhounian jinian kan (Commemorative Volume of the Eleventh Anniversary of the Minsheng Industrial Company). Preface by Zhao Xi. Chongqing: Minsheng gongsi, ca. 1937.

Minsheng shiye gufen youxian gongsi (Minsheng Industrial Company). *Chengke xuzhi* (Essential Information for Passengers). Chongqing: Minsheng gongsi, 1936.

Mittler, Barbara. *A Newspaper for China? Power, Identity, and Change in Shanghai's News Media, 1872–1912*. Cambridge, MA: Harvard University Asia Center, 2004.

Morgan, Stephen L. "Scientific Management in China, 1910–1930s." University of Melbourne Department of Management Working Paper Series 2003/10012.

Morse, Hosea Ballou. H.B. Morse Papers. MS Chinese 3.1 Transcript of Letter Books. Houghton Library, Harvard University.

———. *The Gilds of China: With an Account of the Gild-Merchant or Co-hong of Canton.* 1909. Taipei: Chengwen, 1966.
———. *The International Relations of the Chinese Empire.* New York: Paragon Books, 1960.
Motono, Eiichi. "The 'Traffic Revolution': Remaking the Export Sales System in China, 1866–1875." *Modern China* 12:1 (Jan. 1986): 75–102.
Munro, J. Forbes. *Maritime Enterprise and Empire: Sir William Mackinnon and his Business Network, 1823–93.* Woodbridge UK: Boydell Press, 2003.
Murphey, Rhoads. "The Treaty Ports and China's Modernization." In *The Chinese City between Two Worlds*, ed. Elvin and Skinner, 17–72.

Nagoya shōgyō kaigisho (Nagoya Commercial Association). *Shinkoku shinkai kōjō shōgyō shisatsu hōkokushō* (Report of an Inspection of the Commerce of the Newly Opened Ports of China). Nagoya: Nagoya shōgyō kaigisho, 1896.
Nakano Kozan. *Shina tairiku ōdan yū shoku zasso* (Notes of a Trip across the Chinese Mainland to Sichuan). Tokyo: Rokumeikan, 1913.
Nayar, Baldev Raj. *The State and Market in India's Shipping: Nationalism, Globalization, and Marginalization.* New Delhi: Manohar, 1996.
Negishi Tadashi. *Baiben seido no kenkyū* (A Study of the Comprador System). Tokyo: Nihon toshō kabushiki kaisha, 1948.
Nie Baozhang, ed. *Zhongguo jindai hangyun shi ziliao, 1840–1895* (Historical Materials on Modern Chinese Shipping, 1840–1895). 2 vols. Shanghai: Shanghai renmin chuban she, 1983.
Nie Baozhang and Zhu Yin'gui, eds. *Zhongguo jindai hangyun shi ziliao, 1895–1927* (Historical Materials on Modern Chinese Shipping, 1895–1927). 2 vols. Beijing: Zhongguo shehui kexue chuban she, 2002.
Nisshin Kisen Kabushiki Kaisha (Japan-China Steamship Company). *Kankō jijō* (Conditions in Hankou). Tokyo: Nisshin Kisen Kabushiki Kaisha, 1914.
———. *Nisshin Kisen Kabushiki Kaisha sanjū nenshi oyobi tsuiho* (The Thirty-Year History of the Nisshin Kisen Kaisha and Addenda). Tokyo: Nisshin Kisen Kabushiki Kaisha, 1941.
North China Daily News. Shanghai, 1864–1945.
North China Herald. Shanghai, 1870–1941.

Ōsaka Shōsen Kabushiki Kaisha (Osaka Commercial Shipping Company). *Shinkoku Chōkō unsōgyō genkō* (Conditions in China's Yangzi River Shipping Business). Ōsaka: Ōsaka Shōsen Kaisha, 1900.
Osterhammel, Jurgen. "Britain and China, 1842–1914." *The Oxford History of the British Empire. Volume III: The Nineteenth Century*, ed. Andrew Porter. Oxford: Oxford University Press, 1999.
———. "British Business in China, 1860s–1950s." In *British Business in Asia since 1860*, ed. R. P. T. Davenport-Hines and Geoffrey Jones. Cambridge: Cambridge University Press, 1989.
———. "China." In *The Oxford History of the British Empire. Volume IV: The Twentieth Century*, ed. Judith M. Brown and William Roger Louis. Oxford: Oxford University Press, 1999.

———. *Colonialism: A Theoretical Overview.* Translated by Shelly L. Frisch. Princeton, NJ: Markus Wiener, 1997.

———. "Semi-Colonialism and Informal Empire in Twentieth-Century China: Towards a Framework of Analysis." In *Imperialism and After: Continuities and Discontinuities*, ed. Wolfgang J. Mommsen and Jurgen Osterhammel, 290–314. London: Allen and Unwin, 1986.

Otte, Friedrich. "Shipping Policy in China, Part I." *Chinese Economic Journal* 8:4 (Apr. 1931): 346–58.

———. "Shipping Policy in China, Part II." *Chinese Economic Journal* 8:5 (May 1931): 486–501.

Peattie, Mark R. "Japanese Treaty Port Settlements in China, 1895–1937." In *The Japanese Informal Empire in China, 1895–1937*, ed. Duus, Myers, and Peattie, 166–209.

Pelcovits, Nathan. *Old China Hands and the Foreign Office.* New York: King's Crown Press, 1948.

Percival, William Spencer. *The Land of the Dragon: My Boating and Shooting Excursions to the Gorges of the Upper Yangtze.* London: Hurst and Blackett, 1889.

Perry, Elizabeth J. *Shanghai on Strike: The Politics of Chinese Labor.* Stanford, CA: Stanford University Press, 1993.

Pomeranz, Kenneth. *The Making of a Hinterland: State, Society, and Economy in Inland North China, 1853–1937.* Berkeley: University of California Press, 1993.

Pope, Andrew. "British Steamshipping and the Indian Coastal Trade." *Indian Economic and Social History Review* 32:1 (Jan. 1995): 1–21.

Pye, Lucien. "How China's Nationalism Was Shanghaied." *Australian Journal of Chinese Affairs* 29 (Jan. 1993).

Rankin, Mary Backus. *Elite Activism and Political Transformation in China: Zhejiang Province 1865–1911.* Stanford, CA: Stanford University Press, 1986.

———. "Nationalistic Contestation and Mobilization Politics: Practice and Rhetoric of Railway Rights Recovery at the End of the Qing." *Modern China* 28:3 (July 2002): 315–61.

Rao, T. S. Sanjeeva. *A Short History of Modern Indian Shipping.* Bombay: Popular Prakashan, 1965.

Rawlinson, John L. *China's Struggle for Naval Development, 1839–1895.* Cambridge, MA: Harvard University Press, 1967.

Rawski, Thomas G. *Economic Growth in Prewar China.* Berkeley: University of California Press, 1989.

Ray, Rajat K. "Asian Capital in the Age of European Domination: The Rise of the Bazaar, 1800–1914." *Modern Asian Studies* 29:3 (1995): 449–554.

———. *Entrepreneurship and Industry in India, 1800–1947.* Delhi: Oxford University Press, 1992.

Reinhardt, Anne. "'Decolonisation' on the Periphery: Liu Xiang and Shipping Rights Recovery at Chongqing, 1926–38." *Journal of Imperial and Commonwealth History* 36:2 (June 2008): 259–74.

———. "Lu Zuofu and the Teaboy: The Impact of the Minsheng Company's Management Practices on Yangzi River Shipping Companies, 1930–37." In *Guojia Hanghai* [National Maritime Research], ed. Shanghai Zhongguo hanghai bowuguan, 12. Shanghai: Shanghai guji chuban she, 2015.

———. "Treaty Ports as Shipping Infrastructure." In *Treaty Ports in Modern China*, ed. Bickers and Jackson, 101–20.

Remer, C. F. *Study of Chinese Boycotts: With Special Reference to their Economic Effectiveness*. Taipei: Ch'eng-wen, 1966.

Reynolds, Douglas R. "Training Young China Hands: Tōa Dōbun Shoin and Its Precursors, 1886–1945." In *The Japanese Informal Empire in China, 1895–1937*, ed. Duus, Myers, and Peattie, 210–71.

Ristaino, Marcia R. "The Russian Diaspora Community in Shanghai." In *New Frontiers*, ed. Bickers and Henriot, 192–210.

Robinson, Ronald. "Non-European Foundations of European Imperialism: Sketch for a Theory of Collaboration." In *Imperialism: The Robinson and Gallagher Controversy*, ed. William Roger Louis. New York: New Viewpoints, 1976.

Rogaski, Ruth. *Hygienic Modernity: Meanings of Health and Disease in Treaty Port China*. Berkeley: University of California Press, 2004.

Sasaki Masaya, ed. *Shimmatsu no haigai undō: shiryō hen* (The Anti-Foreign Movement at the end of the Qing: Volume of Historical Materials). Tokyo: Iwanando shōten, 1970.

Sha Weikai. *Zhongguo maiban zhi* (China's Comprador System). Shanghai: Shangwu yinshuguan, 1927.

Shanghai shangye chuxu yinhang luxing bu (Shanghai Commercial Savings Bank Travel Department), ed. *You chuan xu zhi* (Essential Information for Ship Travel). Shanghai, 1924.

Shanghai Tōa Dōbun Shoin (Shanghai East Asia Common Culture Academy). *Shinkoku shōgyō kanshū oyobi kinyū jijō* (Chinese Commercial Customs and Financial Conditions). Shanghai: Tōa Dōbun Shoin, 1904.

Shao, Qin. *Culturing Modernity: The Nantong Model, 1890–1930*. Stanford, CA: Stanford University Press, 2003.

———. "Space, Time, and Politics in Early Twentieth Century Nantong." *Modern China* 23 (Jan. 1997): 99–129.

Sheehan, Brett. *Industrial Eden: A Chinese Capitalist Vision*. Cambridge, MA: Harvard University Press, 2015.

Shen bao. Shanghai, 1872–1949.

Shih, Shu-mei. *The Lure of the Modern: Writing Modernism in Semicolonial China*. Berkeley: University of California Press, 2001.

Shu Xincheng. *Shu you xinying* (Impressions of Travel to Sichuan). Shanghai: Zhonghua shuju, 1924.

Smith, Paul J. "Commerce, Agriculture, and Core Formation in the Upper Yangzi, 2 A.D. to 1948." *Late Imperial China* 9:1 (June 1988): 1–78.

Stoler, Ann Laura. *Carnal Knowledge and Imperial Power: Race and the Intimate in Colonial Rule*. Berkeley: University of California Press, 2002.

Stoler, Ann Laura, Carole McGranahan, and Peter C. Perdue, eds. *Imperial Formations.* Santa Fe, NM: School for Advanced Research Press; Oxford: James Currey, 2007.

Sun, T. H. "Lu Tso-fu and His Yangtze Fleet." Reprinted in Anthony Kubek, *The Amerasia Papers: A Clue to the Catastrophe of China, vol. II,* 1176–83. Washington: U.S. Government Print Office, 1970–.

Sun Yatsen. *San Min Chu I: The Three Principles of the People* (English edition). Taipei: China Publishing, 1963.

Swire Group Archives. Institute for Business History. Shanghai Academy of Social Sciences. Shanghai, China.

Tajima Shigeji. *Yōsukō kisengyō chōsa hōkoku* (Report on a Survey of the Yangzi River Steam Shipping Business). [Tokyo], 1906.

Tan Shi-hua (Deng Xihua). *A Chinese Testament: The Autobiography of Tan Shi-hua.* Trans. Sergei Tretiakov. New York: Simon and Schuster, 1934.

Thampi, Madhavi. *Indians in China, 1800–1949.* New Delhi: Manohar, 2005.

Tōa Dōbunkai (East Asia Common Culture Association). *Shina shōbetsu zenshi* (Gazetteer of China's Provinces). Tokyo: Tōa Dōbunkai, 1917–20.

Tōa Dōbun Shoin (East Asia Common Culture Academy). *Shina keizai zensho* [Compendium of China's Economy]. Tokyo: Tōa Dōbunkai, 1907–8.

———. *Fūsan ushuku* (It Will Be Advantageous to Cross the Big Stream). Shanghai: Tōa Dōbun Shoin, 1917.

———. *Kinsei gyokushin* (Knowledge and Virtue Fully Endowed). Shanghai: Tōa Dōbun Shoin, 1923.

———. *Kohan sōtei* (Solitary Sailboat with Cloven Feet). Shanghai: Tōa Dōbun Shoin, 1913.

———. *Koketsu ryūgan* (Tiger's Den, Dragon's Jaws). Shanghai: Tōa Dōbun Shoin, 1922.

———. *Moku'u shippū* (Hardships amid Wind and Rain). Shanghai: Tōa Dōbun Shoin, 1914.

———. *Sokuseki: Dai ryokō kinenshi* (Footprints: Commemorative Chronicle of the Big Trip). Shanghai: Tōa Dōbun Shoin, 1930.

Tong Shaosheng. "Huiyi Minsheng lunchuan gongsi" (Recollections of the Minsheng Steamship Company). *Chongqing wenshi ziliao,* vol. 17. Chongqing, n.d.

———. "Minsheng lunchuan gongsi jilue" (A Brief Account of the Minsheng Steamship Company). *Sichuan wenshi ziliao,* vol. 10. Chengdu, 1963.

Tongwen Hu bao sui bao (Common Language Shanghai News, supplement). Shanghai: Tongwen Hu bao she, ca. 1900–1906 (copy in Tōyō Bunko, Tokyo).

Torrible, Graham. *Yangtsze Reminiscences: Some Notes and Recollections of Service with the China Navigation Company, Ltd., 1925–1939.* London: John Swire and Sons, 1975; 1990.

Van Slyke, Lyman P. *Yangtze: Nature, History, and the River.* Reading, MA: Addison-Wesley, 1988.

Vogel, Ezra F. *One Step Ahead in China: Guangdong under Reform.* Cambridge, MA: Harvard University Press, 1989.

Waiwu bu (Qing Foreign Ministry) Archives. Institute of Modern History. Academia Sinica. Taipei, Taiwan.

Waley-Cohen, Joanna. *The Sextants of Beijing: Global Currents in Chinese History.* New York: Norton, 1999.

Wang Guang. *Hangye yu hangquan* (The Shipping Industry and Shipping Rights). Shanghai: Xueshu yanjiu hui, 1930.

———. *Zhongguo hangye* (China's Shipping Industry). Shanghai: Shangwu yinshu guan, 1933.

———. *Zhongguo hangye shi* (A History of China's Shipping Industry). Taipei: Haiyun chuban she, 1955.

———. *Zhongguo shuiyun zhi* (Gazetteer of Chinese Navigation). Taibei: Zhongguo dadian bianyin hui, 1966.

Wang Jianping. *Zhongguo hangquan wenti* (Problems of China's Shipping Rights). N.p.: Dadong shuju, 1931.

Wang Jingyu. "Shijiu shiji waiguo qin Hua shiye zhong de Huashang fugu huodong" (The Activities of Chinese Merchants in Buying Capital Shares in the Aggressive Foreign Enterprises of Nineteenth-Century China). *Lishi yanjiu* 4 (1965): 39–74.

Wang Ya'nan. *Zhongguo ban fengjian ban zhimindi jingji xingtai yanjiu* (A Study of China's Semi-Feudal, Semi-colonial Economic System). Beijing: Renmin chuban she, 1957.

Wang, Zheng. *Never Forget National Humiliation: Historical Memory in Chinese Politics and Foreign Relations.* New York: Columbia University Press, 2012.

Wasserstrom, Jeffery N. *Global Shanghai, 1850–2010: A History in Fragments.* Abingdon, UK: Routledge, 2009.

Wei Qizhang. *Wan Qing haijun xingshuai shi* (The Rise and Fall of the Late Qing Navy). Beijing: Renmin chubanshe, 1998.

Wei Yingtao and Zhou Yong, eds. *Chongqing kaibu shi* (History of the Opening of Chongqing). Chongqing: Chongqing chuban she, 1983; 1997.

Woodhead, H. G. W. *The Yangtsze and its Problems.* Shanghai: Mercury Press, 1931.

Wray, William D. "Japan's Big-Three Service Enterprises in China, 1896–1936." In *The Japanese Informal Empire in China*, ed. Duus, Myers, and Peattie, 31–64.

———. *Mitsubishi and the N.Y.K. 1870–1914.* Cambridge, MA: Harvard East Asian Monographs, 1984.

Wright, Mary C. *The Last Stand of Chinese Conservatism: The T'ung-chih Restoration, 1862–1874.* Stanford, CA: Stanford University Press, 1957.

Wright, Stanley F. *China's Struggle for Tariff Autonomy, 1843–1938.* 1938. Reprint, Taipei: Ch'eng-wen, 1966.

———. *Hart and the Chinese Customs.* Belfast: Wm. Mullan and Son, 1950.

Wright, Tim. *Coal Mining in China's Economy and Society, 1895–1937.* Cambridge: Cambridge University Press, 1984.

———. "The Spiritual Heritage of Chinese Capitalism: Recent Trends in the Historiography of Chinese Enterprise Management." In *Using the Past to Serve the Present: Historiography and Politics of Contemporary China*, ed. Jonathan Unger. Armonk, NY: M. E. Sharpe, 1993.

Wu, Guo. *Zheng Guanying: Merchant Reformer of Late Qing China and His Influence on Economics, Politics, and Society.* Amherst, NY: Cambria Press, 2010.

Wu Jianren. *Ershi nian mudu zhi guai xianzhuang* (Strange Events Witnessed over Twenty Years). 3rd ed. Shanghai: Shanghai wenhua chuban she, 1957.

Wu Ling and Zhao Bizhen, trans. *Zuijin Yangzi jiang zhi da shi* (Recent Major Events on the Yangzi River). N.p., 1903.

Wyman, Judith. "The Ambiguities of Chinese Antiforeignism: Chongqing: 1870–1900." *Late Imperial China* 18:2 (Dec. 1997): 86–122.

Xin shijie (New World). Chongqing: Minsheng Industrial Company, 1932–37.

Xingcha zhoukan (Star-Raft Weekly). Chongqing: Chuanjiang hangyun guanli chu, 1930–31.

Xinmin bao (New People's Paper). Chongqing, 1938.

Xinyun dao bao (Guiding the New Life Movement), 5–6. Nanjing: Xin shenghuo yundong cujin zonghui, 1937.

Yan Xuexi. "Lu Zuofu he Zhang Jian: Jindai Zhongguo liangwei jiechu de aiguozhe" (Lu Zuofu and Zhang Jian: Two Patriots of Modern China). In *Lu Zuofu yu Zhongguo xiandai hua yanjiu* (Studies of Lu Zuofu and China's Modernization), ed. Yang Guangyan and Liu Chonglai. Beipei: Xinan shifan daxue chuban she, 1995.

Yang Tianhong. *Kou'an kaifang yu shehui biange: Zhongguo zikai shangbu yanjiu* (The Opening of Ports and Social Change: Research on China's Self-Opened Treaty Ports). Beijing: Zhonghua shuju, 2002.

Ye Xiaoqing. *The Dianshizhai Pictorial: Shanghai Urban Life, 1884–1898.* Ann Arbor: Center for Chinese Studies, 2003.

———. "Shanghai before Nationalism." *East Asian History* 3 (June 1992): 33–52.

Yeh, Wen-hsin. "Corporate Space, Communal Time: Everyday Life in Shanghai's Bank of China." *American Historical Review* 100:1 (Feb. 1995): 97–124.

———. "Huang Yanpei and the Chinese Society for Vocational Education in Shanghai Networking." In *At the Crossroads of Empires: Middlemen, Social Networks, and State-Building in Republican Shanghai*, ed. Nara Dillon and Jean C. Oi, 25–44. Stanford, CA: Stanford University Press, 2008.

———. *Shanghai Splendor: Economic Sentiments and the Making of Modern China, 1843–1949.* Berkeley: University of California Press, 2007.

Yonesato Monkichi. *Chōkō kō'un shi* (History of Yangzi River Shipping). N.p., 1927.

Yung Wing. *My Life in China and America.* New York: Holt, 1909.

Zanasi, Margherita. *Saving the Nation: Economic Modernity in Republican China.* Chicago: University of Chicago Press, 2006.

Zhang Houquan, ed. *Zhaoshang ju shi: jindai bufen* (History of the China Merchants Company: The Modern Period). Beijing: Renmin jiaotong chubanshe, 1988.

Zhang Jin. *Quanli, chongtu yu biange: 1926–1937 Chongqing chengshi xiandaihua yanjiu* (Power, Conflict, and Change: A Study of Chongqing's Urban Modernization). Chongqing: Chongqing chuban she, 2003.

Zhang Renjie, ed. *Guomin zhengfu qingcha zhengli Zhaoshang ju weiyuanhui baogao shu* (Report of the Nationalist Government Committee to Investigate and Reorganize the China Merchants Steam Navigation Company). Nanjing, 1927.

Zhang Shouguang. *Lu Zuofu nianpu changbian* (The Chronicle of Lu Zuofu). 2 vols. Beijing: Zhongguo shehui kexue chuban she, 2014.
Zhang Zhongli, Chen Zengnian, and Yao Xinrong. *The Swire Group in Old China*. Shanghai: Shanghai People's Publishing House, 1992.
Zhaoshang ju lunchuan gufen youxian gongsi dang'an (Archives of the China Merchants Steam Navigation Company, Ltd.), 1872–1949. Second Historical Archives, Nanjing, China.
Zheng Bicheng. *Sichuan dao you* (A Guide to Sichuan Travel). [Chongqing]: Zhongguo luxing she, 1935.
Zheng Dongqin. "Minsheng gongsi chanye jieduan jilue" (A Brief Account of the Minsheng Company's Formative Stages). *Chongqing gongshang shiliao*, vol. 2, 1983.
Zheng Guanying. "Shengshi weiyan" (Warnings to a Prosperous Age). (1890). In *Zheng Guanying ji*, ed. Xia Dongyuan. Shanghai: Shanghai renmin chubanshe, 1982.
Zheng Guohan. *Shu cheng riji* (Diary of a Journey to Sichuan). [Shanghai Library], 1915.
Zhongguo haiyuan gonghui quanguo weiyuan hui (China Seamen's Union National Committee). *Zhongguo haiyuan gongren yundong da shi nianpu* (Chronology of Major Events in the Chinese Seamen's Workers' Movement). N.p., 1984.
Zhongguo shixue hui (China History Association), eds. *Yangwu yundong* (The Western Affairs Movement), vol. 6. Shanghai: Shanghai renmin chuban she, 1961.
Zhongyang yanjiu yuan jindaishi yanjiu suo (Academia Sinica Institute of Modern History), ed. *Haifang dang: shen: goumai chuanxiao* (Archives of Maritime Defense, Part I: Purchase of Ships and Guns], vol. 2. Taipei: Zhongyang yanjiu yuan jindaishi yanjiu suo, 1957.
Zhu Huisen, ed. *Hangzheng shiliao* (Historical Materials on Shipping Administration). Taibei xian Xindian shi: Guoshiguan, 1989.
Zhu Yin'gui. *Guojia ganyu jingji yu Zhong-Ri jindai hua* (State Intervention in the Economy and Sino-Japanese Modernization). Beijing: Dongfang chuban she, 1994.
———. *Zhongguo jindai lunchuan hangyun ye yanjiu* (Studies on China's Modern Shipping Business). Taizhong: Gaowen chuban she, 2006.
Zhu Ziqing. "Haixing zaji" (Various Notes on Ocean Travel). In *Zhu Ziqing quanji* (Complete Works of Zhu Ziqing), 104–9. Jiangsu jiaoyu chuban she, 1988.
Zongli Yamen Archives. Institute of Modern History. Academia Sinica. Taipei, Taiwan.

Index

Harvard East Asian Monographs
(most recent titles)

314. Jacob Eyferth, *Eating Rice from Bamboo Roots: The Social History of a Community of Handicraft Papermakers in Rural Sichuan, 1920–2000*
315. David Johnson, *Spectacle and Sacrifice: The Ritual Foundations of Village Life in North China*
316. James Robson, *Power of Place: The Religious Landscape of the Southern Sacred Peak (Nanyue 南嶽) in Medieval China*
317. Lori Watt, *When Empire Comes Home: Repatriation and Reintegration in Postwar Japan*
318. James Dorsey, *Critical Aesthetics: Kobayashi Hideo, Modernity, and Wartime Japan*
319. Christopher Bolton, *Sublime Voices: The Fictional Science and Scientific Fiction of Abe Kōbō*
320. Si-yen Fei, *Negotiating Urban Space: Urbanization and Late Ming Nanjing*
321. Christopher Gerteis, *Gender Struggles: Wage-Earning Women and Male-Dominated Unions in Postwar Japan*
322. Rebecca Nedostup, *Superstitious Regimes: Religion and the Politics of Chinese Modernity*
323. Lucien Bianco, *Wretched Rebels: Rural Disturbances on the Eve of the Chinese Revolution*
324. Cathryn H. Clayton, *Sovereignty at the Edge: Macau and the Question of Chineseness*
325. Micah S. Muscolino, *Fishing Wars and Environmental Change in Late Imperial and Modern China*
326. Robert I. Hellyer, *Defining Engagement: Japan and Global Contexts, 1750–1868*
327. Robert Ashmore, *The Transport of Reading: Text and Understanding in the World of Tao Qian (365–427)*
328. Mark A. Jones, *Children as Treasures: Childhood and the Middle Class in Early Twentieth Century Japan*
329. Miryam Sas, *Experimental Arts in Postwar Japan: Moments of Encounter, Engagement, and Imagined Return*
330. H. Mack Horton, *Traversing the Frontier: The* Man'yōshū *Account of a Japanese Mission to Silla in 736–737*
331. Dennis J. Frost, *Seeing Stars: Sports Celebrity, Identity, and Body Culture in Modern Japan*
332. Marnie S. Anderson, *A Place in Public: Women's Rights in Meiji Japan*

333. Peter Mauch, *Sailor Diplomat: Nomura Kichisaburō and the Japanese-American War*
334. Ethan Isaac Segal, *Coins, Trade, and the State: Economic Growth in Early Medieval Japan*
335. David B. Lurie, *Realms of Literacy: Early Japan and the History of Writing*
336. Lillian Lan-ying Tseng, *Picturing Heaven in Early China*
337. Jun Uchida, *Brokers of Empire: Japanese Settler Colonialism in Korea, 1876–1945*
338. Patricia L. Maclachlan, *The People's Post Office: The History and Politics of the Japanese Postal System, 1871–2010*
339. Michael Schiltz, *The Money Doctors from Japan: Finance, Imperialism, and the Building of the Yen Bloc, 1895–1937*
340. Daqing Yang, Jie Liu, Hiroshi Mitani, and Andrew Gordon, eds., *Toward a History beyond Borders: Contentious Issues in Sino-Japanese Relations*
341. Sonia Ryang, *Reading North Korea: An Ethnological Inquiry*
342. Shih-shan Susan Huang, *Picturing the True Form: Daoist Visual Culture in Traditional China*
343. Barbara Mittler, *A Continuous Revolution: Making Sense of Cultural Revolution Culture*
344. Hwansoo Ilmee Kim, *Empire of the Dharma: Korean and Japanese Buddhism, 1877–1912*
345. Satoru Saito, *Detective Fiction and the Rise of the Japanese Novel, 1880–1930*
346. Jung-Sun N. Han, *An Imperial Path to Modernity: Yoshino Sakuzō and a New Liberal Order in East Asia, 1905–1937*
347. Atsuko Hirai, *Government by Mourning: Death and Political Integration in Japan, 1603–1912*
348. Darryl E. Flaherty, *Public Law, Private Practice: Politics, Profit, and the Legal Profession in Nineteenth-Century Japan*
349. Jeffrey Paul Bayliss, *On the Margins of Empire: Buraku and Korean Identity in Prewar and Wartime Japan*
350. Barry Eichengreen, Dwight H. Perkins, and Kwanho Shin, *From Miracle to Maturity: The Growth of the Korean Economy*
351. Michel Mohr, *Buddhism, Unitarianism, and the Meiji Competition for Universality*
352. J. Keith Vincent, *Two-Timing Modernity: Homosocial Narrative in Modern Japanese Fiction*
354. Chong-Bum An and Barry Bosworth, *Income Inequality in Korea: An Analysis of Trends, Causes, and Answers*
355. Jamie L. Newhard, *Knowing the Amorous Man: A History of Scholarship on* Tales of Ise
356. Sho Konishi, *Anarchist Modernity: Cooperatism and Japanese-Russian Intellectual Relations in Modern Japan*
357. Christopher P. Hanscom, *The Real Modern: Literary Modernism and the Crisis of Representation in Colonial Korea*
358. Michael Wert, *Meiji Restoration Losers: Memory and Tokugawa Supporters in Modern Japan*

359. Garret P. S. Olberding, ed., *Facing the Monarch: Modes of Advice in the Early Chinese Court*
360. Xiaojue Wang, *Modernity with a Cold War Face: Reimagining the Nation in Chinese Literature Across the 1949 Divide*
361. David Spafford, *A Sense of Place: The Political Landscape in Late Medieval Japan*
362. Jongryn Mo and Barry Weingast, *Korean Political and Economic Development: Crisis, Security, and Economic Rebalancing*
363. Melek Ortabasi, *The Undiscovered Country: Text, Translation, and Modernity in the Work of Yanagita Kunio*
364. Hiraku Shimoda, *Lost and Found: Recovering Regional Identity in Imperial Japan*
365. Trent E. Maxey, *The "Greatest Problem": Religion and State Formation in Meiji Japan*
366. Gina Cogan, *The Princess Nun: Bunchi, Buddhist Reform, and Gender in Early Edo Japan*
367. Eric C. Han, *Rise of a Japanese Chinatown: Yokohama, 1894–1972*
368. Natasha Heller, *Illusory Abiding: The Cultural Construction of the Chan Monk Zhongfeng Mingben*
369. Paize Keulemans, *Sound Rising from the Paper: Nineteenth-Century Martial Arts Fiction and the Chinese Acoustic Imagination*
370. Simon James Bytheway, *Investing Japan: Foreign Capital, Monetary Standards, and Economic Development, 1859–2011*
371. Sukhee Lee, *Negotiated Power: The State, Elites, and Local Governance in Twelfth-Fourteenth China*
372. Foong Ping, *The Efficacious Landscape: On the Authorities of Painting at the Northern Song Court*
373. Catherine L. Phipps, *Empires on the Waterfront: Japan's Ports and Power, 1858–1899*
374. Sunyoung Park, *The Proletarian Wave: Literature and Leftist Culture in Colonial Korea, 1910–1945*
375. Barry Eichengreen, Wonhyuk Lim, Yung Chul Park, and Dwight H. Perkins, *The Korean Economy: From a Miraculous Past to a Sustainable Future*
376. Heather Blair, *Real and Imagined: The Peak of Gold in Heian Japan*
377. Emer O'Dwyer, *Significant Soil: Settler Colonialism and Japan's Urban Empire in Manchuria*
378. Martina Deuchler, *Under the Ancestors' Eyes: Kinship, Status, and Locality in Premodern Korea*
379. Joseph R. Dennis, *Writing, Publishing, and Reading Local Gazetteers in Imperial China, 1100–1700*
380. Catherine Vance Yeh, *The Chinese Political Novel: Migration of a World Genre*
381. Noell Wilson, *Defensive Positions: The Politics of Maritime Security in Tokugawa Japan*
382. Miri Nakamura, *Monstrous Bodies: The Rise of the Uncanny in Modern Japan*
383. Nara Dillon, *Radical Inequalities: China's Revolutionary Welfare State in Comparative Perspective*

384. Ma Zhao, *Runaway Wives, Urban Crimes, and Survival Tactics in Wartime Beijing, 1937-1949*
385. Mingwei Song, *Young China: National Rejuvenation and the* Bildungsroman, *1900-1959*
386. Christopher Bondy, *Voice, Silence, and Self: Negotiations of Buraku Identity in Contemporary Japan*
387. Seth Jacobowitz, *Writing Technology in Meiji Japan: A Media History of Modern Japanese Literature and Visual Culture*
388. Hilde De Weerdt, *Information, Territory, and Networks: The Crisis and Maintenance of Empire in Song China*
389. Elizabeth Kindall, *Geo-Narratives of a Filial Son: The Paintings and Travel Diaries of Huang Xiangjian (1609–1673)*
390. Matthew Fraleigh, *Plucking Chrysanthemums: Narushima Ryūhoku and Sinitic Literary Traditions in Modern Japan*
391. Hu Ying, *Burying Autumn: Poetry, Friendship, and Loss*
392. Mark E. Byington, *The Ancient State of Puyŏ in Northeast Asia: Archaeology and Historical Memory*
393. Timothy J. Van Compernolle, *Struggling Upward: Worldly Success and the Japanese Novel*
394. Heekyoung Cho, *Translation's Forgotten History: Russian Literature, Japanese Mediation, and the Formation of Modern Korean Literature*
395. Terry Kawashima, *Itineraries of Power: Texts and Traversals in Heian and Medieval Japan*
396. Anna Andreeva, *Assembling Shinto: Buddhist Approaches to Kami Worship in Medieval Japan*
397. Felix Boecking, *No Great Wall: Trade, Tariffs, and Nationalism in Republican China, 1927–1945*
398. Chien-Hsin Tsai, *A Passage to China: Literature, Loyalism, and Colonial Taiwan*
399. W. Puck Brecher, *Honored and Dishonored Guests: Westerners in Wartime Japan*
400. Miya Elise Mizuta Lippit, *Aesthetic Life: Beauty and Art in Modern Japan*
401. Brian Steininger, *Chinese Literary Form in Heian Japan: Poetics and Practice*
402. Lisa Yoshikawa, *Making History Matter: Kuroita Katsumi and the Construction of Imperial Japan*
403. Michael P. Cronin, *Osaka Modern: The City in the Japanese Imaginary*
404. Soyoung Suh, *Naming the Local: Medicine, Language, and Identity in Korea since the 15th Century*
405. Yoon Sun Yang, *From Domestic Women to Sensitive Young Men: Translating the Individual in Early Colonial Korea*
406. Michal Daliot-Bul and Nissim Otmazgin, *The Anime Boom in the United States: Lessons for Global Creative Industries*
407. Nathan Hopson, *Ennobling the Savage Northeast: Tōhoku as Japanese Postwar Thought, 1945–2011*
408. Michael Fuller, *An Introduction to Chinese Poetry: From the Canon of Poetry to the Lyrics of the Song Dynasty*

409. Tie Xiao, *Revolutionary Waves: The Crowd in Modern China*
410. Anne Reinhardt, *Navigating Semi-colonialism: Shipping, Sovereignty, and Nation Building in China, 1860–1937*
411. Jennifer E. Altehenger, *Legal Lessons: Popularizing Laws in the People's Republic of China, 1949–1989*
412. Halle O'Neal, *Word Embodied: The Jeweled Pagoda Mandalas in Japanese Buddhist Art*
413. Maren A. Ehlers, *Give and Take: Poverty and the Status Order in Early Modern Japan*